Urbanus Rhegius

GERMAN PROTESTANT REFORMER

A History & Genealogy (1489 – 2001)
From Langenargen to Finkenwerder to the U.S.A.

English Translation by
Linda Schwartau Simonton
Jack Kirchner, Walter König

ORIGINAL GERMAN TEXT
Der Reformator Urbanus Rhegius
Chronik einer Familie zwischen Langenargen und Finkenwerder

BY WALTER KÖNIG
In collaboration with
Magdalena König, Rudolf Meier, Bertha Brockmann

Urbanus Rhegius: German Protestant Reformer
A History & Geneology (1489 – 2001), From Langenargen to Finkenwerder to the U.S.A.:
English Translation

2023 by Linda Schwartau Simonton, Jack Kirchner, Walter König

Published by Urbanus Rhegius Press

For ordering information and permission requests, write to the publisher by contacting: UrbanusRhegiusPress@gmail.com

ISBN: 979-8-218-14769-3

Printed in the United States of America

Cover and interior design by: Colleen Sheehan

Cover Attribution: Stained Glass Window Photo

The Urbanus Rhegius memorial stained glass window in the Evangelische Friedenskirche Langenargen [Lutheran Peace Church], dedicated in 2001, is an initiative of Museum Langenargen. Designer: Diether F. Domes. Glass artist: Andreas Dierig. Photo used with permission of Museum Langenargen.

Dedicated to
our ancestors

Table Of Contents

Urbanus Rhegius
1ST and 2ND Generation US Descendants
Schwartau Family, Red Wing, MN, 1903

Back row, left to right: Margaret, Ann, Rudolph, Henry, John
Front row, left to right: Adolph, Catherina, Helen, Laura,
Carsten Hinrich, George, Clara

Preface

THE ACCIDENTAL ENGLISH TRANSLATION

I'm a 16TH generation descendant of Urbanus Rhegius via my great-grandfather, Carsten Hinrich Schwartau, who emigrated from Finkenwerder, Germany to Red Wing, MN in 1879. On a 2013 trip to Germany with my Schwartau second cousins, following in Urbanus Rhegius' footsteps, we were introduced to *Der Reformator Urbanus Rhegius* by Walter König, the primary author and a fellow Rhegius descendant.

I wanted to read the book, but I didn't get far before realizing my college German minor had sadly faded. Fortunately, I had recently begun taking German lessons from Jack Kirchner, a fluent German speaker and grammarian. Jack had honed his German skills as a translator for US Army Military Intelligence Services in West Germany prior to the Berlin crisis. As the book translation progressed, he was even able to recall the old German language and script he'd been required to learn for his M.A. in German Language and Literature.

Jack loved to translate, and with my journalism degree, I loved to write – and to learn German language, history, and genealogy along the way. This accidental translation turned out to be a much bigger project than either Jack or I had expected, but we both learned so much, it was well worth our time and effort.

Acknowledgements

Our heartfelt thanks to:

- Our German Rhegius descendant relatives for writing this book and for their genealogical persistence in discovering that the 400-year-old candle holders on the Finkenwerder church altar identified Finkenwerder Pastor Sebastian König (Bastianus Regius) as a grandson of Urbanus Rhegius, thereby establishing our connection to Rhegius and expanding our family tree.

- Anne Pudas, Schwartau cousin and former English teacher with a red pen, for editing an early draft, not once, but three times.

- Professor Eduard Hindelang and the Museum Langenargen am Bodensee for invaluable contributions to the content and publishing of the German text.

- Walter König for enthusiasticially supporting our translation efforts, reviewing the entire manuscript and endnotes for German language accuracy, and donating copies of the German version to key libraries and institutions. We couldn't have done it without you!

For Our Readers

It's our hope that through this translation, other English speakers will now be able to learn the inspiring story of Urbanus Rhegius and the turbulence, high points, and sorrows of his life and the lives of his descendants.

LINDA SCHWARTAU SIMONTON
Des Moines, Iowa
November 2022

Introduction

While translating this book we learned several things that may be helpful to English-speaking readers, and we want to pass them along.

Translating the German Title

Der Reformator Urbanus Rhegius: Chronik einer Famile zwischen Langenargen und Finkenwerder literally translates as *The Reformer Urbanus Rhegius: Chronicle of a Family Between Langenargen and Finkenwerder*. This title describes how Urbanus Rhegius was born in Langenargen in the south, moved with his family to Celle where he did most of his work, and had a grandson who was a pastor on the northern island of Finkenwerder, where the authors' families are from.

As you read the Rhegius translation, you'll discover there's much more to be learned than the German title suggests because it's actually three books in one. We chose the English title to reflect these three topics:

- Urbanus Rhegius – his life, key role in the German Reformation, and the historical events surrounding the Reformation
- Rhegius' immediate family (children, grandchildren), their lives and times

· The lives and times of more recent Rhegius descendants, especially those who have ties to the north German Island of Finkenwerder

The German edition also includes a separate family tree that traces descendants with the surname "König" back to Urbanus Rhegius.

Inconsistent Spelling of First and Last Names

The spelling of many German names in this book is not consistent. Sometimes different spellings even occur within the same paragraph because in the past, there were no spelling rules. Instead, people spelled phonetically. For example, the Finkenwerder church registry contains nine different spellings of the König family name: Koning, Koniges, Koninges, Konig, Köning, Konings, Könings in 1630, König in 1667, and Königs. From 1679 on, it is usually spelled König, but once in 1714 the name appears as Köhnig. Other examples in the text are: Hostmann/Horstmann, Linnemann/Lindemann, Fock/Focke/Focken/Vock/Vocke, and Harms/Harmens.

There is also no uniform spelling of first names. A woman's name, Anna, in the text can also be Anntje or Annke, while Catharina becomes Catrina or Trina. Sebastian becomes Bastian, Susanna becomes Sanna, and Margarethe becomes Grete, Gretje, or Gretsche.

Location on the Family Tree

In the text, some people's names are followed by a number in parentheses. This number indicates the location of the person on the Rhegius family tree, a copy of which is enclosed with the original German version of this book.

Some Words are in German and Capitalized

The following types of words in the translation are in German rather than English so that English-speaking individuals who might wish to pursue additional information will be more easily able to do so. The first time the German word appears in the text, it is followed by the English translation in brackets. Many of these words also appear in the German-English Glossary included in this translation.

- Exact names of buildings, for example, Augsburg Dom
- Denominations of money (no English translation is provided)
- Geographical locations, such as:

Bayern	Bavaria
Bodensee	Lake Constance
Konstanz	Constance
Nordsee	North Sea

Österreich	Austria
Sachsen	Saxon
Schwaben	Schwabia
Tirol	Tyrol
Türkei	Turkey
Ungarn	Hungary

There is no German word for "Lutheran," so the German "Evangelisch" is used.

Some Words are Shown Once in German and Thereafter in English

These are:

- Royal titles
- Job titles
- Groups, organizations, affiliations, assemblies
- Wars, treaties
- Books, pamphlets, and other writings

Other

- The numbers within the marginal tabs Page 13 refer to the page in the original German text.

- Since this translation does not include the German edition's 130 illustrations, these illustrations are noted in the approximate location where they appear in the German text.

- This translation also does not include the 66 appendices in the German edition. Many of these appendices show original German documents.

- The original German text has footnotes. These are now endnotes. The original footnotes contain both source citations and explanatory information. In the endnotes, the source citations have been maintained in German, and the explanatory information has been translated into English and bracketed.

- The endnote superscripts may at times appear out of order due to placement of illustrations in the text.

German-English Glossary

Some words in the German text are "old" German and are not found in current dictionaires. Primary author Walther König has graciously provided definitions of some of these words.

AMTMANN	Senior civil servant. Historically, senior servant of a duke or senior servant in the castle
AMTSVERWALTER	Governmental department administrator
BAUER	Farmer
BISCHOF	Bishop
BURG	Castle
BÜRGERAUSSCHUSS	Citizens' committee
BÜRGERMEISTER	Mayor
CANZLER	Archaic for chancellor. See Kanzler
CHOR	Chancel. The area surrounding the altar, including the choir and sanctuary. Also means chorus, depending on the context
CHORHERR	Canon
CHRONIST	Chronicler

CHURFÜRST	Elector. (7 electors elected the emperor in the Holy Roman Empire of the German Nation. They have been the most important princes of the respective territory, but also from the Church, e.g. the Cardinal of Mainz).
COLLEGIUM	Old form of Kollegium, meaning college. College is an individual, Collegium or Kollegium is a team or committee, often used in universities
CRAMER	Merchant
CÜSTER	See Küster
D.Ä	The elder, to differentiate fathers and sons with the same name
DEKAN	Superintendent
DIAKON	Deacon
DIEMAN	Haystack
DIENER	Servant
DOM	Cathedral
DOMHERR	Member of the cathedral chapter
DOMKAPITEL	Cathedral chapter
DOMPREDIGER	Cathedral preacher
DOMPROPST	Cathedral provost
DÖNG	A very old-fashioned living room, in old low German
ERZBISCHOFF	Archbishop
ERZHERZOG	Archduke
EVANGELISCH	Evangelical, meaning that only the scripture in the Bible is the truth, not the Church in Rome's interpretation
FESTUNG	Fortress
FINANZVERWALTER	Financial administrator

FISCHER	Fisherman
FREIE REICHSSTADT	Free Imperial City (see "Expanded Definition" on pg. xxii)
FREIHERR	Baron
FÜRST	Prince (the rank below king or emperor)
FÜRSTENTUM	Principality
GASTHOF	Inn
GASTWIRT	Innkeeper
GEISTLICHE	Clergy
GEMACHL, GEMAHLIN	Consort. Polite, aristocratic word for "wife." Has a noble implication
GENERALSUPERINTENDENT	Supervisor over many superintendents
GESCHLECHTER	The prior generations. In some contexts such as "Die Augsburger Geschlechter" it means the rich, dominant families ruling the town, both commercially and politically
GESELLEN	Journeymen, people who have completed an apprenticeship
GESINDE	Domestic workers, common workers
GRAF	Count (British earl)
GRAFF	Low German word for "Grab," meaning tomb or grave
GRÄFIN	Countess
GRAFSCHAFT	Count's land, British earldom
GROSSER RAT	Superior council
HARNISCHMEISTER	Armor master
HAUPTMANN	Leader, captain in the military
HAUSHOFMEISTER	Senior servant to the court
HAUSMANN	Homeowner
HAUSVOGT	Administrator, probably of lesser importance than Vogt

HEIMATDICHTER	Regional poet
HERRSCHAFT	Ruler's territory
HERRSCHER	Ruler
HERZOG	Duke
HERZOGTUM	Duchy
HISTORIKER	Historian
HOF	Court, farm
HOFDIENER	Court servants
HOFGERICHTSPROKURATOR	Advocate or lawyer for the court
HOFMEISTER	Senior servant to the court
HOFRAT	Honorary title for senior civil servants
HOFSINGER	Court singer
JURIST	Lawyer, jurist
KAISER	Emperor
KAISERLICHER EINNEHMER	Treasurer to the emperor
KÄMMEREI	Treasury
KAMMERMAGD	Lady's maid
KAMMERMEISTER	Treasurer
KAMMERSEKRETÄR	Secretary to noblemen
KANONIKER	Canon, someone who lives by canonical rules
KANTOR	Choirmaster and organist
KANZEL	Pulpit
KANZLEI	More formal word for "office." Often used by lawyers and the nobility
KANZLEISCHREIBER	Secretary, clerk of the Kanzlei (office)
KANZLER	Chancellor (in government, universities, and diplomatic service)
KAPELLE	Chapel
KAPELLMEISTER	Conductor of an orchestra

KAPLAN	Chaplain (Rank below priest. Urbanus' father was a Kaplan in Langenargen.)
KARDINAL	Cardinal
KAUFHERRENSTUBE, KAUFLEUTESTUBE	Merchants room (Kaufherren and Kaufleute are almost the same; Kaufherren is nobler)
KIRCHE	Church
KIRCHENGESCHWORENER	Member of local church council. Same as Kirchenjurat and Kirchenvorstand
KIRCHENJURAT	Member of the local church council. Same as Kirchengeschworener and Kirchenvorstand
KIRCHENPROBST	Superior to the pastors or priests, same as Probst
KIRCHENVORSTAND	Modern word for Kirchgeschworener and Kirchenjurat
KLEINER RAT	Lesser council
KLOSTER	Monastery
KOADJUTOR	Co-assistant in court
KOLLEGIATSSTIFT	Foundation or convent of members who have equal rights (a foundation for colleagues). They had their own rules to help each other in difficult situations or when they became old
KOLLEGIUM	Current form of Collegium, meaning college
KÖNIG	King
KÖSTEREI	Old word for Küsterei
KRAMER OR KRÄMER	See Cramer
KRUG	Archaic word for "inn"
KRÜGER	Owner of a Krug (inn)
KÜRASS	Cuirass. A piece of armor consisting of breastplate and backplate fastened together
KURFÜRST	Current term for Churfürst
KÜSTER	Sexton

KÜSTERY, KÜSTERI	Sextonry
LANDESBISCHOFF	Bishop of the country
LANDESFÜRST, LANDESHERR	Sovereign prince
LANDFISCAL	Manager responsible for state finances
LANDGERICHTSBEISITZER	Assessor to a regional court
LANDGRAF	Landgrave
LANDSKNECHT	Mercenary, Lansquenet
LANDVOGT	Administrator of a large, possibly imperial, province
LANDWIRT	Farmer
MARKGRAF. MARKGRAF'S WIFE: MARKGRÄFIN	Margrave. Wife: Marchioness
MESSBUCH	Missal or mass book
MÜNSTER	Cathedral, originally with a monastery
NOTAR	Notary
OBERBEFEHLSHABER	Commander-in-Chief
OBERHAUPTMANN	Head leader, senior leader, main leader
PAPST	Pope
PÄPSTLICHE LEGAT	Papal legate
PATRIZIAT, PATRICIAT	Wealthy, influential "town fathers"
PFALZGRAF	Count palatine
PFARR, MORE OFTEN PFARRE, PFARREI	Parish or parish office
PFARRER, PFARRHERR	Parish priest (Catholic). Evangelical pastor, vicar, minister
PREDIGER	Preacher
PROBST	Superior to the pastors or priests, same as Kirchenprobst
PROBSTEI	The region for which the Probst is responsible
RAT	City council

RATSHERR	Councilor
RECHNUNGSFÜHRENDER JURAT	Member of the local church council responsible for finance
RECHTSGELEHRTER	Expert on law, jurist
REICH	Empire
REICHSERZMARSHALL	Imperial Arch Marshall
REICHSKANZLER	Imperial Chancellor (1871 – 1918), Chancellor of the Republik of Germany (until 1933), then Reich Chancellor (1933 – 1945)
REICHSTAG	Parliament
REKTOR	Headmaster of a school
RENTMEISTER	Treasurer (word no longer used)
SCHIFFSZIMMERMAN, SCHIFFSZIMMERLEUTE	Ships carpenter, carpenters
SCHLOSS	Castle
SCHLOSSKIRCHE	Castle church
SCHMIED	Blacksmith
SCHWIBBOGEN	Flying buttress
STADTPFLEGER	Early word for Bürgermeister, mayor
STADTSCHREIBER	Writer-in-residence. Writes down what is happening in town. In older times, was a valuable source of history
STALLMEISTER	Head groom
STIFT	Foundation, monastery, convent
STIFTSAMTMANN	Senior civil servant of the foundation, monastery, or convent
STIFTDAME	Lady or member of the foundation
SUPERINTENDENT	Superintendent
SYNDIKUS	Legal advisor
UNIVERSITÄT	University

Expanded Definition of Freie Reichsstadt (Free Imperial City)

Free Imperial Cities were under the direct rule of the emperor and only responsible to him. Other cities had one or more titled individuals such as a count, prince, or even a king between the city and the emperor. Residents of Free Imperial Cities elected their own parliament that was their "town government." At that time, there was not yet pure democracy, so only wealthy and influential people could be elected. In Augsburg, for example, this would be wealthy merchants like the Fuggers and others.

The Free Imperial Cities were more developed than other cities because their residents tended to be freer and more open-minded, as well as having a better grasp of what was going on in the world.

Some of the Free Imperial Cities mentioned in this book are: Augsburg, Hamburg, Lindau (small, but with important connections to Italy across the Alps), Strassburg, and Freiburg (where Urbanus studied).

Urbanus Rhegius

GERMAN PROTESTANT REFORMER

A History & Genealogy (1489-2001)
From Langenargen to Finkenwerder to the U.S.A.

English Translation by
Linda Schwartau Simonton
Jack Kirchner, Walter König

ORIGINAL GERMAN TEXT
Der Reformator Urbanus Rhegius
Chronik einer Familie zwischen Langenargen und Finkenwerder

BY WALTER KÖNIG
In collaboration with
Magdalena König, Rudolf Meier, Bertha Brockmann

1

Table of Contents

Note: Page in original German book in Parenthesis

[PHOTO] Professor Eduard Hindelang, Founding Director of the Museum Langenargen, Honorary Citizen of Langenargen, Publisher of this book. (Photo: Anja Köhler, Friedrichshafen).

* Page number tabs refer to the original page in the German version.

Foreword

It has always been my desire and joy to keep the spiritual and cultural heritage of Langenargen alive. Urban Rieger, who later changed his name to Urbanus Rhegius, was born here in 1489. In this spirit, we have honored Urbanus Rhegius with a stained glass window in the Langenargen Evangelische Kirche [Lutheran Church].

Currently, our museum member, Walter König, in collaboration with Magdalena König, Rudolf Meier, and Bertha Brockmann, offer a comprehensive work on Urbanus Rhegius and his family.

By following generations of Rhegius' descendants, this work allows the sweeping, radical, historical, and philosophical changes arising out of the world of the 1500s to develop before our eyes.

According to Urbanus Rhegius' biographer, Professor Maximilian Liebmann, Urbanus Rhegius is among fewer than one hundred people responsible for the success of the Reformation in Germany. He advocated renewal of the Church rather than separation. In spite of great personal sacrifice, he was not granted fulfillment of his life's goal.

Urbanus Rhegius has left behind over 100 writings that are preserved today in archives in Hamburg, Riga, Philadelphia, Budapest, St. Petersburg, Uppsala, Prague, Paris, Dresden, Jena, Lindau, and other cities. Thirteen of these writings, which the members of the Church Council were supposed to read, have been in the Vatican since 1536. All this is reason enough that the people from his birth city of Langenargen not only continue to care about remembering him, but also care about understanding his message and importance.

As the authors take us along on the life journey of our Langenargen fellow citizen, Urbanus Rhegius, we experience new information about his background, his wife Anna Weissbrücker from the old established Augsburg merchant families, their 13 children, his connection to the Grafen [Counts] von Montfort, his meetings with Luther, his role in the 1530 Reichstag zu Augsburg [Imperial Diet of Augsburg], and finally the family's long journey from the Bodensee [Lake Constance] to Northern Germany, within sight of the towers of Hamburg on the Elbe.

Over six generations, several of Rhegius' family members have served the Counts von Montfort and the Herzögen [Dukes] von Braunschweig and Lüneburg. Rhegius' father, Conrad Rieger, was a Kanoniker [canon] in Oberstaufen and a Kaplan [chaplain: the rank below priest] in Langenargen. Urbanus Rhegius himself contributed to the lineage as a theologian and reformer in Augsburg and Celle. Later descendants include Amtmänner [senior civil servants], Kammermägde [lady's maids], Hofsänger [court singers], Historiker [historians], Vögte [administrators], and Bauern [farmers]. One of these descendants was a Pfarrer [pastor] in the Dom [Cathedral] zu Königsberg and a grandson was a pastor on the Elbe Island of Finkenwerder for 30 years.

The authors of this book richly deserve my admiration for their many years of research, which closes the information gap about one of

Langenargen's most distinguished citizens. I wholeheartedly thank the museum's donors and patrons for their commitment to the art and culture of the Bodensee during this increasingly difficult time.

PROF. EDUARD HINDELANG

Museum Langenargen

Fall 2006

Maria Kunig—Whose Name No One Mentions

[Refers to Urbanus Rhegius' mother. See page 169.]

A Word at the Outset

A low pressure weather system over the Nordsee [North Sea] sends the fall's first high water storm surge up the Elbe River, pushing wind and waves high onto the crowns of the dikes. Rain showers sweep over the roofs and streets, and the few passersby on the dikes hurry home. The people of the town who are seafarers feel thankful not to be on the decks of ships on the high seas, but instead coming home to hearth and family.

We experience something similar. On Finkenwerder's northern dike, we are cordially welcomed by our host. We sit down on old carved wooden chairs at the rustic wooden table, encircled by our host's excellent library. We dine on herring, bread, cheese, and wine. Soon we forget wind and weather.

Our common family history has again brought us together. Each reports about his or her most recent archives visits, letters to contacts, and newly discovered documents. Our family tree extends into the ancient Finkenwerder courtyards, to Fischern [fishermen], Gastwirten [innkeepers], and Schiffszimmerleute [ship's carpenters]. Eventually our family tree converges with Pastor Sebastian König, who was written about by the Chronisten [chroniclers]. He was already living in Finkenwerder by 1590 and presumably died in office there in 1621.

Genealogical research is like archeology. One digs deeper and deeper into the layers of the past, holds up to the light what has long been forgotten, gets an increasingly clearer picture of the life circumstances of our ancestors, and experiences for oneself another world in a different time.

Our mosaic fills out, and soon we are in earldoms and cities, together with dukes and emperors whose history crossed paths with our ancestors. Impatient waiting is replaced by surprising new discoveries. We decipher old handwritten documents, examine coins, explore archives from Schleswig to Basel, search enrollment registries of the old universities, and unexpectedly find ourselves in the midst of events of the Reformation. We have gone back more than 14 generations to discover our ancestor, Urban Rieger, who later changed his name to Urbanus Rhegius. He was born in Langenargen on the Bodensee in 1489, before Columbus discovered the New World.

This book will tell about the reformer, Urbanus Rhegius, his family, and his descendants, as well as the turbulence, high points, and sorrows of their lives. They are our forebears, who mastered their lives in their own times, each according to his or her own talents. The clearer become the traces of our ancestors that time has not buried, the more our respect for their lives' work grows.

Work on genealogy is never finished. And yet – so we believe – we can now shape our acquired perspectives into a form. We would especially like to invite interested readers to provide us with corrections, amendments, and additions leading to greater understanding.

This book originates from a Northern German perspective framed by our family's chronology. It has taken us from the Island of Finkenwerder in the Elbe River to Langenargen on the Bodensee and back to the North.

It has taken curiosity and stamina to bring this work into being. It would please us if we could also arouse your curiosity!

WALTER KÖNIG
Tuttlingen
1998 – 2006

Introduction

A Historical Overview

The year is 1500. The winds of change blow through Europe. In the endless gloomy centuries of the Middle Ages, most people live in poverty and are anxious about salvation, patronizing treatment, and serfdom. Education is a privilege of the few.

Opposition to the powerful beliefs and demands of the Church begins to stir, first hesitantly, then irresistibly. In 14TH century England, John Wycliffe singlehandedly criticizes the Church's striving for property and urges a Church based on the Bible rather than on Church rules. Jan Hus, the Czechoslovakian reformer, is put to death at the stake for similar ideas during the 1415 Council of Konstanz.

Humanism arises in Italy in the late Middle Ages. During the Renaissance, art works portray a new image of men and women that changes the previously rigid scholarly forms of the Middle Ages. People begin to slowly break out of the old order and grasp the concept of individuality.

Humanism also has followers in France, England, and the Netherlands, the most influential of whom is Erasmus von Rotterdam.

In Germany, Humanism becomes a forerunner of the Reformation. Erasmus becomes the "Humanistenfürst" [Prince of the Humanists], admired and revered by the scholars of his time. He teaches a deep, Christ-like, moral philosophy and criticizes the many superficialities of the Church's daily activities. Erasmus puts forth a pure, unadulterated set of beliefs and, in doing so, engages with the groundswell of the Reformation. Huge hopes rest upon him. Also, Erasmus himself demonstrates proof of the ideas of the Reformation. First, however, his 1524 work on free will distances him from Luther. In 1517 Luther posts his 95 theses on the door of the Wittenberg Schlosskirche [castle church]. That act of demanding Church reform sets in motion a movement that keeps the whole century in suspense.

The world circa 1500 is in flux. Several decades earlier, Gutenberg invented the printing press. New ideas can now be printed and distributed many thousand times throughout the world. This rapid dissemination of knowledge is revolutionary, similar to computer technology in our time. In 1492, Columbus discovers the New World under orders from the Spanish king and queen. People on the old continent begin to look beyond its borders. Kaiser [Emperor] Karl V inherits an empire upon which "the sun never sets." Art, science, and discoveries are everywhere. The Italian Renaissance artists create timeless, immortal works of art. In 1506, Nürnberg citizen Martin Behaim creates the first globe of the world. The Spanish and Portuguese divide up the lands of the earth.

Our family is soon caught up in the radically changing times between the Middle Ages and the new era. During the discovery of our family history, it becomes clear that our history is intertwined with the larger events of the times. Just as written history is the memory of an entire people, the genealogy of one family is the origin of family members' identity and self-knowledge.

In 1489 in Langenargen am Bodensee, our ancestor, Urban Rieger, is born. By 1521, he has changed his name to Urbanus Rhegius and is a Domprediger [cathedral preacher] at the Augsburg Dom [Cathedral]. There, he witnesses the beginning of the Reformation at the 1521 Diet of Worms. Still, no one knows where his journey will lead. Along with Philipp Melanchthon, he becomes a fighter in the formulation of the Augsburger Glaubensbekenntniss [Augsburg Confession] and meets with Martin Luther in Coburg Schloss [castle] - an experience that makes a lasting impression on him.

Rhegius' way to Northern German begins in 1530 with the Imperial Diet of Augsburg. Here, he becomes acquainted with Herzog Ernst der Bekenner [Duke Ernst the Confessor].

Page 13

Duke Ernst is from Celle, and Rhegius pledges himself to him. As the Reformation develops in the Fürstentum [principality] of Lüneburg where Celle is located, Rhegius is appointed the first Generalsuperintendent [supervisor of many superintendents]. His assignment is to make the Reformation a success in the region.

Throughout generations, members of the Rhegius family have served various Landesherren [sovereign princes] as Geistliche [clergy], Amtmänner [senior civil servants], Kanzleischreiber [office clerks], Historiker [historians], Vögte [administrators], and as members of Kirchenjuraten [local church councils]. We meet a Rhegius daughter who is a Kammermagd [lady's maid], a grandson who is a Hofsinger [court singer], a Pfarrer [pastor] of an Evangelisch [Lutheran] church in Königsberg, and three Finkenwerder brothers who are Heimatdichter[regional poets].

Over the years, there are frequent connections between the Rhegius/König family and ruling houses. While there are detailed accounts in historical documents of a close relationship between

Duke Ernst the Confessor and Urbanus Rhegius, little is known about Urbanus' connections to the counts von Montfort and the dukes von Braunschweig und Lüneburg in Calenberg-Göttingen, Wolfenbüttel, and Harburg.

None of the Finkenwerder chroniclers report that Sebastianus Regius (a Rhegius grandson who in 1588 changes his name to Sebastian König) comes to the Elbe Island of Finkenwerder, a few miles downstream from Hamburg. There he looks after the interests of the Harburg lineage and solidifies in difficult times the young Reformation on the northern boundaries of the duchy of Braunschweig und Lüneburg.

Page 14

ILLUSTRATION 1: "Schloss Argen im Bodensee." Rebuilt after the fire of 1473. In the background are the Swiss Alps.[6]

Section I:
The Reformer
From Langenargen

Urbanus Rhegius (1489 – 1541) (201)[1]
HUMANIST, POET, THEOLOGIAN, REFORMER

The Political and Ecclesiastical Environment in the Grafschaft [Earldom] of Montfort am Bodensee
(TIME PERIOD APPROXIMATELY 1490 – 1540)

All of Urbanus Rhegius' biographers identify Langenargen am Bodensee as Rhegius' birthplace. In 1562, his son, Ernestus Regius, publishes his father's Latin works and writes:

23

"Natus est Vrbanus ad lacum Brigantinum, illa agrorum parte, quae Generosorum Comitum a monte forti dominatum agnoscit: Arga Longa ... "[2]

The history of the Counts von Montfort has its roots in the Earldom of Bregenz and the Count Palatinate of Tübingen. In the 12TH century, Gräfin [Countess] Elisabeth von Bregenz, the daughter of the last descendant of the long-established Earl of Bregenz's family, marries Hugo, the Palatine Count of Tübingen. The reason behind the marriage is that Hugo is securing claim to his wife's land. When Count Hugo dies in 1182, his sons, Rudolf von Tübingen and Hugo I, rule jointly. Hugo I then changes his title to Count von Montfort.[3]

Count Hugo I becomes founder of one of the most important aristocratic families in Schwaben [Swabia].[4] His property lies mainly in the Southern German area of the Bodensee with scattered property in Switzerland and Austria. Present day Liechtenstein also originally belongs to his estate. The family line, however, does not enjoy political autonomy for long. Arguments soon begin with Count Rudolf of Habsburg. In 1298, the Habsburgs militarily subjugate the Montforts. Over the centuries, the Montforts remain bound to the powerful Habsburg dynasty in multiple ways, until the house of Montfort is finally absorbed by the Habsburgs in 1780.

In 1343, Count Wilhelm II von Montfort, who obtains considerable wealth in Milan, completes construction of a castle on a small, off-shore island at Langenargen.[5] A bolt of lightning causes a fire that burns down the castle in 1473. After the castle is rebuilt, it appears approximately like the 1647 sketch by Matthias Merian (Illustration 1).

The castle stands amidst all the chaos of the times. It is a place for lavish celebrations, serves as residence for some members of the

Montfort family, and is a wartime weapons depot, warehouse, and fortress. With the decline of the Montfort Earldom in 1780, the castle falls to Austria in 1780, to Bayern [Bavaria] in 1805, and finally to Württemberg in 1810. The castle then lies in ruins for many years, until it is acquired in 1858 by König [King] Wilhelm I von Württemberg. He erects the current Moorish-Italianate style Schloss Montfort, which remains a prominent Langenargen landmark.

It is a Habsburg emperor who on January 8, 1453 declares Langenargen to be a city with its own ordinances and privileges. In this year, Count Haug (Hugo XIII)[7] accompanies Emperor Friedrich III to his coronation in Italy and, through this opportunity, obtains from him the above privileges favoring Langenargen.[8]

Page 16

The area of the castle becomes fortified and expanded under Count Hugo XIII, who rules from 1444 – 1491. He not only efficiently expands his property and estates, but also founds the Spital zum Heiligen Geist [Hospital of the Holy Ghost] in Langenargen, helping countless needy people over a period of 500 years.

The hospital's founding charter of October 12, 1491 entrusts it with performing the "öwige frühmess" [eternal mass] at the St. Fridolins-Altar in the hospital's Kapelle [chapel].[9] At this point, the Rieger (later Rhegius) family's association with the Counts von Montfort in Langenargen is mentioned for the first time. On April 28, 1492 the Church's Patron, Count Hugo XV, appoints a new chaplain of the St. Fridolins-Kapelle. His name: Conrad Rieger, father of Urban Rieger (Urbanus Rhegius), and currently the oldest known ancestor of our family.[10]

Urbanus Rhegius' connection to the House of Montfort becomes very important. Langenargen is a haven for him in difficult times. He occasionally lives in Langenargen by invitation of the Countess Magdalena from the nearby Schloss Tettnang and profits from the counts' close connection with the Universität [University] Freiburg, where the Montforts are generous patrons.

Humanism comes over the Alps from Italy in the 15TH century. It finds early acceptance in the nearby Reichsstadt [Free Imperial City] of Lindau. A 1478 treaty with the Habsburgs secures the route to Italy for Lindau and allows the exchange of goods and ideas to blossom, an excellent foundation for well-being, culture, and world interchange. Later, the people of Lindau welcome the Reformation. Isny, also a Reichsstadt in Oberschwaben [Upper Swabia], is the only place in the vicinity of Lindau where Luther's teachings are completely introduced.

Meanwhile, the Counts von Montfort remain strong Catholics. Their close connections to Habsburg emperors leave them no alternative. The emperor's Catholic views are also reinforced and supported by the activities and imperial entitlements of the brothers Johann II, Wolfgang I, and Hugo XVI. These three Montforts are contemporaries of Urbanus Rhegius. From their biography:

Count Johann II von Montfort (reigns 1520 – 1547)

- Born prior to 1489, student in Freiburg of Ulrich Zasius, who was the most well-known jurist of the time
- Served as administrator of Tirol [Tyrol] and counselor to the emperor

- Fought for the Habsburgs in 1532 in Ungarn [Hungary] against the Türken [Turks]
- As judge on the Supreme Court in Speyer, led the highest court in the empire and represented the power of the emperor's upper legal echelons
- Known as a scholar and eloquent orator[11]

Count Wolfgang (reigns 1520 – 1541)

- Born prior to 1489, senior civil servant of the government in Upper Austria
- Member of the Habsburg Imperial Regiment (1524 – 1530)
- Led 7,000 men in battle against the Turks in Hungary and was decorated by the emperor with the Order of the Golden Fleece[12]
- As the emperor's representative at the Imperial Diet of Augsburg on July 10, 1530, negotiated with the Evangelisch[13]

Count Hugo XVI (reigns 1520 – 1564)

- Studied law in Freiburg with Ulrich Zasius
- Initiated the Weingartener Vertrag [Treaty of Weingarten] from 1525 until the conclusion of the military action in the Bauernkrieg [Peasants' War]
- Served as counselor to the emperor at the Kasierlicher Rat und Reichsrat [Federal Council] and, as such, was often the diplomatic emissary for Emperors Karl V and Ferdinand

- Was the emperor's envoy to the Konzil vom Trient [Council of Trient] in 1552

- Accompanied Emperor Karl V in 1552 while his majesty fled from Kurfürst [Elector] Moritz of Sachsen [Saxony] via Innsbruck to Villach[14] (also included in the entourage was Duke Otto I of Harburg)

- While the brothers Johann and Wolfgang remained primarily in the service of the emperor, Hugo was in charge of governmental affairs for the Montforts

These few selected points clarify the status of the Counts von Montfort under the Habsburgs. At the end of the 16TH century, however, the decline of the Montforts' power and influence begins. Division of inheritances, a desire to continue building, and opulent appearances lead to increasing indebtedness from generation to generation. In 1592, as an indication of the decline, Wasserburg has to be sold and Montfort finally given over to the House of Austria (by now also Habsburg). Count Anton von Montfort dies in 1787, the last of the Montfort family line.

The Herrschaft [territory] of Argen remains under the rule of Austria for only a quarter century. While Bayern and Württemberg, which are Napoleon's allies, increase their land and influence, Austria gives up land in the Pressburger Frieden [Peace of Pressburg] on December 27, 1805. Montfort now belongs to Bayern. And the wheels of history turn further when in 1810 Argen becomes part of Württemberg, through a treaty between König [King] Friedrich of Württemberg and Bayern.

ILLUSTRATION 2: From the lineage table of the
four Counts von Montfort-Rothenfels showing the
members of the House mentioned in the text.[15]

ILLUSTRATION 3: The Counts von Montfort Coat of Arms.[16]

A red church flag is at the top, with three golden
rings in a silver field. On the shield is an open helmet,
which is topped by a Bischof's [bishop's] cap. The
corners of the helmet are silver and red.

Page 18

A Childhood in the Shadow of Montfort Castle

Considering the wide scope of Urbanus' life's work and his seem-
ingly effortless connections to the famous Humanists of his time, the
crowned heads, and the important Augsburg merchants, one could
suppose that from the cradle, such a life path must have been laid out
before him through birth and ancestry. Some things about Urbanus
will remain forever unknown. Some are due to the circumstances
into which he was born, others are produced by the radical changes
of his time, and still others are due to his latent talents.

The only sources of information about Urbanus Rhegius' birth
year are two of his letters from July 14, 1535. One is directed to
an Augsburg preacher. The other is to the Augsburg Bürgermeis-
ter [mayor] and Rat [city council], in which he says, "I am now 46
years old."[17] This statement suggests his birth year is 1489. Ernestus Regius, in his 1562 publication of his father's works, tells us that

his father got his Christian name only because his godparents had forgotten the name given to him by his parents. Also, the clergyman performing the baptism did not know which saint was born on that day. [The baby would traditionally be named after that saint.][18] So, the clergyman selected the Day of St. Urban, May 25, which was the saint's day closest to the baptism. From that, Liebmann concludes that Urbanus Rhegius' birth date had to be a few days prior, between the 20TH and 23RD of May, 1489.

The conditions at the start of Urbanus' life are anything but good. Like Erasmus von Rotterdam, Urbanus is the illegitimate son of a priest.[19] According to the Zeitgeist [spirit of the times], to be the illegitimate son of a priest is a serious personal defect. The priest who fathers an illegitimate child faces punishment from the Church, and his family is reviled.[20] The father might lose his position and all his possessions. This is among the most lenient punishments. At most, he loses his honor in the community. "Aside from our own body, our spouse, and our worldly possessions, we still have a treasure we cannot bear to lose; namely our good reputation," writes Luther in the eighth commandment in his Grosser Katechismus [Large Catechism]. That belief was also valid before Luther.

This is certainly one reason Urbanus mentions his mother, but not his father. Also, his son, Ernestus, in his 1562 edition of Urbanus' work, writes nothing about Urbanus' illegitimate birth. He states only that Urbanus "was born to honorable parents on the Bodensee." We may assume Ernestus knows more, but to protect the family's honor, he would not allow it to be publicly reported. Hence, Conrad Rieger intentionally becomes a forgotten man.

Nothing is known about Conrad Rieger's punishment. Also, nothing is known about what his official position may have been at the time of the birth. In 1492, however, three years after the birth of Urbanus, Conrad Rieger is appointed chaplain of Langenargen by Count Hugo XV, patron of the Church. This indicates an untroubled relationship with the House of Montfort, not adversely affected by the illegitimate birth of Urbanus. When Conrad Rieger fathers an illegitimate younger brother to Urbanus, the relationships in Langenargen apparently continue unaffected.[21]

Ernestus Regius reports in his father's *Vita* that Urbanus was "brought up in Lindau and went to school there." He comes to Lindau and its Latin School in about 1503. "Instruction was in Latin. The instruction hours were mornings from 7 – 9 in the summer, 8 – 10 in the winter, and afternoons from 1 – 3.

Page 19

On Saturdays and the evenings before holidays instruction was only in the morning, and, of course, on Saturdays was only an hour so that parents could require their children to assist at market. On Sundays and holidays the children were led in a procession by the teacher to listen to a sermon and sing Psalms in German ... Bathing in the lake was strictly forbidden. Resistant students could expect punishment, however, students were not to be hit on the head or other parts of their body where they could be injured."[22]

Even at that time, the school is steeped in tradition. Among the famous students who studied at the school to prepare themselves for the great universities from Heidelberg to Wittenberg to Krakau, Urbanus Rhegius is recognized in a 1928 school commemorative volume as "one of the theologians who distinguished himself at the 1530 Imperial Diet of Augsburg."

ILLUSTRATION 4: Urbanus attended the Lindau
Lateinschule [Latin School] from about 1503 until 1508.
Pictured here is the school building in 1528. (Ferd. Eckert:
Die Geschichte der Lateinschule Lindau, 1928.)

Are Urbanus' Studies in Freiburg Supported by the House of Montfort?

Throughout his life, Urbanus had fond memories of his student days in Freiburg. Ernestus reports that Urbanus Rhegius' professor, Ulrich Zasius, a Konstanz [Constance] native and distinguished professor of law at that time, loved Urbanus like a son. Zasius, the Humanist among the judiciary, is multi-faceted in his learning. His students praise his ability to inspire them. "We are fortunate to have found a teacher who admires France, marvels at Italy, glorifies Spain, and loves the Germans ... "[23] Zasius' Humanist friends come from far away. The atmosphere at Zasius' home is exuberant, and the world of antiquity comes to life before the eyes and ears of his listeners.

ILLUSTRATION 5: Ulrich Zasius, (1461 – 1535). Urbanus
Rhegius lives as a student in his house and is one of his favorite
pupils. A portrait of Zasius still decorates the façade of a
house on Kanzlei Street in his native city of Konstanz.[24]

Urbanus is permitted to use the private library in Zasius' home. In his 1861 book, Urbanus Rhegius – Leben und Ausgewählte Schriften [Life and Selected Writings], Gerhard Uhlhorn reports, "Urbanus made his own copious notes in the margins of Zasius' written manuscripts.

Zasius jokingly says that Urbanus is stealing his erudition." Urbanus often worked far into the night and then fell asleep with his head over the books on the table. When Zasius, who suffered from insomnia, found Urbanus in such a posture, he would sometimes stack books on Urbanus' shoulders. When Urbanus woke up, the books would noisily fall off, divulging the secret as to who had stealthily played a trick on him."[25]

Page 20

ILLUSTRATION 6: Scholarships must be paid back ... whenever the student ... comes into a great deal of money.[26]

In Zasius' house, Urbanus first comes into contact with the Humanists with whom Zasius exchanges exciting ideas. Among them are such famous names as Wimpfeling, Peutinger (Augsburg), and above all, Erasmus. Urbanus is fascinated by this world. Here he lays the foundation for many later friendships.

He enrolls in the Universität Freiburg on June 19, 1508 under the name "Urbanus Rieger de Argow." He apparently lives free of charge with Zasius.[27] Other students pay an annual fee of 30 Gulden, a sum Urbanus' mother cannot come up with. How does a student receive such preferential treatment? A few months earlier, on November 19, 1507, Count Johann II von Montfort also enrolls in the Universität Freiburg. Like Urbanus, Count Johann studies with Zasius.[28] It is difficult to believe that this is merely a coincidence because it is Count Johann's father, Count Hugo XV, who appoints Urbanus' father chaplain of Langenargen in 1492.

Count Johann and Urbanus are about the same age. It is not too much of a stretch to imagine that they played together as children in the shadow of the castle in Langenargen. We put forth this assumption because we also believe that Urbanus' mother served the Montforts, which we will later examine in more depth.[29] Thus, Urbanus grows up in a privileged world closed to outsiders.

ILLUSTRATION 7: Count Johann II, von Montfort-Rothenfels, from a 1523 portrait panel by Bernhard Striegel. (National Gallery of Ireland, Dublin). Count Johann is a contemporary and fellow student of Urbanus in Freiburg.

It is not only Urbanus' diligence and talents that open doors for him in Freiburg, but also the House of Montfort's recommendations, since the Montforts have longstanding close ties to the university.[30] Urbanus' good relationship with the Count's family is noteworthy and will be clarified later. In 1521, Urbanus dedicates to Countess Magdalena his German-Latin translation of Erasmus von Rotterdam's *Auslegung eines Paulusbriefes* [*Explanation of One of St. Paul's Letters*].[31] And his friend in Ulm, Wolfgang Rychard, writes Urbanus on January 11, 1522, "ex arce Tetnang," from Burg [Castle] Tettnang. A stay at the castle is impossible without an invitation from the countess.

Urbanus' studies in Freiburg lead to an extremely important acquaintance that would have the utmost significance for his future path. He becomes an enthusiastic follower of Johann Mayer von Egg,

soon known as Johann Eck, who had lectured in philosophy and theology in Freiburg since 1502.

Page 21

Urbanus gets to know Eck at Zasius' house, where Eck is a "well-
liked guest."[32] Urbanus calls Eck "a star among scholars" and says
that "there will be no greater name in his time."[33] Urbanus writes
exuberant poems praising Eck, which soon leads to difficulties for
Urbanus.

In Freiburg, Urbanus acquires the so-called baccalaureate degree,
the lowest academic degree, somewhat comparable to the "Abitur"
degree in Germany today. The date is May 22, 1510. Liebmann concludes that Urbanus must have been a very gifted student because it
takes him only a year and a half to complete his degree.[34]

Eck has to leave Freiburg in 1510 because of a quarrel with the
scholastics who stick to the old rules. This creates a problem for
Urbanus as well. He follows Eck to Ingolstadt and enrolls in the
university there on May 11, 1512. At that time, no one suspects that
a bitter feud will soon break out between them.

In the spring of 1516, Urbanus receives his master's degree. He
has to promise to lecture in Ingolstadt for two more years. Among
the themes of his lectures are the works of Aristotle, St. Augustine,
St. Thomas Aquinas, Erasmus von Rotterdam, and others. Some of
his lectures are preserved, and Liebmann confirms that Urbanus "is
astonishingly well versed in Aristotle's scientific thinking."

Overall, the years in Ingolstadt are very productive for
Urbanus. He becomes a member of the "Bayrischen Litterarischen
Gesellschaft" [Bayern Literary Society], which promotes poetry and

history.[35] But beyond the membership, Urbanus also profits from an assignment from the vice chancellor of the university, Duke Ernst von Bayern. The assignment is to contact Erasmus von Rotterdam and persuade the renowned Humanist to come to Ingolstadt.[36]

Urbanus can offer Erasmus a considerable salary of 200 Gulden and further considerations, but the attempt fails. Erasmus wants to keep his independence and will not pledge himself anywhere. In spite of this, Urbanus is honored by the letter from the "Prince of Humanists" in which Urbanus is extolled as "smart, eloquent, educated, in sum, he is gifted and multi-talented."[37] It is important, however, to view this statement in the context of the times, in which Humanists shower each other with praise. On the other hand, Erasmus does seem to be impressed by Urbanus, because he writes to the Canon von Botzheim in Konstanz to send his regards to "Optimo Patrono meo vrbanissimo Vrbano plurimam ex me salutem dicito."[38] (Approximately translated as: to my very best supporter Urban, who has a fine, sensitive, discriminating mind.)

... "by this act, the emperor crowned me ... "

Being crowned poet laureate by the emperor seems strange to us today, like a relic from times past. In antiquity, poets put on the laurel garland with pomp and circumstance.

"Poeta et orator laureatus" – poet laureate and orator. When this ancient tradition is revived in the Middle Ages, Petrarca, the Italian leader of the Humanist movement, receives his laurel garland on the steps of the capitol in Rome on Easter Day, 1341.[39] The award honors his literary works. In Germany, it is the Frank, Conrad Celtis, who is first awarded this honor. He receives the laurel wreath in 1487 from the hand of Emperor Friedrich III at the Burg Nürnberg. Schottenloher speaks of the ceremony publicly recognizing Humanism, "which could make those present experience what it was like at the court and in high society."

Page 22

ILLUSTRATION 8: This painting by Martersteig (1860) shows the Emperor Maximilian I crowning Hutten.[41]

Page 23

Emperor Maximilian I, an important promoter of Humanism, founds his own "Dichterkollegium" [College for Poets] in Vienna to encourage the arts of poetry and oratory. "The one who is being crowned poet laureate should foremost be well-known as a poet, and he should enjoy all the privileges that come to a person who is crowned by the emperor.[40] Maximilian asserts that students should learn "to be critical thinkers, skeptical until acceptable proof is provided, able to entertain revolutionary ideas, and free to seek the truth."

In 1517, Ulrich von Hutten and Urbanus Rhegius are the last, but not least, among the long list of important people crowned by Maximilian. Ernestus Regius reports: "Maximilian highly praises Urbanus, personally crowns Urbanus Poet Laureate and Orator in the customary ceremony,[42] and bestows upon him all the privileges associated with that title, even though Urbanus has not yet earned his theology degree."[43] Unfortunately, the official directive is not preserved, but Ernestus reports that it was signed by the emperor himself.

Liebmann dates the crowning between August 20 – 22, 1517. Even more precisely, we find noted in the *Genealogia* [*Genealogy*] the date " ... August 21, 1517." [44] Here the exact date is established. Uhlhorn and Liebmann do not mention the names of those present. "The emperor presented the laurel garland and ring and gave him the right to teach the subjects of poetry and oratory in all schools as well as bestowed upon him all the privileges, rights, honors, favors, and freedoms that poets and orators crowned by the emperor enjoy either through the rights of law or by birth." [45]

It is astounding that a 28 year old student is being honored by the emperor, who, next to the Papst [pope], is the most powerful man in the Holy Roman Empire of the German Nation.

ILLUSTRATION 9: Emperor Maximilian I in the year 1519. Portrait by Albrecht Dürer, Kunsthistorisches Museum, Vienna (above). On August 21, 1517, Urbanus Rhegius receives from the hand of the emperor the symbols of crowned poets and orators: laurel wreath, beret, ring, and staff[46] (below).

Page 24

When in a November 8, 1517 letter Rhegius writes to Vadian, his friend in St. Gallen, it sounds as if Urbanus himself initiated the honor: "In short, it is as if I were urged by Apollo to go to the emperor's court to ask for the laurel wreath of poet-orator from the invincible emperor and after most graciously being granted the honor, I left. The most distinguished people from all over were there. Quite a few benefactors were present. The most prominent was Jacobus Spiegel, a friend and patron of the arts." [Translated from the Latin into German and then into English.]

Who is this highly distinguished Jacob Spiegel? He is a student of Ulrich Zasius in Freiburg until 1504. In 1512, he becomes the confidential secretary to Emperor Maximilian I. He then serves Karl V beginning in 1520. Two years later, through the intercession of Erasmus, he becomes secretary to Erzherzog [Archduke] Ferdinand, where he distinguishes himself as highly influential.[47] Spiegel has a work by Rhegius in his large library,[48] and Spiegel always maintains close contact with his teacher, Zasius. Therefore, it is probable that Urbanus and Spiegel know each other through Zasius and that Urbanus asks his friend to intercede with the emperor on his behalf.

Spiegel probably has the emperor's ear enough to recommend a student of Zasius and thereby also bestow an honor. "Within the circle of important men who are in close contact with Maximilian is Zasius, not only a legal scholar and Humanist, but also an outstanding jurist..."[49] So, we come full circle.

It is not known for which of his works Rhegius is considered outstanding and therefore being honored by the Emperor. According to the information Urbanus shares with his teacher, Johannes Rhagius Aesticampianus on April 4, 1518, the emperor decrees the following in an addendum to the ceremonial crowning " ... through this act the emperor crowned me, thereby making me a Christian poet, so that I sing the praises of the gods, more zealously than the evil spirit." [Translated from the Latin into German and then into English.]

The day of this event, August 21, 1517, is only a few weeks before October 31, 1517 on which date Martin Luther nails his 95 theses on the Wittenberg Schlosskirche door and the Reformation begins. What does it mean for Urbanus to be a "Christian poet" in the ensuing years of the dispute between the emperor's Catholic dynasty and Luther, the reformer?

From Konstanz, Tübingen, and Basel on the Way to Augsburg

Urbanus Rhegius spends six years in Ingolstadt. There he obviously has a difficult beginning, because for the first time he is on his own and misses the support he had enjoyed in Freiburg. Now he must earn a living to maintain himself. To do that, he tutors young noblemen. The young noblemen, however, do not pay, and Urbanus is pressured by his creditors. He knows no way out other than to become a paid foot soldier. Johann Eck, his teacher, finds Urbanus in this difficult situation in the marketplace among other young men looking for work. Eck rescues Urbanus at the last minute, using his own money to help Urbanus.[50]

As the year 1518 turns into 1519, Urbanus leaves Ingolstadt. Although he is very thankful for the city and the university, his life there apparently does not suit him. The city has nothing but cabbage, beets, and beer to offer, whereas he writes eloquently in a departing poem that Swabia, Franconia, the Rhineland, and his home on the Bodensee are "endowed with wonderful gifts and wreathed with vines."

Apparently, Urbanus soon prepares for his return to the Bodensee because on October 30, 1518 he is already awarded the position of "chaplain of the St. Georg-Altar at the St. Stephan-Kirche in Konstanz."[51]

Page 25

Properties in Unterbuhwil near Bishopszell, pastures in Wollmatingen, and a house in the Hinteren Khrenck in Konstanz belong to the chaplaincy.[52]

In the Freie Reichsstadt [Free Imperial City] of Konstanz, just as in Lindau, there is much interest in Luther's ideas. A few years later, in 1525, the city is Evangelisch. Sacrificed to the conflict are these icons in the St. Stephan-Kirche: 14 altars broken to pieces, liturgical books destroyed, and the church's treasures melted down.[53] No trace of the St. Georg-Altar remains.

In the spring of 1519 Urbanus is ordained as a priest, which probably takes place in Meersburg.[54] Bishop Hugo von Landenberg promotes him to vicar to the bishop in Konstanz.[55]

Urbanus' work at St. Stephan's is apparently of short duration because in July 1519 he has already been appointed to the chaplain position at "St. Konrad beim Heiligen Grab" [St. Konrad at the Holy Tomb] in the Konstanz Münster [Cathedral]. Because there is danger of plague, Urbanus cannot keep the appointment and leaves town.[56] The St. Konrad-Altar has special significance. It is located in the deeper vaults of the cathedral next to the so-called Mauritius-rotunde [rotunda], and it is a replica of the holy tomb in Jerusalem (1260).

Despite the honor of this assignment on a historic site - the Council of Konstanz (1414 – 1418) was convened in this city in the presence of religious and secular dignitaries from all of Europe - Urbanus appears to pursue other interests. After a few months, he gives up the benefits associated with his position and on August 20, 1519 enrolls in the Universität Tübingen. Nothing is known about his studies there.[57] His stay must have been very brief because of all the other activities he is undertaking.

At Easter 1520 Urbanus is deep in the study of Greek. Under the guidance of the Ravensburg Humanist, Michael Hummelberg, he learns Greek together with Johann Fabri, the Konstanz vicar general, and Johann von Botzheim, the canon of the cathedral. These names represent the Humanist circle of Konstanz.[58] While the gentlemen study in Hummelberg's residence, Fabri receives a letter from Johann Eck in Rome. He reports about his work on behalf of the Päpstliche Bulle [papal bull] against Luther. Eck explicitly says that Fabri may give the letter to Urbanus to read. "With that, Rhegius becomes among the very first people in the German-speaking world know about the papal bull that condemns Luther's teachings."[59] The letter must have shifted the group into a state of high excitement, a first bolt of lightning on the horizon of the early Reformation.

Yet, all is still calm. Urbanus is engaged in scholarship. He criticizes the clergy's insufficient knowledge and writes an instruction book for clergy education. Liebmann calls it a "document for the Humanistic education of the clergy that is highly interesting and beyond compare ... ".[60]

Urbanus is now 30 years old. His diverse, somewhat short-lived activities reveal his inner unrest. How should his path unfold? Can he become someone more influential than a simple priest? What should he do in a time when upheaval is dawning?

Page 26

In Augsburg, the position of cathedral preacher is announced. Urbanus applies for the position. On July 1, 1520 he delivers a trial sermon and a second trial sermon on July 8. He is hired as cathedral preacher on July 9 "on the condition that he earn his Doctor of Theology degree before his appointment."[61] The Augsburg Domkapitel [cathedral chapter] again emphasizes that he will not get the position unless he has his doctorate and that his income will be determined accordingly. He loses no time and goes to Basel, where he is 19TH among the 22 students of Ludwig Bär who attend Bär's lectures from May 1 to October 17. He arrives late, about three months into the current semester.[62]

ILLUSTRATION 10: In the summer of 1520, Urbanus Rhegius enrolls in the Universität Basel. "Dominus Urbanus Rhegius, artium liberalium magister, orator et poeta laureatus ex Lindaw dioc Const." He is in a hurry to earn his doctorate. (Universitätsbibliothek Basel).

On November 21, 1520 he can assume the position of cathedral preacher in Augsburg, from which we can deduce that he now has his doctorate because it is a prerequisite for the position. He later signs his public documents with a "D." (Doktor der Theologie) or "der hayligen schrifft Doctor" [Doctor's Degree of the Holy Scripture].

1521 – A Turbulent Year in Augsburg

Having lived in the Imperial Free Cities of Lindau, Konstanz, and Freiburg, Urbanus is used to new, free ways of thinking. In these cities, people are open to new things and curious about new ideas. Of course, up until now, the Humanists are an elite circle of men who view and explain the world with new eyes. But, they do not change things. Now a young monk comes from Wittenberg and shakes the foundations of the prevailing order.

Augsburg, also a Free Imperial City, is more than a beloved place. Emperor Maximilian I prefers it to other cities and comes almost yearly to the "beautiful, merry, graceful, well-built, clean city endowed with happy people and especially beautiful women."[63] He comes not only to celebrate, but also because conferences are held here and important decisions are made. It is also the wealth of the Fugger merchant family that repeatedly draws the Habsburg emperor to the city of merchants.

Finally, Augsburg is the city to which the 35 year old Luther is summoned by the papal legate, Kardinal [Cardinal] Cajetan, in October 1518. Luther is the guest of Johann Frosch, prior of the Karmeliterkloster [Carmelite Monastery] of St. Anna. Luther hopes for a discussion with the cardinal, however, the cardinal insists on one word only: "revoco." [I recant.] Luther does not recant. The meeting with the Augsburg cardinal leads to Luther's expulsion from the Roman Catholic Church and the 1521 summons to the Reichstag zu Worms [Diet of Worms].[64]

As Urbanus assumes his position in Augsburg at the end of 1520, the papal bull threatening Luther with excommunication is official and to be proclaimed in all churches. Urbanus encounters an exceedingly delicate situation because the cathedral chapter is divided over this pronouncement and tries to delay it.[65]

Page 27

Finally, after four weeks, on December 30, 1520, Urbanus is required to ascend the Augsburg Dom pulpit and read the text out loud. The cathedral chapter explicitly states that he should defer only to the pope and the bishop, not to the cathedral chapter.[66] Moreover, the cathedral chapter's position is that it will have nothing more to do with the proclamation of the papal bull. Urbanus stands alone. The cathedral chapter's tactics must have been a confirmation of Urbanus' own reservations.

Here is an excerpt from the cathedral chapter's text that Urbanus presented:

"Regarding the Christian burial and penalty[67] for those who were disrespectful and/or those who defamed, behaved improperly, acted brazenly against the law, or committed other transgressions against either the spiritual or civil law, these people are to be fettered. Any Christian, no matter what his social standing or title, also will be chained if he has any accursed commodities and/or if he endorses, supports, praises, furthers, or keeps the false teachings of these wretched sinners, the same punishment applies. In addition, anyone, by legal order of the penalties prescribed above, who secretly or publicly has booklets containing these heretical, wretched ideas, or who embraces, prints, sells, adopts, or supports these booklets will likewise be so punished. Sinners who sustain these profane defilements shall answer to their righteous, respectable bishops, their vicars or others designated by the bishop. These bishop appointees shall collect said booklets and shall burn them before the clergy and the people assembled by order of this edict."[68]

The threatened punishments are harsh. Whoever possesses Luther's books will be denied a Christian burial, and heretics shall receive the same punishment. The books must be surrendered and publicly burned. The people are uneasy, irritated, and unsure. The city council fears the unrest. Urbanus himself is part of this inflammatory atmosphere. He composes a pamphlet that says it is not Luther, but rather the papal bull that causes "irreparable harm."[69] And the Augsburg chronicler, Rem, notes that Rhegius begins " ... to preach Luther's views." The writing is dedicated to the Humanist Jacob Näf (Nepos) from Tettnang, a professional colleague of Erasmus and authority on ancient languages. He is a confidant of Zwingli.[70] One does not err in assuming that by this act Rhegius wants to draw the attention of the people in his homeland to the progress of the Reformation.

His personal situation at the time is very comfortable. He lives in the house of the bishop of Augsburg and earns a respectable salary of 200 Gulden. The Universität Ingolstadt had not even offered Erasmus more money than that. This is a high annual salary that makes him envied by some and attacked by others.[71] His position as cathedral preacher appears secure since he also receives a 100 Gulden allowance from the cathedral chapter for renovation of the house he is living in.

His public endorsement of Luther soon causes him trouble. On the papal side, the cathedral chapter is instructed to see to it that Rhegius recants his "utterances." The threat is added that whoever endorses "Luther's errors" will be treated as a heretic.[72] Rhegius is warned. He knows the Church's history and also knows that the Roman Catholic Church's power is nothing to be fooled with. What should he do? What can he do?

In 1521 Emperor Karl V invites delegates to the Imperial Diet of Worms. Martin Luther must answer for and recant his theses before the assembled dignitaries of the nation and the emperor. What happens? He appears calm and self-assured: "Here I stand. I cannot do otherwise. God help me. Amen."

Page 28

The emperor, always concerned about preserving the unity of the Roman Catholic Church and the Catholic empire, reacts strongly and imposes an imperial ban on Luther. In order to prevent his imminent arrest on the way back to Wittenberg, Kurfürst Friedrich der Weise [Elector Friedrich the Wise] takes Luther into protective custody in Wartburg Castle.[73]

As a Free Imperial City, Augsburg is represented with a delegation at Worms. Some authors report that Rhegius was a member of the Augsburg delegation. This is not documented, however, and most likely is an error.[74] If he had been present, he certainly would have written about these important events in his letters or other writings. The only verifiable meetings with Luther take place in 1530 in Coburg and 1537 in Schmalkalden.

How closely Rhegius follows the events in Worms is attested to in a pamphlet he writes in 1521 under the pseudonym Simon Hess. He composes a dialogue with Luther that takes place during the Diet of Worms.[75] "I may be killed, but the truth is invincible," responds Luther in the dialogue to a question about why he comes to Worms after being repeatedly harassed. Although Rhegius' presence at Worms is fictitious, Duke Otto I actually is a delegate and must have been representing the principality of Lüneburg's interests against the emperor. Duke Otto writes, " ... When I came to Worms, the emperor sent for me the next day ... "[76] Duke Otto I knows Luther from his student days in Wittenberg, where with his brother, Ernst, he enrolls in the university in 1512. Otto lives in Wittenburg until 1516. He knows Luther and certainly also knows Luther's stance against the Roman Catholic Church.[77]

The Augsburg delegation is under the leadership of Bishop Christoph von Stadion, so Rhegius no doubt quickly becomes informed about the events in Worms. Being just 30 years old, how should he confront this situation? How should he negotiate this slippery slope? Does he believe that his position as cathedral preacher and the indications of support for Luther in Augsburg give him enough clout to take Luther's side? Has he not dreamed for years with his Humanist friends on the Bodensee, in Freiburg, and Ingolstadt about going in a new direction and breaking down entrenched behaviors? And has Emperor Maximilian I not said that one should "think critically, be skeptical until acceptable proof is provided, entertain revolutionary ideas, and be free to seek the truth?" Is this now the opportunity?

ILLUSTRATION 11: On December 30, 1520, Urbanus Rhegius ascends the pulpit of the Augsburg Dom and reads aloud the papal bull threatening Luther with excommunication. (From Franz Häussler: Die Kaisermeile – Augsburgs Prachtstrasse, Augsburg 2000).

He does not deliberate for long. During Pentecost in the Augsburg Dom on May 30, 1521, while Luther is translating the New Testament into German at Wartburg Castle, Rhegius gives a sermon against the selling of indulgences that stirs up a hornet's nest. Pentecost is traditionally the time when the most indulgences are sold. That the cathedral preacher himself argues at this time against indulgences absolutely does not sit well with the cathedral chapter members. Loss of revenue is feared. The Domprobst [priests' superior] and Rhegius' special benefactor, Gerhard Adelmann von Adelmannshausen, join in. Rhegius receives a "dressing down," as Liebmann puts it.

One assumes that Urbanus will now step back to buy time and find fellow supporters. But instead of pacifying the cathedral chapter and presenting himself as more moderate, he makes his anti-indulgence speeches public.[78] In the process, his assertions become stronger and he acquires a larger sphere of influence – a non-acceptable affront to the cathedral chapter.

Added to the agitated mood in Augsburg, the following scene takes place in the cathedral, as described by Heimbürger:

" ... as he (Rhegius) left the pulpit, he was approached by a Domherr [member of the cathedral chapter], who sought to have a word with him and in doing so, struck him across the face with the large ring of keys he was carrying and set off a huge tumult. After that, Dr. Rhegius left ... "[79] Uhlhorn describes further details about the incident. As Urbanus preaches against the abuses of the church and comes down from the pulpit, a cathedral canon approaches him, starts to exchange words with him and accuses him of Luther's heresy. Rhegius' answers anger the cathedral canon so much that he strikes him in the face with a large ring of keys and then a huge fracas breaks out ... [80] An unknown artist recaptures the scene.

The situation becomes even more difficult. In July, Urbanus is reprimanded again, however, the differing views seem irreconcilable. Beginning in September 1521, he applies for a leave of absence because he wants " ... to go into a natural spa" to rejuvenate himself. His leave of absence is denied because the plague is rampant in Augsburg, and the cathedral chapter maintains that his presence at the current time is essential.[82]

Urbanus is persistent and submits a second leave of absence request, to which the cathedral chapter responds with the proviso that if Urbanus wants to resign, he must name his own replacement. It is surprising how fast everything now progresses. By September 20th his house is already disposed of. On October 2, the cathedral chapter asks whether the preacher from Eichstädt, Matthias Kretz, would come to Augsburg as cathedral preacher. Three days later Rhegius' resignation is recorded in the cathedral's records.

The important point is that Rhegius is giving up a highly endowed position in order not to have to accommodate others. Does he believe that going public on his own in 1521 will make it possible for him to achieve even more influence than did his preaching in the cathedral? He travels through Ulm to his home on the Bodensee.

Page 30

ILLUSTRATION 12: When Rhegius is speaking too much truth ... "a member of the Augsburg cathedral chapter approaches him and strikes him in the face with a large ring of keys." [81]

Home Refuge on the Bodensee

The small town of Langenargen's solitude and the expanse of the Bodensee create a fitting place for Urbanus to revitalize and reflect upon what has happened and what is coming.

It does not appear that Urbanus is just resting. He revives his old personal connections and writes on January 4, 1522 to Erasmus von Rotterdam:

"Just as we hoped, you are the sunshine that will drive away the inner and therefore the most dangerous darkness in our world. I say to you that whoever denies that you are the founder of the new theology is a liar and an ingrate.

You are the first theologian who has advocated for returning theology from the murky depths of the scholastics to its source in the Holy Scriptures and have done it with such humility that not once have enemies been injured by your healing and necessary admonitions.

Above all, you have spurred a return to the old theology, from which you then led us cautiously to canonical writings, which are the clearest source. Lastly, with your untiring learned work you have brought so much understanding that no kind of academic study can advance progress more than the holy theology ... "[83] Urbanus diligently ponders the various types of Humanistic thought and its new theology. Enthusiasm emanates from his words and from his conviction that the way forward must be pursued.

Here in his home territory he seeks to win over the Montfort Earldom to Luther's ideas.[84] He dedicates his German translation of the Cyprian explanation of the Lord's Prayer to the spiritual Madam Amalie von Danckenschwyl, who is a family member of the administrators of Langenargen.[85] Among these activities and dedications is his German translation of a Latin work by Erasmus and an interpretation of Paul's Letter to Titus, which he dedicates to Countess Magdalena von Montfort.[86]

While he is writing to Erasmus from Langenargen, a few days later, on January 11, 1522, he is in the Castle Tettnang and writes his friend, Dr. Rychard, the city doctor in Ulm.[87] Tettnang is the residence of Countess Magdalena of Montfort-Tettnang, who was born the Countess of Öttingen. She plays an important role at this time. After the death of her esteemed husband in 1520, she astutely recognizes that she wants to become regent of the Tettnang lineage. We see Rhegius strive to make contact with the person in the highest possible position.

The countess is very interested in spiritual questions. Also, Rhegius previously interpreted the Psalms at her request and dedicated the interpretation to her.[88] They have a long-standing relationship based on mutual esteem.

Page 32

ILLUSTRATION 13: The first page of the dedication to Countess Magdalena von Montfort: "I often think of Your Grace's interest from years ago in listening to my interpretation of the Psalms."

Rhegius may have promised that through such an advantageous connection he could get Luther's thinking accepted in his home territory. Despite his ties to the countess his ambitions cannot be realized because of the House of Montfort's political sympathies with the Catholic Church. Magdalena dies on April 22, 1525.

While Rhegius is studying Luther's writings and corresponding with Zwingli and Vadian, he again seeks employment. In Strassburg he is among three "exceptional preachers" who have been put forward for the position of preacher for the famous Münster [Cathedral] Strassburg. He is, however, not chosen for the position.[89] Urbanus is familiar with Strassburg from a previous visit in 1510 while he was there on behalf of his Professor Zasius. He would definitely have gladly gone to this magnificent Free Imperial City.

"Have you fed the hungry?"
BETWEEN HALL IN TIROL AND AUGSBURG

Then the unexpected happens. In September 1522 we find Rhegius in Hall, Tirol. He becomes the Prinzipalkaplan [principal chaplain] and preacher in the Hall Heiltumkapelle [Holy Chapel] of the St. Nikolaus-Kirche. The original appointment document, dated September 19, 1522, is in the Bischöflichen Archiv [Bishopic Archives] in Brixen.

Liebmann surmises that Rhegius comes to Hall through the intercession of Blasius Hölzl, an influential official in Emperor Maximilian's employ. Hölzl is friends with the Augsburg Stadtschreiber [writer in residence] and Humanist, Peutinger, who knew Urbanus as cathedral preacher there.[90] There is, however, another possible explanation for the connection. The Hall marketplace has been a center for book purchasing in Tirol since the 1520s, especially for books about the Reformation.[91] The Augsburg book printers know Rhegius through his publications there. This possibility is also conceivable.

The overriding point is that there is thriving trade between the merchant city of Augsburg and Hall, with its important market rights – and privileges. Augsburg merchants are among the most important visitors to the Hall annual fair.[92] That Rhegius comes to Hall through one of these opportunities seems plausible, however, which possibility is factually correct we cannot ascertain today.

Through his candidacy for the position in Hall, Urbanus indirectly meets "his" emperor, Maximilian I. The basis of Urbanus' chaplain position in Hall is tied to a donation by the Florentine, Waldauf von Waldenstein, who is an advisor to the emperor.

Page 33

The donor clearly specifies the preacher's responsibilities, not all of which may please Rhegius. He must conduct more masses each week, ensure veneration of the relics, and support the indulgences – a sensitive point that will soon create problems for him.

His income in Hall is about 208 Rheinishe Gulden. In addition, the chapel provides the chaplain and preacher "a cheerful, well-planned residence with a courtyard, garden, abundant fountains, and all necessary belongings situated in the city of Hall in Yntal. The taxes, upkeep, surveillance, and all other expenses are completely free."[93] Hence, Urbanus receives accommodations, a house, and garden at no charge so that his income is tax-free. His mother, who travels from Langenargen to Hall with him, oversees his household.

All is well arranged, as it was previously in Augsburg. In Hall, Urbanus has the same beliefs and convictions he had in Augsburg. Again he risks his well-ordered life. He severely pushes back against or ignores his sworn chapel duties. In one of his fledgling sermons he strongly attacks the indulgences ... "On the most recent day he will not ask how many false gods have you worshipped ... but rather, have you fed the hungry?"[94] It is a renewed attack against the established practices of the Roman Catholic Church.

April 10, 1523 becomes an important day for Urbanus. Ferdinand, Archduke of Austria, Count of Tirol, Infant [Heir Prince] of Spain, and brother of Emperor Karl V, visits Tirol as Landesfürst [Sovereign Prince] for the first time following transfer of the earldom to him by his brother on February 7, 1522. The citizens prepare a great reception for their new Fürst [prince]. The city is decked out, and the citizens are festively dressed. Delegations in colorful uniforms ride to meet him and await him outside the city – all in magnificent regalia. Urbanus heads the Church's delegation. The relics from the holy chapel are brought along and are presented to the people and their ruler. Franz Schweyger, the Hall city chronicler, describes a colorful picture of this day:

"At the edge of the fields of Hall are all the clerics in their official robes, also Doctor Urbanus Rhegius, the preacher, as well as the holy relics. There are also the children of the dignitaries and wealthy young men of the citizenry with a banner ... which they bring before the prince. Wolfgang Waltnhofer, the mayor, ... greets him in Latin and honors him with a gift from the city. The prince and his Gemachl [prince's consort][95] ride into the St. Nikolaus Kirche. Everyone sings the Te Deum Laudamus ... Afterwards Ferdinand is invested as Prince of Tirol in the city of Hall."[96]

Ferdinand's riding into the church can be taken quite literally. This is the Herrscher's [ruler's] prerogative. What exactly does Schweyger say about the proceedings in the church? Ferdinand is indeed invested in the St. Nikolaus Kirche as Sovereign Prince and Count of Tirol. Rhegius attends this historic event and sees everything up close.

Page 34

> ILLUSTRATION 14: On April 10, 1523 the 20 year old Archduke Ferdinand comes to Hall. He is "a lively, friendly young man, blond, grey-eyed, and slight, who looks nothing like a ruler."[97] Urbanus and the clergy greet him in front of the city gate.

Only two weeks later Rhegius visits Augsburg. On the one hand, the first problems arise in Hall because of his support for Luther. On the other hand, "he longs for" Augsburg. From his letter of September 16, 1524 we learn what sort of longing this is ... Urbanus is in love! He congratulates his old friend and teacher, Wolfgang Fabricius Capito, who is en route to Strassburg to his own wedding and adds: "I would have married over a year ago if the storms of persecution had not been against me. I am still being tossed about by them." (See Appendix 1.)

We learn that the marriage has been planned since 1523. And who is the bride? She is Anna Weissbrücker, to whose father, Kaspar Weissbrücker, Urbanus dedicates two of his works in 1523. The agreement between names and dates leaves no doubt that he already wanted to marry Anna in 1523.

It sounds dramatic when Urbanus mentions "the storms of persecution," but they are real, and they delay the marriage for two years. Before he leaves Augsburg, he receives a warning from the Hall senate. He should not yet come back. The bishop of Brixen has turned Ferdinand against Rhegius, and the Archduke is so angry, Rhegius would not be safe in Hall. He sends Ferdinand a letter of apology via the Hall city council, but it is not heard.[98]

In the letter to his friend, Capito, we further learn that Rhegius preaches three times a week to the Augsburg Carmelites and that, at the Fuggers' request, he acts as a substitute for Father Speiser in St. Moritz, where the Fuggers have been patrons since 1518. It has long been well known that the Fuggers are the financiers of the Catholic emperor. On the other hand, the Fuggers are open to the world and respect Rhegius, called the "Merchants' Preacher" from Augsburg.[99] The distinction between Evangelichen [Protestants] and Katholischen [Catholics] is not yet firmly established.

Rhegius uses his extended stay in Augsburg to write additional publications. His *Himmlischer Ablassbrief* [*Holy Indulgences Letter*] is informative, a pamphlet which he publishes in 1523 on the Feast of Corpus Christi. Only God can forgive sins – and He does it without demanding money! Because Rhegius wants to stand up for his acts, he signs the document: "Proclaimed and certified by Doctor Urbanus Rhegius from Augsburg."

Here he resumes his life's calling. Liebmann calls Rhegius' *Himmlischer Ablassbrief* a "remarkable document for its time ... a clearly defined turning point in western history." Liebmann is convinced that Rhegius purposely releases his *Himmlischer Ablassbrief* at the same time the papal indulgences are offered on the Feast of Corpus Christi in the church where Rhegius preaches.[100]

Page 35

ILLUSTRATION 15: The Himmlischer Ablassbrief.
Rhegius assures the faithful that true forgiveness of sins
comes only from God, not from paying indulgences.[101]

His move is both ironic and daring. Papal indulgences are offered
at the same time as Urbanus' *Himmlischer Ablassbrief*. Both promise
forgiveness of sins, which from Urbanus costs nothing because true
forgiveness comes only from God ... "and not for the sake of money."
When one considers that through similar remarks he lost his position as Augsburg's cathedral preacher and placed in jeopardy his
second position in Hall, one cannot deny his honest convictions and
courage.[102] (Remember that the purchase of indulgences is an essential source of church income and of Urbanus' own economic foundation.)

In about July or August Rhegius returns to Hall, where the situation is so volatile, he has to be led to the pulpit under guard.[104] He
writes friends that the Senate and the people want him, however, the
bishops of Trient and Brixen try to bring him down in every possible way. He hurriedly flees from Hall and returns to Augsburg. He
comes back to Hall on November 9, 1523 because he believes the
situation is now safe.

On the contrary, Hall is not safe. On November 13, 1523, the pre-
siding bishop in Brixen, Sebastian Sprenz, issues an arrest order on
the grounds that Rhegius' "preaching and other unfortunate measures
cause great harm and insurrection."[105] Rhegius has fortune in misfortune – the Hofrat [senior civil servants] in Innsbruck on Novem-

ber 18, 1523 refuse the arrest order because the archduke in Hall on April 10, 1523 "handled the matter of Doctor Urbanus himself,"[106] which probably means Rhegius could not be arrested and imprisoned without Archduke Ferdinand's consent. Did Ferdinand learn through a brief conversation with Urbanus during his April visit that six years previously, Ferdinand's grandfather, Emperor Maximilian I, had crowned Urbanus poet laureate and that according to the statutes surrounding the poet laureate coronation, crowned persons like Urbanus are under the sole and direct jurisdiction of the emperor? Urbanus' incarceration order is dismissed. However, through his connections, Bishop Sprenz succeeds in forcing Urbanus to leave Hall. Again he goes to his home territory of Tettnang and Langenargen as a temporary residence.

Page 36

Urbanus' activity in Hall, Tirol lasts about 15 months, not much longer than his approximately 11 month stay in Augsburg.

ILLUSTRATION 16: Heiltumkapelle in Hall, Tirol. Urbanus Rhegius is entrusted with the veneration of the numerous relics, but criticizes them at the same time. It is not a question of the number of idols one worships, but rather: ... "have you fed the hungry?"[103]

A New Beginning in Augsburg

Urbanus stays in Langenargen for several months. In the summer of 1524 he is back in Augsburg, preaching here and there and generating more publications.

It is an unsettling summer. Minor incidents are already creating havoc. We are still in the first decade of the Reformation, and it is not surprising that no direction is firmly established. In 1517, Luther nails his theses in Wittenberg. They cause curiosity, unrest, and excitement, while requiring new ways of thinking. Different viewpoints develop in the Reformation camp. Zwingli has a loyal group of followers in Augsburg. As many others come forth, so does Urbanus. He stands with Luther, but not unconditionally and not in agreement with every point. Zwingli has tremendous influence in the upper German region, and Urbanus is also sympathetic toward him. Meanwhile, the Evangelisch supporters come to view Erasmus critically because he does not want to be aligned with either side.

Liebmann brings Urbanus' situation during this time period into focus with the summary that Urbanus is "critical of Luther, receptive to Zwingli, and distancing himself from Erasmus."[107] About Erasmus, whom he had previously held in high regard, Urbanus writes:

> "I mourn the fate of Erasmus, who, as long as he remains true to his calling, is, with all due respect, a great figure. Namely, he has, with original brilliance, restored what had been misrepresented for many centuries due to a lack of linguistic skills.

... he struggles fearfully; he does not wrestle his way through. Either he publicly illuminates an unknown facet of scripture, or he portrays himself in an ungodly way because he collaborates with the papists. He praises actions. I do not know what he says from his own free will. Hopefully this fine man will not suffer persecution. He might be setting aside the message of the cross ... "[108]

In August 1524 Rhegius is entangled in a difficult quandary. The controversial populist monk, Johann Schilling, preaches at the Barfüsserkirche [Church of the Barefooted (Poor)]. He is beloved by the common people because he spares neither the city council nor the clergy from his attacks. With a severance payment of 20 Gulden he is to be banished from the city, but 1,800 people gather in front of the city hall and ask that Schilling stay. The city council will not agree to that and offers the crowd "another good" preacher: Urbanus Rhegius.

Page 37

After three days Urbanus wants to give his first sermon in the Barfüsserkirche and ascends the pulpit, but his words are drowned out by the people's shouts – the crowd demands Johann Schilling! The situation gets out of control, the city council is warned about rumors of rebellion, and in no time, 4,000 people armed for battle assemble in front of the city hall.

The city council cannot enforce order and allows the banished monk to preach again in order to appease the crowd. Soon, however, the city council clamps down hard. Three ringleaders of the insurrection are seized, two are beheaded in the fish market, and one is severely whipped and banished from the city.[109]

In the fall of 1524, Rhegius becomes preacher at St. Annakirche [St. Anna Church] in Augsburg. Now he begins a productive and also personally significant time because his wedding is approaching.

The Marriage to Anna Weissbrücker

WHILE THE BAUERNKRIEG [PEASANTS' WAR] RAGES JUST OUTSIDE THE TOWN

We can thank a fortunate stroke of luck for the colorful description of Urbanus' marriage to Anna Weissbrücker on Corpus Christi in 1525. The Augsburg chronicler, Clemens Sender, captures the day in his writing.[110] It is June 16TH – coincidence or not – three days after Luther marries Katharina von Bora in Wittenberg.

While Luther chooses his house for his wedding, Rhegius decides to hold his in the St. Annakirche, thereby uniting his public function with the wedding and giving it a demonstrably official character. The most prominent people of Augsburg, led by Mayor Ulrich Rehlinger, accompany the wedding procession. The city's pipers go first, and one can imagine how the passersby run alongside, in order to see the spectacle. That a priest gets married so publicly and with the support of the city fathers is unusual enough. The bridal couple and guests enter the St. Annakirche and are joyfully greeted with the "Te Deum Laudamus."

Let us listen to Sender, the chronicler, in modern German: (For the original text see Appendix 2.)

"On Friday, June 15TH, after Corpus Christi, Urbanus Rhegius, a priest's son from the Konstanz Diocese, Poet Laureate and Doctor, married a young woman in St. Anna's.[111] Next to him were Mayor

Ulrich Rechlinger and Dr. Frost (Frosch). Behind them were Cris-toff Herwart; Hans Schmid, the Lutheran pastor from St. Ulrich; Laux Welser; and the insurgent preacher from the Barfüsserkloster, Michael Keller. Following them were Dr. Ambrosi Jung and many other citizens and distinguished women and men who attended the wedding. The city pipers were also there.

ILLUSTRATION 17: Dr. Johann Frosch (Rana) [Frog], former prior of the Karmeliterkloster St. Anna and host in 1518 to Luther in Augsburg, presides at the marriage of Urbanus Rhegius and Anna Weissbrücker on June 16, 1525 in the St. Annakirche.

As soon as they entered the St. Annakirche, the organ played the "Te Deum Laudamus." Then Dr. Frosch went to the altar and gave a short sermon, in which he highly praised the honorable institution of marriage. Afterwards he invited the bride and groom to the altar and spoke to Dr. Urban: honorable gentleman and Christian brother, do you take Anna to be your wedded wife?

Page 38

Give me a sign. He says, 'Yes.' Then he spoke to the bride: Do you take this honorable gentleman and Christian brother, Dr. Urban, as your wedded husband? Give me a sign! Then she says, 'Yes.'

After that, he married them according to the old custom. Together they took the Holy Sacrament in both forms[112] and left the church for the Wägelin-Haus [House], from which they had previously departed. After lunch a dance followed. Among many others who joined in were Mayor Ulrich Rechlinger's daughter, Laux Welser's daughter, Cristoff Herwart's daughter, and Dr. Conradt Peutinger's daughter."

Dr. Frosch conducts the wedding ceremony with the same ritual Urbanus had used to perform Dr. Frosch's wedding ceremony in the spring of 1525. Urbanus uses his own wedding as an occasion to present his work, *Sermon of Marriage*, which gives his views on the marriage of priests.[113] Urbanus closes his writing with the ritual he had previously used in conducting Johann Frosch and his wife's wedding ceremony. Frosch now uses the same ritual for the wedding of Urbanus and Anna.

Here is a colorful picture of the wedding day. The chronicler tells us the wedding luncheon and dance take place in the Wägelin-Haus. Hans Wägelin is the owner of the house on Anna Street, where the District Savings Bank is currently located. The wedding guests walk only about 100 steps from the main door of the St. Annakirche to the house. The house is recognizable on the city map drawn up by Georg Seld.

At this time, a priest's marriage is a huge risk for both partners. The cleric goes against not only the rights of the church, but also against those of the state since the church's celibacy rules are embodied in the laws of the empire.[115]

ILLUSTRATION 18: In the foreground is the St. Annakloster and the St. Annakirche as seen from the west. Diagonally across to the left is the Wägelin-Haus, where the wedding ceremony and dance are held.[114]

Also, it is a great risk for the wife because most priests who take these steps face dire consequences. Often, they will be banned from the city and must make due elsewhere with a lesser paying position. An example is Jakob Griesbeutel. On August 26, 1523 in Augsburg, he becomes the first priest to marry. He has to leave the city and struggle to survive among strangers.[116]

Despite these dangers, Anna and Urbanus resolutely support the Evangelisch cause. For the third time in four years, Urbanus swims against the tide of the times. Outmoded structures are being questioned. Previously, in 1521 in Augsburg and 1523 in Hall, he did not shy away from risks, even though in both cases his actions resulted in the loss of well-endowed positions. Now 36 years old, he goes yet a step further and, with his public wedding, makes his opinions known to everyone.

Three months prior, Urbanus performed the marriage of his colleague, Johann Frosch, also known as Johann Rana. He is the former prior of the Karmeliterkloster St. Anna and Luther's 1518 host in Augsburg.

Page 39

ILLUSTRATION 19: The Karmeliterkloster St. Anna presents the bridal couple with two Gulden "in gold," similar to these coined in Hamburg. These gold pieces are valid throughout the entire empire because of their gold content. (Photo: Rudolf Meier).

ILLUSTRATION 20: In Augsburg's St. Annakirche,
the most beautiful Renaissance church of its time north
of the Alps, Anna and Urbanus exchange vows. [117]

Frosch knows Luther very well because in 1516 in Wittenberg Luther conferred a Doctorate in Theology on Frosch. This is a direct connection to Luther. It is understandable that Frosch, through his closeness to Luther, also exercises a certain influence on Urbanus in favor of Luther.

Konrad Peutinger, Augsburg's famous Humanist and writer in residence, does not attend the wedding himself, however, he sends his daughter, Felicitas, to the wedding dance as a sign of his support. Felicitas is a nun in the Kloster St. Katharine, which she leaves of her own free will, hardly to the joy of her famous father and her mother, Margarete Welser. Divided beliefs run through the familes.

We know much less about Anna Weissbrücker's fundamental motives. We can safely assume her family favors the Evangelisch position because in 1523 her father, Caspar Weissbrücker, is a guest at the wedding of another priest, Jacob Griesbeutel. Nothing is known about Anna Weissbrücker's birth year. The chronicler speaks of "a young girl." Compared to Urbanus she is clearly younger – about 20 years old at the time of the wedding, so it can be assumed she was born in 1505.[118] Caspar Weissbrücker is described as a "respected, wealthy citizen."[119] For that time, his daughter, Anna, has an above-average education. Everything indicates it is a progressive, well-situated home without financial worries. The combined love, similar inclinations, convictions, and heritage point toward a fruitful, independent union.

Page 40

ILLUSTRATION 21: Urbanus Rhegius in 1524, the only portrait from his lifetime. The grammatical form of his name, "D. Urbanum Rhegium,"[120] indicates that the portrait is dedicated to him. Perhaps it is a gift from his bride, Anna, who arranged for it before their forthcoming marriage. The artist is probably a wood carver working for an Augsburg printer. Despite intensive research, he remains unknown.

Page 41

The names of the wedding guests and the Weissbrücker's acquaintances allow us to infer from which side Urbanus and Anna receive support. There is Mayor and City Trustee Ulrich Rehlinger (Sender, the chronologist, spells it "Rechlinger"). The mayor's family (von Rehlingen) belongs to the "eight original forefathers," who have been in Augsburg since 1302. Ulrich Rehlinger is among the first to have Evangelisch sympathies. He corresponds with Zwingli and promotes Evangelisch beliefs in Augsburg, however, he is also influenced by the Anabaptists.[121]

Lukas (Laux) Welser Jr., member of the Welser-Vöhling Company, also owns important estates in Schwaben and is married to Ursula, the only daughter of Augsburg Mayor Sigmund Gossenbrot.[122] Lukas owns an exceptionally elegant mansion at 15 Mauerberg, in which the Margraf [Margrave] Casimir von Brandenburg-Kulmbach celebrates his wedding in 1518.[123] In 1520, Lukas assumes the important rank of Kaiserlichen Einnehmer [imperial collector] in the city government and is a member of the inner circle until 1533.

The Weissbrücker family lives at 17 Mauerberg. They are close neighbors of the Welsers, and the families are friends in both private life and business. Urbanus dedicates his 1523 work, *Von Reu, Beicht und Buss* [*Of Repentance, Confession, and Atonement*], to Lukas Welser.[124] Lukas Welser is among Urbanus' early acquaintances in Augsburg, and one can infer that Urbanus met Welser at the Weissbrücker's home.[125]

"The revolutionary preacher in the Barfüsserkloster" referred to by the chronologist, Sender, is none other than Michael Keller. "A sharp-tongued, popular, crude preacher with a passionate temperament quickly gains influence with the people."[126]

Last, but not least, Ambrosius Jung is among the wedding guests. He comes from a famous line of physicians. His father, Dr. Johannes Jung, is personal physician to Emperor Maximilian I. In 1494, he is made a nobleman by the emperor. In the same year, Ambrosius, who is barely 25 years old, becomes physician to the Augsburg cathedral chapter. During Ambrosius' tenure, he mentions Rhegius and the Adelmann brothers to the Cathedral Preacher Oecolampiadus and the Bishop of Stadion. From 1510 – 1522 Ambrosius is also the city physician, and in 1536 he becomes the superior to the priests.

ILLUSTRATION 22:

LEFT: Dr. Ambrosius Jung, physician of the cathedral chapter and city physician in Augsburg. He is a wedding guest of Urbanus Rhegius and Anna Weissbrücker.[127]

RIGHT: Konrad Peutinger is a Humanist, advisor to the emperor, and city writer in residence. He represents Augsburg at the Reichstag zu Worms [Imperial Diet of Worms] and tries to persuade Luther to recant.[128]

In 1520 Karl V elevates the Ambrosius brothers and Ulrich Jung to the nobility. He names Ulrich as his and King Ferdinand's personal physician when they are visiting Augsburg. In 1538, both brothers, along with Dr. Conrad Peutinger and Anton and Raymund Fugger are received into Augsburg's patrician class.[129]

Lucas Gassner, Sr. is an especially close friend of Urbanus. Between 1521 and 1525, Urbanus dedicates six of his works to him! This is highly unusual because only twice does he dedicate two works to a single person, and he usually dedicates only one work to a person. Lukas is the most important merchant of this wealthy Augsburg family and is married to the daughter of patrician Jakob Rehlinger. He is a partner in Tirolian copper and silver mines and leaves a 50,000 Gulden dowry to his only daughter, Veronika, who has been married to Ulrich Fugger since 1516.

There is no doubt that Urbanus understands how to collect influential people as friends. There is also no doubt that most of his friends are also friends of Zwingli because Luther fears that Rhegius is completely on Zwingli's side. Luther writes Urbanus on July 7, 1528 " ... that we had been of the opinion that you are completely estranged from us ... " (See Appendix 3.) Luther is now pleased that Rhegius is again on his side and eagerly awaits an answer. As Urbanus does not yet have these contacts himself, there are new possibilities regarding his acquaintance with Luther (through Frosch), Zwingli (through Keller, Rehlinger, and Jung), and similarly the emperor and king (through the physician brothers Jung). His contacts with the Fuggers might come through the Gassner family.

While Urbanus and Anna enjoy the most beautiful celebration of their lives, the Grosse Teusche Krieg [Great German War] rages outside the Augsburg city gates and elsewhere. This war is better known as the Bauernkrieg [Peasants' War], (1524/1525). The peasants rise up against bondage, oppression, burdensome taxes, and serfdom. They interpret Luther's *Freiheit Eines Christenmenschen* [*Freedom of Christians*] to also be a symbol of personal freedom, and they demand it. Rhegius preaches twice on this theme and publishes his 1525 sermon before Luther and Melanchthon write their comments about the Peasants' War.[130]

To the peasants, Urbanus preaches patience and suffering. He warns the peasants that by revolting, their suffering will only get worse. He tries to explain that a Christian can be free in his beliefs even though he is a serf and that there was also serfdom in biblical times. In the second section, he appeals to the masters' consciences. They also have a Master to whom they are accountable, and they should keep in mind that they themselves are free men who are "governing free men" [noblesse oblige]. In closing, he suggests that freeing the serfs might be an act of Christian love. This is really the first expression of his own beliefs.[131]

Luther adopts Rhegius' public position in his, *Ermahnung zum Frieden auf die zwölf Artikel der Bauernschaft* [*A Call to Freedom from the Twelve Articles of Peasantry*]. He recommends Rhegius' viewpoint: "My master and friend, Urbanus Rhegius, has written sufficiently and well on this topic, and you should read it."[132]

Merchants, Gold Traders, Businessmen — Anna Weissbrücker's Ancestors

THE WEISSBRÜCKER AND FENDT FAMILIES IN AUGSBURG

The tax records stored in the Augsburg City Archives go back to 1346 and are complete, with the exception of the period 1599 – 1619. They provide insight into the citizens' property. References to the tax districts allow for reconstruction of where the taxpayer lives. We can also find relationship designations, such as "son, daughter, or son-in-law." [133]

For us, the most important question is whether Caspar Weissbrücker is Anna's father (Vater), cousin (Vetter), or another relative (Verwandter). [134] Previous authors use cousin or relative. They support their use with the following text from the 1547 Augsburg tax record, page 72a:

"On April 3, 1548 Anna Wissbruggerin, widow of Herrn Doctor Urban Kunigs, preacher in Zell in Sachsen, inherits 959 R in gold from Caspar Wissbrugger, the local merchant, her father. As heiress, she had to pay a tax of 86 R in gold. However, the honorable town council reimbursed her for half of that sum through the mayor [135] because the aforementioned doctor has been preacher here for many years."

We interpret the original German text, "Caspar Wissbrugger dem Cramer alhie ihrem Vatern ererbt" to read in English: "Caspar Wissbrugger the local merchant her father...".

Caspar Weissbrücker appears in the Augsburg tax records of 1504 – 1541. Previously no one with this name is recorded. If Caspar were Anna's cousin, her father's name would also have had to appear in the records unless he lived in another city.

ILLUSTRATION 23: Original entry in the Augsburg tax record, page 72a, about Anna Weissbrücker's inheritance of 959 Gulden. Here Urbanus is called "Urban Kunig."

A clear picture is gained by Caspar Weissbrücker's tax payments in the 1520s:

1525. Page 39a: "30 pf. 5ff, 45 kr."
1526. Page 40c: "30 pf. 5ff, 45 kr. his son-in-law receives 2 Pf."
1527. Page 41d: "30 pf. 15ff, 45 kr. his son-in-law" ("his son-in-law" is crossed out).
1528. Page 41d: "30 pf. 7 R, 45 kr."[136]

Page 44

Urbanus Rhegius is mentioned in the tax records:

1528, Page 2c: "Wunderhaus [House of Miracles], Doctor Urban Regius and his mother."

A small circle in front of the name means the person is not a citizen of the city and therefore is charged only a minimal tax. Rhegius is employed by the Free Imperial City and is free from tax! The following are the connections:

> 1525: Urbanus and Anna marry.
> 1526: After the wedding, they live with Caspar Weissbrücker, "his son-in-law" is Urbanus.
> 1527: "Son-in-law" is crossed out: Urbanus and Anna now live in the "Wunderhaus," an addition to the St. Anna-kirche, later the Mesner house, today Schlosser'sche Buchhandlung.
> 1528: "Son-in-law" no longer appears because Urbanus is registered, tax-free, in the "Wunderhaus" with his mother (and certainly his wife, Anna).

If Urbanus is the son-in-law, then Anna must be the daughter. The circumstances seem to rule out that a different Urbanus could be the son-in-law, especially considering Anna's later inheritance as Caspar's only female heir, so that other children (and sons-in-law) are excluded.

Further evidence is revealed by Anna Weissbrücker's family's inheritance. Caspar dies in 1542, and his wife, Ursula, in 1546/47. Both inheritances are distributed about the same time. Anna appears to inherit from Caspar Weissbrücker. Anna's mother, Ursula Fendt, has two heirs: Ursula's brother, Jerg Fend in Basel, and Urusla's cousin, Lucas Fend, in Mühlheim:

Anna Weissbrücker receives from Caspar W.	959 Gulden
Her daughter, Afra, Leonhart Auffgeber's wife in Munich	100 Gulden
Jerg Fend in Basel receives from Ursula Fendt, his sister	477 Gulden
Lucas Fendt in Mühlheim receives from Ursula Fendt, his cousin	238 Gulden
TOTAL INHERITANCE	1,774 Gulden

The division of the funds is an indication of the degree of the relationship. If Anna receives twice as much as her mother's brother, her relationship to her parents must be closer than that of her mother and brother. That is the case between parents and children, just as between Ursula Fendt and Anna.

The convoluted conditions of the inheritance show in retrospect that the parents probably sold their holdings and possessions and that they dissolved or sold their business. That is how they solved their inheritance problems.

From the Weissbrücker and Fendt families' entries in the Augsburg tax records, we get the following picture of Anna's parents and grandparents:

Bartholomäus Weissbrücker (Wissbrugker) is in the "Vom Diepolt" tax district in 1504, at Mauerberg 17, only two blocks from the cathedral, perhaps a 3 – 4 minute walk. (See also Illustration 24.)

At the same time Bartholomäus appears in the tax records, "Caspar, his son" is also recorded. In 1503 and before, there are no Weissbrückers in the tax records. Thus, both probably came to Augsburg in 1504.

ILLUSTRATION 24: The Augsburg city plan in 1626, according to Kilian. The "Vom Diepold" tax district is outlined in yellow. It is on the left border of the street in Mauerberg where the Weissbrücker house stood.

In 1508, father and son are registered in the "Vom Diebold" tax district. From 1508 on, Caspar is registered in "Vom Ror," and from 1512 on he is registered in "Vom Zimerleuthhaus." All of these tax districts are near one another in the inner city.

In 1523, Caspar Weissbrücker appears again as a taxpayer in "Vom Diepold," also in Mauerberg. Bartholomäus, his father, is mentioned by name, but without a tax charge. In 1524, Bartholomäus is listed as "free." Caspar returns to his father's home four or five years before his father's death and has to pay taxes.

For the first time in 1529, Bartholomäus' widow, "Bartholomeo Wissbruggerin," appears as a taxpayer. Bartholomäus died in 1528.

Caspar's mother appears under the name, "Bartholomeo Wiss-bruggerin" until 1539. (The wife is given the family name with the suffix "in.") From 1540 on, "according to the will of Petronella W" is added to her name. Thus, it is indicated that Caspar's mother's first name is Petronella and that she probably dies in 1539/1540. An executor of her will pays her remaining taxes.

After Caspar Weissbrücker's death, his wife, Ursula Fendt as Caspar Wissbrugkerin, pays taxes until 1546. As of 1547, her taxes are paid by an executor, so Anna's mother would have died in 1546 or 1547. In 1548, Anna receives her inheritance as mentioned above.

Anna spends the first year of her childhood at Mauerberg 17, her grandparents' and parents' house, a short distance from the cathedral, in the vicinity of Lukas Welser's mansion. Also, the tax districts "Vom Ror" and "Vom Zimerleuthhaus" are located between the cathedral and the St. Annakirche. [137]

From an incident during Anna's childhood in 1514, we learn something about her father's business. On April 28, 1514, an official from the city of Strassburg writes to the Augsburg city council, which we are translating into present day German to make it more understandable:

> "We are informing our honorable, wise, good friends and
> Augsburg city council, Ludwig Böcklin, Knight for the
> Masters, and the Strassburg city council about our service.

> Dear Friends, We have read your cordial letter concerning
> an evil-doer who is accused of having taken some gold from
> your citizen, Caspar Weissbrugger. We discovered the
> aforementioned thief had stolen nothing but silver objects
> and broken goblets. We will return the stolen goods to
> their owners. We would further like to inform you the
> investigation has not revealed further details as contained in
> the papers of the court case.

Page 46

> Our dear and good friends, we will do everything in our
> power to help you. Written on the Wednesday after St.
> Jörgen's Day, in the year 14" (April 28, 1514). (For the
> original text, see Appendix 4.)

The document appears to be an interim report. When the Strassburg city council writes to the Augsburg city council, the situation is taken seriously. Unfortunately, no further correspondence between the two cities can be found.

We see that Caspar Weissbrücker travels great distances to do business in gold. It takes more than a week to travel approximately 300 km from Augsburg to Strassburg. During the Renaissance, the commercial centers for artistic gold and silver pieces are in Spain and Italy. "From these commercial centers the work of these artisans spreads across Europe. Augsburg becomes an important jewelry and silver center."[138]

Do the Weissbrückers and the Fendts become acquainted through the gold business? In 16TH century Augsburg, there are several goldsmiths named Fendt: Mathäus, born in 1545; Hans, born in 1575; and Jonas, who marries in 1623. Thus, we can surmise that the Fendt family is traditionally in the gold business. Also, through these family connections, we may be able to explain Anna's good education and her large inheritance.

Caspar is a well-known merchant in Augsburg. When the tax records list him as a merchant, that designates him as someone who is a businessman. He is a member of the Kaufleute Stube [merchant's room], which is somewhat comparable to a guild. In the merchant's room's records, which begin around 1540, it states: "Caspar Wispruckher died on April 21, 1542."[139] Membership does not depend only on bloodline, but also on economic qualifications and the businessman's reputation. (See Illustration 25.)[140]

ILLUSTRATION 25: Caspar Weissbrücker
is a member of the Augsburg Kaufleutestube.
(Illustration: Augsburger Stadtlexikon)

Caspar's mother dies about the same time as he. In the 1541 tax records dated May 19, 1542, it is noted that the executor of Caspar's mother's estate has to pay an inheritance tax on 3,386 Gulden that were left to her by a non-resident. About 1,000 Gulden remain to be paid "on debts and possessions thought to be left in Vienna by Wissbruggerin." (See Appendix 5.)

The proceedings raise questions. Caspar's mother, Petronella Weissbrücker, inherits this large amount from Vienna. Does she come from Vienna, and what inheritance is it? Why does her son, Caspar, not inherit anything? Because he died before her will is settled? And if that is the case, why is his daughter, Anna, not included?

Page 47

Our attempt to answer some of these questions in Vienna were not successful. The proceedings are not known in any of the Vienna archives we searched, e.g., Finanz-und Hofkammerarchiv Wien, Wiener Stadt- und Landesarchiv, Heraldisch-Genealogische Gesellschaft "Adler," Wien.

Since the name Weissbrücker does not appear in the Augsburg sources before 1504,[141] the proceedings about Petronella's inheritance can be an indication that she and her husband, Bartholomäus, come to Augsburg from Vienna around 1500. The exact wording, "left behind debts and household goods" could mean that she still has possessions in Vienna.

What is known about the Fendt family, from which Anna's mother originates? The name "Fendt" first appears in 1251 in Augsburg as Ulricus Fundanus. The family and its coat of arms are first mentioned in a 1762 book by Paul von Stetten, Doctor of Jurisprudence: *History of the Noble Lineages in the Free Imperial City of Augsburg.* He writes:

"In the oldest documents in which the names of the Augsburg citizens are found, the name Fundanus also appears, which is 'Fendt' in Latin. Ulricus Fundanus is the first civil witness in the 1251 contract between Bishop Hartmann and the city, whereby one can infer that although he is not a Stadt-Pfleger [mayor], he is a very respected man. Also, Ulrich Fende is mayor in 1282.

We also find Conrad Fenden, Peter Rhelinger's father-in-law, who may have lived in about 1320. But there is no one else by that name until the establishment of the extended family's business enterprise is announced in 1368. This family was probably descended from both the nobility and from artisan guild members. No record can be found of the original founding member of the family, however, the last member of the Fend family, Johannes Fend, was head of the Zunft der Salzfertiger [Salt Traders Guild] in 1382, 1385, and 1388. In 1478, Brother Conrad Fend was Guardian of the Barfüssern. One surmises he was the last of his clan. Perhaps what happened is that his name is missing in the list of community townspeople because a long time later his name appears again.

A gravestone in Rome is said to be inscribed: Johann Vende, Patricus Augustanus Vindelicior, along with the Fend coat of arms. From the title "patricius," which was infrequently used after 1368, I surmise that this Johannes died after that year. Perhaps he died in the 15TH century."

The Johann(es) Fend mentioned above, along with Johann Gossenbrot, is also cited in an old document from 1324 mentioning the mayors:

"Mr. Johann Fend and Mr. Johann Gossenbrot were mayors. In 1382, they had been in office for four years. In 1384, there was a huge death toll in Augsburg, in which more than half the population died. Clergyman carried all the holy relics throughout the city. With great piety, all the citizens, both men and women, piously followed the processions."[142]

ILLUSTRATION 26: The Fend family's coat of arms (left) and the Gossenbrot coat of arms (right) in an undated Augsburg document, probably from the 16TH century.

Page 48

There are two known painters from the Fendt family. Bernhard Fendt appears in the tax records from 1480 – 1515. He is aligned with the Hans Holbein d. Ä [The Elder] school of art and works for churches and monasteries. Leonhardt/Lenz Fendt is one of the artists of basilica paintings in the former Augsburg Katharinenkloster (today the Staatsgalerie Augsburg). The six ogival arched paintings on boards were created between 1499 and 1504 by Hans Holbein d. Ä, Hans Burkmair, and an Augsburg painter with the initials L.F. (Leonhardt Fendt?), all artists of the Hans Holbein school.

We know Ursula Fendt's brother, Jerg, Doctor of Jurisprudence, because she willed him some of her possessions, and we know he lived in Basel. It is perhaps a bold assumption that in Basel he associated with the sons of Hans Holbein, Ambrosius and Hans, because they had an art studio there. Jerg Fendt d. Ä, is likely the father of the aforementioned Jerg Fendt, Doctor of Jurisprudence, because the names are so similar. He lives in the tax district "Nattans Garden." He would be Ursula Fendt's father and Anna's grandfather.

It remains a challenging task to establish a family relationship among the artists, goldsmiths, and/or the mayor, Johann Fendt.[143]

An Unknown Painting Tells the Church History

The year of the marriage closes with a significant event in Augsburg church history. At the Christmas celebration in 1525, church members gather with their extended families and guilds in the St. Annakirche and celebrate communion with Urbanus Rhegius and Johann Frosch, according to the Lutheran rites: Rhegius offers the chalice of wine, Frosch the bread.

As unspectacular and normal as this sounds today, it is revolutionary for the people a mere eight years after Luther nails his theses to the church door. Until then, the priest distributed only the bread to the congregation. The priest then drank the wine symbolically for everyone. Luther ordered communion "in both forms," i.e. in the form of bread and the form of wine, so that all took part in communion, according to Jesus' teachings. Communion "in both forms" is a protest against the Roman Catholic Church and a public espousal of Luther's interpretation.

In 1524 communion is offered in individual cases according to the Evangelisch ritual, however, after the 1525 Christmas communion: " ... the first public, celebratory form makes apparent the split with the old Church."[144] The painting in the St. Annakirche by an unknown artist becomes a symbol of the proceedings. The original, painted in colorful oils on copper, measures "one Schuh [shoe] high and one Schuh two Zoll [inches] wide." Nothing is known about the whereabouts of the original, but an impressive 1741 reproduction is preserved.

Underneath the painting is the description of the characters and the story: "This painting depicts the chancel of the St. Annakirche in the morning, in which the so-called high altar is represented. In front, Doctor Regius is holding the chalice and Doctor Rana [Latin for "frog"] is holding the bread. Some of those kneeling are from the lineages, others are people from the guilds, as identified by their coats of arms. The first coat of arms is the Manner family, second is the Vehlins, third is the Peutingers, fourth is the Langenmantels, fifth is the Pemmels. The year is 1525, and the letter 'W' appears. Above, one sees the coat of arms of the Haugens."[146]

Page 49

ILLUSTRATION 27: The 1525 Christmas celebration depicting Urbanus Rhegius and his colleague, Johann Frosch, distributing communion "in both forms." The participants are men and women from Augsburg lineages and guilds, identified by their coats of arms. (The description is in the manuscript Chronica Ecclesiastica Augustana between pages 60 and 61.)[145]

Page 50

If we assume this painting is historically correct, we learn a bit of Augsburg church history. All participants in the depiction are well-known Augsburg personalities:

· The young woman, far left, has the coat of arms of the merchant family Haug above her head. The family has been in Augsburg since 1346. In 1507, she becomes a member of the merchant's room. One of her daughters marries Anton Pymel.

· The woman without a coat of arms, second from left could possibly be Anna Weissbrücker, since she is not associated with anyone else depicted.

· The gentleman with the coat of arms of the Manner family, third from left, drinks from the chalice held by Doctor Rana.

· The woman with the Vöhlin family coat of arms, fourth from left, is receiving bread from the hand of Rhegius. The Vöhlins are an old Augsburg lineage. Johannes, Paulus, and Conrad Vöhlin are members of the Augsburg city council. They are all Evangelisch. There is a relationship to the Freiherr [Baron] von Illertissen, the Langinger family, and the Welsern family. The Vöhlins own extensive property.[147]

· The man with the Peutinger family coat of arms, fifth from left, could be Conrad Peutinger, the important Humanist, writer-in-residence, and advisor to Emperor Karl V. If so, then his participation in this communion service is highly significant. In June of the same year, he allows his daughter to attend Urbanus and Anna's wedding dance. Here we see a further sign of his leanings toward the Reformation.

· The man and woman with the Langenmantel family coat of arms are sixth and seventh from the left. The family has been in Augsburg since 1272 and belongs to one of the old patrician lineages. One member of the family is the previously mentioned chronicler.

· The woman and man with the Pemmel coat of arms are eighth and ninth from the left. It is very likely that the man is Anton Pemmel or Pimmel, who is called Anthoni Bimel by Sender, the chronicler. He was born in 1475. His mother is Ursula Fugger, which is why the coat of arms is similar to the Fugger's. Beginning in 1518, Anton is in the Kleinen Rat [lesser council] a Zunftmeister [head of the guild] of the Weaver's Guild, in 1528 he is an architect, and in 1529 he is mayor of Augsburg. Through marriage in 1531 he assumes a stake in his father-in-law's (Haug mentioned above) business. In religious matters, "He changes with the wind." He is a very successful merchant and leaves his daughters a large fortune.

Strikingly, Anton Pemmel is the only one who is elegantly dressed. He is probably showing that not only is he a wealthy merchant, but also that he wants to be recognized as a donor of the painting. Above all of the characters, in the third line above the painting, it is noted that the owner of the original painting is one "Monseigneur Bemmel, Painter."[148]

The Latin texts to the left and right clarify the matter:

"Ordained by an act of God" (above left)

"The Lord's Supper [Holy Communion] in both forms, offered for the first time in the St. Anna/ Carmeliter (Kloster) during the 1525 Christmas celebration" (above right)

It is obvious that Rhegius' and Frosch's uncompromising advocacy on behalf of the Reformation has great influence on the Augsburg citizenry. This plays an inciting role in the religious schism of the following years. Rhegius comes into even deeper conflict with the old doctrines.

Page 51

The quarrel with Johann Eck, his old teacher and patron, becomes more bitter. They meet by chance at the Augsburg wine market, and a lively discussion ensues. Rhegius proposes a public debate in which they each defend their thesis, but Eck refuses.[149] An exchange of letters follows, led by Eck's exceptionally sharp attacks against Rhegius' beliefs. Rhegius answers politely and inserts his former esteem into the exchange:

"Because even today, Eck is so often thought of, I must openly state that there is no one in the whole world whom I prefer and respect more for his scholarship and great understanding than Eck ... "[150] The chasm between them remains unbreached. Neither polemics nor patience can bring them to the table together again.

Neither slander nor intentionally spread falsehoods are off limits. We find a sample of these in a letter Urbanus writes to Zwingli on April 1, 1527.[151] Early in the year 1527 hoarseness hinders Urbanus' preaching, and he stays at home. A rumor spreads throughout the city that he was caught in "an act of adultery with a married woman from a distinguished family" and was stabbed three times. His frightened mother hurries to his side. She finds him happily engaged with his children, unharmed and in good condition. When Rhegius confronts the man who allegedly started the rumor, the man invites Rhegius to dinner in order to completely dispel all suspicions.[152]

The Augsburg Confession Bears His Signature

THE YEAR 1530 IS THE HIGH POINT OF HIS WORK

The last five years in Augsburg focus on disputes with the Anabaptists and preparation for the Imperial Diet of Augsburg. To combat the Anabaptists, the city council hires reform-minded preachers and chooses Urbanus Rhegius as the leader.[153] The Anabaptists allow only adult baptism. They want to restore "true Christianity and a righteous social order." The Reformation is a side issue which the Anabaptists strenuously oppose.

The literature reports an incident in which Rhegius harshly reproaches an Anabaptist woman. There are 100 Anabaptists imprisoned in Augsburg. One of the women prisoners wishes to speak with Urbanus. She is summoned from the prison and brought before the city council and Rhegius, who lays out her "errors." She does not accept his interpretation and answers him:

> "Brother Urbanus, you sit on a soft cushion next to the mayor, and your speeches are accepted as if they were spoken from heaven. But I, a poor, imprisoned woman, sit on the ground and must defend myself bound by shackles and handcuffs." To that Urbanus replies: "You, dear sister, have been freed from the Devil's service, at considerable cost, through Christ, yet you have again put yourself under the Devil's yoke. You have been duped

by the Devil and you have led others from the path of righteousness."[154]

The example clarifies how very seriously people take religious matters and how strongly held beliefs control people's lives. The entire city council is consumed by the Anabaptist question and attends the confrontation between Urbanus and the Anabaptist woman. If the testimony of the Anabaptist woman is to be taken literally, that she was led out in shackles, then the severity of the proceedings is harsh.

Page 52

In the proceedings above, Rhegius distinguishes between "the naïve, poor people, who, without malice, fell into these traps" and the movement's leaders. For the followers, he pleads for mercy, but he says the leaders should be reprimanded by the city. This is moderate compared to corporal punishment usually applied to Anabaptists.[155]

In 1529, as the high point of the Reformation in 1530 approaches, Landgraf [Landgrave] Philipp von Hessen invites the most important reformers to Marburg for a "Concordie" [religious conference to reach agreement]. Its purpose is to bridge the schisms among the groups. Rhegius is also invited. He writes to Landgrave Philipp on September 12, 1529, thanking him for the invitation ... "and I want to attend, but I am concerned about my health. For the entire year I have had fluid in my head so that I can hardly breathe the air." (The complete text of the letter is in Appendix 6.)

Rhegius' premonitions about his health come true, and because of it, he cannot travel to Marburg. He will deeply regret his absence, because the only meeting between Luther and Zwingli takes place in Marburg. Philipp der Grossmütige [Philipp the Magnanimous], as the landgrave is also known, surprisingly declares to his guests "that he was won over to the Reformation by the writings of Urbanus Rhegius."[156] Through his influence with the landgrave, who is 15 years younger than he, Rhegius advances the Reformation in Hessen. Perhaps, with this he initially ignites it. Although this meeting takes place without Rhegius' presence, his influence over Landgrave Phillip is probably the most meaningful, long-lasting successful outcome of his efforts because it alters Germany's religious and political landscape.

In the meantime, the day of the Imperial Diet approaches. In 1530, Emperor Karl V invites the dignitaries of the Imperial Diet to Augsburg to resolve religious issues. The invitation is conciliatory in that everyone is allowed to state his own opinion. The highest ranking political and religious members of the Heiligen Römischen Reiches Deutscher Nation [Holy Roman Empire of the German Nation] arrive: "An emperor, a king, four electors, 42 princes, five cardinals, 90 Counts, 98 Abgesandte [emissaries], 60 individuals with doctoral degrees, and a large group of knights and noblemen from inside and outside. In all, over 1,200 people of the highest and lowest ranks of the nobility are there."[157]

ILLUSTRATION 28: Landgrave Philipp der Grossmütige von Hessen (from a portrait by Hans Krell at Wartburg Castle). The landgrave (b. 1504 in Marburg, d. 1567 in Kassel) and the Saxon princes are the driving force behind the Reformation.

The princes arrive, accompanied by their theological advisors. The entire German Evangelisch clergy is present – only Luther is not allowed to take part because he is the subject of a ban and was excommunicated. He is in Coburg, which at that time is located on the outermost edge of Sachsen, where he can be certain of his elector's protection. He awaits an exchange of messages. Although he is enduring forced idleness, he keeps his sense of humor. He compares the quarreling and cawing of jackdaws and crows outside his window to the activities of the black-clothed clergy at the Imperial Diet.

Among the Imperial Diet's significant decisions for Germany and all of Christendom, we wish to single out those with which Urbanus Rhegius was directly or indirectly involved. He is among the preachers who most often give sermons between the time of the advance party of princes' arrival in Augsburg and the emperor's summit, that is, from the beginning of May until the middle of June. Here, Urbanus soon learns that it is not solely about God's word, but rather about practical politics.

Saxon Elector Johann commissions Urbanus to conduct the Pentecost festival service on June 5, 1530, in the Kirche der Dominikanerinnen St. Katharina [St. Katharina's Dominican Church]. This prestigious honor is bestowed after Emperor Karl V asks the elector on May 24TH to remove Rhegius as one of the selected preachers in Augsburg.[158] The elector sees himself as the spokesperson for the Evangelisch in Augsburg. Urbanus' sermons are an offense to the emperor because they go against his explicit wishes.

Saxon Elector Johann and many high ranking dignitaries are present at the Rhegius' Pentecost festival sermon. A handwritten document from Augsburg reports that the bishop of Strassburg welcomes the elector in the church's chancel. After the sermon, the elector asks the bishop if he liked the sermon, to which the bishop answers: " ... yes, and it didn't bother me that I listened to him so long." The elector then says: "And this sermon should be forbidden by the emperor?"[159] Rhegius does not hear this exchange. Still, according to Liebmann's supposition, Rhegius becomes involved in the Sachsen elector's religious politics.

During this time, Urbanus may see himself not as taking position in the center, but rather as a mediator of the divergent interests. Around May 20, 1530, Landgrave Philipp von Hessen, who is well-disposed toward Rhegius, invites him to dinner. They debate about the Last Supper for two hours. They discuss Luther's interpretation, "This IS my blood," which is opposed to Zwingli's version, "This SYMBOLIZES my blood."

In a letter to Luther in Coburg on May 21, 1530, Rhegius immediately reports the outcome of the discussion.[160] The landgrave does not support Zwingli's side of the argument. Also, the landgrave is ready to proceed on the fundamental questions in the Augsburg Confession of Faith and to sign it based on Melanchthon's position.[161] The landgrave's faith in Rhegius may have been strengthened because Rhegius can point out his close connection to Melanchthon. In his above mentioned letter to Luther, Rhegius writes that he confers daily with Melanchthon. Melanchthon is entrusted with editing the Augsburg Confession, and he pulls in Rhegius and Brenz as his closest collaborators. We cannot rule out that Rhegius tries to influence Melanchthon to adopt one or the other viewpoints of Land-grave Philipp regarding which version of the Last Supper to choose.

Page 54

In the aforementioned letter to Luther dated May 21, 1530 Rhegius says: "Daily, as often as work allows, I have conversations with those who love your soul – with Philippus (Melanchthon), Jonas, Eis-leben, and Spalatin. I have no other respite from my studies other than the scholarly discussions with such men. If you were also here now, I would have felt complete joy. May Christ grant that I see you soon."[162]

Rhegius loves this kind of work. This is the impression given by his many contacts and activities. He is not a folksy preacher who sways people, rather he is among those who calmly mediate, debate, make peace, and work on theological and scientific matters. Many of his sermons have timely themes such as serfdom, the relationship between subordinates and those in authority, foundations of Evan-gelisch teachings, and various questions of faith. He wants to gather as many people as possible into the faith by expanding their knowl-edge of these issues.

Meanwhile, the Imperial Diet proceeds. Emperor Karl V comes to Augsburg directly from his coronation in Bologna. Here is what Uhlhorn writes about the day:

"Finally, the emperor himself arrives on June 15TH in all his splen-dor, as seldom seen before. With his entrance, he made it clear that he came as the Vogt [administrator] of the Roman Catholic Church. Holding nothing back, the emperor, from his first greeting, unleashed his power and majesty. This show of power made the Evangelisch look like a tiny, ineffectual group.

The princes receive the emperor on the Lech Bridge. The Cardinalerzbischof [cardinal archbishop] of Mainz made the welcoming speech. Nearer the city, the Augsburg city officials awaited the emperor. The group was comprised of Mayors Ulrich Rehlinger and Anton Pymmel, accompanied by four city councilmen. Councilman Dr. Peutinger made the welcoming speech to the emperor. Augsburg displayed its imposing military might: 12 cannons with the musketeers alongside, citizens clothed in black with close-fitting velvet jackets, merchants in ash colored garments with satin jackets and yellow feathers, four squads of servants dressed in armor and carrying weapons, and finally knights, mercenaries in grey, citizens in black, merchants in buff colors, and the Fuggers' servants with their families' colors on their sleeves. The wide Lech plain blazed in the evening sun from the gleam of the weapons and the magnificent regal jewelry. A huge crowd from all nations pressed together. Here one got the feeling that the emperor of the Holy Roman Empire of the German Nation was lord of the world.

As cannons thundered, trumpets blared, drums rolled, and bells pealed, the emperor himself approached the city ... First came the representatives of the empire, then the princes, electors, and, some distance before the emperor, the Reichserzmarschall [arch marshall], the elector of Sachsen, with an unsheathed sword. Today the emperor himself appeared in splendor such as he ordinarily detested: he rode a white Polish stallion decorated with gold cloth. Following the emperor were King Ferdinand and the Päpstliche Legat [papal legate] Campegius. At the red gate, six of the emperor's councilors led the emperor under a silk canopy in the city's colors of red, green, and white."[163]

In the church, the Roman Catholic protocol is followed throughout the ceremony. At the Bernhardskapelle the emperor is greeted by Bishop Christoph von Stadion, and the Easter choir sings the traditional Easter hymn: "You have come, for whom we have longed, and awaited in the darkness ... "[164] This is the song with which the Church for centuries pays homage to Christ the King. Now the words are used to greet the earthly emperor, which violates the beliefs of Rhegius and many others.[165] In November 1530 he writes on this theme and publicly condemns the action as blasphemy.[166]

Page 55

The ban of all sermons is passionately debated in Augsburg. Shortly after his Pentecost sermon, Rhegius recommends to the city council that it not give in on this issue. Also, he speaks privately with the mayor, who was a guest at Rhegius' wedding five years previously. The city still vacillates. He expects the city to back him, but he is denied this, even though he is the city's ordained preacher. This deeply wounds Rhegius. Also, his life is in grave danger in the city, where the empire's Spanish soldiers invade his home and want to kill him.[167]

On June 18, 1530 the emperor issues a universal decree generally forbidding the sermons "under the most severe punishment." Only clergy personally appointed by the emperor may preach. Rhegius had preached two days previously - the last time from a pulpit in Augsburg. He is greatly disappointed, but on the other hand, the new situation frees him for a new assignment, which will become the most important of his life. For the next two months he can devote all his efforts to the collaborative shaping of the statement of beliefs, the Augsburg Confession.

He eagerly throws himself into the new assignment. Osiander reports an example in which Rhegius acts as a mediator between Melanchthon and him. It concerns the doctrine of justification by faith. [This is a very strong belief of Luther's. It means God's act of removing the guilt and penalty of sin while at the same time declaring the sinner righteous through Christ's atoning sacrifice. In the Evangelisch belief, righteousness from God is viewed as being credited to the sinner's account through faith alone, without works.] The scholars are deadlocked over the translation from ancient languages. When Melanchthon further questions a translation of Osiander's, the latter suggests that on a convenient day, " ... they should go to Doctor Urbanus Rhegius, who has a Hebrew and Chaldean Bible with commentary, so that we can clearly understand it." Soon afterwards, Osiander, Melanchthon, and Brenz sit down with Urbanus, who shows them the disputed place in his *Bibles of Ancient Languages*.[168]

When the great Melanchthon, the Schwabian colleague Brenz, and the strident Osiander come to Rhegius' house and sit together pouring over his books, it is an indication of how esteemed Rhegius is in this small scholarly circle.

ILLUSTRATION 29: Philipp Melanchthon (born 1497 in Bretten, dies 1560 in Wittenberg). He is Luther's most important colleague and author of the Augsburg Confession. Urbanus Rhegius is an important collaborator in the wording of the text. (Albrecht Dürer, 1526, Berlin Copper Print).

ILLUSTRATION 30: Title page from
the 1530 Augsburg Confession.

Page 56

Productive days as these are mixed with new challenges. Johann
Eck publishes his 404 *Article*, an indictment of the Reformation. Eck
cites 12 of Rhegius' works and points out his heretical views. Only
Luther's and Zwingli's works are cited more often. "In this way,
Eck brands Urbanus Rhegius as the third greatest heretic present in
Augsburg. The papal legate also receives a copy of Eck's charge ... .in
a letter to the emperor, Rhegius is specifically mentioned as spread-
ing both orally and in writing 'this cursed, devilish, and heretical
plague' named after Luther."[169]

The remaining time until the reading of the Augsburg Confession is hectic. Rhegius tirelessly strives for mutually agreeable solutions to controversial questions. On June 23, 1530, a day before the
official reading of the Augsburg Confession, the princes arrive from
Sachsen, Hessen, Brandenburg, and Lüneburg (Duke Ernst and his
brother Franz) along with the envoys from Nürnberg and Reutling-
en together with their advisors and theologians, for the purpose of
establishing a definitive text. Rhegius is present when the text that
is to be presented to the emperor the following day is agreed upon.

In a private conversation in Langenargen in September 2001, Professor Liebmann says the Augsburg Confession "is the most important Evangelisch document." Melanchthon authored the document
and Rhegius made significant contributions. Liebmann calls the previously mentioned Thursday, June 23, 1530 "the absolute zenith of
Rhegius' importance in the Reformation."[170]

The presentation of the written Augsburg Confession to the emperor, assembled imperial dignitaries, and their theologians occurs a day later, on June 25, 1530. Landgrave Philipp tenaciously insists that the document not only be given to the emperor, but that it also be read aloud. Urbanus has no official function at this time and is not present. It must be gratifying for him, however, that the land-grave, whom he so greatly influenced, no longer "leans" toward the Reformation, but is a strong advocate for the Evangelisch cause in this historic hour.

ILLUSTRATION 31: Reading of the Augsburg Confession in the bishop's palace. Rhegius is fortunate that "his" landgrave insists that it is read aloud to the emperor. (Represented on a 1730 medallion. Photo: Rudolf Meier).

In the meantime, Rhegius begins to smooth the way for his and his family's future. Since 1528, Margrave Georg von Brandenburg-Ansbach has been asking him to "lay the foundation for an Evange-lisch religious organization in his lands."[171]

Page 57

Luther recommended Rhegius for this position, however, Rhegius is non-committal. Also, Rhegius has health problems and has to put aside his work every couple days. The margrave raises the salary offering from 100 to 150 Gulden, but no arrangement is agreed upon. Rhegius says that the city of Augsburg will not release him from his contract.[173]

From a genealogical perspective, it is interesting that by October 1528, three years and four months after their marriage, Urbanus and Anna have four children. Twins are not mentioned, but it can be assumed that two young girls are members of Urbanus' household. And he mentions his "very old" mother. How old she really is he does not say. Urbanus is 39 years old at this time, so his mother would be about 60.

ILLUSTRATION 32: " ... a married woman, four small children, a very old mother, and two young girls. It is not good to travel with so many people,"[172] writes Rhegius to Margrave Georg von Brandenburg-Ansbach on October 11, 1528, declining the offer of a position.[174]

Presumably the first conversation with Duke Ernst zu Braunschweig and Lüneburg, later known as Ernst the Confessor, and his younger brother, Duke Franz, both of whom sign the Augsburg Confession, takes place in July 1530.[175] During the dukes' stay in Augsburg they hear many of Rhegius' sermons and soon recruit him for their duchy.[176]

On August 26, 1530 Rhegius and his family leave Augsburg. He will never see the city again.

"The Most Wonderful Day of My Life"
RHEGIUS MEETS LUTHER AT COBURG CASTLE

How should we imagine the day of the departure from Augsburg? The night before, Urbanus is still conferring with Melanchthon and the Nürnberg representatives. Anna single-handedly prepares for the departure. We learn later that at this time, she is pregnant and probably already has five children.

How many chests and baskets are there to be packed? There are clothes, shoes, kitchen utensils, necessities for the children, a few toys, cherished personal items, her husband's valuable library, and a bag of her parents' gold pieces for the long journey to the North.

And how does Anna feel, leaving the city of her birth, the wealthy trade and Free Imperial City of Augsburg, where, as a child, she played in the streets and visited her grandparents? Augsburg engenders a feeling that, "In this city beats the pulse of the world." Goods from the Orient and expensive spices from the Far East come here via Venice, cloth is traded, and gold and silver jewelry is created.

Page 58

Wealthy patricians build palatial mansions. Emperors and kings sweep through with colorful entourages. There is always something new and exciting. Women wear the latest fashions. Now Anna climbs into the covered wagon, leaves her birth house, her youth, and her parents behind to journey to a distant, unknown land.

Nürnberg is the first stop. The Nürnberg envoy, Kress, escorts Anna. On August 29TH and 30TH, the city honors Rhegius with a special reception. He is welcomed both in the city hall and at a banquet in the outer courtyard.[177] The latest news from the Imperial Diet is very important to the people of Nürnberg. They want to know how things stand with those who support the "old beliefs" and the discussions to find common ground with Zwingli's followers. Urbanus can give the answers, even if the answers are not optimistic.

Urbanus has been looking forward to a personal meeting with Luther for a long time. Now, while traveling to the North, he can fulfill his dream and meet with Luther at Coburg Castle. In the distance, he and Anna can already see the fränkishe Krone [Frank Crowns], one of the largest castles in Germany. Luther has been in Coburg Castle for six months, protected by 12 armed guards. We do not know how the visit goes, but certainly he welcomes Anna and embraces the children. He knows how to charm people and above all, he knows Anna and knows about her education in ancient languages.

"What Rhegius leaves to posterity about these days is the highest praise for his contemporary, Luther. Four years later, with effusive words, he tells an Augsburg friend about the meeting:" [178]

ILLUSTRATION 33: Rhegius and his family visit Martin Luther at Coburg Castle. (Photo: Walter König).

"When I came to Sachsen, I spent a whole day with Luther, the man of God, who was brought to Coburg Castle, and I had the most wonderful day of my life. Luther is such a great theologian that no century has produced anyone comparable to him.

...Luther was always great, but now, to me, he is the greatest of all." [179]

In another letter Urbanus writes:

> "I judge, no one who knows Luther can hate him. His books demonstrate his apostolic spirit, but when you have heard him up close, how he speaks about godly things, you would say: 'In person he is greater than his reputation'. Luther is so great, that no one is entitled to look down on him.

Page 59

> I know what I am talking about. I, too, have written books and religious tracts, but compared to Luther, I am an elementary school pupil. This judgment flows not from my love for Luther, but rather my love for Luther flows from this judgment. I despise no one, and I would rather be despised than praised. But I will not tolerate Luther being despised because he is the chosen implement of the Holy Spirit. He is a theologian for the whole world. I know him more deeply now that I saw him myself and listened to him."[180]

Luther's room at Coburg Castle is very well preserved. The ceiling panels are still original. Luther and Rhegius probably sit on the benches against the window. Such "window benches" provide better light for reading and working. To visit the castle and recreate the day is a sublime feeling.

ILLUSTRATION 34: In this room in Coburg Castle Luther and Rhegius meet in early September 1530 and discuss the Reformation's progress. (Photo: Kurt Gramer Bietigheim).

In the book, "Fürstentag" [Princes' Day], the following description of his room is attributed to Luther: " ... I sat in the venerable Coburg Castle, as previously I sat in Wartburg Castle, half a prisoner. Oh, but I was a sick man. The other half of me was a free man, in a princely room in which a wedding could take place. All walls, ceilings, and floors were paneled in artistic wood. It was a joy to look at ... there are small pieces of wood. Nothing is painted. Everything is carved out of colorful wood, inlaid, and smoothly planed. If we were seeing it from afar, it would represent the finest heraldry."[181]

Can Luther and Rhegius look at and enjoy these amenities? Each has worries. Luther is beleaguered both by the papal bull that banishes him and the emperor's ostracism of him. He is an outlaw. Anyone can kill him without being punished. He is troubled by the lack of unity among supporters of the Reformation. Rhegius leaves Augsburg frustrated by the vacillation of the city council. Also, "his" city has not signed on to the Augsburg Confession. The last negotiations among the different groups on the Evangelisch side result in a stalemate. In the end, he and Melanchthon are alone in their views. The feeling of not being able to reach the desired goal because of the schism must sadden him.

So, the beautiful panoramic view of the countryside from the Coburg Castle battlements is overshadowed by thoughts about the Reformation's progress.

Nevertheless, this day on the threshold of a new life for both Urbanus and Anna is an encouraging sign that they are on the right path. Rhegius' words show clearly the effect of Luther's personality on him. His enthusiasm for his day with Luther strengthens his heartfelt convictions.

Page 60

By Covered Wagon into the Unknown North

As the journey to the North proceeds, the picture book German land-scape unfolds: the heights of the Thüringen forest, the mighty Wart-burg Castle near Eisenach, the turbulent brooks and cliffs of the Harz Mountains, church steeples and venerable cathedrals, Hildesheim and Hannover, farmers harvesting their crops, beggars and sick people, religious people and travelers, gifts joyously received, noisy sleep-ing quarters, the first North German sheep, and the juniper bushes of the Lüneburg heath. The farther north they go, the more the lan-guage changes. Urbanus and Anna often have to ask people to repeat questions because they do not understand them. Plattdeutsch [Low German] is spoken here, and Urbanus asks himself for the first time how the people are supposed to understand him when he preaches to them.

Today's modern technology makes it possible to drive the 359 kilo-meters from Coburg Castle to Celle in four hours and 36 minutes, half a day with ample rest stops. A journey by covered wagon in 1530 requires two weeks, depending on the weather, the stops at the innumerable toll stations between the principalities, and possible repairs to the wagon and wheels. Most roads are in bad condition. The wagons often get stuck in the quagmire and must be pulled out. Such services and assistance are a business for farmers, blacksmiths, and wheelwrights. It is a "business" for highway robbers as well.

We do not know the family's exact route. Most likely it is the old trade route, with places to rest, stay overnight, and change horses.

The expert coachman takes the familiar, less dangerous roads. To guard against surprise attacks by robbers, he bands together with other travelers and wagons. This provides better protection in case of attack because safety is assured only within city gates.

Anna and Urbanus get their first glimpse of the countryside, around which their lives will center. The principality of Duke Ernst the Confessor is poor and deeply in debt because of the political conditions. His father, Duke Heinrich, caught in the middle of an untenable political conflict, fled to France.[182] Urbanus describes the 1532 situation of the Lüneburg farmers as follows:

> "The peasant labors at backbreaking work day and night and lives in a smoky hut like Noah's Ark: dogs and cats, cows and calves, stallions, sows, chickens, and sheep, all close together by the fire. When he comes home cold, sick, and tired, he does not have enough wood for the fire. He subsists on tough, raw, rotten bacon, hard bread, and water. His careworn sleep is fitful and uncomfortable. What little he earns by the sweat of his brow, he must give to the monastery."[183]

The description of the conditions sounds drastic. One can read between the lines what Urbanus is trying to say: that this is not acceptable. He knows that in the South, where he comes from, life is not so hard. He specifically denounces the required payment to the monastery.

Even though outward conditions in the North are more modest for Urbanus, they have advantages over Augsburg. There, at any time, a vacillating city government can withdraw its support from him. Here, he is backed by a duke who has been on the side of the Reformation from the very beginning. Duke Ernst's studies with Luther in Wittenberg have been alluded to previously. Also, the duke is closely related to the Sachsen elector.

Page 61

As a child, Duke Ernst was raised at the Sachsen court. His mother, Margarethe, is a sister of Friedrich des Weisen [the Wise], Luther's protector.[184]

At the beginning of the Reformation, Duke Ernst has to proceed cautiously so as not to become the object of the emperor's wrath. He and his brother, Franz, are practiced in the art of diplomacy. Beginning with the 1527 Landtag zu Scharnebeck [Diet of Scharnebeck], they shape events toward acceptance of Evangelisch beliefs. During Duke Ernst's subsequent trip to Torgau for Sachsen Elector Johann Friedrich's wedding, he meets Luther. Their discussion of further action assures the duke's support and the progress of the Reformation in his principality. Now it is time to implement the Reformation, by developing new church and school organizations, dissolving the monasteries, and above all, reframing education for Evangelisch pastors.

In contrast to Augsburg, where the Evangelisch teachings are popular with the people and the authorities vacillate, in the principality of Lüneburg, the Reformation is ordered by the authorities and the people still need to be convinced. Duke Ernst is preparing Rhegius for this task. When Duke Ernst returns to Celle from the Imperial Diet and his courtiers ask him what he brings back, he says he brought back a magnificent treasure for the whole country. This "treasure" is Urbanus Rhegius. Duke Ernst says, "Rhegius is an expensive man, but do not begrudge him the money and the large additional sums we have paid to have him come here."[185]

This is the environment in which Urbanus finds himself after his arrival in the North, in Celle, the city where Duke Ernst lives. A decade of hard work lies before him.

First Diplomatic Assignment in Lüneburg
THE CITY THAT FIGHTS AGAINST THE REFORMATION

Rhegius' signatures confirm that his primary title is "Pastor of Celle." As Rhegius already anticipated, it is the Low German language of the North that is a problem for him, a Schwabian from Southern Germany. In the northern cities, Low German is spoken and preached from the pulpits. Hochdeutsch [High German] is spoken only in courts of the nobility and in their churches. It is evident that the language is a problem for the whole family, so Urbanus seeks a tutor from Northern Germany for his children.[186]

Rhegius' first assignment is in the city of Lüneburg, which, at the high point of its history, is among the richest members of die Hanse [Hanseatic League]. Salt is the basis of the city's wealth, and the established patricians defend their influence and money, stubbornly holding onto power against new political groups. The first difficulty for Urbanus in Lüneburg is that the people of Lüneburg want to hear the Sunday Evangelisch sermons in their native language, Low German, rather than in the High German spoken by Urbanus.

In October 1530, the city council invites Rhegius to Lüneburg, but he declines. "I can get no respite from nasal dripping and catarrh, so I can by no means stand fresh air." After Christmas, his health condition and his wife's impending delivery of their next child still prevent him from accepting. He cannot leave her alone in Celle, but says he will come, "as soon as the days become longer."[187]

In approximately March 1531 Rhegius is in Lüneburg, the largest city in the principality. Duke Ernst has little influence in Lüneburg because the entrenched interests in this mighty city are very strong. The introduction of the Reformation in Lüneburg is especially important to Duke Ernst. He covers Urbanus' travel costs and lets him live in his Lüneburg house, called "Hertogen Husz" [duke's house] in the old German language. In 1381, the city built the house for its nobility, however, it is without a kitchen so the current duke has to depend on the hospitality of the city council when he stays there. Perhaps by having no kitchen in house, the city council wants to keep the duke's visits to Lüneburg short.

Page 62

Urbanus soon presents an education and church organizational plan in which he carefully advances the Evangelisch beliefs, yet leaves many aspects of the old plan untouched.[188] He subdivides the text into sections: phases of school development, care for the poor, and church customs and instruction.

He returns to Celle in the summer, but is soon called back to Lüneburg because differences among rival groups have recurred. On September 1, 1531 he is again in Lüneburg. The school and church plans will come before the city council and the citizens on September 4th.[189] Rhegius spends the winter of 1531/32 in Celle.

In the spring of 1532, Rhegius is called back to Lüneburg for the third time. The people of Lüneburg probably hear that Rhegius intends to move to Hamburg and remind him of his promise to them. "In any case, Rhegius points out that it is not the Lüneburg city council, but rather two members of the Bürgerausschuss [citizens' committee] – Hans Polde and Helmig Lampe – who successfully sought out Duke Ernst and Rhegius in Celle. On March 24, 1532 they were able to take Rhegius back to Lüneburg with them where he begins his superintendent duties Easter 1532."[190] His family comes with him, and no definite time for their departure is established.[191] He lives in the Lüneburg superintendent's Probstei [dwelling of the priests' supervisor], across from the Johanniskirche's main entrance.

The new educational plan seems to be Rhegius' most pressing task. For the Lateinschule [Latin School] St. Johannis, founded in 1409, he recruits highly qualified teachers, among them Hermann Tulich and Lucas Lossius, who is also Rhegius' secretary. In Rhegius' view, both of them are great support for the new instruction and training program. Tulich works closely with Luther and is professor of philosophy in Wittenburg. Hiring him is a huge victory for Lüneburg. Few people today are aware that it was primarily the monastery schools that supervised the spiritual growth and instruction of the sons of the upper class. Now the monasteries and their schools are shut down. Reorganization of the school system is therefore of primary importance to the Reformation. Rhegius indicates in the educational plan that a city needs an educated school master, a devout preacher, and a wise city council. Capable people are necessary for the common good so that later there will be pastors, writers-in-residence, school masters, jurists, mayors, city councilmen, doctors, etc.[192] Also, poor children should be taught "because occasionally they, too, have received a fine mind from God." Behind Rhegius' diplomatic words lie instructions that education is no longer to be a privilege of the upper classes, but rather, is open to all.

Page 63

The young girls should have a special training school "so that they learn wise Christian virtue, writing, reading, and understanding of the Catechism."[193]

The city council and citizens should better supervise and organize what has up until now been the more or less haphazard care of the poor. Monies collected by the monasteries must not be diverted, but must be spent on the poor. Furthermore, begging by young people who are capable of working is forbidden.

Reorganization of the Church's operations is an even bigger task, and it conflicts with people's historical traditions. In the reorganization, all aspects of the operation must be completely regulated: from financial matters to the collection and use of the Church's possessions and holdings; to spiritual fellowship; to discussing and resolving the important and thorny question regarding dissolution of the monasteries. Talented clergy, who at least know the basic Lutheran teachings, have to be educated and supervised. Salaries for the clergy need to be determined. The clergy will be relatively well paid. The superintendent makes 300 Marks, his assistant superintendent 200 Marks, every pastor 180 Marks, and the chaplain 150 Marks.[194] These are standard annual salaries.

Above all, the Latin worship service that hardly anyone understands has to be replaced by one in German. Marriages should be publicly performed. Cemeteries are to be located outside the city because of the risk of disease ... The preacher should not only preach the Gospel, he should also live it ... , clergy should be forewarned that they will be punished or dismissed for violations. The superintendent should dismiss the current supervisor of the Catholic priests and enforce the new regulations.

This list illustrates how sweeping the changes are. Rhegius assigns the churches the task of bringing unity to Church practices in accordance with the new beliefs of the Reformation. On such occasions, he does not forget to point out their own obligations to those in power. Every Easter the superintendent is to preach a special sermon to the council members reminding them of their responsibilities.[195]

On September 24, 1532 there is a public discussion in the St. Johanniskirche about the most important changes. The church is packed. Members of the council, among them Hieronymus Witzendorf, the mayor, as well as the assistant mayor, the notary, Rhegius, and the numerous city preachers, sit in the Chor [area in the front of the church where the choir usually sits].[196] Rhegius opens the discussion: "Dear Brothers and Sisters, I ask you in the name of God that before and after the discussion you respect God's holy name ... we must not have the discussion with envious hearts, rather the discussion must take place in freedom and unity and serve the search for the truth."

The propositions for discussion are read in Low German, so that all those present understand them.[197] Surprisingly, no one strenuously objects. Others ask only minor questions so there is no substantive debate. As a result, the city council can now advance the tenets of the Reformation, for example, the fraternal societies and guilds are converted to the Evangelisch way of thinking. Now Rhegius can press the issue of assuring that the poor receive a good share of the collected monies.

Page 64

ILLUSTRATION 35: The center aisle of the St. Johanniskirche am Sand. Here Rhegius leads the discussion and presents the contents of the new education and church reorganization plan to the city of Lüneburg. (Photo: Wilhelm Krenzien, Lüneburg).

Page 65

Urbanus stays in Lüneburg until late summer of 1533 "in the middle of the wolf pack," as he writes to Kanzler [Chancellor] Förster in Celle. This shows that he often has to defend himself from many attacks. "In an impressive farewell speech in the prince's drawing room before the city's dignitaries, he admonishes them to be steadfast in their true faith and to defend the Church doctrine."[198] During the Feast of St. Michael in September 1533, he returns to Celle.

After the Hanseatic League cities of Hamburg, Lübeck, and Rostock, Lüneburg is one of the cities in which the Reformation is firmly established, and Rhegius can rightly be called the Reformer of Lüneburg.[199]

Going to Hamburg as Superintendent?
ANNA TRAVELS TO THE HANSEATIC LEAGUE CITY

On July 20, 1533 Urbanus writes a letter from Lüneburg to "the virtuous, Christian women, Hilken Reders, Gesske Hugs, and Wermelke Tonagell, my dear sisters in Christ in Hamburg."[200]

He thanks them for their friendship, which they extended to his wife, Anna, in Hamburg. The "sisters in Christ" are probably wives of Hamburg city councilmen. Matthias Reders is councilman in 1529 and mayor in 1547. Johann Huge is councilman in 1523.[201]

What happened? In the three years from September 1530 to September 1533, Rhegius is in Lüneburg for about 20 months, sometimes alone, sometimes with family. Are Urbanus and Anna unsure whether they should stay in Lüneburg? Are Anna or both of them being drawn to the more attractive Hanseatic city of Hamburg? Or, is the initiative coming from Hamburg? The latter is possible because two preachers have gone to Lüneburg from Hamburg.[202] Does Hamburg want to "get revenge" and take a preacher from Lüneburg?

What is the status of the Reformation in Hamburg? Johannes Bugenhagen, born in Pomerania and one of Luther's closest collaborators in Wittenberg since 1521, arrives in Hamburg on September 29, 1528 and stays until June 9, 1529. During this time, Bugenhagen writes the educational and church organizational plans and thereby changes the Hanseatic city "like no one else before him."[203]

"Above all, we need a good superintendent, who is a good organizer, if we can get one. Such people are expensive ... " writes Bugenhagen in the church organizational plan. The city would prefer to hire Bugenhagen himself, but he is indispensable to Luther in Wittenberg.

It is very difficult for the Hamburg city council to find a qualified candidate upon whom they can all agree, until in 1530 it turns to a "famous and meritous scholarly man of God from the local area, namely, Doctor Urban Regius." Regius has been living in Celle since 1530 as the general superintendent of Duke Ernst's principality of Braunschweig-Lüneburg ... and has already garnered considerable attention from the Hamburg city council.[204] The author of the previously mentioned lines adds that "it would be a stroke of luck for Hamburg to recruit Regius."

Page 66

The call to Rhegius is not recorded in the chronicles, but Rhegius does answer via his own messengers on February 19, 1532. (See Appendix 7.)

He thanks them for the call "to the preacher position in the illustrious city of Hamburg, in which I would be very seriously interested and also would willingly serve as superintendent, as per your wisdom, in all matters you desire." He points out, however, that he is still in Duke Ernst's service and is busy as superintendent in Lüneburg. He would have to discuss the proposal with "his most gracious lord," Duke Ernst.

The Hamburg city council understands. It writes on the Monday after Invocavit Sunday, the sixth Sunday before Easter, that Rhegius might finish his work for Lüneburg and "negotiate to bring your wisdom here to us and take on the office of superintendent." [205] (See letter in Appendix 8.)

Rhegius answers on March 1, 1532. Duke Ernst's father has died, and the duke has not yet returned.[206] Rhegius says he will reply as soon as possible. (The letter is in Appendix 9.)

One month later, Rhegius turns down the call. He writes on April 2, 1532, "Honorable Hamburg Mayor and Councilmen," that he must travel to Lüneburg on an assignment from his lord, the duke, which he promised a year ago to undertake. With "advice and fervor" he offers to help and writes, "May God protect and keep Your Eminences and the whole city of Hamburg in the right teachings and true beliefs." (See Appendix 10.)

The first Hamburg superintendent post goes to Johann Hoeck (Aepinus) on Pentecost Sunday 1532. Rhegius meets him five years later in Schmalkalden, when both consult with the Schmalkaldisher Bund [Schmalkaldic League] and sign the Schmalkaldische Artikel [Schmalkald Articles]. Surely they talk about the development of the Reformation in Hamburg and share their experiences. At this point, Urbanus can not foresee that five decades later, his grandson, Sebastian, will come to Finkenwerder as pastor.

The friendly ties with Hamburg, which Anna previously experienced during her first trip there, continue for many years. In 1536, Urbanus dedicates one of his Latin works to Hamburg Senator Joachim Moller.[207] In 1537 Urbanus reflects upon his own noble work reforming the schools.[208]

Duke Ernst the Confessor and Rhegius

Much has been written about the good relationship between Duke Ernst and Rhegius. After a year as pastor in Celle, the duke names Rhegius general superintendent of the principality of Lüneburg-Celle. As the reigning prince, Ernst is also head of the Church there.

Immediately after Rhegius informs the city of Hamburg that he cannot accept the superintendent position, he promises Duke Ernst that he will remain in Celle forever. In gratitude, the duke gives Rhegius one of his family's houses. The house is located in what was then the suburb of Blumlage. Today it is Bergstrasse 1A and 1B. The house, built by Duke Ernst in 1530, was demolished in 1705. The carved wooden thresholds, the old lateral profile brackets, and the wood from the pillars used in constructing the half-gabled framework were re-used. The duke's undated letter sent along with the gift of the house states:

Page 67

ILLUSTRATION 36: Duke Ernst gives Rhegius this house, built in 1530. It is inheritable property. Its current address is Bergstrasse 1A and 1B.[210]

"After Dr. Urbanus Regius has pledged himself to us and after trusting to stay with us for a lifetime has decided to continue to serve industriously in future godly pursuits and to accept the offer of the position of superintendent of the entire principality according to the best of his abilities and to govern faithfully to the glory of God. We have promised him to provide for the welfare of his wife and children. As there is mutual trust between us, along with shared Christian values and love, and as a sign of our good faith, with the advice of our chancellor, we have made him a gift of the house on Blumen Strasse, in which he is living, and which Dr. Rhegius and his wife may bequeath to their heirs in perpetuity."[209]

It is reported that Rhegius wrote Bible verses for his children in big letters on the walls of his house: "Memento Jesum resurrexisse" (Remember that Jesus is risen) and on the door posts: "Memento vocis Archangeli, tubae Dei ac tribunalis Domini" (Remember the voice of the Archangel, God's trumpeter, and God's most recent revelations). Writing on walls is not an unusual practice at that time.

We have already noted that Countess Magdalena von Montfort and Luther at Coburg wrote on walls.

The duke makes no decisions regarding the Church without Rhegius' consent. Their relationship is deep and trusting. It is recorded that many of the duke's decrees begin like this: "We, Ernst, Duke of Braunschweig and Lüneburg and Urbanus Rhegius ... " He instructs Rhegius to handle questions about church affairs that often require expert counsel and to develop procedures for issues stemming from local conditions.

On June 16, 1533 Rhegius sends the duke, per his request, an expert opinion about the future council in which the Evangelisch nobles and dignitaries will have to clarify unresolved questions of the Reformation.[211] In 1533, Rhegius is still in Lüneburg. He sends a letter along with his highly political opinion, adding a few very personal words at the end: "Lüneburg is not in another world. My heart is with Your Princely Grace.[212] With God's help, may my body also be there with you soon. In brief, Your Princely Grace, please be steadfast in the belief that if God is with us, who can be against us? Your Grace has a young son, a Prinz [Prince], and I had a young son named Paul...[213]

St. Paul is Rhegius' favorite apostle. Liebmann considers it possible that when Rhegius fled from Hall, he was lowered over the city wall in a basket, as was Paul in Damascus.[214] It may be that this is more in the realm of speculation, but it is nevertheless striking how often Rhegius preaches about Paul. His lectures in Augsburg about Paul's letters are so popular that he often has to give them publicly.[215]

As an aside, Rhegius' son, Paul, later becomes a soldier and dies in the 1552 Belagerung von Metz [Siege of Metz]. Rhegius never gets over his son's death. How much pain it must have caused Rhegius that a young life is sacrificed for an emperor who fights the Reformation through every possible means. Even Emperor Karl V himself regrets Metz. In his farewell address in Brussels on October 25, 1555, the emperor says: "After the king of France and several princes failed to capture me, I tried in the middle of winter to win back Metz for the kingdom. Cold, dampness, and snow brought things to a standstill ... now I will have to surrender the Niederlände [Netherlands] to my son, Phillip, and the empire to Ferdinand ... "[216] This is an important moment in world history, but a great sorrow for Anna, the grieving mother. Perhaps she remembers in this moment her husband's words about "the poor young men" who meet such a tragic end.

These years in Celle are fruitful for Urbanus, especially the year 1535. To the three brothers, Duke Otto I (Harburg), Duke Ernst the Confessor (Celle), and Duke Franz (from 1539 in Gifhorn), Urbanus writes:

Enchiridion

or

Handbuechlin eines Christlichen Fürsten
[Handbook for a Christian Prince]
to guide him in his position of authority
according to God's holy word
Handbook assembled in brief
by Doctor Urbanus Rhegius
Wittenburg 1535

Rhegius views the rulers' power as God given. Then, as now, it is natural for hereditary rulers to govern. Carefully, Rhegius works toward getting rulers to be ethical because "the Holy Scriptures demand that rulers be lawful and just and that they view all individuals as God's children. Therefore, a prince must be strong, wise, and prudent; administer the law; and have a courageous heart."

Rhegius rightly takes this opportunity to emphasize the importance of the sermon. Because a Christian prince should conduct himself in his office according to God's word, he is duty bound "to use his power in his principality to preach what is right and to counter opposition contrary to this."[217]

ILLUSTRATION 37: First page of the
Handbüchlein eines christlichen Fürsten
dedicated to Dukes Otto, Ernst, and Franz.

These admonishments also pertain to Duke Otto I, the oldest of the three brothers. When the *Handbook* is published, Duke Otto has lived in Harburg for seven years and is building his official residence there. Whether Rhegius and Duke Otto meet in person is not known. Duke Otto is a courageous supporter of the Reformation.

Page 69

It is Duke Otto who first takes up the Evangelisch resistance following the Evangelisch defeat at Mühlberg by superior Catholic forces at the start of 1548.[218]

The education of Evangelisch pastors is Rhegius' forte. It is understandable that shortly after the Reformation, there is a real shortage of educated Evangelisch pastors. Luther also frequently complains about this. On February 8, 1532 Rhegius writes to pastor Johann von Amsterdam in Bremen: "It is my view that a pastor must also read the writings of the original teachers who are true believers. To read only current writings is to stay an uninformed child."[219] Uhlhorn calls Rhegius' great interest in the Church founding fathers "the origin of the study of Church history.[220]

ILLUSTRATION 38: Duke Ernst the Confessor (1497 – 1546) from an oil painting in the Lutherhalle [Luther Hall] in Wittenberg. (Copy by Lucas Cranach the Elder).

In 1535, out of these thoughts, comes one of Urbanus' most frequently read works. It is an instruction book for young pastors, which Urbanus publishes in Latin and a year later in German: *Wie man fursichtiglich und on ergernis reden soll...* [*How one should speak carefully and without malice ...*] He recommends pastors in training learn to conduct mass, be discrete, avoid overzealousness, and study the Bible.

Meanwhile, Rhegius becomes accepted by all sides as a leading reformer. His opinion is sought. The people of Strassburg are still working on an agreement with the Southern Germans and the Swiss. In December 1534, Bucer and Melanchthon come to Kassel to present a unification plan. Luther basically agrees with this plan, but wants Rhegius to be consulted.

Likewise, in Augsburg a "Konkordie,"[concordance] should be reached. People here remember Rhegius and want him back. Gereon

Sayler, the city physician, and Huberius, the city council's representative, travel first to see Luther in Wittenberg and then to Celle, where they urge Rhegius to return to Augsburg. We do not know what Urbanus really thinks about a return to Augsburg. On one hand, Augsburg appeals to him and especially to Anna, but in the principality of Lüneburg-Celle, he has a free hand in his work as well as the appreciation and high regard of Duke Ernst.

The two representatives from Augsburg inform Rhegius of Luther's wishes that he accept the call to Augsburg. Duke Ernst, however, tells the visitors that he would "rather lose one of his eyes than give up Rhegius." Turning to Rhegius he says, "Dear Father, stay with us. You may be more highly paid in Augsburg, but you will certainly not have more love than you have from us."[221]

Page 70

ILLUSTRATION 39: A 1524 wood carving
of Urbanus Rhegius, from an unknown
publication (Bomann-Museum, Celle).

Page 71

On July 14, 1535 Rhegius writes a letter to the Augsburg mayor and city council. He thanks them "for remembering his former faithful service" and says that he would gladly help them in any possible way. "But I have unfinished assignments, which I cannot in good conscience put off. Up until 1535, I have not made any promises in Sachsen, but a half year ago I was obliged to face all kinds of emergencies, so that I have agreed to stay in my gracious lord's service, for God has blessed me and my wife with nine children, and I am now 46 years old, half of which I have spent seeking a religious city in which to serve Him ... " The full text can be found in Appendix 11. Incidentally, it contains the only reference to Rhegius' age. His comment that he is 46 years old places his birth in the year 1489.

Augsburg's mayor and city council answer Urbanus on September 8, 1535: "We have not forgotten your former faithful service to us and would like nothing more than for you to return to Augsburg and elevate the Evangelisch faith in our city."

Luther acknowledges the effort to recruit Rhegius. He writes to Augsburg: "We have also diligently written to Dr. Urbanum Regium and would gladly return him to you. But he will not leave the pious Duke Ernst."[222]

The Wittenberg Concord is signed on May 29, 1536. Rhegius is not there; he has never been in Wittenberg. According to Uhlhorn, Rhegius "signed in absentia." Presumably, his signature is secured in Naumburg.[223] Correspondence between Luther and Rhegius at the end of 1535 could be related to these events. Urbanus again has health problems and writes Luther about them. It is interesting how Luther reacts. He is "not distressed" that Rhegius is suffering "because I know you are made in the image of God's son ... " The letter is a psychological masterpiece. Luther does not address Rhegius' suffering, rather he interprets it according to Rhegius' expressed beliefs that as Christ suffered, so must we suffer. Then he almost apologizes that he talks too much. "Only a brother must address another brother and extend his hand to him." Luther understands that he has to put friends on the same level he is. He understands people! (The letter is in Appendix 12.)

Prinzess [Princess] Apollonia as Godmother to One of Rhegius' Daughters

Apollonia (1499 – 1571), Duke Ernst the Confessor's youngest sister, enters the Kloster Wienhausen at age five and is strictly brought up there. In 1527, when Ernst proclaims the Reformation in his principality, he allows his sister to leave the monastery for four years. He brings her to her mother, Margarethe von Sachsen, in the Sachsen court at Meissen. Margarethe is the sister of Friedrich der Weise. Apollonia remains close to her brother. In 1541, she takes over the upbringing of Ernst's children when Ernst's wife dies. The trustees of the Meissen Castle force her to leave the court. With a paltry pension, she passes her life in Uelzen until her death in 1571.

It is not known how the princess and Rhegius become acquainted. She is said to have read some of his writings, especially those pertaining to the Reformation and the nunneries. From his perspective, Urbanus could have thought that the princess is a "key person" who could potentially provide entrée to the nunneries, because nunneries are a very difficult place in which to present the ideas of the Reformation.

Page 72

Getting people living in monasteries to leave them goes against centuries of customs. Rhegius and Duke Ernst visit some of the monasteries together. Ernst's brother, Franz, often accompanies them, as does Chancellor Förster. Might Rhegius have received a promise of support from Princess Apollonia? Such a possibility is not plausible.

She is deeply committed to life in the monastery and struggles with the Reformation her whole life.

Therefore, the relationship between Urbanus and the princess must be one of mutual trust and respect. Urbanus' dedication of one of his works to her is more effusive than usual, and it demonstrates a heartfelt bond with the Princess: "To the illuminating, noble princess and mistress Apollonia, born Hertzogin [Duchess] of Braunschweig and Lüneburg, my gracious princess and dear sponsor."

Anna and Urbanus name one of their daughters after the princess, who is also her godmother. In 1537, Rhegius dedicates a major work to her: *Dialog von der schönen Pedigt, die Christus Luc. 24. von Jerusalem bis gen Emmaus den beiden Jüngern am Ostertag getan [Dialogue of the beautiful words in Luke 24 that Christ delivered to his two disciples on the walk from Jerusalem to Emmaus on Easter day].*[224] In the extensive text, Urbanus and Anna have a dialogue in which they participate as equals, which is very unusual for that time. In the preface, Urbanus clarifies that the women in the Bible have achieved great things. This is a clear criticism of the current convention in which women do not participate in public discussions.

In the preface to the *Dialog* Rhegius says to the princess: "After I have received many kindnesses from Your Grace, it is time that I acknowledge your kindnesses again. But because I know that Your Grace has no greater uplifting joy than to hear God's word, I look upon you as a source of God's goodness. Out of the joyful garden of the Holy Scripture, I am gathering beautiful, fragrant flowers. Your Grace, with spiritual joy in your heart, may you continue to enlighten many people." With this dedication and in the *Dialog*, Rhegius captures the life circumstances of the princess, which surely offers her the compassion she never received from her family.

ILLUSTRATION 40: Princess Apollonia dies on August 31, 1571 in Uelzen. On her grave marker in the St. Marien-Kirche in Uelzen, she is depicted in Spanish dress within the four corners of the coats of arms of her grandparents. (The four corners represent the principalities of Welfen, Sachsen, Nassau, and Bayern.) Photo by Rudolf Meier.

Page 73

In the *Dialog*, Anna appears as an educated woman and a "sincerely pious soul," who has read the Old Testament in its "original" language.[225] At the end of the *Dialog*, Anna says: "All worldly possessions are vain and are nothing compared to these Christian beliefs. I desire for my dear children no other dowry and paternal inheritance than the true enduring beliefs of this sermon." What Rhegius recommends to his young theology students he himself practices in his parsonage in Celle. At the beginning of the *Dialog* he says: "If I were to secretly or publicly shame my wife and the other women in my household, that would be against the Evangelisch teachings, and I would completely and totally lose the immeasurable treasure of Christian free will." In his forward to the first Latin edition, Luther praises the *Dialog* between Anna and Urbanus as an example of true piety.[226]

The original text of this work already exists in 1532, when Urbanus spends several months in Lüneburg with his family. Good friends urge him to publish the work.[227] Reading the 636 pages today takes some effort, especially because of the flowery "Baroque" academic style and the minutely detailed instructions. Nonetheless, the basic tenor of the history, like the disciples from Emmaus emerg-

ing from the darkness into the light and rapture, is clearly a classical model.

"Ego Urbanus Rhegius Subscribo"
RHEGIUS SIGNS THE SCHMALKALD ARTICLES

At the end of January 1537, Rhegius is on his way from Celle to
Schmalkalden. He is with Duke Ernst the Confessor and his followers, who are on horseback. Duke Ernst is a founding member of the
Schmalkaldischer Bund [Schmalkaldic League], which was formed
in 1531. The Evangelisch princes and cities have joined together to
defend the Augsburg Confession and, in fact, the league is the most
powerful inner circle of Evangelisch strength.[228] Duke Philipp von
Hessen and Elector Johann Friedrich von Sachsen are the driving
force and co-leaders of the league.

Schmalkalden is a Hessian exclave [a portion of a state or territory geographically separated from the main part by surrounding
alien territory] in Thüringen. It has a favorable location at the confluence of Medieval trade routes between Franken, Thüringen, and
Hessen. The duke and the elector each travel half way from their res-
idences in Kassel and Torgau. We do not know which route Duke
Ernst and his followers take. The 330 km route from Celle, probably
through Hildesheim, passing the Harz Mountains through Göttingen, Witzenhausen, Eschwege and up to the knolls of the Thüringen
Forest, takes the procession about 10 days in winter. It is reported
that Luther's journey starts in Wittenburg on January 31, 1537 and
that Melanchthon, Spalatin, and Bugenhagen accompany him. They

reach Schmalkalden on February 7TH.[229] They take eight days for this approximately 270 km trip, an average of about 33 km per day.

Luther's entourage goes to Torgau at the invitation of Sachsen Elector Johann Friedrich. They then proceed together through Weimar, Arnstadt, Waltershausen, and Friedrichroda to Schmalkalden.[230] Ludwig Bechstein reports in his 1834 historical romantic publication, *Der Fürstentag* [*The Prince's Day*] that Duke Ernst from Lüneburg and his entourage, including Urbanus Rhegius, join Luther's and the elector's procession prior to reaching Schmalkalden and ride into the city to enthusiastic cheers.

Page 74

The small town of Schmalkalden is full of anticipation and excitement.[231] Each day, elegantly and colorfully dressed dignitaries and their processions enter the city. Electors, counts, mayors, and advisors from the Imperial Free Cities all have to be officially welcomed and housed. "The dignitaries from Braunschweig are housed with Lorenz Kürschner,"[232] reports Ludwig Bechstein. Urbanus is part of the delegation.

The Lüneburg delegation is invited to the meeting of the Schmalkaldic League, which is the most important meeting. It begins on February 7 and lasts until March 6, 1537. For Urbanus, it is a welcome opportunity to see good friends and fellow activists from the old days, especially his friends from Southern Germany. The elector of Sachsen is expected, as well as the old league members from Anhalt and Mansfeld, Philipp von Pommern and Ullrich von Württemberg; Philipp von Braunschweig-Grubenhagen; the Count of Schwarzburg, Henneberg, Nassau-Saarbrück; Wilhelm von Til-

lenburg; the Danish representatives; Johann and Georg von Brandenburg; Ruprecht von Zweibrücken; Friedrich von Liebnitz and
Heinrich von Mecklenburg; the mayors and advisors from 22 Imperial and Free Hanseatic League Cities; 42 Evangelisch scholars; and
the entourages of the elector, landgraves, and the duke , along with
their theological advisors and court preachers.[233] Other authors name
18 German princes, representatives from 28 Imperial and Hanseatic League cities, 42 Evangelisch theologians, the emperor's Vice
Chancellor Held, and the Papal Nuncio Peter von der Vorst, as well
as observers from Denmark and France.

The conference opens on February 7TH. As church bells ring
throughout the city, the members' festive procession moves from
outside the city, through its gates, to the St. Georgskirche. Even if
Ludwig Bechstein excessively romanticizes the events in his *Der
Fürstentag* periodical, his description may give an impression of the
morning in Schmalkalden:

"Serious, festive music is heard, trumpets blare like cherubs'
voices, the resounding thunder of drums roars closer and closer. Followed by music and accompanied by Hispanic gentlemen-at-arms,
comes the Herald of the emperor carrying a staff. After him come the
Spanish courtiers with the imperial banners, who gather around the
emperor's ambassador, Dr. Matthias Held, the Vice Chancellor of
the Empire. Two standard bearers follow him, carrying the Hessian
and the elector of Sachsen's flags. Then come the current leader of the
League, Landgrave Philipp von Hessen, and the second in command,
Elector Johann Friedrich von Sachsen, who are engaged in serious
conversation. Following them is Duke Ulrich von Württemberg and
the Fürst von Henneberg. Then come Duke Ernst von Braunschweig
and Lüneberg and Duke Philipp von Pommern. After them come

Duke Philipp von Braunschweig-Grubenhagen and Duke Franziskus von Lüneburg."[234]

Then follows the unending procession of rulers. Finally come
"priests in their dark robes or theological scholars in their academic
gowns. At the forefront are the most learned, Dr. Martin Luther and

Page 75

Georg Spalatinus. Following them are Philipp Melanchthon and
Justus Jonas. Then come Bugenhagen and Johann Agricola, Kruciger
and Nicolaus Amsdorf. Doctor Urbanus Rhegius, superintendent and
reformer of Lüneburg, and Stephan Agricola walk near each other,
as do the Nürnberg clergymen, the spiritual Andreas Osiander and
M. Veit Dietrich ... "[235]

Superintendent Johannes Aeppin and Johannes von Amsterdam,
whose names have been previously mentioned, are participants from
Hamburg and Bremen.

As the working sessions begin, the theologians meet in the late
Roman style Hessenhof [Hessen court] on Neumarkt, the administrative seat of the dukes of Hessen. The civil representatives meet
in the drawing room of the city hall, built in 1472.[236] Both buildings are still standing.

For Urbanus it must be an overpowering experience to be with
the most highly respected reformers and influential theologians of
the times for four weeks to debate, organize, negotiate, or simply
exchange opinions over wine or beer after the day's work is done.
There are not only serious events, but also pleasurable ones. The city

is alive with itinerant people performing for money: exhibitors, enter-tainers, artists, and actors. The wine merchants also profit.

The 1537 city accounts report that about 1,000 liters of wine are provided to conference participants.[238]

ILLUSTRATION 41: The Hessenhof in Schmalkalden, administrative seat of the Hessen government. In 1537 it is the meeting place of the Evangelisch theologians.[237]

What is the reason for so many prominent figures and so much expense? Throughout the entire time of the Reformation, the Evange-lisch reformers want a convention in which the important unresolved theological questions should be discussed and decided. Originally, it was planned for May 1537 in Mantua, but it takes place eight years later in Trient. In preparation for the convention, elector Johann Frie-drich von Sachsen had asked Luther to write out the tenets of the Evangelisch position and the points that are non-negotiable.[239]

The "Schmalkaldischen Artikel" [Schmalkald Articles] come out of this mandate. For posterity, Luther himself writes this complete personal testament of faith. Since Luther is plagued by kidney stones he is very concerned about dying. The elector's wish is similar to his own. Luther wants to firmly lay out his position in case he dies prior to the convention.

Page 76

During the four weeks, the most famous theologians of the time preach daily in the Schmalkalder Stadtkirche [City Church]. Luther,

Nikolaus von Amsdorf, and Urbanus preach twice. Bucer, Spalatin, Melander, Schnepf, Ambrosius, Blarer, Brenz, and Osiander also preach from the pulpit.[240] What a contest of words, ideas, confessions of faith, and visions among these men of the early Reformation!

Ludwig Bechstein reports which of the theologians gave the first sermons in the Stadtkirche St. Georg after the opening of the conference.[241] The following is verbatim: "After Luther, Dionys Melander preached; on the Sunday before Lent Urbanus Rhegius; on the Monday before Shrovetide Erhard Schnepf; on Shrove Tuesday Martin Butzer."[242]

Luther makes a pun to chide Urbanus after a sermon that was too long: "hoc neque urbanum neque regium fuit" (roughly translated as "neither profound nor exciting"). During a short city tour of Schmalkalden we ask the woman tour guide about this episode. She is knowledgeable and answers spontaneously: "Luther suffered greatly from kidney stones. Because of this, he was impatient and not always gracious. It was the middle of winter and a heated stone was brought into the church to keep Luther warm." Luther's views about speaking are delivered in this witty remark: "Tritt forsch auf, machs Maul auf, hör bald auf!" [Literally: "Step up soon, open your mouth soon, and stop soon!" It means to say something serious in a nice way.] Luther could not tolerate long sermons.

German history is being written at this meeting in Schmalkalden. Compromises are presented to preserve future relationships among the Evangelisch congregations. The question of whether the Schmalkalden League should participate in the church council convened by the emperor plays an important role. For quite some time, Urbanus has advocated for a role. One must be courageous and consult with everyone "because all of Christiandom has a right to expect much from us. Considering all our power and capabilities, we owe that to Christianity."[243] In 1536, he had published *Dialogus* [Dialogue], an entertaining and useful conversation about the upcoming Concilio [Council] of Mantua in which he pled for the participation of all.[244] Now the sentiment has changed. The Evangelisch side has become self-assured and decisive. The conflict with Rome is clearer than ever. Participation in the council is rejected. The conference's refusal to sustain the Schmalkald Articles is an important turning point in the Church schism that Rhegius has fought against. Now everything is pulling in another direction.

Rhegius looks forward to seeing Luther again. He has not seen Luther for seven years, since their meeting at Coburg Castle. Still, the joy of the reunion is also clouded by Luther's poor health. Concerns are openly expressed, and questions about the future are asked. How would things go forward without Luther, the rock in the turbulent waters, the fearless fighter? Luther himself fears that after his death, his Wittenberg colleagues could become split by conflict.[245]

Twice Urbanus stands in the chancel before the assembled Evangelisch princes of the realm, the mayors, and the councils from the Imperial Free and Hanseatic League cities who are jointly preparing to oppose the emperor and the pope. Not only the princes of the realm, but also his Evangelisch colleagues, foremost of whom is Martin Luther himself, are looking up at him from the church pews. This is a high point in his life, an auspicious hour. For a short time, he is in the spotlight and this gives strength to his words.

ILLUSTRATION 42: Twice Urbanus Rhegius preaches in the Stadtkirche St. Georg before Luther and the assembled princes of the realm. The sermon is too long for Luther, who is suffering from kidney stones. (Lithograph from the Biedermeier period).

What thoughts may be occurring to Urbanus Rhegius? Does he make "only" a theological presentation, or at the last second, does he make political suggestions and an appeal to uphold Church unity? We do not know his thoughts, yet we cannot help but be fascinated by this scenario in the Schmalkalden Stadtkirche.

Meanwhile, outside in the market and the streets, colorful preparations for Schrove Tuesday are progressing. Luther is staying in a house owned by Balthasar Wilhelm. Here, the text of the Schmalkald Articles is being finalized. This house is now called the Lutherhaus [Luther House], but at that time it was the Töpfermarkt [market where pots are sold]. Because of his illness, Luther invites his friends and fellow reformers, including Urbanus Rhegius, to his quarters.[246]

In this house on February 21, 1537 a famous sermon takes place because Luther is too weak to go to the Stadtkirche. He invites the electors, the counts, and all his friends to his quarters to once again bear witness to his beliefs. His strong will overcomes the weakness of his body. Luther preaches with his usual vigor, however, those present, including Urbanus, worry about Luther's condition and discuss the necessity of signing the Schmalkald Articles soon.[247]

ILLUSTRATION 43: The Lutherhaus in Schmalkalden.
On February 24, 1537, the Evangelisch theologians, among
them Urbanus Rhegius, sign the Schmalkald Articles.

Seven years ago, the Augsburg Confession still set the tone for
the connection between the old church and the Evangelisch church,
whereas the Schmalkald Articles are written with greater clarity and
emphasize opposition to the Roman Catholic Church. Since these
articles are a theological confession of belief, they are not signed by
the princes and the cities as was the Augsburg Confession, but rather
by the theologians, including Rhegius. The text is the foundation of
the Lutheran Church's beliefs, which today every pastor confesses
at his or her ordination.[248]

Page 78

Because of Luther's illness, the signing must take place in his quarters. It is February 24, 1537, two days before his departure. He signs
first, followed by Jonas, Bugenhagen, Crutziger, Amsdorf, Spalatin,
and Melanchthon; then Agricola, Didymus, and Urbanus Rhegius
(the first three signature lines).[249]

ILLUSTRATION 44: "Ego Urbanus Rhegius. D.
Ecclesiarum In Ducatu Lunoburgensi Superintendens
subscribo meo et fratrum meorum nomine et Ecclesiarum
Hannopherane."[250] ("I, Urbanus Rhegius, Doctor of
Theology and Superintendent in the principality of Lüneburg,
sign for myself and in the name of my fellow officials as
well as in the name of the Church in Hannover.")

Rhegius is authorized to sign the articles in the name of the Hannover Church. The previous year, he led Duke Ernst's commission there. The problems were similar to those he had encountered in Lüneburg: to develop a city plan for school and church reform. The highest level diplomatic skills were needed in Hannover because it did not belong to Duke Ernst's principality, but rather to the principality of his relative, Erick I of Calenberg-Göttingen. With Rhegius' signature on the document, it shows that Hannover stands with the Schmalkaldic League rather than with the lands of Calenberg-Göttingen, the largest city in the principality.[251]

After the signing of the Schmalkald Articles, written by Melanchthon, the document is read aloud to the assembled rulers and papal dignitaries. This document is signed by everyone, including Urbanus Rhegius.[252]

ILLUSTRATION 45: Title page of the Schmalkald Articles. (Published by Christian Rödinger, 1554).

Page 79

The return trip from Schmalkalden to Celle through the wintery countryside is very difficult. On April 18, 1537 Urbanus writes to Luther from Braunschweig that he has heard through Melanchthon that Luther had a good trip home and is doing better.[253] Urbanus himself rode from Schmalkalden back to Celle and caught a very bad cold. He hopes Luther will write the forward to his *Dialogus über Lukas 24* [*Dialogue About Luke 24*]. This forward, in Latin, is published by Johann Freder in 1542 after Rhegius' death.[254] That

Urbanus can ask Luther to write this forward attests to the close relationship between them.

Religious Dialogue on the Way to Hagenau – The Last Journeys

Following his return from Schmalkalden and Braunschweig, Rhegius is soon called to Westfalen to help the cities of Soest, Lemgo, and especially Minden. In August, he delivers an "extremely powerful and fiery sermon"[255] in Minden, which he publishes at the request of his friends there.[256] "Watch out for false prophets who come to you in sheep's clothing, but inside are flesh-eating wolves who will tear you apart ... ," he warns the congregation. As it has been years ago in Augsburg,[257] the main concerns here are the Anabaptists.

Meanwhile, there is no letup in the political maneuvering. The emperor again asks for help fighting the Turks and simultaneously tries to clarify the contentious religious questions, in order to win over the power of the Evangelisch followers to his side. However, the mood between the Roman Catholic Church and the Evangelisch becomes increasingly irritable and irreconcilable. Final efforts are undertaken to avoid a major conflict, a war. A religious dialogue scheduled to take place in 1539 in Nürnberg, to which Rhegius is also invited, is cancelled.

The next convention is planned for 1540 in Speyer, but is changed to Hagenau in Elsass. Duke Ernst asks Rhegius to write an opinion about the convention's prospects, which Rhegius assesses as fair to poor. "He becomes deeply aware how great the divide is, and with new eyes, he sees a lasting schism in the church."[258] His spirits are dampened by physical suffering and awareness that part of his life's work, the preservation of church unity, will not be fulfilled. In this state of mind, he rides on with Duke Ernst and 15 knights to Hersfeld, where they meet with the Hessian and Sachsen theologians, in preparation for the journey to Hagenau.

From Hersfeld, Urbanus writes to the elector of Sachsen on June 22, 1540 that he has been instructed to stay in a suburb of Hagenau. Urbanus fears that this is because " ... they could be more easily attacked." He remembers the threats to him in Augsburg and thinks " ... that a small band of 15 men could easily be taken prisoner." [259] The elector answers immediately and tries to calm Urbanus.

In Hagenau, the Roman Catholics inundate the Evangelisch with unacceptable demands. Just as in 1530 in Augsburg and 1537 in Schmalkalden, Rhegius tries to mediate. He has known the participants for many years. He himself had many opportunities to personally connect with King Ferdinand. Seventeen years ago, when Ferdinand was a 20 year old archduke, Urbanus rode to meet him at the outskirts of Hall and welcomed him in the name of the Church.

Page 80

Substantive discussions do not take place in Hagenau. The convention is adjourned until October 1540. The participants want to meet again in Worms. Urbanus' name is still on the invitation list, but because of his poor health, he cannot attend. From Hagenau, he returns to Celle. A few months later he is dead.

Early Death in Celle – Burial in the City Church

It appears that Urbanus' strength is sapped at the start of his sixth decade. We repeatedly hear about the fluctuations in his health. He himself speaks about it more frequently. The period in which he was born, with its fundamental changes and spiritual awakening, over-taxes him, but at the same time, it opens great opportunities for him. He sees the challenges of the times and wants to surmount them. He grows through challenges, is eager, and always gives his best. Deeply held convictions, a strong will, and also perhaps ambition drive him. He does not allow himself rest and recovery.

Frequent moves, dangerous journeys via horseback or covered wagon, animosity from his political opponents, a large family, and a host of assignments that cause unforeseen new developments demand his attention and strength. We are amazed by the volume of his work. In his bibliography of Urbanus, Liebmann lists 92 manuscripts and 139 publications. Some are only single pages, others are more than 300 pages. He does most of his writing at night when his children are asleep and the house is quiet. Then, with paper, quill, and ink, he sits down at his desk in the candlelight. His wife's admonish-ments do not deter him from what he considers his duty. It sounds like an apology when, along with the date, he remarks, "in haste," or "in great haste" as if he wants to say, "If only I had more time."

All authors of Urbanus' Latin *Vita* probably owe their information about his last days to the detailed accounts of his son Ernst. Ernst surely got these details from his mother, since he was only five years old at his father's death.[260]

The bad cold that Urbanus has on his return from Hagenau is attributed by doctors to a "Fluss," an old term for stroke, rheumatism, or gout. The "Fluss" begins in Urbanus' head and goes down into his whole body. A wound breaks out on his right leg, which the doctors say should be left unbandaged.[261]

In May, the wound heals. The doctors have no further advice. Urbanus reads his *Dialogus von den Emmausjüngern* [*Dialogue of Emmaus Disciples*] and consoles himself with what he himself wrote to console others. On Sunday, May 22, 1541, he once again celebrates communion with his congregation. Monday morning, he falls out of bed. A stroke paralyzes his right side.

His wife, children, colleagues, and close friends gather around his death bed. They try to comfort him with words from the Holy Scriptures, but instead, he gives more comfort to those present. He asks them

Page 81

ILLUSTRATION 46: Rhegius' final resting place in the chancel of the Stadtkirche Celle. (Photo: Dietrich Klatt, Celle).

not to be distressed by his departure because after a life of work and effort, he is ready to die. After three hours he falls peacefully asleep. No one knows his last words, but they may have been to ask God to continue to bless his young family.

His wife is 36 years old, the same age as Urbanus when they got married in 1525. Total responsibility for the children rests on her young shoulders. On Ascension Day, her husband will be laid to rest during a large funeral in the chancel of the Stadtkirche Celle. Anna is pregnant when she has to get through this difficult day.

Urbanus, as general superintendent, is the highest ranking church official in the principality after the duke. The burial ceremony of someone of this rank is very precisely prescribed. It is a celebration honoring his life and work. Usually, it is attended by the highest ranking church and civic representatives of the city in which the court is located. It is led by Duke Ernst the Confessor, his family, and probably also his brother Franz.

Duke Ernst provides the widow with an annual pension of 40 Gulden and six "wichhimpten" rye, as well as care for four children (two sons and two daughters) for four years and a grant for one of the sons if he wants to pursue religious studies.[262] Whether the Duke gives additional support to his godchild, Ernst Regius, is not documented, but it is likely. When Duke Ernst dies in 1546, his sons Heinrich and Wilhelm probably provide support for Ernst Regius. In the preface to Ernst's German translation of his father's works, which he dedicates to Princes Heinrich and Wilhelm, he thanks them for the "great support and kindnesses given to him and his family by Your Gracious Majesties."

Where presumably is Urbanus' grave in the Stadtkirche? The Fürstengruft [princes'crypt], which still exists today, was first laid out in 1576 by Duke Wilhelm dem Jüngeren [the Younger] (1535 – 1592). In previous years, members of the duke's family were interred "auf dem Chor" [chancel, near the area in front of the church where the choir sits]. Page 260 of a Celle manuscript indicates that Rhegius "lies buried about two steps from Duke Ernst and his Gemahlin [consort]."

This statement is corroborated by F. Bonnels' work.[263] "West of the Fürstengruft in the chancel lie the graves of 1. Urbanus Rhegius (Died May 23, 1541), 2. Duke Ernst the Confessor (Died 1546), 3. His Consort Sophia (Died June 8, 1541), 4. Duke Friedrich (Died 1553), and 5. Duke Franz Otto (Died 1559). The site of these graves was verified in 1891/2 by Pastor Kreusler."

The aforementioned princes' crypt was built by Duke Ernst's son, Duke Wilhelm dem Jüngeren under the chancel, in which he and his consort, as the first members of the Welfenhaus [House of Guelph] are buried.[264]

Page 82

In 1626, the oldest graves, including Rhegius", were given up. The grave stones were placed in the chancel wall behind the altar. Whether Rhegius' grave stone was also there is not mentioned.[265]

The grave sites are shown in the following sketch from the works mentioned above:

ILLUSTRATION 47: Urbanus Rhegius lies buried in the chancel of the Stadtkirche Celle, "two steps" from Duke Ernst. The sketch shows the grave sites: 1. Urbanus Rhegius, 2. Duke Ernst, 3. His consort Sophia, 4. Duke Friedrich, 5. Duke Franz Otto.

Martin Luther greatly mourns the early death of Urbanus. Luther's preface to Urbanus' *Dialogue* appears in Johann Frede's 1542 Latin edition of the work. It is a memorial to the beloved deceased:

"For many reasons, it causes me great pain to hear of the death of pious men, especially the demise of those who publicly or privately demonstrated their talents to others. First of all, I am sorry that the Church, the state, and their families into which they were born and developed, have been robbed of their protectors. I speak only about the Church and how much the Sachsen churches[266] have lost with the death of Urbanus Rhegius. In truth, he has been a bishop to neighboring lands, in which he has sown the seeds of true Evangelisch beliefs. Urbanus has purified the people's worship services and customs and quelled the flatterers' false ideas. With distinction, he has led many pious followers of the Church and worldly regents with his teachings and counsel.

Many congregations feel like a flock without a shepherd. When I think about the deaths of such men, bitter pain overcomes me again. Then, in the spirit of the Holy Ghost, I look upon the congregations across the land and embrace them in my prayers. With many qualms I think about how few gifted servants of the Church there are. How much weakness lies within those who put themselves forth to lead others. Some of these 'leaders' even have wrong beliefs.

When such admirable members in Christ are called from this life, I also feel it is a sign that because we all will be judged on Judgment Day, God takes certain people from the crowd beforehand. As Isaiah says: 'The righteous will be gathered up so that they do not see evil, but will come in peace and tranquility into their chambers.'

Although one must mourn when the Church is robbed of its defenders through the death of pious and learned men, one must also fervently wish them Godspeed on their journey home. Blessed are the dead who die in the Lord. Thus, we know that our Urbanus is holy. He was called by God, always lived Christian beliefs, faithfully served the Church, and graced Evangelisch beliefs with piety and moral purity. We know that he has eternal joy in the company of Christ and the heavenly hosts, among whom he openly learns, and stands and hears what he himself preached here, according to God's words. As he earlier with his esteemed wife, children, and all his followers enjoyed discussing the teachings of the Church forefathers and the prophets, he himself now hears the old teachers and Christ preach in heaven as he had preached on earth. He rejoices that his faith agrees with the teachings of Christ and the Church forefathers.

It behooves us to preserve Urbanus Rhegius' memory by enthusiastically reading his writings."[267]

Anna Weissbrücker Remains in Celle

During her 16 year marriage and afterwards, Anna does not try to become a public figure. With 13 children, she hardly has the time or opportunity. But there is sufficient material about her life for us to form an image of her character.

She grows up in a progressive Augsburg merchant family where the Reformation finds acceptance early on. With her marriage to Urbanus in 1525, Anna shows that she strongly adheres to Evangelisch teachings, and she is a great support to her husband during uncertain times. In letters from Luther and Melanchthon, who often send her greetings, she is described as an extremely well-educated woman. In a letter to Urbanus from November 1, 1537, Melanchthon compares Anna to the biblical "heroines," Sara, Rebecka, and Elisabeth.[268]

There is a suggestion that Anna might be Jewish because she is educated in ancient languages. Aside from that, when we work through her family history, we come upon another possibility. In the previously cited *Dialogue*, it is mentioned that Anna studied Hebrew in Augsburg with Rabbi Antonio Margaritha.[269] When can that have been? From the Universitätsmatrikel [university registry] in Leipzig where Margaritha was a "Lektor der heiligen Sprachen" [lecturer in holy languages] in 1532, the following picture emerges:

"Antonius Margaritha, born in Prague to a distinguished Jewish family, was baptized into the Lutheran faith in the Bayern city of Wasserburg in 1522...He was promoted to lecturer in holy languages – Augsburg 1523, Meissen 153? (illegible), Leipzig 1532, and professor in Wien 15?? (two numbers are missing)."

Margaritha is therefore a Jew who converted to Christianity. His Jewish name is Samuel Margolis. In 1523, he teaches in Augsburg, where Urbanus and Anna certainly hear about him. Urbanus has a great deal of positive interest in Judaism. Scott H. Hendrix reports that Urbanus clearly distances himself from Luther's statements about the Jews. Especially in Braunschweig, Rhegius makes an effort to meet and talk with the Jews and wants to convert them. He absolutely cannot understand that they do not want to accept Christ, since all arguments support Christianity and stem from the Bible.[270] He even writes a letter in Hebrew to the Jewish congregation in Braunschweig.[271]

ILLUSTRATION 48: In a letter of recommendation
dated July 9, 1543, Duke Ernst the Confessor requests
the mayor and the Augsburg city council support the
widow of "the very learned Doctor Urbanus Rhegius"
in her business affairs. (Stadtarchiv Augsburg).

When Anna studies Hebrew in 1523 in Augsburg with Rabbi
Margaritha, there is automatically a tie to Urbanus. Because Margaritha is specifically named as her teacher, it follows that she begins
to learn Hebrew in 1523. Margaritha's acquaintance with Rhegius
quickly grows through Anna's interests. Urbanus is happy that such
a learned man as the rabbi converts to Christianity and that he hopefully will bring the Jews into the Christian faith through "the right
arguments."[272]

Margaritha does not appear in the Augsburg tax records. He,
like Urbanus, pays no taxes because he is not an official resident
of the city. He is often a guest of the Peutingers. Their own children are home-schooled, eventually with other children. It is only a
five minute walk from the Peutinger's house to the Weissbrücker's
house on Mauerberg. So, there is a good possibility that Anna has
her Hebrew lesson at the Peutinger's house.

Das Allgemeine Gelehrten-Lexikon [Common Dictionary of Scholars]
notes that Anna had a conversation with Margaritha in Leipzig in
1531.[273] Anna, however, is already in Celle in 1531 awaiting her baby
at the beginning of the year. That she would undertake such a long
journey in 1531 sounds very unlikely since both Margaritha and Anna

live in Augsburg until 1530. The comment in *Das Allgemeine Gelehrten-Lexikon* that Anna is also fluent in the Chaldean language is also reported in other sources.[274] She is interested in the roots of Christianity, and her proficiency in ancient languages leads her into interpretation of the Bible. Thus, there are good reasons that Urbanus writes his *Dialog* as a conversation with Anna. He introduces her publicly in this work as an equal partner.

Bringing up the children and managing the large household are primarily Anna's responsibility after she is left alone following Urbanus' death. There is not yet an organized school system so much of her time is spent teaching her children to read and write. She knows how important that is.

Her financial burden is lightened through the duke's previously mentioned promise of a 40 Gulden annual stipend, but especially through her Augsburg inheritance. Also, she enjoys the duke's support. In 1543, she must settle her Augsburg inheritance. She travels to Augsburg with a letter of recommendation from Duke Ernst to the mayor and city council "to expedite and render her help in every possible way." (See letter in Illustration 48.) A printed version of the letter is in Appendix 13.

[THERE is a photo of the City of Celle coat of arms at the bottom of page 85.]

Page 86

Anna remains in the house on Bergstrasse that was given to her and Urbanus as a present by Duke Ernst. After Urbanus' death, it belongs to Anna. Why then in 1553 does she buy the house at Stech-bahn 10, (today the Volksbank)? There must be a good reason for this. Karl Schottenloher reports that Urbanus' library burns.[275] That happens shortly before 1553, which explains the reason for Anna's purchase of the Stechbahn 10 house.

ILLUSTRATION 49: Anna Weissbrücker buys this house in 1553, located today at Stechbahn 10, in the city center of Celle, across from the Stadtkirche. (Photo: Walter König).

We do not know what Anna lost besides her husband's valu-able library. A house fire is always a tragedy. The home where the family lived, with all its accompanying memories, is lost forever, not to mention the material loss.

Anna's 1553 house purchase is noted in the Celle city register. She pays 225 Gulden in cash to the seller, Jürgen Sonnemann. The text is included in Appendix 14.

The house is a good purchase for Anna. It is in the center of the small city, much more so than the house on Bergstrasse. From the gable windows she can view the Stadtkirche. Now she is much closer to her deceased husband. The worship service is only a few steps away.

In the ten years surrounding her husband's death, other import-ant people in the Evangelisch movement also die. In January 1546, Duke Ernst, sponsor, friend, and protector of the family, passes away. Martin Luther dies only a month later. Anna witnesses the Schmal-kalden Krieg [War] in 1547, at the end of which everything appears to be lost. She lives to experience the Augsberger Religionsfrieden

[Peace of Augsburg] in 1555. She is happy and proud that the empire's law recognizes the Evangelisch teachings with the name of the city of her birth. Finally, she also sees the beginning of the Counter-Reformation. It remains a turbulent century.

Anna outlives her husband by 28 years! There are differing accounts about the year of her death. The earliest chronologists, for example, Bytemeister, give the year as 1569,[276] as does *Das Allgemeine Gelehrten-Lexikon* by Jöcher and Rotermund. In contrast, Clemens Cassel in his two volume, *Geschichte der Stadt Celle* [*History of the City of Celle*], gives the year of Anna's death as 1566.[277] Most later authors have adopted Cassel's date, however, it is an error. Our own research shows that the "old" authors are correct that 1569 is the year of Anna's death.

Clemens Cassel writes: "The years 1567 – 1569 were the Plague Years. Listed among the dead in 1566(!) were Pastor Ondermark, who was Urbanus Rhegius' loyal assistant, Rhegius' wife, and the prince's financial advisor, Simon Hoppener."

How is the year of Anna's death accurately determined?

Page 87

ILLUSTRATION 50: "Doctor Urban's wife" is listed in the Glockengeldregister [bell registry of those who have died and names of people who paid money to have the church bells rung for the deceased] with those who died of the plague between 1567 and 1569. Pastor Ondermark is also listed (first entry, right side above, without an amount of money indicated. For Urbanus' wife, see the area marked in yellow.)[278]

Preserved in the sacristy of the Stadtkirche Celle is an ancient iron-clad chest containing old Church documents. Among the documents is the *Glockengeldregister* [*bell registry*] indicating on pages 168 – 176 the fee charged for the Church bells to be rung for those who died of the plague between 1567 – 1569. All the deceased are registered without individual dates. On page 175 we find in the right column: "Dr. Urbanus' loving wife..." After her, only 22 names are listed, a sure sign that she is one of the last to fall victim to the plague in this time period.

Further proof of 1569 as the year of Anna's death is the entry of the death of Pastor Ondermark in the eleventh position before Anna's. The year of his death is known to be 1569. The same applies to Simon Hoppener, noted on page 173. It is highly likely that Clemens Cassel made a mistake in writing down 1566 since he knows that Ondermark and Hoppener died in 1569.

Uhlhorn's assertion that Anna, "with her numerous children and their many needs" lives in Calenberg in 1588 is disproven by Eckard Weinberger in 1989.[279] A thorough examination of Church records reveals that Elizabeth Dransfeld listed as the "Widow of Urbani Rhegii" is actually the wife of Urbanus Rhegius, *Junior*.

The Children of Urbanus Rhegius and Anna

Acccounts vary as to the number of their children. The previously mentioned *Genealogia* lists 11 children (but Afra and the last born child who died early are not included). Some sources indicate 14 children, without providing their names.[280] Thirteen is the well-documented number of children that has prevailed. Ernst Regius says in his father's *Vita* that during his parents' marriage, 12 children were born and that one birth occurred after his father's death, but the child soon died. Even if the *Vita* contains some vague information, Ernst is talking about his siblings, and who should know them better than he does?

Eckard Weinberger, himself a Rhegius descendant from the Königsberg line, states there are 12 living children. He describes them in a thought-provoking article on the 500TH anniversary of Urbanus' death.[281] There are reliable birthdates for only two of the children. Largely because of nomenclature, we came across series of names which differ from Weinberger's, nevertheless, we have accepted many of his assertions.

1. MARIA (301). Born around 1526 in Augsburg. Year of death unknown. 1543/44 lady's maid to Countess Elisabeth at Münden Castle. Married the Evangelisch preacher, Johann Algermann, Beedenbostel, Celle District (302). Her descendants include: "Court singers, Kanzlei-schreiber [office clerks], historians, Finanzverwalter [financial administrators], notaries, and poets. Rhegius' grandson, Franz Algermann, is multi-talented."

   In the traditional way of naming children, the oldest daughter is named after her paternal grandmother. That is the case here, especially since Urbanus' mother always moved with him and managed the household. She lived with the family in Augsburg until 1529. It is likely that Urbanus honored and thanked his mother with the birth of his first child. From this, we can deduce that Urbanus' mother was named Maria.

2. URBANUS (303). Born about 1527 in Augsburg. Died after 1569, but before 1572. Senior civil servant at Schloss [Castle] Münden and Nienover. Detailed description in chapter 11 "Urbanus Regius, Jr." Married Elizabeth Dransfeld, Göttingen (304). She lived as a widow in Münden in 1588. Children:

    2.1 SEBASTIANUS REGIUS, changed his name to SEBASTIAN KÖNIG in 1588 (401). Pastor on the Island of Finkenwerder in the Elbe River, 1588 – 1621. Born after 1554, but before 1559 in Münden. Died 1621 in Finkenwerder. For descendants, see Rieger –R(h)egius - König.

Page 89

    2.2 CHRISTOFF REGIUS (404). Born around 1561/65 in Münden or Nienover. Year of death unknown. Senior civil servant in Reinhausen near Göttingen. On September 22, 1595 married Anna Spangenberg (405), daughter of Wilhelm Spangenberg from an old Münden family. Beginning in 1540 was in the Münden office. 1546 was secretary and special advisor to Countess Elisabeth. Later secretary to Duke Erich II. In 1573, because of his outstanding service, was awarded three "Hufen"[hides] of land in Grone near Göttingen.[282] [A "hide" is Anglo-Saxon for the amount of land it takes a family with a plow to support itself.] Christoff was the co-heir of his Uncle Ernst Regius. (See chapter: "Urbanus, Jr. Leaves Behind Three Underage Children."). For descendants see Appendix 15.

2.3 ERICH REGIUS (406). **Born about 1563/67 in
Münden or Nienover. Date of death unknown.
Soldier. Enlisted May 25, 1589 in the Göttin-
gen Academy. Co-heir of his uncle, Ernst Regius.
(See chapter: "Urbanus, Jr. Leaves Behind Three
Underage Children.")**

3. URSULA (305). Probably born around 1528 in Augsburg.
Year of death unknown. Stiftsdame [member of the foun-
dation] of Walsrode Monastery. In 1537/38 Duke Ernst
replaced the Catholic order there with the Evangelisch
order.[283] In Lüneburg, all the women's monasteries were
maintained for the care of the daughters of the nobility and
citizens. Because old customs continued, the term "nun"
was still used long after the Reformation, as can be seen in
the *Genealogis*. The reason Ursula Regius goes to the monastery is unknown. Personal records from this period in
Walsrode have not been obtained.

   As the second daughter, she is named for her maternal
grandmother, Ursula Fendt (St. Ursula was martyred in
452 in Köln. In Augsburg there was a Dominican women's
monastery by this name.) Ursula is present at the sale of her
mother's house and garden in Celle on July 16 and 20, 1569.

4. ANNA (306). Probably born in 1528 in Augsburg. Date of
death unknown. Married Balthasar Wettmer, Celle (307).
Named after her mother, Anna Weissbrücker or after St.
Anna, Augsburg. Anna, mother of the Virgin Mary, is
among other things, the patron saint of goldsmiths (see
chapter: "Merchants, Gold Traders, Businessmen – Anna
Weissbrücker's Ancestors").[284]

5. AFRA (308). Born around 1529/30 in Augsburg. Date of
death unknown. Married prior to 1548 to Leonhard Auff-
geber, München (309). She inherits 100 Gulden from her

grandfather, Caspar Weissbrücker, see chapter: "Merchants, Gold Traders, Businessmen – Anna Weissbrücker's Ancestors." She is probably named for St. Afra, who was martyred in 304 in Augsburg and made a saint in 1064. She is patron saint of the Augsburg Diocese. St. Afra's grave was a shrine visited on pilgrimages.

6. EUPHROSINE (310). Born around 1530 in Augsburg or Celle. Date of death unknown. Named in the July 16TH and 20TH sale of her mother's house and garden as "Ephrosine Regia." Probably unmarried. Euphrosyne is one of the three Charities in Greek mythology (after Charis = charisma, charity, philanthropy). The Charities are: Aglaia (Beauty or Splendor), Euphrosyne (Joy or Mirth), and Thalia (Good Cheer).

7. SOPHIA SARA (312). Probably born after 1530 in Celle. Date of death unknown. In about 1553/54 married Georg Ebel, Münden (313). He is present at the 1569 sale of his mother-in-law's house and garden in Celle. Sophia is Greek for wisdom. Sara is the wife of Abraham in the Bible. Children:

   7.1 GEORG. Later lives in "Ferlein" (Fehrlingsen district of Nordheim).

   7.2 HANS MARX (MARKUS). Barber.
   Children:

   7.2.1 JOHANN. Born in Münden about 1575. In 1589 enrolls in the Göttingen School, 1580 – 97 lives in Münden.

   7.2.2 DAUGHTER. Name unlisted

   7.2.3 SON. Name unlisted

   7.2.4 SON. Name unlisted

   7.3 SIDONIA. Married Peter Rauch

   7.4 ANNA.

Page 90

8.   FRANZIKUS OTTO (314). Born after 1530 in Celle. Died "in Prussia" (see *Genealogy*). Possibly named after Duke Ernst's two brothers (Otto I. of Harburg and Franz of Gifhorn). Or, more likely, after Franziskus Otto, Duke Ernst's son, to whom Rhegius dedicated his Catechism at Christmas in 1540. Princes Franziskus Otto, Friedrich, and Heinrich interpret the holy scriptures using a question and answer format, in which Franziskus Otto, as the eldest, gives the explanation.[285]

For Franziskus-Otto's descendants, see the following chapter: "Franziskus-Otto Regius as Founder of the Königsberger Lineage."

9.   APOLLONIA (316). Born after 1530 in Celle. Date of death unknown. Named in the sale of her mother's house and garden in Celle on July 16TH and 20TH, 1569. Goddaughter of Princess Apollonia, Duke Ernst's sister, to whom Rhegius in 1536 dedicates his *Dialogue*. Marries (Ernst) Hermann Quedlenburg (317). Prior to 1555 he was a teacher in Osnabrück. From 1555 – 1583 he was pastor in the Obershagen district of Burgdorf.[286] Children: Ernst, Hans, Sophia, Anna, and name not listed.

One of these daughters, which one is not known, marries Georg Scharffenberg on December 11, 1588. He works as a wood carver for Franz Algermann, known as the illustrator of the illustrious members of the Guelph branch of the family. See chapter: "Court Singer, Office Clerk, Franz Algermann..."[287]

ILLUSTRATION 51: Welfischer Kathechimus. Title
page of the German edition from 1858 "at the most
gracious bequest of his Majesty, King Georg V."

10. PAULUS (318). Born shortly before June 16, 1533 in Lüne-
     burg. His death at age 19 in 1552 during the Siege of Metz
     is verified through a letter from Urbanus to Duke Ernst.
     He is named after his father's favorite Apostle.

11. MARGARETA (319). Probably born in 1534 in Celle.
     Date of death unknown. Present at the sale of her moth-
     er's house and garden on July 16ᵀᴴ and 20ᵀᴴ, 1569. Marries
     Hironimus Sofart (320). Whether Margareta is named for
     "Margaritha," her mother's Hebrew teacher, is merely a
     guess.

12. ERNST (321). Born in Celle in 1536. Died July 19, 1581
     unmarried, in Hagenau/Elsass. Registered in Wittenberg
     on June 15, 1554, Doctor of Jurisprudence. "Helped educate
     young gentlemen, nobility, and respected boys from good
     families." In 1562 he published two separate volumes of
     his father's works in Latin and in German."[288] The Latin
     edition contains his father's *Vita*, which is often quoted.

Page 91

   Ernst probably collects his father's works during his
studies in Wittenberg. He has outstanding contacts there.
Bugenhagen, one of Luther's closest collaborators, lives in
Luther's city of Wittenberg until April 1558. Melanchthon
lives there until April 1560. Effner calls Ernst an "erudite,
well-taught student of Melanchthon."[289]

After finishing his studies, Ernst travels to France as Hofmeister [senior servant to the court] of a Count von Eberstein. They stay in Strassburg for a long time. Marbach and Sturm, who are the directors of the church and school there, ask Ernst to lecture because of his excellent knowledge of languages. From those lectures, a longer tenure evidently ensues at the Akademie Strassburg, the forerunner of the university, founded in 1621.

In 1566 – 68 Ernst is professor of ethics and, at times, also of Greek, "two or three hours a week." He has problems with colleagues who have not yet obtained their degree. They do not want to earn their degree under Ernst, but rather under Sturm. In 1567 he becomes Dekan [superintendent] and one of the nine members of the Kommission zur Reformation der Akademie [Commission for the Reformation of the Academy].[290] On March 24, 1568 he becomes advisor to Count Jakob zu Zweibrücken-Bitsch and lives during this time in Ingwyler. Ernst dies as "Cancellarius Veldenzensis" [Chancellor of Veldenz].[291]

In February 1556, Ernst writes to Melanchthon in Wittenberg, who recommends Ernst's poem to Duke Franz Otto. Ernst asks Melanchthon to have it printed, since in five or six weeks he will be traveling through Wittenberg to Augsburg. On the way, they pass through Bad Pyrmont, newly discovered mineral springs near Hameln.[292]

13. NAME NOT LISTED (322). Ernst Regius reports that the 13TH child was born after his father's death and died soon after. The child's name is not given.

ILLUSTRATION 52: Title page of the volume, Deutsche Bücher und Schriften [German Books and Writings] by Urbanus Rhegius, published in 1562 by his son, Ernst Regius

It is extremely unusual that 12 of 13 children reach adulthood. Eight children marry, so that Anna is delighted to have many grand-children.

Of the four sons, only Urbanus and Franziskus Otto marry. Paulus dies as a soldier at age 19, Ernst remains unmarried. The Regius name is carried on only through the Urbanus, Jr. lineage – which starting in 1588 continues through Sebastian under the name König – and through Franz Otto, who founds the Königsberg line.

Franziskus Otto Regius as Founder of the Königsberg Lineage

Eckard Weinberger reports that one Zacharias Regius, born in 1684 in Königsberg, in 1720 is a Diakon [deacon] and zweiter Pfarrer [assistant pastor] of the cathedral there.

Page 92

He is known as a "descendant of the well-known theologian, Urbanus Rhegius."[293] Zacharias' grandfather, also named Zacharias Regius, is Kantor [choirmaster and organist] and Lateinlehrer [Latin teacher] at the Kurfürst's [Elector's] School in Joachimsthal (district of Angermünde/Eberswalde) from about 1606 – 1610.[294] This classical grammar school was founded in 1604 by Prussian Elector Joachim Friedrich and opened in 1607. It is located in the elector's castle. It is famous for its music curriculum under its first choir director and organist, Zacharias Regius.[295]

If Zacharias is choir director, organist, and Latin Teacher in about 1607, he might have been born between 1570 and 1580. It is more likely that he is the son of Franziskus Otto Regius, born approximately between 1530 and 1535. It is highly unlikely that another generation could have interceded.

Under what circumstances could Franziskus Otto have gone to Prussia? Duke Erich II allows everyone in his territory of Calenberg-Göttingen who is opposed to the 1548 Augsburg Interim to be persecuted, including Göttingen preacher, Dr. Joachim Mörlin. [The Augsburg Interim is an imperial decree ordered on May 15, 1548 at the 1548 Imperial Diet of Augsburg, after Holy Roman Emperor Charles V defeated the forces of the Schmalkaldic League in the Schmalkaldic War of 1546/47.] In 1550, Mörlin, who is one of the Interim's strongest critics, must flee. He receives help from Countess Elisabeth, who sends him a horse as he flees to Prussia. Elisabeth's daughter, Anna Maria, is married to Duke Albrecht of Prussia.

Elisabeth has her steward accompany Mörlin to Erfurt. From there, he travels via Arnstadt to Schleusingen to the Count von Henneberg and eventually to Königsberg. The chronologist Lubecus reports: "As the Doctor was moving toward Königsberg, more and more citizens followed him – the pious, faithful children of the pastor ..."[296] The Regius family very personally experiences all this. Urbanus, Jr., the brother of Franziskus Otto, is at this time in the Münden office. Urbanus, Jr.'s wife, Elisabeth Dransfeld, comes from Göttingen. So, there is a good possibility that Franziskus Otto went to Königsberg in 1550 as a young man, probably also with a recommendation from Countess Elisabeth.

Mörlin arrives in Königsberg on August 25, 1550. From Albrecht I, the countess' son-in-law, he receives the opportunity to give a sermon to determine if they want to hire him as cathedral pastor.[297] We do not know anything about Franziskus Otto and his activities there. He must be on a successful path similar to that of his brother, Zacharias, who is a choir master, organist, and Latin teacher. The descendants are listed in Appendix 16 along with their occupations.

PHOTO: Der Dom [Cathedral] zu Königsberg

Page 93

The "Urbanus Coat of Arms"

Heimbürger mentions in his 1851 Rhegius biography, that Urbanus has a coat of arms "with a golden beam slanting to the right with the letters C M T (Christus mundum transigit). In every corner is a white rose."[298] Ten years later Uhlhorn speaks about a "seal" and gives the same description.[299] Both authors have made an error in their assumptions.

How could this happen? In the *Reformations Almanach von 1817* [Almanac of the Reformation of 1817] another version of the coat of arms is provided by Professor Johann Crotus (Crotus Rubianus, Rekto [Rector] of the Universität Erfurt in approximately 1520). The *Almanac* commemorates Luther's stop in Erfurt on his way to the Imperial Diet in Worms.[300] Johann Crotus puts his own coat of arms in the middle and surrounds it with 16 coats of arms of his Reformation and Humanist friends. It begins in the upper left with

Martin Luther, followed by Ullrich von Hutten, Erasmus von Rotterdam, Philipp Melanchthon, and so forth. Below in the middle appears "Urbanus Regius, at that time professor at Ingolstadt, thereafter Evangelisch preacher in Celle..." The depicted coat of arms is described as "Vrb. Reg." That presumably verifies the preceding description – which is probably the source for Heimbürger and Uhlhorn.

Our joy over this discovery is short lived. A close look at the Erfurt registry, which contains the original, gives us better information. The coat of arms ascribed to Urbanus Rhegius actually belongs to "Heinrich Urban, Crotus' friend and a member of the Cisterciensers [Spanish Order of Cisterciensers]."[302] The original is in old German handwriting. The coat of arms is labeled with the incorrect family name. The mistaken description could only happen in this way: The writer asks whose coat of arms it is and receives the answer, "Urban." Since he knows only Urbanus Rhegius and not Heinrich Urban, he assumes Urbanus Rhegius is correct.

There is further confirmation in 1858 by Kampfschulte and in a detailed 1997 *Studie zum Erfurter Humanistenkreis* [*Study of the Erfurt Humanistic Group*] by Eckhard Bernstein.[303] Bernstein reports that Heinrich Urbanus' real name is Heinrich Fastnacht and that he calls himself Urbanus after his place of origin.

Rieger, Kunig, Rhegius, König
EVOLUTION OF A FAMILY NAME

ILLUSTRATION 54: "Herr Urbanus Regius, otherwise
called König, came here from Basel in 1520." Description
encircling a picture of Rhegius by Johann Konrad Stapf
(1642 – 1702), Städtische Kunstsammlungen Augsburg.

Page 94

In the writings about Rhegius, the view persists that his name
"is really König." A picture by Johann Konrad Stapf (1642 – 1702),
for example, is circumscribed: "Herr Urbanus Regius, otherwise
called König, came here from Basel in 1520."

ILLUSTRATION 53: Das Rektorenblatt [Rector's Record]
also called the Humanistenblatt [Humanist Record]
of Professor Johann Crotis, in the Universität Erfurt's
Matrikelverzeichnis [matriculation register]. In the middle,
under the coat of arms, is hand written "Vrb. Reg," however,
it is actually the coat of arms of Heinrich Urban.[301]

Wilhelm Havemann writes in 1837: "During his stay in Augsburg,
Ernst met the preacher at that time, Urbanus Regius (König)."[304]
Heimbürger says: "Named after his original family name of König, he

changes his name...to the Latin 'Rhegius.'"[305] Uhlhorn summarizes: The family perhaps loses track of the reason that they later changed the Latin name back to the German name "König.'"[306]

Havemann, Heimbürger, and Uhlhorn probably got their information from the Celle manuscript. There it is pointed out: "Part of the family stayed in Celle and its vicinity. After a time, those from Celle took the name König."[307] On the next page: "Leznerus also found a Werner König, lawyer and doctor from Münden and the principality of Braunschweig and Lüneburg, adviser at Wolfenbüttel. This is somewhat like the example of those from Celle who changed their name back to their beloved German and like his ancestors from Langenhagen (meaning Langenargen, Anm. d. Verf.)."

It appears that the reference to the name change from Rhegius to König orginates with Leznerus. Certainly, he makes a mistake in the example of Dr. Werner König from Münden, whose Münden family was known by the name König beginning in 1452 and who is not related to Rhegius from Langenargen. This error likely results from the fact that Werner König is listed in February 1581 in the matriculation registry of the Universität Helmstedt as "Wernerus Rhegius, Mundensis." During his student years, he Latinized his name.[308]

Anticipating the Latinization of names, Ernst Regius (406) registers on May 25, 1589 at the Göttingen Pedagogical Academy as "Ericus Regius, Urbani ex ejusdem nominis filio nepos Mundens" (approximate translation: Erich Regius, grandson of the Urbanus family).

As far as the change from Rhegius to König is concerned, Sebastian (401) is the only one of those previously listed who does this. How does the name König or Kunig (the old form) enter into the discussion? There are several sources on this question. One is the entry about Anna Weissbrücker's estate in the Augsburg tax records:

"On April 3, 1548 Anna Weissbrücker, blessed widow of Dr. Urban Kunig, Pastor in Zell [Celle] in Sachsen, [309] ..." (See chapter: "Merchants, Gold Traders, Businessmen – Anna Weissbrücker's Ancestors.")

The entry suggests that Urbanus is known as "Kunig" by the Augsburg treasury. We will learn how this happens in the chapter after next: "She bears the entire burden – but nobody mentions her name."

The second source goes back to the actual roots. Ernestus Regius (320) writes about it in his preface to the Latin edition of his father's *Vita*:

"Natus est Vrbanus ad lacum Brigantinum, illa agrorum parte, quae Generosorum Comitum a monte forti dominatum agnoscit: Arga Longa opida, quad ut nomen ostendit exporrecto amaenosqu. ductu ripam Brigantinam occupant, et Arcem in ipso lacu adjunctam habet: parentibus pijs ac honestis, cuius familiae reliquias superesse pleriqu. meminerunt. Majores eius familliaequ. consortes

Regum cognomine appellati fuerent, inde usqu. a prima
eiuse domus memoria. Sed cum et obnoxium inuidiae et
lusibus aptum hoc tenui rerum statu nomen Vrbanus fas-
tidiret, leni deflexu superbae uoculae et iocantium sales
declinauit, et limis se inuidorum subtraxit oculis: ex Rege
(quod non iniocundo multorum risu persaepe exposui),
factus est Reguis."

Translation:

"Urbanus was born on the Bodensee (Bregenzer See)
[Lake Constance], in the part of the Herrschaft [terri-
tory] which belongs to the noble Counts von Monfort;
in the city of Langenargen, which, as the name suggests,
is on a long and narrow stretch of land bordered by the
lake. His parents are pious and respected. Many members
of his family remember that there are still relics.[310]

The ancestors and members of his family were known by the
surname König [King][311] since the beginning of the lineage ... But
because Urbanus did not like names prone to envy or jokes, which
he experienced as he grew up [because he was the illegitimate son
of a priest], he avoided jibes about his name by gently changing the
pompous sounding name to Rex,[312] meaning king in Latin (as I very
often heard explained with friendly laughter). That is how the name
"Regius" originated."

A more detailed version of this explanation is:

1. The ancestors and members of his family bore the name
    König. The word "Regum" used in the original text is the

Latin genitive plural of Rex = König (in German). Ernestus is not playing on the name Rieger, but rather on his
mother's name, Kunig/König.

2. "...since the first memory of his lineage," the Rieger line
    is completely left out. The reason for this may be that
    Urbanus' father dies in 1494, while his mother lives in
    the family home until 1528/29. Anna Weissbrücker knows
    Urbanus' mother for several years. It is because of her that
    Ernestus, the author of the *Vita*, knows the most about his
    family.

3. "...the dislike of what was to him a pompous sounding name
    creating envy and jokes." This statement again pertains to
    the name "König." If one imagines that an illegitimate child
    is named König [King], then one can easily imagine "a king,
    and then an illegitimate birth. What kind of king is that?"
    "through moderate change...and with skillful transforma-
    tion," he changed it. He does not call himself Rex. That
    would be too close to König (King).

Page 96

4. The most important point: "Out of Rex, Regius is formed."
    Here is Urbanus' preferred "moderate change" from the
    word Rex to Regius (ex rege, which literally means "from
    the king," in the Latin ablative case).

5. "what I often heard with friendly laughter." One sees
    Ernestus looking bemused as he writes this. A little pride
    in his father also comes through.[313]

6. Ernst Regius' version is so convincing, that there can be no
    doubt that the family name König stems from his mother.

He never mentions his father, but Urbanus is a linguistic expert. In the name Rhegius, Urbanus also conceals his father's name, Rieger, as a so-called "phoenetic Latinization." If his life circumstances do not allow him to honor his father, he can succeed in doing so by combining both family names – a linguistic stroke of genius.

Conrad Rieger and "Maria Kunig" – The Deepest Roots (101/102 on the family tree)

PRAYER FOR THE SALVATION OF THE COUNT'S SOUL

We find the first information about Urbanus' father, Conrad Rieger (101), in the *Brudershaftbuch Grünenbach* [*Grünenbach Brotherhood Book*].[314] Konrad Rieger, in his "propia manu" (own handwriting), enters his name as a member of the St. Nikolaus Bruderschaft in Isny in 1490.

ILLUSTRATION 55: Konrad Rieger enters his name as a member of the St. Nikolaus Bruderschaft in Isny in 1490: "Ego Cunradus Rieger Canonicus In Stouffen pnti (in presenti) recognosco propria manu scripto cyrographo huius egregiae fraternitatis statutaet statuenda fideliter seru(v)are Dolo et fraude remotus Anno 1490."[315]

Translation:

> "I, Cunradus Rieger, presently canon in Oberstaufen, pledge, in my own handwriting, to preserve the statutes and future decisions of the excellent brotherhood faithfully and without trickery and deception. In the year 1490."

An inconspicuous remark on the document's right edge states that he died in 1494 in Langenargen and was chaplain there (Obiit Anno 94 zu der langen argen et fuit ibidem Capellanus). What is implied by this declaration? What is the meaning of the St. Nikolaus-Bruderschaft in Isny? What is motivating Conrad Rieger to join and why in 1490?

Brotherhoods serve the common prayer needs of their members. They are formed to carry out a specific brotherly purpose on a daily basis and for members to participate in church programs. The prayer not only addresses members' current concerns, but also their concerns about the dead. Mankind is trapped in the fear of eternal damnation and qualms about hell. Through prayer, the eternal judge is said to be pleased and eternal salvation achieved.[316]

The 1463 St. Nikolaus statutes give us a glimpse of members' duties. Also, it shows that Konrad Rieger would like his brothers to pray for him after his death and for his journey into the afterlife. (See Appendix 17.)

The year he joins the brotherhood deserves careful attention. In 1490, his son, Urban, is now a year old! Is Conrad being attacked? Is he looking for support? Does he want to soothe his conscience? As a priest, does he fear the consequences?

The Counts von Montfort have governed the village of Staufen and their holdings since 1311. In 1328, Count Hugo of Montfort "for his and his ancestors' salvation" founds the Kollegiatsstift Staufen [Foundation for Colleagues. Each foundation developed its own operating rules. The purpose was to help each other in difficult situations or when they became old]. There were six priests and the priests' superior in the Kollegiatsstift Staufen. They all shared the institution's income.[317]

According to the Kollegiatsstift's founding documents, it is among Conrad's duties to pray for the salvation of the count and his ancestors. The priest's superior and the canons do not lead monastic lives. Each is in charge of his own household and has an obligation to manage his portion of the foundation's proceeds. Stables, cattle, and fields must be cared for and cultivated. So it is not completely wrong when it says on Urbanus' epitaph in Hannover, "He was born the son of Rhegius, a farmer." It is, to be sure, only a half truth.

The dates when Conrad was canon in Oberstaufen as well as his birth year cannot be determined. Since he is canon in 1490, he may have been born between 1450 and 1460. A 1680 fire in the foundation buildings leaves the whole town of Oberstaufen in ashes, with the exception of five houses. A house at what is today Hugo-von-Königsegg-Strasse 1 is still decorated with the Counts von Montfort's coat of arms. An old stone points to the foundation. All old documents were destroyed in the fire. Nothing is known about Conrad Rieger and his transfer to Langenargen.

In 1492, Conrad Rieger is living in Langenargen on the Bodensee, a day's ride west from Oberstaufen. On March 31, Count Hugo XV of Montfort names him chaplain of the St. Fridolinskapelle in Langenargen.[318]

We have to surmise his duties as chaplain. And what about his income? The previously mentioned chaplain position is established in 1442 by head pastor Jodok Gessler, citizen and landowner in Langenargen, to "advance the service of God and the world's needs."

Page 98

In addition, "the head clergyman at Argen...should have an assistant." The founder endows the position with "a country house in Schlatt; a wine garden in Hagnau; 2 Eimer derived from the wine, in perpetuity; 6 Schillings a year from a wine garden in Tettnang; 10 Schillings annually from Hans Schmid of Gohrheim (Gohren) from his meadow; 10 Schillings given by Günther from Rettersham (Retterschen); 3 Schillings given by Hans Eglin of Argon; 3 Schillings from Hans Kohler from Niederweiler; and 2 Schillings from Kaspar Scherer from Argon. All together this is 300 Pfund Heller."[319]

ILLUSTRATION 56: The house, which today is the Propstei-Apotheke in Oberstaufen/Allgäu, was the previous location of the foundation. The Chorherren [canons], including Conrad Rieger, pray here daily for the salvation of the Counts von Montfort.

ILLUSTRATION 57: Gotischer Opferstock [Gothic offering box] in the Pfarrkirche St. Martin, Langenargen, from the 1500's, possibly stood in the St. Fridolinskapelle during Conrad Rieger's time. (Photo: Walter König).

Page 99

It is not likely that Conrad Rieger himself cultivated the yard of the country house in Schlatt and managed the wine garden in Hagnau. He probably receives his share of the meat when it is slaughtered. He gets his daily needs met from the fruits of the fields and corn for baking bread, not to mention the wine from Hagnau. The money from the previous financial supporters either arrives at definite times or he collects it himself.

On October 12, 1491, a year before Conrad comes to Langenargen, Count Hugo XIII of Montfort-Rothenfels establishes an endowment for the Spital zum Heiligen Geist [Hospital of the Holy Spirit].[320] He combines the chaplain's position with those of the foundation, but makes no other changes. The chaplain, who previously lived in the clergyman's country house, keeps only an apartment "in the upper chamber of the house next to the Fridolinskapelle."[321] Conrad Rieger lives here beginning in 1492.

His duties are prescribed directly by the count. Along with responsibilities associated with the foundation hospital, Count Hugo wants a "daily early mass." The chaplain, Conrad Rieger, must conduct four masses a week, assist the pastor with the Sunday and holiday masses, and participate in the processions, but he has none of the usual clergyman's benefits.

The Kapelle [chapel] is large and has three altars. It was torn down in 1718 and replaced with the current Pfarrkirche [parish church] St. Martin Platz.

We do not know whether Conrad's transfer to Langenargen is arranged according to his wishes, with assurances of future benefits there. In any case, he is in Langenargen with his family, however, the young family's luck changes drastically in two short years when Conrad dies in 1494.

ILLUSTRATION 58: Langengargen in 1698. In the foreground is Schloss Montfort. Halfway to the left above it is the Kapuzinerkloster [Capuchin Monastery]. Halfway to the right in the long wall is the St. Fridolinkapelle, on the site of the current St. Martins-Kirche. In the background is the oldest depiction of Tettnang, with the ruins of the old castle that was burned down in 1633. Urbanus Rhegius was a guest of the Countess Magdalena in Tettnang in 1522.[322]

Page 100

She Bears the Entire Burden - But Nobody Mentions Her Name

After Conrad Rieger's early death, Urbanus' mother singlehandedly bears the entire responsibility for the daily care and upbringing of five year old Urbanus and his younger brother. Soon their education is added to her load. It is extremely difficult to be an unwed mother in that society. We cannot imagine today how despised she is. Is she only able to fulfill her responsibilities by aligning herself with the House of Montfort?

Urbanus and Count Johann II are classmates, which explains Urbanus' ties to the count's family. Does this show an additional connection between Conrad Rieger and the Montforts? Could Urbanus' mother have been taken into service in Schloss Montfort? There are good reasons to assume this premise.

Count Heinrich VII of Montfort (1456 – 1512), a brother of the count who employed Conrad Rieger in Langenargen, is a member of the Augsburg cathedral chapter. The Counts von Montfort are well established in the city of the wealthy Fugger family. Count Johann of Werdenberg, a brother of Heinrich's mother, is elected bishop there in 1469. Now Heinrich VII should advance very quickly there.

As member of the cathedral chapter, Heinrich VII must spend 13 weeks a year in Augsburg. In 1487, he also becomes a member of the cathedral chapter in Konstanz. Now he has to divide his time between both cities, but he resides primarily on the Bodensee. He is also a member of the cathedral chapter in Strassburg (about 1506), but does not appear to have significant duties there.

"Usually, Count Heinrich spends the year until the end of August in Konstanz. In September he travels to Augsburg and returns to Konstanz at Christmas."[323] It is possible that in Augsburg Urban's mother begins serving the cathedral council member, Count Heinrich. She might travel with him to Konstanz and eventually end up in Langenargen.

ILLUSTRATION 59: In the painting, Mariä Verkundigung [The Annunciation of Mary], Hans Strigel, d.J, depicts the family of Count Hugo XIII in 1465 along with his consort, Countess Elisabeth of Werdenberg, and their six children. In the foreground is the couple. Also in the foreground, above the couple, is Count Heinrich VII, member of the Augsburg cathedral chapter (with banner). Diagonally to the left above him is his brother, Count Hugo XV, who in 1492 installs Conrad Rieger in Langenargen. (From Langenargen Geschichte(n), chapter 4).

This assumption is unverifiable up to this point, but there is a lot of evidence to support it. In the oldest Langenargen records, the family name Kunig/König is not known before 1500. In Augsburg, it is the exact opposite. There, Jerg Kunig is a member of the bakers' guild and sits on the Kleinen Rat [lesser council], whose members in actuality run the city.[324] The Grossen Rat [superior council] also has a function, and it is where the guilds are represented. Jerg's father, Peter Kunig, is also a baker.[325] These are significant indications that Peter Kunig's daughter, Maria Kunig, is employed by a member of the Augsburg cathedral council.

Jerg Kunig appears in the Augsburg tax records as executor of a will. As a trustee, he pays a tax in 1521 to St. Wolfgang's for Ulrich Meuting.

He lives on Frauentor Street near the Cathedral and dies in 1531/32.[326]

Page 101

Members of the councils also serve as "cross-examiners" in trials for punishable offenses (lower judicial matters). Appendix 18 lists eight trials between 1521 and 1527 in which either "Kunig" or "Jerg Kunig" is named as a cross-examiner.

Is there a connection with Urbanus' mother's family? Age-wise, Jerg could be her brother. That would explain Urbanus' name being entered as "Doctor Urban Kunigs" in the 1548 Augsburg tax records. Although his name is Rhegius, in Augsburg he would be associated with the Kunig family. Did the Kunig family initiate Urbanus' call to Augsburg? As member of both the lesser and superior councils, Jerg Kunig had many opportunities to put in a good word for people. Is this the reason Urbanus' mother gladly returns to Augsburg?

Strengthened by these connections, we feel encouraged enough to name Maria Kunig as Urbanus' mother.

Who is "Dr. Urban's Brother"?

In the Augsburg court records there is a document dated August 26, 1526 that lists the name "Sixt Pferfferlin" in which "Doctor Urban's brother" is also mentioned. We cannot determine in what capacity.[327] It appears to be an earlier minor case concerning four youths and a weapon. "Doctor Urban's brother" was involved.

The court records dated August 25, 1526 contain the following sentence (translated from Old German):

> "On August 25, 1526, Augustin, brother of Dr. Urbanus and a carpenter by trade, is cross-examined. His sentence prohibits him from drinking wine in any tavern in the city of Augsburg and within one mile of its environs for

one year. After closing time and during the night, he is not to be on the public streets. He may not carry any weapon, other than those legally approved for the populace to carry. Also he should be on peaceful terms with S. Pfefferlin and his sons. By order of Georg Vetter, councilman and mayor."[328]

This description is particularly noteworthy as it is similar to an entry in the 1527 Augsburg district tax records. "In Koch's Lane:" "Augustin Rieger, Carpenter, fined 30 Pfennig."[329]

Augustin Rieger, Dr. Urban's brother, a carpenter, lives in Augsburg in 1526/27. There can be no doubt that this refers to Urbanus' younger brother, whom he mentions in a 1516 letter.

Count Heinrich VII, with whom Urbanus' mother probably comes to the Bodensee from Augsburg, dies in 1512. Now that she no longer has a moral obligation to stay in Langenargen on the Bodensee, she travels with her son, Urbanus, to look after the household and to gather her small family in Augsburg, the city of her ancestors.

In Part II that follows, the reader will learn about her return to the Duchy of Braunschweig and Lüneburg and how she carries out her spiritual heritage.

Section II:

The Long Journey From the Foot of the Alps

The Political and Religious Environment in the Principality of Calenberg-Göttingen

(CIRCA 1540 TO 1590)

Under Heinrich der Löwe [the Lion], the Guelphs can unite and advance their power considerably during the 12TH century. Heinrich is Duke of Bayern and Sachsen (somewhat later known as Niedersachsen), which stretches from Münden to the confluence of the Werra and Fulda Rivers, eventually extending into Holstein. After its demise, the House of Guelph must cede considerable ter-

175

ritory. Heinrich's grandson, Otto das Kind [the Child], keeps the imperial fiefdom, which we know as the duchy of Braunschweig and Lüneburg.

Disputes over inheritance in the House of Guelph repeatedly lead to divisions of territory. In 1495, the "Middle House of Braunschweig" is split up between the brothers Heinrich dem Älteren [the Elder], who founds the Wolfenbüttel lineage, and Erich dem Älteren, who founds the Calenberg-Göttingen lineage. Each of these territorial rulers receives the title, Duke of Braunschweig and Lüneburg, and each one's territory has the status of a principality.[330]

Calenberg-Göttingen exists for fewer than 90 years. It has three rulers with whom the R(h)egius family is associated.

Duke Erich I., der Ältere, rules 1495 – 1540.

Countess Elisabeth, his wife, rules 1540 – 1546 (as guardian of her son, Erich).

Duke Erich II., der Jüngere, rules 1546 – 1584.

During this time, two of Rhegius' descendants, Urbanus Regius, Jr. (303) and his sister, Marie-Madeleine (301), are in service in Schloss Münden. Marie Madeleine is lady's maid to Countess Elisabeth, and Urbanus, Jr., is secretary and senior servant of Duke Erich II.

ILLUSTRATION 60: Shows the division into six territories in 1580.[331] A lineage table of the House of Guelph with an overview of the most important land divisions. The names of the dukes cited above are provided in Appendix 19.

Erich I is still pledged to the knighthood. He maintains a close friendship with Emperor Maximillian I, his godfather. He enters Maximillian's service and fights with and for him at the important battles of that time: 1493 against the Turks in Croatia, 1507 in the Italian campaigns, and 1508 in Besancon against the French.

In the 1504 Battle of Regensburg, Erich I is critically injured as he saves the emperor from falling off his horse.

Page 103

As a reward, Maximillian, in front of the assembled Reichsritterschaft [Brotherhood of Knights], makes him a knight of the Holy Roman Empire of the German Nation.[332] Erich I now wears the Orden vom Goldenen Vlies [Order of the Golden Fleece].[333] Erich dies at age 70 at the Reichstag [Parliament] in the Alsacian city of Hagenau on July 30, 1540, where Urbanus Rhegius is present. Erich's imperial diet is left in financial ruin at his death.

In 1525, 55 year old Erich had married his second wife, the 15 year old Imperial Markgräfin [Marchioness] Elisabeth, daughter of Joachim I, elector of Brandenburg. After her husband's death, Elisabeth skillfully consolidates power as regent for her young son, Erich II, who was born in 1528. Her regency lasts until he comes of age in 1546. Elisabeth is praised by many chronologists as a talented, hardworking regent who is also skilled in court politics.

Early on, while her husband, Erich I, is still alive, she leans toward the Evangelisch, for whom she fights with great effort. She continues after her husband dies. In 1538, she aligns herself with the Evangelish and Landgrave Phillip of Hessia, one of Luther's eminent supporters. Then, in 1540 she seizes the opportunity as her son's regent to further the Reformation throughout her entire domain. One of her first actions is a letter to Duke Ernst in Celle, requesting he send Rhegius to her.[334] Elisabeth wants Rhegius to implement the Reformation and win over Calbenberg-Göttingen to the cause. Unfortunately, her letter has not been preserved, but Ernst answers her on September 7, 1540 that this is not possible since "Urbanus is in such poor health he cannot travel."[335] (See Appendix 20.)

With Landgrave Phillip's consent, Elisabeth brings Antonius Corvinus from the Hessian town of Witzenhausen and entrusts him with implementing the Reformation in her lands. In 1542, Corvinus writes church rules for Calenberg-Göttingen, which Duke Otto I also adopts for Harburg.[336]

Countess Elisabeth puts all her efforts into what she believes is a good upbringing for her son, Erich II, and that definitely includes exposure to Evangelisch beliefs. In 1544, when he is 16 years old, she takes him on a trip to the court of the elector of Sachsen. In Wittenberg, Martin Luther is at the table at which the young nobleman has to demonstrate his knowledge of Christianity. Unfortunately, Luther's skepticism soon proves to be accurate. The young boy cannot be protected from the dangers of associating with companions of his own rank and status. He will not be able to grow beyond the beliefs of the Holy Roman Emperor's court.[337]

Page 104

Elisabeth tirelessly dedicates herself to her son's upbringing. She writes an "educational and organizational plan" for him, dated January 1, 1545. It is a highly remarkable document, which Tschackert calls, "the first course of instruction for an Evangelisch state."[338]

It is still worth reading. At the same time, it is touching to read how Elisabeth describes the future responsibilities of her very young son... "from a completely motherly and well-intentioned perspective and a true heart."[339] She summons up the "most highly laudable memory" of his deceased father, cites extensively from Biblical texts and admonitions, warns about a reversion to Catholicism, and encourages good social conduct. Finally, she wishes that her son reigns with "God-given wisdom."

Elisabeth does not stop with admonitions, but describes in detail how she would like the court and administration organized. The office should be filled with capable, hardworking people, who should live at court and "should be unmarried and have their living quarters at the office." "The chancellor, vice chancellor, secretaries, and office apprentices should be at the office by 6 a.m. in the summer and 7 a.m. in the winter." The duties of the Kammermeister [treasurer], senior civil servant to the court, Stallmeister [head groom], Schmiede [blacksmiths], Harnischmeister [armor master] as well as advisors, Hofdiener [court servants], and Gesinde [domestic workers] should be firmly delineated, and they should be treated fairly. It is especially not to be forgotten that all record books should be accurately kept.

Erich II becomes engaged to Sidonia, who is 10 years older than he. Sidonia is the daughter of Duke Heinrich von Sachsen and the sister of the future Electors Moritz and August. It appears that everything is arranged according to his mother's wishes, and her son is in good hands. Erich gets to know Sidonia at the court of Landgrave Philipp in Kassel. Landgrave Philipp could not stop himself from saying, "in this marriage, all kinds of things can happen."[340] The wedding takes place on May 17, 1545 in Münden.

Erich's mother's wishes and vision are not fulfilled. On the contrary, she will be bitterly disappointed. Life has dealt Erich a different hand. He leads his small principality during turbulent times.

In 1546, the parliament in Regensburg falls prey to the glamour of the emperor's court and converts to Catholicism.[341] Emperor Karl V's grandfather, Emperor Maximillian I, had showered the young Duke Erich II's father, Duke Erich I, with honors. Young Duke Erich II was hungry to prove himself through deeds. It was therefore easy for Emperor Karl V to take Erich into his fold and turn him against the Evangelisch believers. Fate takes its course. Erich's first action for the emperor fails. At Drakenburg, after a losing battle against the Evangelisch coastal cities, Erich II can save himself only by swimming to the opposite shore of the Weser River. He leads a restless life, fights here and there, and travels to Spain where he stays with Philipp II for a long time. Phillip awards him the Order of the Golden Fleece for joining up with the Catholics.[342] Erich is criticized by his own councilors for having spent only six months in his principality over the past 14 years.

Events unfold quickly. Emperor Karl V wins an overwhelming victory against the Schmalkaldic League at the 1547 Battle of Mühlberg. All appears to be lost for the Evangelisch cause. In the course of these events, Erich II succeeds in returning his lands to the Catholic faith. He allows the reformer, Corvinus, to be thrown in prison on November 2, 1549. Corvinus suffers many years in the dungeon of the Festung [Fortress] Calenberg, in spite of repeated fervent pleas from Erich II's mother, the countess. Corvinus is finally set free, but he dies a few months later as a result of his imprisonment.

The emperor's victory at Mühlberg is short-lived. Power alliances are shifting. Elector Moritz von Sachsen, who actually was awarded his electorate by the emperor for his combat in the Schmalkaldic War, turns against the emperor. He aligns himself with France and eventually pursues the emperor to Tirol. Duke Otto II of Harburg is also in the elector's army.[343] The emperor escapes only with great effort. The treaty Moritz negotiates in Passau on August 2, 1552 assures the Evangelisch that they can freely practice their beliefs until a final agreement is reached at the upcoming Imperial Diet.

The settlement is concluded in 1555 with the "Peace of Augsburg." It gives the princes of various principalities the right to decide between the two religions. Their subjects must abide by the decision of the prince who rules them, or they must leave. The reconciliation ends the religious battles. Both faiths are considered equal under imperial law, but the written agreement contains grounds for new disputes, which finally break out in 1618 in the Thirty Years' War.

In the year of the Peace of Augsburg, Erich II proclaims that "his subjects must abide by those regulations supporting the Evangelisch teachings regarding the Reformation and Church affairs that were enacted 12 years prior." This is how in 1555 Calenberg-Göttingen again becomes Evangelisch – the third turn-around in 15 years!

Erich II dies in Pavia, Italy in 1584. He has no legal heir. His duchy falls to the House of Wolfenbüttel.

Urbanus Regius, Jr. (302 on the family tree)[344]

SECRETARY AND SENIOR CIVIL SERVANT
AT SCHLOSS MÜNDEN, SENIOR CIVIL
SERVANT AT SCHLOSS NIENOVER

"educated from an early age in
Duke Erich II's Office..."

Preserved in Das Archiv des Predigerseminars [Archives of Pastoral Training] in Celle-Kleinhehlen is a manuscript dating from approximately 1740, designated in the archive's written description of its collection as "Anonyme Handschrift" [anonymous manuscript].[345] It contains over 300 pages listed as "Urbani Rhegii Lebens Geschichte" [The life history of Urbanus Rhegius], collected by Heinrich Philipp Guden. Guden, a tireless researcher and collector, was general superintendent in Celle from 1735 to 1742.[346]

The document contains a repetition of some of Rhegius' works and also provides valuable references to his family, particularly on pages 82 – 87. It is noteworthy that many people were collecting everything that was learned about Urbanus and his family.

Here we find significant information about Urbanus Regius, Jr.:

"Leznerusen, 76TH chapter. According to Meister Johannes Sutelio, it is reported by the first church in Göttingen that Urbanus Regius, a well-educated, well-read pastor, is raised from childhood in the office of Duke Erich II. After that, he is employed in many capacities.

Regius is rewarded with the income of the St. Alban church. He does not take charge himself, but lets others do the administration. Finally, Theodorus Teuffel becomes Regius' curate and administrator and succeeds Regius after his death."

"From his childhood on..." When can that be? Urbanus, Jr. turns 14 when his father dies in 1541. His mother has 12 children to care for and must consider how to lighten her responsibilities. She remembers good friends and certainly thinks about the court in Münden.

Page 106

Anna's husband, Urbanus, Sr., belonged to a circle of reformers and Humanists around Dr. Burkhardt Mithoff, the personal physician to the nobles' family and advisor to the countess. Corvinus, Melanchthon, and all the important names of the Reformation also belong.[347] The name Rhegius is well-known at Schloss Münden.

Besides that, in 1536 Rhegius writes the church organizational plan for Hannover, the largest city in Calenberg, and in 1537 signs the Schmalkald Articles as Hannover's representative.

What can be easier for Anna Weissbrücker than to ask the countess if she can find employment for her son at the castle? In the anonymous manuscript there is also a reference: "Urbanus...is probably first employed in the service of Countess Elisabeth."[348]

ILLUSTRATION 62: Right: The 700 year old St.
Blasius Kirche in Münden, the "home church" of Urbanus
Regius, Jr.'s family. Above: Sebastian Regius (401)
was baptized in the richly decorated 1392 baptismal
font. (Photo: Christoph Drescher, Hamburg).

Urbanus, Jr. is clearly listed in the so-called Rode-Register of 1551 as being in the ducal service.[349] Handbook 43/44 of the duchy's administration has "Urbanus' daughter Marie-Madeleine" as lady's maid for the countess' apartment.[350]

Both siblings, Urbanus, Jr. and Marie-Madeleine, probably witness the magnificent wedding of Duke Erich II to Sidonia, Duchess of Saxony on May 17, 1545 in Münden. The brother of the bride, Duke August von Sachsen, later elector and a descendant of Moritz von Sachsen, accompanies his sister, Sidonia, to Münden.

Another wedding soon follows on June 6, 1546 when Countess Elisabeth at age 36 marries Count Poppo XVIII von Henneberg-Schleusingen after her son, Erich II, becomes duke. They, too, marry in Münden, where Elisabeth has her life-long widow's pension and where the couple lives.[351]

The statement cited above: "...is raised from childhood in the office of Duke Erich and after that, he is employed in many capacities" leads to the conclusion that Urbanus, Jr. was not studying, but rather was employed in the practical work of the office. At first, he was a writer and secretary, and later he was a senior civil servant. In the countess, both brother and sister will have a reliable protector. Also, the countess will be pleased to have two people from the orginal families of the Reformation to depend on.

Just when everything seems to be in order, political developments bring disruption, insecurity, and anxiety. This is especially the case in Calenberg-Göttingen because of Duke Erich II's erratic actions. His own conversion to Catholicism in 1546, the losing battle at Drakenburg, his re-conversion of his duchy to Catholicism in 1549, and the suppression of the Evangelisch teachings all work together to create a disastrous situation.

In these uncertain times, Urbanus, Jr.'s mother, Anna Weissbrücker (202), decides to make a daring move. On April 24, 1548, she lends Countess Elisabeth 500 Goldgulden for two years at a negotiated interest rate of 5%.[352]

Due to the differences in their social standing, the countess will not travel to Celle, so Anna Weissbrücker gladly goes to Münden with the money because she can see her eldest son, Urbanus, Jr., while she is there. It is approximately 200 km from Celle to Münden. A covered wagon travels about 30 km a day, so Anna is en route for about a week. She needs knowledgeable and trustworthy escorts for herself and her valuable cargo. Five hundred Goldgulden is 1½ kg. of gold. Where can one safely stay overnight? Which routes are safe? Is she perhaps traveling with Duke Ernst's knowledge in order to find out what the people in Münden are thinking about religion? Is Duke Ernst providing her with security guards?

The ruling house's financial straits are proverbial. Why does Elisabeth need this loan? She is no longer regent for her son and has been re-married for two years. The contract is between "Boppo, Count and Herr zu Henneberg and Elisabeth, born Marchioness zu Brandenberg and Countess and Frau zu Henneberg" and Anna

Weissbrücker. Elisabeth no longer has the title of Countess of Braun-schweig and Lüneburg. The text of the loan contract is in Appen-dix 21.

At the castle, Anna is the countess' guest. She counts her 500 gold coins on the table. Can we imagine this moment? Is there a witness representing both sides, or is there boundless trust between them? Anna hands over most of her inheritance, which she received after her father's death in 1543.

ILLUSTRATION 63: Anna could have journeyed from Celle to Münden in this manner. (Hans Beham, circa 1528).

Her decision is extremely risky, but Anna has faith in the count-ess. Anna also expects "political" advantages. Through the loan, it is probably Anna's intention to solidify her son, Urbanus, Jr.'s, position at the castle during these uncertain times. (Her daughter, Marie-Madeleine, is no longer in Münden in 1548.) The authors Brauch and Samse have previously reported on the rulers' need for and collection of funds from subjects and this is again underscored. The subjects contribute in order to maintain their positions at the castle.

Problems with the repayment soon begin. By Easter 1552 nothing has yet been repaid, neither the annual interest nor any amount on the principal. In a letter dated "Holy Easter Day 1552" to the treasurer, Heinrich von Rode, Anna Weissbrücker clarifies that she is awaiting payment of 100 Goldgulden. The amount of interest has increased because of the default on the due date. Anna will wait until "Holy Walpurgis Day" on May 1ST.[353] (See Appendix 22.)

ILLUSTRATION 64: Anna Weissbrücker writes
to the treasurer, Heinrich von Rode, that she is
awaiting repayment of the loan. This is the only
written document in Anna's handwriting.

What follows is heated correspondence among the countess, treasurer, and others. Each one points to someone else. According to a
reading of the old papers, there is "not a Heller nor Pfennigk" to be
gotten from the duke and his senior civil servants. Most astonishing is a letter from Countess Elisabeth to Treasurer von Rode dated
early May 1552. The salutation is brief, the language harsh. A righteous anger emanates from the countess' writing. She is, because of
him, beset by "disdain, scorn, harm and disbelief." All this is because
of his forgetfulness. To her, it is highly unpleasant to go back on her
promise to Anna Weissbrücker.[354] Her daughter, Katharina, will
bring the matter to the duke's attention.

From available documents, it is not known whether and when
Anna Weissbrücker gets her money back. The circumstances of the
times are chaotic, and we have reason to assume she loses everything.
In 1552 the plague comes to Calenberg. In Göttingen, 25 victims
are buried each day.[355] In 1553, the flaming sword of war sweeps
through the land. Countess Elisabeth is not completely immune to
the conditions. In the spring of 1553, during a stay in Schleusingen
at the count of Henneberg's, she encounters her relative, Margrave
Albrecht Alcibiades von Brandenburg-Kulmbach. She persuades
him to join in a plan, along with her son Duke Erich II, to oppose

their relative, Duke Heinrich dem Jüngeren. She wants to avenge the humiliation she has experienced at Duke Heinrich's hand.[356]

In her zeal, she offers up gold chains, silver settings, and jewels to supply 600 of her son's cavalrymen. As her own resources are not sufficient, she takes out a 300 Gulden loan from the Hannover city council.[357] She solemnly gives her royal word that either her son will repay the loan or she will not leave the town until the debt is settled.

In 1553, Erich II and the margrave, along with the Harburg troops, fight against Elector Moritz von Sachsen and Duke Heinrich zu Braunschweig and Lüneburg. At the Battle of Sieverhausen, the tragic quarrel reaches its climax. The elector is victorious, but loses his life. Duke Heinrich mourns the death of two sons. All his anger is directed toward the unfortunate Elisabeth, who with her son and the margrave, waged war against him. Heinrich's troops overrun the Calenberg lands. The countess is banished to Hannover. Her possessions in Münden are taken over by Heinrich as war reparations.[358] (In a later agreement, her life annuity is transferred to Erich II.)

Page 109

The days Elisabeth spends in Hannover are sorrowful. Havemann writes: "Thus, Elisabeth's situation was certainly bleak. How circumstances had changed! Once she was the celebrated consort of Erich I, the multi-talented prince favored by the emperor. She was cheerful and happy with her life, the heart and soul of the small but splendid court. Now she is robbed of everything, oppressed, an outcast where she once had ruled."[359]

The year 1555 brings some relaxation of the tensions between Duke Heinrich and Elisabeth, so that she can turn to him for financial assistance. In the following quotation, she is asking him for help in repaying the loan from the city council. "My God in heaven, I only wanted not to be considered a liar! Help me. I honorably put this behind me, and I will be eternally grateful to you, that the believers are not betrayed by me."[360]

> "For two years we have been living in misery here in Hannover and have had to beg to survive... because our funds do not cover the 83 Gulden weekly upkeep of the court." In the autumn of 1554 she is already complaining: "For three weeks we have had no meat in our kitchen and have had to suffer from the cold because of a lack of wood."

If Elisabeth cannot pay back the 300 Gulden loan from the city council, which it is publicly known that she owes, how much less likely is it that she can repay Anna Weissbrücker's 650 Gulden (the 500 Gulden loan, plus accrued interest)?

In her social position, Elisabeth is a child of her times as far as money matters and her upkeep allowance are concerned. Quite often she has been plagued with debts and other related expenses. In 1525, she spends 70 Gulden on wedding expenses and pays for them 21 years later! On the occasion of her daughter's wedding in 1543, she buys expensive gifts, not only for the bride, but also for the distinguished guests. Her son, Erich's, wedding to Sidonia in 1545 costs 2,700 Taler, and just as much is needed for the wedding of her daughter, Anna Maria, to Duke Albrecht of Prussia.[361]

On March 21, 1555, Duke Erich and his mother come to an agreement which stipulates that she will give Erich the home in which she lives as a widow, and she will leave the duchy.[362] In spite of

huge debts, she donates to the Hannoverians a memorial communion goblet and silver bowl inscribed, "ALL THE SORROW IN
MY HEART TURNS TO THE SUPREME HOLINESS OF
GOD" (Marktkirche Hannover). In mid-1555 she goes to Ilmenau
with her second husband, Poppo, Count zu Henneberg, where she
dies on May 25, 1558 at the young age of 48.

For us, the question remains: In 1548, does Anna Weissbrücker
know about the risks associated with her loan, or does she simply
have boundless trust in the countess who so bravely fights for the
Reformation? Perhaps Anna sees only the latter and cannot imagine
that she will not be able to get her money back from the countess,
who is so beloved and popular, especially in Evangelisch circles.
For Anna and her family, it is a huge loss. Five hundred Goldgulden is a fortune at that time. In comparison, Anna paid a total of
225 Gulden in 1553 for her house in Celle![363] Perhaps her "political" aspirations are at least fulfilled, in that the loan strengthens
her son, Urbanus, Jr.'s, position, and forgiving the loan furthers his
feudal tenure at St. Albani.

Page 110

The Feudal Tenure at St. Albani – Honor and Frustrations

In 1554, Duke Erich II issues a letter of feudal tenure favorable to
Urbanus Regius, Jr. regarding the "...clerical position at St. Albani in
Göttingen and all properties and privileges accompanying the posi-

tion...for his excellent and loyal service."[364] (See Illustration 65 and transcribed document in Appendix 23.)

ILLUSTRATION 65: Duke Erich II awards
the parish position at St. Albani to "his dear
loyal servant, Urbanus Regius, for life."

In 1549, Duke Erich II first orders his duchy's return to Catholicism. Later, he awards Regius, who is a member of a "founding Evangelisch" family, a feudally tenured clergyman position. Duke Erich has political reasons for doing this.

ILLUSTRATION 66: Entrance of the St. Albani
Kirche in Göttingen. (Photo: Magdalena König.)

For several years, the Göttingen Kirche has been in turmoil. Joachim Mörlin, a fiery theologian who was once Luther's pastor in Wittenberg, comes to Göttingen in 1544. There, he rants and raves against what is happening. The rules revert to Catholicism so that laymen cannot drink from the communion chalice and priests cannot marry. The Evangelisch believers demand a forthcoming council to resolve these matters. Under pressure from Duke Erich II, Mörlin is dismissed in 1550. He has to leave Göttingen under chaotic circumstances. Countess Elisabeth secures passage for him to Schleusingen, where he is aided by the rulers of Henneberg, until he is called to Königsberg by Elisabeth's son-in-law, Duke Albrecht of Prussia.[365]

After Mörlin's dismissal, Johann Sutelius (Sutel), who was born in Altenmorschen near Melsungen, again becomes influential. He is pastor at St. Albani and also superintendent. Countess Elisabeth promises him feudal tenure for life at St. Albani, but Erich II does not honor it. Franciscus Lubecus, the Göttingen chronologist, states: "In 1554, the council promises a scholarly man the position of pastor at St. Albani in Göttingen. His name is Johan Sutel, magistrate. Sutel promises to stay there for life, since the country's prince and his noble, gracious mother had assured him lifelong feudal tenure."

Page 111

Her Grace, the duke's mother, is not able to keep her word because she is banished from the country, so Sutel does not want to accept the pastor position.[366, 367]

The duke's promise of feudal tenure to Urbanus, Jr. brings with it honors as well as many frustrations. Sutel had received the promised feudal tenure without restrictions. Ignoring his mother's unrestricted promise to Sutel, Erich II gives Urbanus tenure only at St. Albani. If Sutel is granted feudal tenure simultaneously by both Elisabeth and Erich, an unavoidable problem ensues. It is the beginning of a tug of war among the city council, Sutel, and Regius over the feudal tenure and above all, over money.

Sutel refuses to recognize Regius' rights. On November 3, 1554, Regius writes to Duke Erich's wife, Countess Sidonia, most likely because Duke Erich is absent. He points out that he received feudal tenure from Erich II, who is "the reigning legitimate sovereign prince of the country." He is prepared, along with Sutel, "to settle" for a yearly payment. See Appendix 24.

Countess Sidonia sends Urbanus' letter, along with her own, also dated November 3, to the mayor and city council of Göttingen and asks them to instruct Magistrate Sutel, in the name of the duke, to give the parish over to Urbanus, along with all the minor property associated with the principal property or an annual stipend.[368] The letter is signed by Sidonia herself. See Appendix 25.

Her instructions bear fruit. Soon, on November 27, 1554, Urbanus acknowledges that he "for the sake of peace" has reached an agreement with Sutel for a yearly payment of 20 Gulden. He acknowledges a sum of 20 Gulden received from the Göttingen city council. With this, it is clarified that Sutel stays in the financial office, with a priviso in the contract stipulating an annual payment to Regius. See Appendix 26, page 250.

On July 30, 1555, Sutel leaves for Northeim. His successor is the former deacon, Andreas Tappen, an "unworthy successor." In actuality, Tappen was the replacement for Regius. In front of Tappen's fellow officials in 1588, Regius had sharply criticized Tappen for his carelessness and laziness. Regius lets Michaeli deal with Tappen.[369] It is public knowledge that it is in the power of the feudal proprietor, such as Michaeli, to appoint and dismiss clergy. As we know, however, Regius had not studied theology and is therefore technically not a clergyman.

The year 1559 becomes a very important year. Dietrich Düvel, usually called "Devil" in correspondence, becomes Tappen's successor as the pastor in charge of finances at St. Albani. He remains in office for 55 years, until 1614. Now Düvel has the responsibility to pay the 20 Gulden yearly stipend to Regius. We will soon see how carelessly he handles this duty.

In the year Pastor Düvel assumes office, Urbanus, Jr. receives two important pledges from the duke. On June 29, 1559, Duke Erich II grants Urbanus Regius, Jr. feudal tenure for lands and possessions "on credit." Regius' male heirs will assume the feudal tenure contract upon Regius' death. See Appendix 37.[370] The intent of this contract is genuine feudal tenure. This is clearly stated in the text, in which the feudal lord promises to honor his agreement with the tenure recipient. As long as the recipient is "loyal and pious," any damages associated with the feudal items shall be waived. From early times until the present, this is the format of feudal contracts.

Page 112

ILLUSTRATION 67: Duke Erich II grants Urbanus Regius, Jr. feudal tenure for the ducal lands "on credit" and expands the feudal tenure of St. Albani to his son, Bastian.

Page 113

The duke's promised feudal tenure appears to be validated for the first time in 1516. On September 17, 1576, the three sons of Urbanus, Jr., namely, Sebastian, Christoph, and Erich are awarded feudal tenure by Duke Erich II.[371] Unfortunately, further details are unknown. The childen are named as holders of feudal tenure because their father, Urbanus, Jr., died in 1570. Sebastian, the oldest, is about 17 – 20 years old at this time. The terms of the feudal tenure are in the form of a so-called sub-contract that will not be valid for Urbanus, Jr.'s sons' children, so the promise will apparently result in no material gain. It may be possible for Urbanus, Jr.'s sons to get out of the contract. In the meantime, the supposed reasons for the promises of 1559 remain of interest. Several thoughts about these promises will be proposed in the following chapter.

The second promise extends the St. Albani feudal tenure to (Se) Bastian, the oldest son of Urbanus, Jr., whose education should be paid from the proceeds of the feudal tenure, "in order that he may hereafter serve us and our principality." Thus, Sebastian Regius (after 1588 known as Sebastian König) is legally bound to stay in the duchy of Braunschweig-Lüneburg. This is the reason he will go to Finkenwerder as pastor several years later.

Secretary, Office Servant, Senior Civil Servant – A Difficult Life in Calenberg-Göttingen

In the previously cited *Anonymous Manuscript* it says that Urbanus, Jr., "was raised in the office of Duke Erich and after that served in many capacities."

We find confirmed in a wide variety of documents and writings that he "serves in many capacities" and is entrusted with many different assignments:

1551	"in the royal service," according to custom, as cited above.
1554	"our dear, fathful servant," in the original feudal tenure at St. Albani.

1554	"our office servant," in the Countess Sidonia's letter, dated November 2, 1554.
1557	Senior civil servant at Reinhausen Monastery. Administrator as successor to Johann Ruden.[372]
1559	"Our dear and faithful office servant," feudal tenure document dated June 29, 1559.
1559 – 62	"Senior civil servant in Münden," cited in the hospital bills.[373]
1561	Senior civil servant[374] and temporary administrator.[375]
1561	On February 22, original announcement of a contract as "senior civil servant of Munden." (Legal transaction in Boventen. Original register, page 413, number 644.)
1562	As a senior civil servant of Münden and Sichelstein, Regius receives an invitation from the city council to go to Hannover to advise on raising taxes.
1562	On February 27, Regius signs the inventory of the Reinhausen Monastery before it is handed over to senior civil servant Ludolf Fischer.[376]
1564	January 25, 1564, a legal acknowledgement of debt from Erich II to Urbanus Regius "formerly named senior civil servant."
....	"Secretary to Duke Erich II" in the *Genealogia D. Urbani Regij*.[377]
1565	Senior civil servant in Nienover, letter from September 5, 1565 to Duke Erich II.

This mosaic gives us ample evidence to reconstruct the life of Urbanus Regius, Jr. and his family.

"From his youth" in Münden, Urbanus, Jr. was "raised in the office and after that was given many assignments." This leads to the conclusion that he comes to Münden as a very young man and is trusted with many different assignments at the office. In the original feudal tenure documents of 1554 and 1559, the duke refers to Regius as "office servant." The designation "servant" in this instance means a "civil servant."

We encounter Urbanus, Jr. in about 1557 as a senior civil servant in Reinhausen, a place near Göttingen with a monastery.

Urbanus, Jr. is listed in Münden as an official in the hospital billing department's records from 1559/60: [378]

"2 measures of rye from Urbano Regio, officially authorized

4 measures of rye received from Urbano, officially authorized

4... in money, from Urbano, the official

2 golden coins for 2 measures of oats from Urbano"

ILLUSTRATION 68: Duke Erich II rules the duchy of Calenberg-Göttingen from 1546 – 1584. Below he is pictured in about 1573 as a Knight of the Order of the Golden Fleece (Bayrische Staatsgemäldesammlungen, München).

ILLUSTRATION 69: Kloster Reinhausen Monastery in Göttingen, Mathias Merian, 1654.

On January 31, 1562 Regius buys beer, probably not for the hospital, but rather for the castle. Jürgen Lodewiger, court civil servant, acknowledges the receipt of "twenty Daler for 10 kegs of beer from the Honorable and Respectable Urbanus regius, senior civil servant of Munden."[379] It is probably beer from nearby Einbeck that Luther previously enjoyed in 1521 at the Diet of Worms.[380]

Another time Regius buys five kegs of beer from Christoffer Monck, "Respectable Urbano Regio, senior civil servant from Munden," which confirms that Monck "received money" from Urbanus, Jr. The wording confirms that around the middle of the 16TH century, Low German is still the official language. One may wonder about so much beer. Beer is widely known as a "healthy drink" since many people have no access to clean drinking water.

Page 115

ILLUSTRATION 70: "...twenty Daler for ten kegs of beer..."
Urbanus, Jr. buys large amounts of beer. He acknowledges
the receipt on St. Laurentius Day, August 10, 1562.

The evidence shows that Urbanus Regius, Jr. has the responsibility to buy and sell on behalf of the court administration. The castle duties, involve domestic staff and horses, organization of celebrations, regulation of farming and construction, and many more duties, which make us think of a central economic enterprise. The court of Münden in 1530 is described as having 140 people and 126 horses.[381] All of it has to be financed and paid for. With the duke's monthlong and yearlong absences on his military campaigns, one wonders how the whole operation can function.

The Castle in Flames – The Duke in Spain – the Duchy in Debt

March 16, 1561 is a fateful day in Münden. A devastating fire breaks out in the castle. In the evening, flames reach "toward heaven." It will take three days to put them out.

The household staff's living quarters are on the castle grounds, where today a large parking lot is located. Urbanus, Jr. lives there with his young family. We can imagine his wife, Elizabeth, with little Sebastian in her arms, as she frantically looks about the burning castle grounds for her home and family. Will the fire engulf the dwellings and the city? What should they try to save? Where should they run?

Let us listen to Willigerod, whom we heard earlier in this narrative, as he with great emotion describes the fire at the castle:[382]

> "On Monday evening between 5 and 6 o'clock, a horrendous fire broke into uncontrollable flames. It raged for three nights, and not only completely reduced the magnificent castle to ashes, but also cost many people their lives. On the first night, almost all the peasants from the surrounding feudal lands and jurisdictions came immediately to help quench the inferno. They came from Münden, Brackenberg, Friedland, Adelepsen, Harste and Hardegsen. Nevertheless, all efforts were in vain.

Above all, people tried to save the most valuable items from the room where the silver was stored. Many farmers had to force themselves to go in. The poor people! Almost all of them quickly lost their lives when the floor, already engulfed in flames, suddenly collapsed in a raging blaze.

Pitifully they screamed for help, but who could save them? After the blaze was extinguished and the debris was cleaned up, they found 14 dead bodies, not counting those who were completely reduced to ashes.

The benevolent temporary administrator, Urbanus Regius, Jr., personally had three wooden boxes made, into which were put the 14 dead bodies along with many body parts, arms, legs, hands, and feet.

Page 116

The three biers, accompanied by many thousand tears of the mourners, were brought to St. Aegidii Cemetery.

The famous preacher and chronologist, Johann Letzner, whom we thank for the detailed account, gave the funeral oration for the unfortunate souls. He correctly gauged the prevailing spirit, in which all such misfortunes were explained as punishment... the tears of many mothers, which were waiting to be willingly shed, could now flow in abundant profusion."

ILLUSTRATION 71: View of the city of Münden
around the middle of the 16TH century. On the right,
the Fulda and Werra Rivers converge into the Weser
River. In the middle is the city, to the left is the castle.
(Copper engraving by Braun & Hogenberg from the
Niedersachsenbuch '84, Hannover-Münden).

The duke stays in Spain at the time of the fire, returning to
Münden on July 5, 1561. He then departs quickly for the Netherlands and renews his contract to serve Phillip II. In the spring of
1562, he sends construction workers from the Netherlands to work
on Schloss Uslar and Münden.[383] At the beginning of 1563, he brings
his beloved Katharina von Weldam back from Spain to the Calenberg lands. Military campaigns are more important to Erich II than
his duchy and its people. He travels further to Denmark and advances
with a large army across the Elbe to Mecklenburg and Pommern.
He finally returns to Münden in 1566.[384]

Until 1564, Urbanus Regius, Jr. is is occupied with official administrative duties and concerns of the duke's. Albert Brauch summarizes the administrative tasks of a senior civil servant: "During the
16TH century, the senior civil servant is responsible for the administration and financial management of all governmental affairs," and
"The senior civil servant is exclusively the duke's official with major
financial responsibilities, however, he is not responsible for paying
military salaries, etc."[385]

It is well known that many principalities, including Calenberg-
Göttingen, are perpetually short of funds. Calenberg-Göttingen's
financial need increases because of the fire and resulting costs. Even
Urbanus, Jr. is affected by it.

Urbanus, Jr.'s responsibility as senior civil servant for financial revenue is detailed in a decree, the "treasury council's agreement between the dynasty and its lineage." The decree is directed to the civil servants and mayor of the "district of Göttingen." Urbanus Regius, Jr. is senior civil servant for both Münden and Sichelstein. All civil servants are to report to Hannover about what has been received and what is in arrears in the "Twelve Year Tax Increase."

In a letter to the city council dated January 23, 1562, Urbanus asks to be excused because he is overloaded with work and cannot come to Hannover. He has to look after the countess and the supplies for the entire court. Also, the duke is returning soon and therefore Urbanus must remain at the castle. The servants of the Münden district have to travel weekly to Uslar with stones and lime (where the duke began building a castle in 1560). Urbanus has to order firewood for the kitchen, bake house, and brew house. See Appendix 27 for a complete list of his duties.[386]

In the literature, it is partially acknowledged that Urbanus, Jr., is "senior civil servant and advisor" in Münden. Some examples of his daily activities as senior civil servant are cited above, however, we find no clues as to the daily activities of an advisor.

The 1564 Document About Debts

An undated and unsigned list, probably compiled by Urbanus, Jr. in early 1564, states that Urbanus, Jr. has a claim of 685½ Taler owed him by the court. "In my completed computations for the district of

Münden, there is still an additional amount owed..."[387] He implores his "Gracious Prince and distinguished Lord" to have the council put business matters in order "when they have the time and opportunity." See Appendix 28.

Urbanus, Jr. had spent more than 1,000 Taler of his own money, which was only partially paid back. In the left margin of a handwritten note is a remark from the office that the designated sum is "still owed by my Gracious Lord (Erich II) to Urbanus."

Did Urbanus have his mother's experience in mind regarding whether to expect repayment of "princely" debts? It is surprising that he is even able to pay out such a sum. Urbanus, Jr.'s claim of 685½ Taler is more than his mother's claim for her loan. In 1564, Duke Erich is undertaking new "escapades," which almost cost him his duchy. Perhaps this is Urbanus' last cause.[388]

He requests official receipt of his claim and receives it on January 25, 1564. In Duke Erich II's debenture bond [acknowledgement of the debt], there is the surprising phrase, "to my former senior civil servant for the district of Münden and Sichelstein." In other words, Urbanus Jr. has been relieved of his position as senior civil servant! [389] How the negotiations proceed and what arguments are exchanged we do not know. It is widely known that the duke has unpaid debts and that this plays a role in Urbanus' demotion. It is also understandable that Urbanus is extremely anxious to be paid. The negotiation takes place around the year of the castle fire, in which the financial situation becomes even worse than before. The duke's debenture bond is available in Appendix 29.

That Urbanus, Jr. resigns from his position as senior civil servant in Münden in 1564 is verified by the appointment of his successor, Anton von Bardeleben, who is senior civil servant in Münden from 1565 to 1585.[390] Does Urbanus, Jr. stay in nearby Reinhausen, where in 1557 he is selected as senior civil servant and monastery manager?[391]

Page 118

On February 27, 1562 he had already completed the inventory of goods and services for the monastery.[392]

The history of the former Benediktinerkloster [Benedictine Monastery] in Reinhausen dates back to the 12TH century. It eventually comes under the control of the duchy von Braunschweig and Lüneburg. In 1542, this allows Countess Elisabeth to place the monastery and convent under the jurisdiction of the Evangelisch Church order. When the monastery is dissolved in 1574, it becomes the duke's property. Today, it serves as Reinhausen's parish church.[393]

Uhlhorn mentions Urbanus, Jr. as a foundation senior civil servant at St. Blasii in Einbeck beginning in 1564. Therefore, there ought to be a seal of St. Blasii containing three rose stems and the letters U.R.[394] This seal, however, cannot be found in Einbeck.[395]

With the duke's debenture bond in hand, Urbanus believes the money certainly will be repaid soon. How can he be so deluded?

As Senior Civil Servant at Schloss Nienover in Solling

Our assumption that Urbanus left the principality of Calenberg-Göttingen because of its outstanding debt to him cannot be verified, however, we find him about a year later as a senior civil servant at Schloss Nienover in Solling near Bodenfelde on the Fulda River.[396]

At that time it is difficult to leave the service of one ruler and enter the service of another.

Nienover is comprised only of a castle on the mountain and an economic area in the valley. There is no village.[397]

ILLUSTRATION 72: Schloss Nienover during its reconstruction in 1640/56. Merian-Stich, 1654. (From: Erich Weise: Geschichte und Schloss Nienover im Solling).

The old castle's ownership changes frequently, but in 1152 it comes into the possession of Heinrich der Löwe [the Lion]. After Heinrich is overthrown, the castle serves for more than a hundred years as an imperial feudal loan from the Stauffen emperor to the Counts von Dassel.

In the 13TH Century, the counts' expanding lineage soon pushes up against the determination of the Guelph dynasty to regain their previous territory. The Stauffen counts are defeated, thereby losing their re-gained territory. In 1303, Neinover is again a Guelph possession.

In the middle of the 16TH Century, we encounter the previously mentioned Countess Elisabeth. She is the Consort of Erich I and 40 years younger than he. He bequeathes to her not only Schloss Münden, the place for her to spend her widowhood, but also Schloss Nienover. Elisabeth calls the delightful, scenic Schloss Nienover her "dowry for tomorrow." Immediately, she personally manages her new property, which flourishes under her capable leadership.

Page 119

A 1535 document provides an enlightening description of the castle inventory, which still may have existed when Urbanus arrived 30 years later.[398] The 1535 inventory lists the furnishings and equipment for the Catholic religious service, kitchen, bakery, and the area where dairy products are made. The kitchen includes a meat locker, pantry, and a bacon storage area. Near the bakery is a beer cellar. In the main building, 16 beds are kept ready for use. Three of these beds are for "gentlemen." The detailed description of the house, kitchen, and utensils provides a lively picture showing where people lived, conducted business, baked, brewed, drank, and ate. Twelve decorated cannisters are used for chopping. They depict wolves and hawks preying on young animals. Also depicted are armed men fighting thieves, robbers, and plunderers.

There are 118 donkeys, cows, and bulls; 133 pigs; 689 sheep; 26 geese; and 140 chickens. The breeding horses of the duke's riding horses are apparently under separate management.

The wealth of the hunting lodge lies in the extensive beech and oak forests. Logging is important, however, an even more profitable source of income is the acorns used for fattening pigs. The peasants from the five villages of Nienover (two Bodenfeld villages, Wahmbeck, Schönhagen, and Kammerhorn) are permitted by the countess in 1541 to fatten their pigs there at no change. Peasants who live elsewhere pay a grazing fee. In 1547, over 1,000 pigs are recorded as grazing in the Nienover woods.

In the 1550's, Countess Elisabeth loses her retirement property in Münden because of her previously described dispute with her nephew, Duke Heinrich II von Wolfenbüttel. She must also, with a heavy heart, leave Nienover.

During the ensuing administration of her son, Duke Erich II, Urbanus Regius, Jr. assumes the senior civil servant position at Nienover. He has overall responsibility for the castle, the financial operation, all income and disbursements, for planting and harvesting, forestry operations, and personnel.

In a letter to the count in Münden dated September 4, 1565 (Appendix 33), Urbanus complains about the lack of labor "of the fourth type" to plow the fields. That is, the fallow lands must be planted four times between June and the winter planting. For that, residents of the neighboring villages will also be used, and they are not under Urbanus' jurisdiction. He cannot demand that they do this field work. Instead, the residents of the duke's villages ought to do the work. They, however, are rebelling against this, especially those from Bodenfelde and Wahmbeck.

The September 4, 1565 letter is the only reference to Urbanus' daily duties at Schloss Nienover. We assume he stays in Nienover about five to seven years, until his death. As for a quick settlement of his claim against Duke Erich II, he is sorely disappointed. The assignment to a remote place like Nienover is not exactly a promotion compared to Schloss Münden. Does his poor health play a role so that, for example, he cannot risk going back to Celle, where his mother lives until 1569 and the family enjoys a good reputation? Or, has he presented his claim all too vigorously in Münden and ruined his relationship with the duke? We do not know.

The last time we hear about Urbanus, Jr. is in 1569 at the sale of his mother's house, where he is represented by his siblings.

The Mother's Worries About Money

On February 27, 1575, a decade after Urbanus, Jr.'s claim for debt, his widow, Elisabeth Dransfeld, asks Duke Erich for payment of the remainder.[399] She writes that while still living, her deceased husband reminded the duke several times, which she has also done. Her creditors are after her "almost daily," and she has even been sued. She can not settle her own debts and provide for her small children and her poor, aged mother. The duke's debt to her now amounts to 686 Taler. For ten years, the sum owed has remained unchanged. Elisabeth has no way out of the situation. See Appendix 30 for her writing to Duke Erich.

Duke Erich II answers on March 5, 1575, acknowledging the accuracy of her claim. He instructs his advisors to repay the debt, "not in one payment, but in two or three installments," one-half between next Easter and Pentecost. The payment is not to be made to Elisabeth Dransfeld, however, but rather to the advisors who should then pay her creditors directly.[400] Duke Erich personally signs the letter.

The delaying tactics continue. On May 17, 1575, the advisors write to the treasurer requesting payment of the amount, however, nothing happens.[401] A decade later, on on April 8, 1584, Duke Erich II writes his advisors from Pavia, Italy that he "would like to have at least half the debt settled within a year's time."[402] A short time later, on November 17, 1584, Erich II dies in Pavia. Calenberg-Göttingen is now ruled by Duke Julius in Wolfenbüttel.

The duke's aforementioned writings must have preceded further petitions from Elisabeth because her situation reaches a dramatic climax in 1584. Since she has to borrow money in order to fight for her family's survival and she cannot eliminate her debts herself, she is sued by her creditors. The city council deals with the matter. On January 21, 1585, a decision is rendered. Elisabeth is found guilty and has to pay her creditors![403] See Appendix 31.

Elisabeth Dransfeld now makes a request of Julius, the new duke . On July 10, 1585, he sends Eisabeth's letter to his advisors in Münden and requests a report from them. (Her letter is unavailable to us.)

In November 1585, the advisors confirm the validity of the statements in Elisabeth's letter to the duke and apologize by stating that they believed it was a matter of new, not old debts. Moreover, there is no money available to pay the debt.[404]

On October 11, 1585, Elisabeth again requests payment of the unchanged amount. Not once has she added interest to the total sum due. Three times the duke has instructed the advisors to pay. Elisabeth, however, cannot hold off her creditors any longer.[405]

After that, we hear nothing more about the matter. This may be an indication that after more than two decades, Elisabeth finally receives the money, but we cannot be sure. The authorities act arbitrarily. It does not appear that they did anything illegal. For years, Elisabeth feels humiliated. She and her children, Sebastian, Christoph, and Erich suffer financial hardship that dicates their daily lives. It is ever present during the childhood and youth of her three growing sons.

Reminders to the New Ruler (Duke Julius)

The oldest son of Elisabeth Dransfeld, Sebastian Regius, later pastor in Finkenwerder, studies in Strassburg. His studies are supposed to be paid for out of the profits of the St. Albani feudal tenure agreement. Dietrich Düvel [Devil], the pastor of St. Albani, however, is always delinquent in paying the annual reserve sum of 20 Gulden or fails to pay it at all.

Encouraged by Duke Julius' good reputation, Sebastianus Regius writes to him on October 11, 1585 and again writes almost the same letter on September 1, 1586. He complains to the duke about the outstanding payments due. He emphasizes that this is the only income his father, Urbanus Regius, Jr., was able to eke out in many years of hard work and that it was very difficult for him to save even this small amount. See Appendix 32. He has his brother deliver these letters.

ILLUSTRATION 73: View of Strassburg in about 1500, with the Akademie [Academy Sturm], later the Universität. In the background is the Strassburg Münster[Cathedral]. Three Rhegius generations feel a tie to the City.[406]

Both of Sebastian's letters are written by a professional scribe, which is a common practice at the time because most people cannot write. It is certainly the case with Sebastian, who, as a young student, does not want to make any grammatical errors when he turns to the country's highest ruler for help. On October 12, 1586 he writes again, still more urgently. This time, he has his cousin, Franz Algermann, deliver his letter.

From Münden on November 7, 1585, Sebastian's mother, Elisabeth Dransfeld, writes at length to Duke Julius. She addresses the letter, "To Your Princely Grace from your humble servant, Elisabeth, Urbanus Regius' blessed widow." Thus, we know she again lives in Münden.

The issue appears still unsettled because on November 20, 1586 Franz Algermann composes a letter about the matter to the "Prince's Braunschweig Chamber Secretary," Wolf(gang) Ewerd(e)s. See Appendix 34. Algermann addresses him as, "Dear Cousin," which shows their close (perhaps kinship) tie. Wolf, or also Wolfgang, Ewers or Ewerdes – the spelling of the names varies – is one of the most influential chamber secretaries in Wolfenbüttel civil service. There is a deep level of trust between the two of them, because all the royal petitions must pass through Ewer's hands.[407]

The name Wolf Ewers piques our interest in another respect. He is a direct forefather of future Finkenwerder Pastor Daniel Conrad Heinrich Evers, the first chronologist of the Elbe island.[408]

In 1588 Duke Julius makes a church inspection in Calenberg-Göttingen. On March 16 the visitors are in Münden.

Page 122

There is a possibility that Elisabeth Dransfeld can voice her concerns. Here is the protocol:

"Urbanus Regius' widow in Münden delivers a request[409] to Your Supreme Highness[410] which states that pastor Theodoricus Düvelius of St. Albani in Göttingen has not wanted to give her son, a student, money for his education, even though the pastor is ordered to do so. This means that the pastor refuses to do what he does not want to do." The Vice Chancellor writes to his superior that through the death of the original beneficiary, the feudal tenure has become null and void.[411]

According to Elisabeth's statement, Pastor Düvel is again delinquent in paying the stipend out of the reserve profits. Sebastian should let the duke know if he wants to continue in the clergy. If not, the duke will know how to proceed. Enough said!

Uhlhorn mistakenly reports that the above-named widow is Urbanus, Sr.'s wife, rather than Urbanus, Jr.'s.[412]

Urbanus, Jr. Leaves Behind Three Underage Children

The Duke August Bibliothek [Library] in Wolfenbüttel preserves the original manuscript of Urbanus Rhegius, Sr.'s most frequently printed work, *Dialogus von der Schönen Predigt* [*Dialogue From the Beautiful Sermon*]. At the end of this 1537 document is a handwritten family tree, entitled, *Genealogia D. Vrbani Regij* [*Geneology of Dr. Urbanus Rhegius*]. See Illustration 74.[413] The transcribed version is in Appendix 35.

In this document, Urbanus, Jr. is shown as Sekretär [secretary] to Duke Erich II, and we deduce that his wife, whose last name is "Dransfeldis," comes from Göttingen.

ILLUSTRATION 74: The Genealogia D. Vrbani Regij, written inconspicuously on the reverse side of one of his works, is an important key to the Rhegius family history. Eleven of the 13 children are named in it.

Three sons are listed for Urbanus, Jr. and Elisabeth:

1. Sebastian Regius. About 1588. Pastor in Finkenwerder.
2. Christoffer (Christoph). Senior civil servant in Reinhausen.
3. Erich, miles. Soldier.

On October 28, 1572 and March 1, 1573 "the trustee of the blessed children left behind by Urbanus Regius" writes to the city council of Göttingen and accuses Pastor Dietrich Düvel of not having paid the promised sum from the reserves.[414] According to the letters, Urbanus, Jr. dies before October 1572. We surmise that he is born about 1527, which would make him somewhat older than 40 when he dies.

His wife, Elisabeth Dransfeld, must now care for the children by herself. Through her correspondence with Schloss Münden about the money owed her, we know how difficult this is for her.

Her bitterness is voiced in the lines she writes in 1585:

"...and now I am sitting here with my many children, since
I have no funds owed to my blessed husband that will
help me out of my sorrow and fear..."

How much more could she do for her children and how much
better her life would be if Münden paid her the money owed her
for more than two decades! And how unjust she must feel it is that
Urbanus paid the money out of his own pocket while in the duke's
service!

In 1595, Christoph Regius marries Anna Spangenberg in Münden.
She is the daughter of Münden Secretary, Wilhelm Spangenberg.
In 1598 we encounter Christoph as Amtsverwalter [governmental
department administrator] in Reinhausen.[415]

Erich Regius enrolls in the Göttinger Pädagogium [Göttingen
Pedagogical School] on May 25, 1589. He becomes a soldier.

The sons' career choices indicate a very conventional family mind
set. According to an old tradition from pre-Reformation times, the
oldest son becomes a theologian (to show thanks to God), the second
becomes either a civil servant, lawyer, or merchant (to care for the
family), and the third becomes a soldier (to fight for the country).
Here is an example of this sequence:

The first time we again hear about the sons Christoph and Erich
is in January 1592 when they are named heirs of their uncle, Ernestus
Regius. Meanwhile, they are about 30 years old and live in Münden.
Duke Heinrich Julius of Wolfenbüttel succeeds his father, Julius,

in 1589. On January 19TH and 20TH he writes to the Count von Schwendung; to Peter, Freiherr [Baron] zu Morsburg and Befford, Kasierlicher Geheimer Rat [imperial privy counselor]; and to Georg Hansen, Count Palentine bey Rein, Duke in Upper and Lower Bayern, and Count zu Veldentz about employing the two sons.

In the letter to the Count of Schwendung, Duke Heinrich Julius calls both brothers "our subjects with feudal tenure from our city of Münden." Might both of them be connected in some way to the feudal tenure "in Borksbeutell" that they were awarded in 1576? We are unable to find out anything about it, so the question remains unanswered.

The letters mentioned above cannot be completely deciphered so the underlying facts of the case are difficult to understand. On the one hand, the talks concern "properties withheld." On the other, it is about debts to be settled. The three addressees are requested to intercede on behalf of the brothers' concerns. Their uncle died in 1581 which means the brothers have apparently been pursuing their inheritance for some time.

Sebastian, the oldest brother, is not named as an heir in the letter. It is possible that he received financial support from his Uncle Ernst while he was studying in Strassburg.

The name Dransfeld is mentioned as a Göttingen family of advisors and scholars. In 1355, the "von" in "von Dransfeld" was dropped because "von" signifies nobility. The "von Dransfelds" are not nobility so the "von" signifies where the family is from.[416] The origin of the Dransfeld family name is initially the name of a commons, land, or meadow which then became the name of a small city near Göttingen. Seven Dransfelds are members of the Göttingen city council.

Beginning in 1500, several appear in the registries of various universities. Twice the family produced a mayor of Göttingen.

We have yet to establish a connection to Elisabeth Dransfeld.

Page 124

Court Singer, Secretary, Historian, Financial Administrator, Notary, Poet

THE MULTI-TALENTED RHEGIUS GRANDSON, FRANZ ALGERMANN

When Duke Otto II is buried on November 24, 1603 in the Harburg Marienkirche with all honors due an imperial prince, Pastor Sebastian König is in the funeral procession, representing the Lüneburg section of the Elbe River Island of Finkenwerder.

Sebastian's cousin, Franz Algermann, is probably also among the mourners because he has the honor of composing Duke Otto's funeral oration, paying tribute to his life and deeds for posterity. Algermann eagerly sets to work on the task. In 1603, with Phillip von Ohr in Hamburg, Algermann publicly dedicates a 244 line poem to Otto's sons; his widow, Hedwig; and "other assembled princely heirs."[417] He concludes with a slightly altered version of the 90TH Psalm sung to the melody, "Ein Feste Burg ist unser Gott" [A Mighty Fortress is Our God]. Only a few copies of the funeral oration remain. The title page is found in Appendix 36.[418]

Algermann prints his own tribute to the Duke in the form of an anagram. Every other line begins with the first letter of the following words:

"Dem Durchleuchtigen Hochgeborenen Fürsten vnd Herrn, Herrn Otten Hertogen Zv Braunschweig Vnd Lvnebvrg Zw (u) Underthenigen Vnd Lezten Ehren Gestelt"

["To the Enlightened One, The Princes, and Nobley Born Lords. To Otto, Duke of Braunschweig and Lüneburg, all burial honors."]

The dedication contains 122 letters and a total of 244 lines. Those interested in the deceased duke's lineage will find Algermann's detailed text very informative.[419]

Algermann, in one of his exemplary works about the House of Braunschweig and Lüneburg, meticulously establishes the family lineage in the *Prachtstammbaum* [*Magnificent Family Tree of the Guelphs*] (1584). This exerpt from Algermann's work, which is displayed in the Duke August Bibliotek in Wolfenbüttel, is outstanding.[420]

It is a pleasure to delve deeply into this document. Portraits of the most important people are presented along with their coats of arms. The portrait of Duke Otto I is the only depiction personally dedicated to him and is therefore especially valuable. Because she is descended merely from minor nobility, his consort, Metta von Campe, is portrayed without a coat of arms, even though the family possesses one.

ILLUSTRATION 75: Excerpt from the House of Braunschweig and Lüneburg's *Prachtstammbaum*. Duke Otto I with his consort, Metta von Campe, is shown at left. On the right is his brother, Duke Ernst the Confessor, and his consort, Sophia von Mecklenburg.

Page 125

In the *Prachtstammbaum,* Algermann mistakenly calls "Anna von Campe" Metta's cousin.[421]

Anna von Campe is betrothed to Heinrich des Mittleren [meaning he is the Heinrich "in between" two other Heinrichs]. Heinrich des Mittleren is the father of Duke Otto I. Since father and son have a strained relationship, there are certainly problems in their relationship with the female cousins.

Algermann is very careful in representing the House of Braunschweig and Lüneburg as one of the oldest noble lineages. He cites Heinrich der Löwe; Karl der Grosse [Charlemagne]; Sieghard, King of Sachsen; and the Langobard clan, all of whom are blood relatives of the "noble Guelphs." Members of the House of Braunschweig are also close friends or in-laws of the "highest potentates, electors, and princes in Germany, Italy, and France."

The *Prachtstammbaum* is dedicated to Duke Heinrich Julius (1564 – 1613), who in the year of the lineage's origin, is only 20 years old. A year later he marries Dorothea von Sachsen, daughter of Elector August. The two of them further the family line.

The entire *Prachtstammbaum* is bordered by muses and verses, in which the most important persons describe themselves. In addition, the names of the lesser nobility and Guelph bishops of Minden and Halberstadt are listed. In order to demonstrate divine right, the phrase "with the grace of God" appears under the dedication to Heinrich Julius, God the Father with Christ and the Holy Ghost. Below that, Ferdinand II is enthroned over the nobles of the kingdom on whose wings the coats-of-arms of the electors and the highest ranking parliament members are depicted.

In 1589, Algermann writes a clarification to the *Prachtstammbaum*. He chooses to present it in the form of a dialogue. He has Charlemagne awake from the dead and ask what has occurred since his death. Both good and bad happenings are reported to him. As the centuries unfold, new people emerge, four of them are historians. The life of Heinrich Julius is foreshadowed. In the closing monologue, Charlemagne shows understanding of the younger generation's pressure to succeed, however, he also points out the futility of all human endeavors.[423]

Who is Franz Algermann? His lineage comes from the previously cited *Genealogia D. Vrbani Regij*:

GRANDPARENTS:	Urbanus Rhegius. (1489 – 1541). Anna Weissbrücker. (About 1505 – 1569).
PARENTS:	JOHANN ALGERMANN. Date of birth unknown. Died 1549 or 1575.[424] Studies in Wittenberg, 1534 – 1548. Evangelisch minister in Beedenbostel, Celle district.[425] Married in 1545 to Maria Regius, probably the eldest daughter of Urbanus Rhegius and Anna Weissbrücker. Born 1526 in Augsburg. Probably died before 1569. 1543/44 lady's maid to Countess Elisabeth[426]
2 CHILDREN:	1. ERNST. Died young 2. FRANZ (FRANCISCUS). Born about 1548 in Celle. Died 1613 in Wolfenbüttel. In 1578 marries Anna Kelner. Birthdate unknown. Died after 1614. Daughter of the organist Thomas Kelner from Braunschweig.

Page 126

ILLUSTRATION 76: Title page of the *Prachtstammbaum*, designed by Franz Algermann. He traces the origin of the "ancient princely House of Braunschweig and Lüneburg" back to the "...most noble, oldest German, most excellent Guelph."[422]

Page 127

Franz Algermann and Anna Kelner have three children: Hedwig, Franz (who studies in Helmstedt), and Anna.

The previously mentioned *Genealogia* can be found on the reverse side of the last page of the original writing, *Dialogus von der schönen Predigt*.[427] At this point, Franz Algermann has already been in the duke's service for 12 years. It can be assumed that the document was acquired by Franz for the duke .

Who may have written the *Geneologia*? The author has remarkably detailed knowledge about the family, writes in Latin, fully portrays the Algermann family, and must have had access to the original in the duke's archives. From this we assume that Franz Algermann is the author.[428]

The *Geneologia* contains some inaccuracies. Paul is not the first born son. We know that he is born in Lüneburg in 1533. Also, Paul is not the grandfather, but rather Conrad Rieger is.

Uhlhorn mentions Urbanus Rhegius' oldest daughter and therefore we presume it is Maria, "who is already married in 1537 during Rhegius' lifetime." Duke Ernst gave her 50 Gulden as a wedding present.[429] To Rhegius' great joy, Bugenhagen probably attended the wedding. If these assumptions are correct, then Maria is about 11 years old in 1537. What we are dealing with here cannot be a wedding, but rather an arranged promise to marry. Also, in 1543 – 44, Maria would not have been a lady's maid to the countess. We maintain that more likely, the actual wedding takes place in 1545 – 46, which is also supported by information about Franz's birth around 1548 and the early death of Ernst, the first born son.

Franz Algermann studies in Strassburg, Wittenberg (enrolled on July 21, 1566), and Frankfurt/Oder [on the Oder River]. After his studies, he becomes a teacher for a year at St. Aegidien in Braunschweig and a choir director and organist in Neustadt.[430] In 1575, when he is about 27 years old, he arrives in Wolfenbüttel to serve as a court singer for Duke Julius and a bassist in the prince's choir. At the same time, he becomes the office secretary. According to Samse, his salary amounts to 20 Taler. "When the duke has an opportunity to observe Franz's capabilities and good conduct, he values Franz highly. After that, he sends him as a trouble shooter to the city of Braunschweig. The Duke also confides in him in many matters."[431]

It is really astonishing how many different tasks Algermann is assigned during his almost four decades of service to the duke and also how he cultivates his passions. His musical capabilities encompass titles such as court singer, bassist, and choir director. It appears that because of his musical ability he is selected for the prince's choir.

Music, especially spiritual music, is his passion for quite some time. In 1596, he publishes an Evangelisch hymnal containing 36 Latin hymns translated into German and accompanied by recommended melodies.[432]

The contents include the Creator, creation, and Christ as Savior. The appendix contains a 12 stanza "Gebet wider den Türcken" ["Prayer Against the Turks"] and a 13 stanza song about the 44TH Psalm. Inge Mager writes a commemorative celebration of Algermann's German translation of the Latin texts that is worth reading. In it, she says he returns "the sublime, picturesque language in the hymns from the Middle Ages to earth."

Algermann's love of Evangelisch songs is substantiated by the publication of the musical Psalm, "Himlische Cantorey, der Psalter Davids..." ["Heavenly Cantorey of the Psalms of David"]. It appears in Hamburg in 1604, and a second edition appears in Wolfenbüttel in 1610. This side of Algermann is surely formed by his grandparents and their generation. His grandmother, Anna Weissbrücker, lives in Celle near Beedenbostel. It is therefore probable that when he was a child, he was frequently at her home and that she was a role model for him. She can tell her oldest grandchild much about her vast experience. She personally experienced the early years of the Reformation. She knows the turbulence in Augsburg, her husband Urbanus' participation in the Augsburg Confession, the Imperial Diet there in 1530, Urbanus' visit with Luther in Coburg, and the time with Duke Ernst in Celle. When Anna dies in 1569, Franz Algermann is 19 years old.

In a 1598 biography of Duke Julius, Algermann demonstrates his affinity for the House of Braunschweig and Lüneburg as well as his historical knowledge of the Guelphs. He thoroughly revises the work in 1608.[433] Even if the biography is overly positive in praising the ruling authority, Franz's work still provides us a good glimpse into the life of this remarkable prince.

The wording of the title page informs us that Algermann is "the senior official who has a close relationship with the prince and is entrusted with his confidences." What Algermann writes in the book is derived from his own personal experiences with the duke and stems from "his own perspective." Strombeck highlights in his foreward that the work is the first published biography of Duke Julius. The draft must have been hand written over a long period of time because when Algermann completes the first version in 1598, the duke has already been dead nine years.

Additional works by Algermann suggest he studied law or has at least rudimentary legal knowledge. He is Landsgerichtbeisitzer [regional court assessor] for the Harz offices and the Hofgerichts-prokurator [lawyer for the court].[434] He calls himself "Landfiscal" [manager responsible for state finances], a judicial official who represents the financial rights of the country's ruler.

His numerous assignments demand a great deal of travel. In 1584 he compiles a very detailed description of the official duties in Wolfenbüttel, [435] and in 1605 he writes about the city of Braunschweig. He also describes the sub-branches of the River Leine (1583 – 1585).

On August 11, 1585, Algermann reports to the duke that he has received the duke's instructions regarding the sub-branches of the River Leine. Algermann is traveling and becomes very ill during the journey. In his own personal style he writes:

> "Between 11 and 12 at night, after previously feeling good,
> I suddenly took sick, so that everything in the room

swirled about me. Although I got up and walked around for two hours, nothing helped, so that I saw death before my eyes because I could hardly breathe.

Page 129

Thus, I had to delay my journey and set out for home around 12 midnight, in order to be with my family."[436]

Despite his numerous activities on the duchy's behalf, the relationship between Franz and the duke is not without difficulties. On October 20, 1606 the duke announces restrictions on what Algermann can do.[437] The duke justifies the ban on Algermann's publication on rebuilding the city of Braunschweig. The duke disagrees with what Algermann writes about the city of Braunschweig and so Algermann publishes his own version in 1608. Problems were already emerging in 1589 – 90. At that time, Algermann was accused of bribery. On January 8, 1590 he addressed a comprehensive document to the duke declaring that he "is innocent before God and the world."[438] He asks for payment of the salary due him for many years and offers his resignation.[439] He is given additional assignments after that. Following a brief retirement, he dies in 1613 in Wolfenbüttel at age 65.

There is no known portrait of Franz Algermann.

According to what follows in Part III, if Franz Algermann and Sebastianus Regius had met at Duke Otto II's funeral, Sebastian would have invited his cousin to Finkenwerder.

For our readers from the Bodensee, we begin with a glimpse into the political and religious environment in the northern corner of the duchy of Braunschweig and Lüneburg. This may be useful for our readers from Southern Germany. Those readers from Finken-werder may wish to skip these details. On the other hand, such details might interest our readers from Finkenwerder by helping them find closure regarding connections between the North German families and their own Langenargen ancestors.

ILLUSTRATION 77: "Printed and prepared...by Cunradt Horn, Franciscum Algermann and Georg Scharffenberger Anno 1584" (Excerpt from the *Prachtstammbaum*). Beginning in 1582, Georg Scharffenberger works with Franz Algermann on the *Prachtstammbaum*. Scharffenberger makes the wood carving. On December 11, 1588 he petitions Duke Julius to allow him to settle in Wolfenbüttel and marry. The bride is the daughter of Hermann Querenberg and a granddaughter of Urbanus Rhegius.[440]

Section III:

Rhegius' Descendants on the Island of Finkenwerder in the Elbe River

The Political and Religious Environment of Finkenwerder

A divided island in an area between the Duchy of Braunschweig-Lüneburg, the city of Hamburg, and the Earldom of Holstein The Guelphs early on expand their holdings from the towers of Hamburg to the Elbe Island of Finkenwerder. Following the deaths of the Counts zu Stade in 1144, no less than Heinrich der Löwe [the Lion], Duke of Sachsen, adds the territory to his domain.[441] At that time, the Elbe islands are still a unified region extending from Kaltenhof to the Finkenwerder Ness. In 1158 the island region is referred to by the name Gorieswerder for the first time.

Heinrich der Löwe does not completely enjoy his new possession. The archbishop of Bremen also has claims on it since the rulers of Stade in 1063 hold many fiefs and church properties in trust. The feudal tenure of the properties is supposed to go to the church after the Stade lineage dies out, but Henry der Löwe seizes the land by force.[442]

The inhabitants of Gorieswerder abandon Heinrich in 1192 and pledge themselves to the Counts zu Holstein, who likewise have prior claims.[443] In 1111, the islands are divided into Northern and Southern Elbe when the Counts zu Holstein from the House of Schauenberg are given them through the emperor's feudal tenure. The dispute lasts a full 90 years until Duke Heinrich's grandson, Duke Otto das Kind [the Younger], waives rights to the Earldom of Stade. Thus, the archbishop of Bremen receives as feudal tenure Goe Hittfeld, Hollenstedt, and the southern half of the islands of Finken- and Gorieswerder in the Elbe.[444] Since the northern part stays with Holstein, the result is a political division of the island in 1236. This condition continues for 700 years until the Grosshamburggesetz von 1937 [Law of Greater Hamburg of 1937].

In 1236, Gorieswerder is already divided into two islands, according to a document that states, "duas insulas, scilicet Gorieswerder et vinkenwerder"[445] (two islands, namely Gorieswerder and Finkenwerder).

Devastating storm surges from the 12TH to the 14TH centuries tear the former Grieswerder into several islands and destroy the existing cultural landscape. Thus, we find on Lorich's 1568 Elbkarte [Map of the Elbe] the northern part labeled "dikeless Hamburg-Finkenwerder." Residents and landlords lose their struggle with the water for this part of the island.

Ancient chroniclers report that Count Gerhard I von Holstein in 1265 bequeaths the southern part of the Finkenwerder and Altenwerder area to his daughter, Luitgarde, as a dowry upon her marriage to Duke Johann von Lüneburg, the son of Duke Otto dem Kind. This is one of the first connections between the earldom of Holstein and the duchy of Braunschweig-Lüneburg.

Dike construction by the Dutch plays a significant role in the early development of the Elbe marshes. In 1106, an agreement is made between the archbishop of Bremen and the first Dutch settlers whereby the marshes are made suitable for growing crops and ought to be settled.[447] In 1130, the settlement of the Hamburg Elbe marshes begins. Harburg becomes known as "Horeburg" (Sumpfburg) [Marsh]. Kausche believes it is possible that Finkenwerder, at least the southern half, is also settled by the Dutch.[448] Centuries later, Dutch sounding names, like van Rigen, Benit, von Cölln, von Campen, von Dratteln, Fock, and Fink support this assumption.[449]

ILLUSTRATION 78: The Elbe Island of Finkenwerder at the time of Sebastian König's arrival. The Lüneburg section is surrounded by a dike, the Hamburg section is, "dikeless Vinkenwarder." From 1588 to 1617, Sebastian König preaches in the church depicted above.[446]

All Finkenwerder chroniclers extensively report about the storm surges that devastate the island again and again. In the Cäcilien Flood of 1412, more than 30,000 people drown in the lower Elbe. The history of the Elbe island is the history of storm surges and the history of the people's will against the forces of nature. With a single break in the dike, inhabitants have years of hard work ahead of them, and the rulers regularly incur great expense to restore the dike.

So it also goes for Duke Otto II von Hostein after the heavy storm surges of 1420, 1421, and 1426. Huge expenditures are necessary to repair the flood damage. In 1427 he seeks financial relief by mortgaging the northern half of the island to the wealthy Hamburg advisor, Erich von Tzeven.[450] Soon the debt becomes too great even for Erich, and in 1445 he transfers his rights to the city of Hamburg "for 1,200 Rinsche Gulden made of gold, with good weight."[451]

At the same time, Hamburg acquires the royal rights from Holstein so that in 1445, the northern part of Finkenwerder that formerly belonged to Holstein is now politically Hamburg's. It is noteworthy that the church's district of North Finkenwerder remains in Nien-stedten and thus still belongs to Holstein, which has been the case since 1297. Now Finkenwerder is divided into three parts. South Finkenwerder belongs to the church and also to the political district of the duchy of Braunschweig and Lüneburg. North Finkenwerder belongs to the political district of Hamburg and the church district of the Holstein earldom, under the Counts zu Schauenburg of the Itzehoe/Pinneberg lineage.

There is a further significant change in 1459, when the last Earl of Schauenburg from the Rendsburg lineage dies. Through marriage, Holstein falls to the House of Oldenburg, which, beginning in 1449, also rules Denmark. As a result, endless conflict ensues. Hamburg claims control of and tariff rights to the Elbe. The Danish kings claim that Hamburg belongs to the Danish royal domain. Thus, Danish King Christian III vehemently proclaims sovereignty over Hamburg and threatens the city with war. He dies in 1588 as Sebastian König arrives in Hamburg.

Page 132

ILLUSTRATION 79: Excerpt from the Karte der Elbgegend bei Hamburg [Map of the Elbe Region near Hamburg], which Pastor Bodemann provides in his book, Denkwürdigkeiten der Elbinsel Finkenwerder [Memories of the Elbe Island of Finkenwerder]. An older map from Pastor Evers is included.

Since at this time North Finkenwerder belongs to Hamburg and Hamburg belongs to Denmark, Danish claims are inevitably in force in North Finkenwerder. If one follows the Danes' thinking regarding their claim, the Danish kingdom now runs through the middle of the divided Island of Finkenwerder to Hamburg. The inconspicuous ditches become the "boundaries" between the two spheres of influence. In 1768 Denmark recognizes Hamburg as an Free Imperial City (according to the Gottroper Vertrag [Treaty]).[452]

In the decade between 1520 and 1530, the principality of Braunschweig and Lüneburg undergoes important changes that will soon affect Finkenwerder and the descendants of Urbanus Rhegius. In 1519, Duke Heinrich II participates in the election of the Holy Roman German emperor. He chooses the French King, Franz I, which puts him in conflict with the Habsburg Emperor Karl V. In 1520, Heinrich leaves his country and goes to the French court.

In 1521, Heinrich gives the principality of Braunschweig and Lüneburg to Otto and Ernst, his sons in Celle. Otto, the first born, who has been secretly engaged to Metta von Campe, a noble young woman of lesser aristocratic rank, abdicates his right to govern and unites with his brother, Duke Ernst, in 1527. Otto is compensated with Schloss Harburg and its functions.[453]

Duke Otto I thereby becomes founder of the Harburg branch of the Guelph lineage and ruler of South Finkenwerder. His son, Duke Otto II, succeeds him in 1549 – 1603. The Harburg line rules until 1642, when Duke Otto II's son, Duke Wilhelm, dies unmarried. Harburg reverts to Celle.

In the meantime, the Reformation alters Germany's political and religious landscape. Duke Ernst of Braunschweig and Lüneburg, later known as Ernst the Confessor, becomes one of the most ardent proponents of Luther's teachings.

Sebastian König (1554/59 – 1621) (401 on the family tree)[454]

(UNTIL 1586 KNOWN AS SEBASTIANUS REGIUS) PASTOR IN FINKENWERDER, 1588 – 1621

In the Beginning – A Call for Help From Harburg

In 1588, Finkenwerder is an island with fewer than 100 resident and can only be reached by boat. Most residents are farmers and fishermen. There are a few artisans, but no school and no doctor. Only the part of the island that belongs to Braunschweig-Lüneburg is surrounded by a protective dike.

Page 133

The few houses that are protected by quays against storm surges are on the northern half of the island. Sebastian König is the new pastor responsible for the congregation of Finkenwerder's southern half, the "Lüneburg side."

Everything here is new to him. He is about 30 years old. He knows Low German from Münden, his birthplace, but here in Finkenwerder, it sounds different. His ear must become accustomed to the new sound. The people are taciturn, skeptical, and reticent. They struggle for their daily lives, busy with fishing or field work from early morning to late at night.

The contrast could not be greater between Finkenwerder and his family of origin's lifestyle in the wealthy city of Augsburg, through whose gates the dukes and emperors enter and where merchants and emissaries from the rulers of many countries are welcomed into the city. Celle and the friendship between his grandfather, Urbanus Rhegius, and Duke Ernst were also talked about. Celle is also only a small city, but even so, it is a city where nobility reside, and in which the dukes descend from their coaches in front of the castle. Sebastian himself grows up in Münden at the confluence of the Werra and Fulda Rivers and in Nienover on the Weser River. His parents' small, modest official's house stands in the large square in front of Schloss Münden among the other castle servants' houses. Often, he and his two brothers peek over the fence at the splendid, colorful celebrations of the ducal family, who are called the "Calenberg dukes" by the local people.

What other circumstances lead up to Sebastian's coming to the duchy's northernmost point? His father, Urbanus Regius, Jr., had provided for the future and had the 1559 feudal tenure extended to Sebastian. (See the original document in Appendix 37.)

In this document, the name (Se)Bastian is mentioned for the first time. Since he is not named in the feudal tenure of 1554, it means he was born between 1554 and 1559. The duke limits the extension of the feudal tenure rights to Sebastian, under the condition that Sebastian's education be paid out of the profits – and this is important to the duke – that Sebastian must later serve the duchy as pastor.

Sebastian's mother, Elisabeth Dransfeld (304), reports about his education in a letter to Duke Julius of Wolfenbüttel dated November 7, 1585.[455] (See Appendix 38.) She writes:

> "My son has been studying in Switzerland and other places for 15 years, under the assumption that he will undertake...the pastoral duties (namely at St. Albani, Göttingen) which he should occupy and administer. I will write to him that he should arrange to do so as soon as possible..."

This text provides informative clues about Sebastian and his family:

1. After the early death of Sebastian's father around 1570, his mother sees to his education.

2. "Fifteen years of study" is probably the total years of schooling, including study at the university.

3. "In Switzerland." We could not establish any registration date in Switzerland. Despite this, he could have studied there. Due to the cost of the university education, there is often no registration. The opposite may also be valid, in that not every person who registers eventually studies at the university. Many who can afford it register only for the prestige.

4. In "other places" certainly means Strassburg because he writes numerous letters from there in 1585 and 1586.

    Since documents showing matriculation begin only in 1621, when the "L'Ecole Latine et l'Ancienne Academie de Strasbourg" combine to become a university, there is no proof of any enrollment.

Page 134

5. "...that he himself should perform and administer the pastoral duties." It follows that Sebastian is studying theology. Otherwise, he could not assume the pastoral duties at St. Albani.

6. "That he should arrange to do so as soon as possible." His mother probably means he should finish studying and go to work.

Why the impatience, and why so many letters in such a short time? The reasons become clear when we see that Sebastian's oldest son, Johann, is born on January 10, 1587, three months after his urgent letters from Strassburg. A new generation has arrived! Now the needs, especially the financial ones, are great. No money is coming from Göttingen. It is very hard for his mother to support him. Sebastian has to quickly earn money!

There is no information about his wife's origin. The church records preserved in the Stadtarchiv [City Archives] Strassburg show no marriage between the two. At that time, there is no church registry in Münden. So the question remains whether Sebastian's wife is from Strassburg or Münden. The only certainty is that she is not from Finkenwerder.

Sebastian's hopes rest on Duke Julius, who is interested in cultural and religious affairs, founds the Universität Helmstedt in 1576, and knows Sebastian's grandfather, Urbanus Rhegius. Sebastian's chances are fairly good, since Evangelisch pastors are sought after in the decade following the Reformation. Luther himself often complains about the lack of educated Evangelisch pastors.

What is the reaction to the letter, and how could the negotiations in Finkenwerder have been construed? The duchy of Braunschweig and Lüneburg is divided through inheritance into: Grubenhagen, Lüneburg-Celle, Calenberg-Göttingen, and Braunschweig-Wolfenbüttel. In Celle, the lineages split into the Harburg, Gifhorn, and Dannenberg-Hitzacker branches. Yet, the rulers of the family divisions remain in frequent contact at family celebrations, funerals, and other occasions.

In Sebastian's case, there are repeated opportunities to serve Duke Julius and talk with the duke's Harburg relatives. For example, in February 1587, Countess Dorothea dies. The first wife of Duke Heinrich Julius von Wolfenbüttel and the daughter of Elector August von Sachsen, she is only 24 years old. The ducal relatives from Harburg are certainly present at the burial.

In May 1587 two of Duke Julius' sons, Joachim Carl and Julius August, study at Universität Helmstedt at the same time as four ducal sons from the Harburg branch of the lineage. The sons are:

Otto III, Wilhelm, Johann, and Friedrich.[456] (The extremely close tie between the House of Wolfenbüttel and Harburg becomes clear a few years later when two of Duke Otto's sons marry two of Duke Julius' daughters! Christoph marries Elisabeth on October 28, 1604 and Otto III marries Hedwig on April 15, 1621.)

Putting these pieces of the mosaic together, one can more readily assume that at one of these events the suggestion is made to entrust Sebastian Regius with the Finkenwerder congregation. A pastor is being sought there who can be trusted to move forward on the various political church interests dividing the island. The pastor must be loyal to the rulers and to the Reformation. With Sebastian as pastor, the authorities do not need to worry because they have known the R(h)egius family for decades.

It may sound strange to us today that the rulers are personally concerned about who fills the pastor's position, however, the dukes or mayors and city councils in the Imperial Free Cities have not been the chief church officials for very long. They have had this responsibility only since the Reformation, and they are taking it very seriously. Also, the Evangelisch teachings are not yet firmly established.

Page 135

Moreover, based on the Evangelisch teachings, the countries' rulers are trying to free themselves from patronizing treatment by the emperor and the "old church." Thus, the consolidation of the Evangelisch teachings is an important political factor in the selection of the "right" pastor.

There is also word from Duke Otto II that he is personally concerned about who is selected pastor. For example, on September 10,

1562, he writes to Johann Schiedlich, pastor at Mücheln in Mansfeld, about a pastor position in Harburg.[457] Salary and responsibilities are not addressed, rather it sounds more like a command when Duke Otto writes: "It is therefore our gracious thinking that you will get on your horse and that you will henceforth establish yourself with us." Pastor Schiedlich comes and occupies the very first pastor position in Harburg until 1569. He is simultaneously superintendent.[458]

The dukes von Braunschweig-Lüneburg in Harburg have always been close to the citizens. The example shows that the current duke cares about the citizens' opinions. In June 1565, for example, he personally rode to Finkenwerder and "...listened to the concerns of the residents of his duchy."[459]

We hear no more about the profits from the feudal tenure at St. Albani, so we may well conclude that with Sebastian's installation as pastor in Finkenwerder, the old claims no longer exist.

Sebastian may have hoped that all past financial worries have been settled, but he will soon learn otherwise. His letter of April 12, 1588 to Duke Otto II's secretary is an urgent call for help. He lays out his financial need before the duke.[461] He is supposed to get nine Schillings annually from each farmer and five Schillings from each farm laborer, but no one is paying. He writes, "...our pastors depend on it," and are also at the mercy of these circumstances for their pay. The church members might be ordered to pay "my expenses and small salary." He even promises them a gratuity for their trouble.

ILLUSTRATION 80: Duke Otto II with his first consort, Margaretha, Countess of Schwarzenburg (right) and his second wife, Hedwig, Countess of East Friesen (left).[460]

His petition is taken up by the synod of April 8, 1589.[462] They decide that Sebastian should demand his salary and it is up to the parishioners to find the means to pay him.

The previously mentioned letter, which he himself signed, is the first written evidence of Sebastian's activities in Finkenwerder. Appendix 39 contains a copy.

Page 136

ILLUSTRATION 81: Sebastian König's church duties begin with financial problems. He asks the secretary of Schloss Harburg to procure his small salary. He went from house to house and did not collect one cent.

Page 137

From Regius to König

For three generations, the family goes by the name R(h)egius.[463] During the Humanist era, it is traditional for students to register at the university under Latin and sometimes Greek translations of their names. At the conclusion of their studies, most revert to their given names.

The R(h)egius family is different. Sebastian's grandfather, Urban Rieger, still goes by "Urbanus Rieger de Argow" in 1508 in Freiburg, as he does in Ingolstadt in 1515. He calls himself Regius for the first time in 1516 and Rhegius in 1524.

In the third generation, all male descendants go by the name Regius. The Königsberg branch of the lineage keeps the name Regius in succeeding generations, as does the family of Christoph Regius, Sebastian's brother.

As we know from his letters, Sebastian is still calling himself Sebastian Regius in 1586. In the official record of the Harburg Synod of April 16, 1588, he is listed as "Bastian Konig,"pastor in Finckenwerder.[464] He himself writes his names "Kunnicke" with a "u," an indication that the family name could have formerly been "Kunig," rather than "König." He ends his name with "ck," probably because he still has an ear from the Southern German sound, where one says "Kunig/König" with a hard (unvoiced) ending, in contrast to Northern German where one writes "König," but says, "Könich."

We do not know what prompts Sebastian to change his name to "Kunnicke" when he assumes his first pastoral position. (In the official records of Harburg, it is always written "König.") Either he is following the tradition of reverting to his family name after completing his studies, or, more likely, here on this small island inhabited by farmers and fisherman, a plain sounding Northern German sounding name is less likely to create a barrier between him and the island's residents. In any case, he is not trying to impress people with an "upper class" name. Perhaps he prefers to appear pragmatic and "streetwise" rather than "too educated," a perception that will soon prove to be correct.

It is noteworthy that after his name change, he still writes four letters as "Kunnicke" (1588, 1600, 1609, 1610) and one as "Kunningk" in 1600. At the time, it is not unusual to vary the spelling of first names and family names. Spelling and writing are based more on phonetic sound than grammatical rules.

The Official Records of the Harburg Synod
TREASURE TROVE OF WORTHWHILE, FORGOTTEN, AND LUDICROUS INFORMATION

The Niedersächsische Hauptstaatsarchiv [Main State Archives of Lower Sachsen] in Hannover preserves the official records of the Harburg Synod from about 1570 to 1617.[465] It requires a great deal of persistence to work one's way through approximately 350 pages, which are not always in chronological order and are in many different individuals' handwriting and in very small print or illegible. Nevertheless, it is worth a quick glance at the document.

Page 138

ILLUSTRATION 82: The "Stedtlein Harburgk" [village of Harburg] with its castle, where the annual synod takes place, in which Sebastian König participates. In 1613, he preaches in the Marienkirche [Church of Mary].[466]

The official records of the 1571 synod contain a list of books "the Pastors should have."

· The Bible, in Latin and German.
· The *Lüneburgische (Kirchen)-Ordnung (vom Jahr 1564)* [*Lüneburg Church Regulations of 1564*].[467]
· *Katechismen* [*Catechism*] *von Luther.*

- *Confessio Augustana* and *Apologia* [Augsburg Confession and its Legal Justification].

- *Loci communes* (Melanchthon's *Hauptpunkte* [Main Points] combined with Luther's *Rechtfertigungslehre* [Teachings on the Legal Justification] 1520/21).

- *Examen Ordinandorum* (*Examen nach Melanchthon*) [Tests of Ordination by Melanchthon].

- *Wie man fürsichtiglich im Predigen reden soll* [How One Should Speak Carefully in a Sermon] (by Urbanus Rhegius).[468]

Upon his arrival in Finkenwerder, Sebastian König finds a book by his grandfather in the parsonage bookcase. It is dedicated to "The young pastors in the duchy of Lüneburg." In the early years of the Reformation, there are all kinds of zealots. Rhegius reminds the young preachers to exercise restraint. He warns them against being overly enthusiastic. The work is especially significant because in 1576, Duke Wilhelm der Jüngere for Braunschweig-Lüneburg and Duke Julius for Braunschweig-Wolfenbüttel officially decree that the country's two Evangelisch churches must follow the "Corpus Doctrinae" [Body of Doctrines].[469] The importance of this work is already recognized in Harburg in 1571 in that it is required reading for all pastors.

From his preface to Urbanus' book, we quote Duke Julius verbatim. He has "made this useful booklet into a handbook and allowed it to be published" for the young preachers.[470] The close personal relationship between both dukes and the Rhegius family is not to be overlooked. As a child in Celle, Wilhelm der Jüngere, son and heir of Ernst the Confessor, met Rhegius. Duke Julius of Wolfenbüttel employed Franz Algermann, Urbanus Regius' multi-talented grandson, at his court.

The official records of the Harburg Synod provide the first confirmed dates of Sebastian König's position as pastor in Finkenwerder. The synod takes place on April 16, 1588. In the official records, Sebastian is named among the participants as "pastor in Finckenwerder." The following is an excerpt from the official record that deals with the pastors of the Harburg congregations:

Page 139

"Tuesday, April 16, (15)88

...It is hereby made known and noted to comply with legal proceedings that I have beseeched my Gracious Prince and Liege in the past about matters that have been sworn to God[471] and I now bring before the court. It has been especially apparent that the poor peasants do not know what an oath is, what formal requirements are necessary, what it means to swear to God, and what we must fulfill and extol. Therefore,[472] it might be your, my Gracious Prince and Liege's,[473] wish that the clergy not just once a year, but often and repeatedly, whenever the opportunity arises, especially when it concerns an explanation of the Catechism, present the material with their whole heart and soul. The purpose of such preaching is to teach church members the truth and how to carry through on an oath sworn to God because now their oaths are so scantily heeded, some of them might unknowingly sin."

What follows are some contributions or questions from partici-
pating clergymen, for example:

> "Honorable Johann of Altenwerder:
> He complains that Heinrich Piper of Dradenau in the
> Hamburg district no longer obeys canonical law. (For
> instance, he does not attend worship service.) Judgement:
> Be he living or dead, the pastor should not render Piper
> any rights of church membership, as long as Piper behaves
> inappropriately. Also, Johann should lodge a complaint
> against Piper with the country's sovereign prince."

This example shows how strongly the church pressures its
members to fulfill their "canonical obligations." The pastor should
revoke the church's blessings from such a member. The church's
powers are to be respected. Denial of communion, without which
there can be no forgiveness of sins, means social banishment from
the congregation. "Be he living or dead" indicates that he would be
denied a church burial, yet another ostracism from the church community.

> "Honorable Sebastian (König) in Finkenwerder:
> Reports that the official in Blankenesse wants to
> impose a new, unusual tax on travel. He [Sebastian]
> requests it be rescinded..."[474]

Wordly matters are being discussed here. The official from Blankenese represents the district north on the Elbe, across the river bank
from Finkenwerder. It belongs to the country of Holstein. If one

travels from there to Finkenwerder, one arrives in "North Finken-werder," which belongs to Hamburg. A pastor from "South Finken-werder," which belongs to the duchy of Braunschweig and Lüneburg, is concerned about the high cost of the toll. How this case, which one might describe as ludicrous, can be resolved "diplomatically" is not readily apparent.

It cannot be ascertained whether Sebastian comes to Finken-werder together with his young wife. The 300 kilometer trip takes over a week on horseback. While traveling, pastors usually stay over night with fellow pastors or similar officials. When that is not pos-sible, they stay in simple inns. It is possible that Sebastian travels with a letter of recommendation from his cousin, Franz Algermann, officially stamped with the ducal seal of the Wolfenbüttel office.

In 1571, the official records point out a noteworthy event in Finken-werder. On July 16, 1571, Johann von Amsterdam, the pastor at that time, appears at the Harburg office. He reports in the duke's pres-ence that after the sermon on June 15, while reading in his Messbuch [missal], he wants to underline something. Then he notices that some of the pages had been removed. He immediately informs the Admin-istrator Heine Wiper;[475] Jacob Fink, church council member; and "Elder" Heine Rigen. But these members of the congregation did not want to know anything about it.[476]

Page 140

On December 18, 1571, there is a hearing in Harburg. Everyone from Finkenwerder participates except fishermen Hermann Bom, Heinrich Stehr, Jr., and Henneke Schult.

Everyone is questioned, one after the other. (Farmers are designated with a "B" for "Buman" and fishermen with a "K" for "Kötner.")

HEINE WÜPER, VOGT	Buman	I have not cut anything out of the missal.
HEINE RIGEN	Buman	I also do not know whether my wife or children cut pages out of the missal.
HINRICH STEHR	K	
JACOB STEHR	K	
JACOB FINK	Buman	
HEINE KÜLPER	Buman	I also do not know anything.
BARTHOLT FOCKEN	K	
HEINO SCHILTT	Buman	
JÜRGEN SCHULT	K	I have not heard anything either.
HEINRICH HOHE	K	
ALBERT SCHILT	Buman	
CORDT BANNIT	K	
HEINRICH FOCKEN	Buman	I also do not know who may have done it. I also do not suspect anybody. Before God and the world, I do not know anything or what happened to them.
CLAUS HOPEN	Buman	
SIMON MERING	K	
HEINE BOM	K	
VEIT MOLLING	K	
PETER MEYENSCHEIN	K	
HEINRICH FOCKEN, SR.	K	
PETER DINSSDAL	K	

HEINE RIGEN, JR.	K	
HERMAN KÜLPER, JR.	K	
HANS MEWES	K	
MARTIN STEHR	K	I do not remember whose oaths these are and who were the 6 of them who raised their finger but were not allowed to be sworn in.
HERMAN BOM	K	
MARTIN MEWES	K	
UNMARRIED PEASANTS		
JACOB AND HEINE RIGEN		
BARTHOLD PLASS		
HANS DINSTAL		
JOHANN WIPER/ WÜPER		
HENNEKE KRUKEN		
PETER FINK		

Removing pages from a book on the altar is a religious sacrilege. Because of this very significant incident, all inhabitants of the "Lüneburg side" were summoned. From this list, one can get a relatively good account of the number of residents in the decade before Sebastian becomes actively involved.

"Buman" definitely refers to the eight "main farms," which are also mentioned by Bodemann.[477] About 12 people belong to the main farm, as well as married couples, their children, retired older people, serfs, and maids. That would be about 100 people for eight main farms. Concerning the 18 farm laborers, there could be eight people per household, for a total of about 144 people. The four fishermen's families might add up to 24 people.

Page 141

TOTAL FOR THE 8 MAIN FARMS	ca 100 people
For the 18 farm laborer farms	ca 144 people
4 fishermen's families	ca 24 people
6 bachelor farm laborers	ca 6 people
TOTAL	274 people in the year 1571

If we assume the "Lüneburg side" has about 300 inhabitants at this time, we might have a closer estimate of the actual circumstances. (For the year 1658, Bodemann's estimate is 491 residents for the "Lüneburg side" and 305 for the Hamburg side.")[478]

It gives a glimpse of a village community where everyone knows everyone else. The Harburg authorities do not require everyone to take an oath at their hearing about the missal incident, but their group deposition allows us to surmise that they are "a congregation under oath." Not one of them gives the slightest hint as to who the culprit may be!

Perhaps this event and others like it are the reason the duke personally participates in several synods. We find an example in the official records from the synod of April 24, 1593. "The Enlightened, Noble, Prince, and Liege, Duke Otto, has graciously ordered that those officials commanded by God...the church and the schools, be respected and closely listened to. For that reason, Your Gracious Prince wants to attend this synod, especially concerning all kinds of happenings and punishable offenses in the duchy, what I have just said is exactly the same as what we previously shared..."[479]

We see that Duke Otto II takes the church affairs of his territories personally in hand. He speaks directly with the pastors of his communities and issues codes of conduct that make it clear "that everyone who acts contrary to God and his conscience" – and the duke does not forget to add – "and against Your Gracious Prince, will be responsible to Your Gracious Prince and will be punished."

In the official records, the pastors are not directly mentioned even once, however, all pastors must attend the synod. Sebastian König also has to participate in the synod and hear the duke's admonitions. On the following Sunday, the Finkenwerder congregations are informed of the duke's warnings.

In 1593, it is established that "until Pentecost a proper inventory and bill has to be recorded and handed in. It is to list what each church, pastorate, and Küstery [sextonry] has on its grounds and an annual tax paid on them." We do not find such an inventory, however, we do find that Sebastian König begins with the 1595 church bills and in doing so he reconstructs public entries from 1590 on.

What did Sebastian König propose in the course of his official duties during the years he served the synod from Finkenwerder? The following are some excerpts from the official records:

"April 28, 1590:

Sebastian König from Finkenwerder asks that he might have improvements on his home which have already been requested and that the church members should fulfill their oath.

Judgement: The members who took an oath should be so instructed.

April 4, 1592:

Mr. Sebastian König makes it known that Claus Hoppen owes 5 Marks a year. For details, consult 'church property – packing, sale, inter-related business.'

April 29, 1606:

Mr. Sebastian König of Finkenwerder makes it known that the people of Finkenwerder often request eight, nine, ten, or more baptismal sponsors. He requests an official ruling about it.[480]

Also, confession has not yet been repealed, which is contrary to the duke's mandate.[481]

1617 or later:

Concerning the request by the Honorable Sebastian, pastor in Finkenwerder, 1) that he has not been able to obtain his salary from the church council 2) that the parishioners from Hamburg, in spite of their sworn obligation to do so, have not given the money for the badly needed parsonage repairs, for heating the parsonage, and for contstructing necessary buildings.[482]

JUDGEMENT: It is hereby ordered 1) that the salary should be collected[483] by the church council members, 2) concerning the people of Hamburg, because they refused to pay, they should now have to pay double, 3) concerning construction, one should provide the wood and other necessary supplies and build and improve what is needed."

Other official records make public the names of previously unknown Finkenwerder pastors prior to Sebastian's tenure. Bodemann and Finder do name Otto Tynsdal as pastor in 1439, before the Reformation.[484] Tynsdal most likely comes from a Finkenwerder family whose name appears in the Finkenwerder church records for decades.

On December 11, 1571, Johann von Amsterdam is listed as pastor in Finkenwerder in conjunction with the leasing of church properties. He was also involved in the "missal incident." It is noteworthy, too, that in 1537, Johannes von Amsterdam signs the Schmalkald Articles, along with Urbanus Rhegius and other theologians. Johannes von Amsterdam signs for the city of Bremen. Thirty-four years separate the two dates. We have not researched whether both mentions are for the same person, however, it is probable that they come from the same family.

The synod of November 7, 1580 names Jörg Wiechmann pastor in Finkenwerder. How long Johann von Amsterdam and Jörg Wiechmann serve as pastors cannot be ascertained because they are listed only for the years provided above. An actual list of the Finkenwerder pastors is in Appendix 40.

Duke Otto II, Finkenwerder's Benefactor

Church accounting records are a fruitful source of information for those researching family and local history. Church accounting records go back further than other church record books. While the Finkenwerder church records list marriages, births, and deaths beginning in 1621, the church accounting records provide much valuable information about the three prior decades.[485]

The cover page of the church accounting records begun by Sebastian König reveals an interesting event from both a church and local history perspective: Duke Otto II donates 100 Gulden, a large sum for that time, to the church in Finkenwerder.

> "Soli Deo Gloria[486]
>
> Otto, the illuminating, noble Prince and Ruler of Braunschweig and Lüneburg, my Gracious Prince and Liege, on February 22, 1595 A.D.,[487] moved by multi-faceted, princely virtue, grants to the poor church of Finkenwerder, through his gentle, merciful goodness, 100 Gulden in order to pay off a large unpaid debt. Thus, Almighty God wants to bestow upon our Gracious Liege, a regency blessed by good fortune here on earth, a happy, just, long life; and after your earthly sojourn, everlasting complete bliss. Amen Amen Amen. p. 5"

ILLUSTRATION 83: Cover page of the Finkenwerder church accounting records. Duke Otto II is venerated for donating 100 Gulden to "the poor church," to be paid by someone else – because of a prior criminal act. Who is this? The church's accounts reveal the culprit in an encoded format.

The text suggests that something extraordinary must have happened here. Nevertheless, what is the reason for the duke's benevolent gift of 100 Gulden?[488] Sebastian König leaves us puzzled about the "excessive debt," even though he knows the particulars. It is a delicate matter that not everyone on the small island needs to know about. He places an encoded clue in the inconspicuous concluding remarks on "page 5:"[489]

"On February 22, 1595, Henneke Focken is indebted to the church in Finkenwerder – p.1, for 150 Lübsch Marks. Mainly, he is responsible for paying the church 9 lübisch Marks on "Petri Cath" (February 22)."

The note on p.1 refers to the Duke's gift. Within this note, the connection is disclosed. Henneke Focken must pay 150 Lübsch Marks. Since he has no money, nine lübisch Marks in interest are agreed upon.

After the last entry in the church accounting records cited above, it is immediately noted that in 1597 Hennecke Focken pays church members Peter Finck and Heine Wentgen the total amount of 150 Marks plus two year's interest.

Where does the money come from? We deduce the answer from the following entry, in which Jacob von Rigen owed the church 150 Lübsch Marks and has to pay nine Marks a year interest. The amount owed is always 150 Lübsch Marks. The answer is that Jacob von Rigen assumes Hennecke Focken's debt; simultaneously, Focken is relieved of it. The nine Marks annual interest is indeed paid to the church over the course of 19 years. Only in 1616 is Johann von Rigen's total debt paid off, and, to be sure, payment to Heine Wentgen and Johann König.[490] We learn afterward that the sum is "applied to" construction costs of the new church.

The criminal act itself is diplomatically handled by Sebastian König. He directly names neither the act nor the culprit. Only the agreement about sums and dates allows it to be determined that Hennecke Focken is indebted to Duke Otto for the stated amount. Otto waives the debt, to the benefit of the Finkenwerder church. Looking at the agreement from this standpoint, the duke is not spending any money, rather he is only waiving a claim.

Page 144

ILLUSTRATION 84: Portrait of Duke Otto
IVN, [Jr,], on the medallion from 1585.[491]

It often happens that criminal acts are settled monetarily. For example, Matthes, representing the dukes for the fiscal year 1548/49, agreed to accept payment of 306 lübisch Marks for "legal felonies" in lieu of a full payment of 5,246 lübisch Marks.[492]

An essential part of the church's accounts are various expenditures for construction and repair. For example, in 1600, "a barn for the pastorate is purchased," in 1604 a coal burning stove is installed in the parsonage, in 1607 the windows are repaired, and in 1608 a new sextonry is built.

In 1609 – 10, an event transpires that illustrates how things do not always go ideally and peacefully on Finkenwerder. According to church records, the bell tower is being repaired, and 13 Marks are being spent for oak shelves. Here is a letter evidently written by Sebastian König to Johan Bismarck, superintendent in Harburg. Sebastian intercedes on behalf of a carpenter who worked in the church and has been subjected to "disobedient, vile apprentices."[493] They beat the poor carpenter with a chair until he was black and blue, poured several tankards of beer on his face, and stabbed him "to the extent that he did not even have the strength to stand up. All the money he earned was consumed by his expenses related to the event."

The matter recorded in the church's accounts names Hans Basten. He brought the sealed letter to the Harburg office. Sebastian petitions the city council. The letter's very personal salutation allows us to assume that Sebastian has a good relationship with his superintendent in Harburg. The letter's salutation reads, "I wish Your Grace, your beloved wife, and your children a joyous New Year filled with blessed good fortune."

By examining the church's accounts, we get the impression that there are no existing procedural policies in matters like this. Up until the end of Sebastian's records in 1620, we never find a continuous record of income and dispersements, which are listed without differentiating among them. There are no totals or amounts listed. Assets and liabilities appear to be an unknown concept. We also see that the accounts have not been audited. If there is no payment, it is recorded as "unpaid debt" or along with the debtor's name, "indebtor." It is only much later, around 1660, that accounting is more exact. From 1660 on, compound interest is calculated and outstanding claims are noted.

Church Land – Leasing, Sale, Complex Entanglements

Bodemann reports that the church's assets are "insignificant," and the income so small that it seldom covers ongoing expenses. "Yes, the single piece of arable land, which the church previously owned in Osterfeld, and which in 1590 was still leased to Claus Hoppen for 5 Marks a year, is sold to Claus Hoppen in 1605 for 105 lübisch Marks.[494]

Page 145

Such a gift of fallow land as a liquid asset, which slips through the fingers, like a bird, never to return, has to appear to us as an immense lack of thought...[495] Pastor Evers also critically alludes to the sale.[496] He mistakenly lists 100 Marks instead of 100 Gulden, which corresponds to 150 lübisch Marks.[497]

Bodemann and Evers, both pastors in Finkenwerder, criticize the church's politics at that time as well as their predecessor, Sebastian König. We will try, with a look behind the scenes, to shed some light on these complex entanglements.

To which predecessors do the sale of church land pertain? The first entry in the church financial records states that the church land has been leased to Claus Hoppe since 1590:

> "On Michelmas in 1590, church council members Peter Fink, in the presence of Jacob van Rigen, the administrator; Heino Wulff; and Henneke Focken consent to lease out the church's entire acreage in Osterfeld to Claus Hoppen for 5 lübisch Marks per year."[498]

But Claus Hoppe does not pay on time. In the official record of the 1596 synod, Sebastian König reports that Hoppe has not paid for four years and his debt totals 20 Marks. The synod presents the matter to the duke and requests his decision.

The duke's intervention, effective in 1598, reveals that "the administrator should inform Claus Hobbe of Finkenwerder that he should deliver or pay the money to the church within 14 days or be taken by the head and immediately put in the stocks until he pays.[499] We do not know if this official threat was carried out. In any case, Claus Hoppe pays nothing until 1605.

Before the land is to be sold in 1605, there is a dispute in the congregation. Sebastian König writes to Hermann Möller, secretary at Schloss Harburg that "behind my back some of the people in Finkenwerder want to approve giving Claus Hoppen the land and want to deny my managing it in any way..."[500] The letter is available in Appendix 41.

The pastor would like to manage the land himself. Hoppe unites his friends among the farmers in opposition to Sebastian. In Sebastian's letter to Harburg, he reminds the duke's secretary that the deceased Duke Otto II summoned Hoppe to court and rendered a judgement against him. Sebastian hopes that "my gracious Prince and Liege," who is Duke Wilhelm since 1603, will not reverse Otto II's decision.

Once again, the matter is up to the duke to decide. The church's accounts verify that Hoppe certainly has not lived up to the conditions of the lease. But suddenly, he has the money to buy the church's land for 100 lübisch Marks and at the same time pay the outstanding leasing fee for 10 years (50 Marks), which is a total 150 lübisch Marks. The church members and Administrator Jacob van Rigen agree to the above. Finder remarks that the cost of protecting the church land in Osterfeld by building dikes is too great for the congregation to bear, and that is the reason to sell it.[501]

Page 146

Now Hoppe has his own land, yet, what happens to the proceeds? The church's accounts state: Sebastian König receives the money. Sebastian, in turn, uses some of the money to purchase an acre from Simon Küper, which he, Sebastian, may now manage.

From the money remaining after the land purchase from Simon Küper, Sebastian is to pay the church 7 Marks 8 Schillings tax, at the usual rate of 5%. He must fulfill the following conditions: "And these 150 Marks...should be paid back to the church on demand out of his own funds, be he living or dead, from his personal estate and his real estate."[502] He is liable with all his possessions.

No reason is stated why the pastor receives the proceeds from the sale of the church's land and from it buys a different parcel of land. Does he need land in order to feed his family, and does this give him persuasive arguments as he negotiates with Schloss Harburg?[503] After all, he can point out that the proceeds from management of the church's lands are part of his salary.

Sebastian has expressed the wish for his own land for quite some time. In 1604, he tries to acquire a parcel of land "...in order to be able to erect a home for his widow..."[504] From his parents' experience, he remembers all too well how unreliable it can be to receive assistance after serving the princes for years. Thus, he would like to provide a place for his wife to live in case he dies before she does.

The conditions under which Sebastian receives the money specify, to be sure, that he has to pay interest, but there is no mention of paying back the principal sum of 150 Marks. Sebastian has definitely paid the interest due to the church through the year 1606. From 1607 until his death, he no longer pays interest, but we find no evidence that anyone objects to this.

In 1620, Sebastian's handwritten church accounts cease without a specific conclusion. It is possible that he could not work any more due to illness. At that time, he is over 60 years old.

A handwritten entry by someone else first appears on January 18, 1632: "Let it be known that both appointed church members, Hinrich von Rigen and Johan von Rigen, on the one side, and on the other side, the heirs of the Honorable Sebastian Koning (Johan Koning, Hinrich Steers, and Johann Wulff) meet in the parsonage..."[505] They maintain that the amount of 150 Marks and annual taxes of 7 Marks 8 Schillings from 1607 onward are still due. Beginning in 1621, the year of Sebastian's death, the annual tax is raised to 9 Marks. The resulting taxes are 211 Marks 8 Schillings.

As a result of the discussion, it is ascertained that in 1607 Sebastian König paid 160 Marks 13 Schillings for repairs to the church's buildings and 50 Marks 11 Schillings to Jacob Decken, carpenter in Harburg, for work on the sextonry. With the disbursement of both these sums, the taxes are fully paid. Again, it is not a question of repaying the 150 Marks.

A full ten years later on January 9, 1642, the church council members again gather in the parsonage. Johann König, who is Sebastian's son and now Lüneburg administrator, is absent due to illness.[506] Gerd König (503), his brother and heir to the land, should pay 10 years' back taxes. Here, for the first time, the original sum of 150 Marks is demanded. Gerd has no money and is indebted for both sums.

Page 147

In 1650, a list of church claims is presented. The claim against Gerd König, who died in 1645, amounts to 150 Marks, plus 63 Marks in taxes dating back to 1644. Because of a calculation error, the sum is reduced by 9 Marks.[507] In 1650, the outstanding church claims are solidified.

In the following years up to and including 1663, Henneke Linneman pays an annual tax of 9 Marks. In 1647, he marries Gret-sche König (627), Gerd König's daughter, and becomes heir to the parcel of land as documented by his tax payments. Whether the 150 Marks are included can not be deduced from the present documents.

Are Evers' and Bodemann's previously mentioned criticism of Sebastian justified? One has to take into account the conditions at that time. That a money matter remains unregulated for so long can only be explained by the Zeitgeist [spirit of the times]. We have seen that the dukes themselves do not take the repayment of borrowed money very seriously. Lack of money is the constant companion of both those in power and the common folk. One gets the impression that indebtedness is completely normal and not at all a blemish on one's honor.

Between Spiritual Welfare, Dike Construction, and "Iron Cows"

The archives contain much information about church activities, quarrels among the inhabitants, and similar matters, but little about spiritual welfare itself. Other than Sebastian König's letters to the Harburg office, we have only his handwritten church accounting notes. In 1621, his successor starts compiling the register that lists weddings, baptisms, and causes of death, from which some things about life and death can be inferred.

The register shows the high child motality rate, the frequent deaths of young mothers in childbirth, and frequent loss of possessions and goods during storm surges, but the human suffering and the material hardship of the time remain mostly hidden from us. Sebastian is not an eloquent writer like his grandfather, Urbanus Rhegius, who left us over 100 writings. Rather, he seems to be a practical man of action, a helping hand. On one of the islands in the Elbe dominated by Mother Nature's power, one does not live in the "ivory tower of science," but one is immersed in life. Sebastian may often remember his grandfather, who warns in a 1522 sermon that on judgement day God will not ask how much you have prayed in church, but whether you have fed the hungry.[508]

We find Sebastian anywhere people need someone who can read and write. He is probably the only person on the island who can do so. Then there are the money problems of the farmers to solve, questions of inheritance to administer, and disputes among the residents to settle. He even has to deal with questions about the dikes. Next to the administrator, the pastor is the one the residents can turn to in all cases. People from the time of the Reformation are used to the church's dominant authority. Thus, the clergy continue to fulfill these traditional roles for many years.

Only once do we read about a sermon of Sebastian's. In 1762, Pastor Evers reports in his previously cited manuscript: "In 1613 he (Sebastian) preaches at the Harburg Synod,[509] as noted by Preacher Theodoricus Möller in an annual report from the synod." Theodoricus Möller is pastor in Sinstorf from 1604 to 1629. There should be more documents written by him, but in spite of our numerous efforts to find them, we are unable to do so.[510] His handwritten documents were most likely destroyed in a 1630 Sinstorf fire.[511]

Page 148

At the end of his notes, Pastor Evers paints an impressive picture of his own and his predecessor's experiences in Finkenwerder. He writes that it is not a prime location for a preacher to live, because the residents "do not become more docile" as a result of their numerous misfortunes. The residents have, at times, come to church with axes and knives and he himself sometimes in 1762 still notices large knives in the confessional. Thefts and lewdness also occur. At the death of Evers' predecessor's predecessor, Pastor Oberbeck (1742), no one had a Bible. The schoolmaster at the time was threatened with a beating if he required the children to learn Bible verses. He praises the island people's industrious work ethic because one would either have to starve or move away. "The richest land owner works side by side with his serfs." We include Evers' conclusions in Appendix 42.

In 1617, 1621, and 1622, Duke Wilhelm gives detailed instructions to his pastors about how he wants God to be worshipped.[512] In the office, there should be no reprimanding and unnecessary quarreling. Rather, the sick should be visited, the Catechism duly respected in all congregations, and sermons should be easy to understand. In Altenwerder and Finkenwerder the Catechism should be read aloud in the afternoons. The pastors are ordered to report various items of information to Harburg, for example, whether during the service beer and brandy are drunk by the parishioners.

The duke's orders contain two important dates for Finkenwerder: "Sextons are to be installed"[513] (instruction from 1617) and "a book is to be kept at every church in which the names of the children who are baptized, people who take communion,[514] and people who die are listed." This is the instruction for starting a church register. Sebastian's successor, Pastor Schulze, starts one on November 4, 1621 in Finkenwerder. The first one in Alterwerder begins in 1641.

In the first year of his time in Finkenwerder Sebastian König already experiences a taste of the problems that will often occupy him. On May 23, 1594 two high officials from the Harburg office, Marschallek Melchior von Lohe and Trobaldus Grummer, come to the parsonage to hold a meeting of Simon Külper's creditors, who are also church members.

A total debt of 2,401.2.6 Marks has accumulated.[515] Negotiations reduce the amount owed to creditors in Hamburg, Sinstorf, Altenwerder, and Finkenwerder to 2,161.11.6 Marks. The pastor is to retain 8 Schillings for recording the agreement. The high officials from Harburg insist that Simon Külper must sell five tracts of land, thereby giving Finkenwerder the certainty that its dikes are free from outside creditors. Five interested farmers are immediately found who will draw lots to purchase the five parcels of land.[516] The purchase price is 300 lübisch Marks per tract. Incidental expenses total 99.8 Marks. Sebastian König is assigned to reconcile these amounts. He gets entangled in the financial settlements.

Page 149

We did not investigate the subsequent developments in this matter, but it is conceivable that out of the 1605 sale of church land, Sebastian König buys a parcel from Simon Külper. From this, we can conclude that Sebastian König has a renewed need for money.

A second case of excessive debt involving the court appears in 1594. This time, in 1629, Hermann Külper, also called Harm or Harmen, is listed as a building sub-contractor.[517] The meeting of the creditors takes place on August 14, 1594 in the parsonage. The debts have risen to 1,697.1 Marks. Negotiations with the creditors reduce the debt to 1,391.9.6 Marks.

Among the list of creditors we find Sebastian König is owed 61.10 Marks – a considerable sum. In payment of this amount, wood is to be delivered. Surprisingly, Sebastian is listed as a land purchaser. To pay off his debts, Hermann Külper must have agreed to sell various parcels of land: One of them is bought by Sebastian König.

"...[Hermann Külper] relinquished and then sold to Mr. Sebastian König, ½ Morgen and 55 Ruhtten of land.

Harmen Külper, in the legal bill of sale with the pastor, has a maximum of three years to pay the debt to the three buyers and reclaim the land."[518]

Sebastian is to pay 191 Marks for this land. Bodemann mentions that in 1629 Sebastian's wife, Susanna, owns land from the former property of the building sub-contractor Harm Külper, so that the land stays in the König family.[519] How can Sebastian come up with this considerable sum? We assume that he marries for a second time in Finkenwerder and the money is possibly part of his second wife's dowry.

The end of the creditors' statement indicates that the pastor should receive 10 Marks, because the creditors' meeting takes place in the parsonage. For most of the creditors, a lot of money is at stake, thus, we can imagine the lively to boisterous arguments that take place. Ten Marks for hosting the meeting is a large sum, when one thinks, for example, that at that time, a cow costs about 20 Marks. The meeting lasts a long time and the pastor's wife certainly has to continuously provide food and an ample supply of drinks.[520]

There are many reasons for the farmers' financial distress. Farming using one's own money was and is fraught with risk. In Finkenwerder, floods from storm surges add to the danger. In his impressive portrayal of Mother Nature, Harold Schloz skillfully describes the circumstances that have existed since the 12TH century.[521]

A few years before Sebastian arrives in Finkenwerder, the All Saint's Day Flood of November 1, 1570 ravages the entire North Sea coast from France to Denmark... "after which other deluges occurred. It originates with a northwest wind at the time of the new moon and is then reinforced by a surging tide. On the night of October 25, 1570, a terrible storm began, so that several ships in the Elbe capsized. Near Hamburg, the dikes broke...No man had ever experienced such storm surges. The floods came unceasingly one after the other and did not recede."[522]

The chroniclers all report the rebuilding of the dikes on the Hamburg side of the island – shown on Lorich's 1568 Elbkarte [Map of the Elbe] as "unprotected." Certainly, from 1603 – 1612,[523] the construction of a dike on the Lüneburg side in Osterfeld was joined with the existing dike on the western half of the island belonging to Lüneburg. The realization of this huge project is credited to Duke Wilhelm of Braunschweig and Lüneburg, who in 1603 takes over the reign of his deceased father, Duke Otto II.

Page 150

On May 30, 1600, Sebastian König reminds the secretary of the Harburg office that he has already spoken to him about building the dike. The people from Hamburg, including Harburg officials, must come to Finkenwerder to contribute their expertise and to begin making decisions at the site.

It is further reported in the letter that Michael Witte of the Lüneburger Deichverband [dike association] would like to be included, however, his brother Claus Witte, the administrator of the Hamburg side, would not allow this.[524] In 1600 there is already talk about a dike association on both sides of the island. There is evidence that the common dike project was in the planning stages or actually begun during Duke Otto II's lifetime, possibly at the urging of Wilhelm, who in 1600 was not yet ruler. The letter mentioned is in Appendix 43.

On February 14, 1602, the so-called Fastelabendsflut [Flood on the Evening of Lent] breaks out over the Elbe islands, followed by a summer storm on August 15, 1602. Both events may have encouraged the dike construction to proceed as quickly as possible. Considering the limited technical capabilities of that era, one certainly has to recognize the superhuman effort required from the island's inhabitants since every new storm surge would adversely affect the construction already completed.

We learn about the Flood on the Evening of Lent indirectly from Sebastian König's February 7, 1609 letter to Johann Bismarck, Lüneburg superintendent in Harburg. Sebastian urgently advocates for making necessary repairs. It is pouring down rain. The church's roof is leaking. Strangers are coming to the church, "who have already suffered enough." His rooms are "so miserable" because of "the great floods recurring for the last seven years."[525] The damage has not been repaired since that time.

What does it look like in Finkenwerder in the decade of major dike construction? By far, the greater part of the work is being done on the Hamburg side, but inhabitants of all divisions of the island are engaged in this project. As the only pastor on the island, Sebastian is called upon to listen to and settle many disputes. Certainly everyone is pleased when the work is finally completed. As cited previously, when Sebastian is permitted to preach at the 1613 Harburg Synod, it may be in recognition of his untiring effort during these years.

Meanwhile, the new dike does not protect the inhabitants from more havoc. Finder reports that in the next two centuries 64 dam burstings and ship capsizings are recorded.[526] In fact, a few years after completion, Duke Wilhelm has already begun lodging complaints about the dike's neglected condition. He writes on March

20, 1619 "to the pastor in Finckenwärder, the Honorable Sebastian König, to warn you seriously about our people in Finckenwärder. In no other place is there such laxity and disobedience by some of our people as in Finckenwärder." The dike association members are elected, but are assigned no specific duties and no oath of support is required of them. The duke wants to bring attention to these conditions once again, however, "the pastor is instructed to warn our subjects and to report such people to the dike association, which is entrusted with rectifying the matters."[527] The letter is reproduced in Appendix 44.

Duke Wilhelm energetically intercedes from Harburg. He wants his work to be protected and to have it saved. If the harvests are wiped out by catastrophic floods, the farmers cannot afford to pay their taxes. The duke is not opposed to the election of the members of the dike association, but the pastor should see to it that the "right" people are chosen.

Page 151

Since the pastor is assigned multiple duties, one might assume he would receive additional compensation, but from all appearances, that is not the case. No definite amount of compensation is specified. The pastor's salary in the duchy of Lüneburg is derived from three combined sources. First, there is the so-called quarterly payment described in Sebastian König's previously cited letter of April 12, 1588. Secondly, the pastor may cultivate church land. The so-called "support fees" for official duties such as baptisms, weddings, funerals, and confessions constitute the third source.

The regulations consequently result in each pastor's income being highly variable, depending on the largess of the land owner and the number of official duties requested by the members of the congregation.[528] The situation depicted in the previous chapter regarding land clarifies once again how important the land income is from the clergy's overall perspective. It shows why Sebastian receives replacement compensation when the land is sold.

The 1667 Harburg Erbregister [inheritance register] for Finkenwerder indicates that three acres of land belong to the parsonage.[530] The land is plowed and harvested without pay by renters from both sides of the island, in accordance with their long-standing duties. The pastor himself sows the seeds. From their own harvests, main tenants bring a whole Dieman [haystack] of oats or barley to the parsonage and sub-tenants bring a half haystack.[531]

Bodemann reports on the parsonage's income in 1626.[532] We hear about corn, smoked meat, pigs' heads, and homemade breads being delivered. At Easter, every main tenant must bring 20 eggs to the parsonage and every sub-tenant must bring 10.

ILLUSTRATION 85: The church district circa 1600. 1) Old parsonage, 2) Lüneburg cemetery with the old church (up until 1881), 3) parsonage land which the pastor farms, 4) parsonage meadow, 5) church land sold to Claus Hoppe, 6) the current church with parsonage[529] (Drawing by Ria Henning).

The parsonage has much in common with a farm. One is reminded of Katharina von Bora, Luther's wife, who manages the household with great skill and diligence and knows how to make something out of everything in the garden. Sebastian certainly has a horse because how else can he get to Harburg when he has business at the office? And, in the stalls are two "Eiserne Kühe [iron cows], which, according to Pastor Schulze, have belonged to the parsonage since time immemorial.

The "iron cows" are a definite "iron clad" component of Sebastian's salary. That is the way it is in Finkenwerder up until Sebastian's time. The congregation must continually provide the pastor with two cows. If the cows are no longer giving milk and breeding, they have to be replaced with new cows.

Page 152

When Pastor König dies in 1621, the congregation's two cows are sold. His successor, Pastor Schulze, (506), does not have the cows as part of his salary. He complains about this in a detailed report, unfortunately undated, addressed to the "Honorable Administrator of the principality of Braunschweig-Lüneburg in Finkenwerder." The administrator is his brother-in-law, Johann König (501), whose sister Ilsche König, marries Pastor Schulze. His request is approved by order of the administrator:

> "Upon studying my brother-in-law's genuine and excellent report stating that the Lüneburg congregation members in Finkenwerder are not fulfilling their pledges to the pastor for an unthinkable amount of time, in order to improve his living conditions from this date forward, and to honor with Christian gratitude a valid debt, it is hereby recommended that he keep two good cows, called 'iron cows.' They are truly immortal because they never should have been taken away from the pastor." [533]

Pastor Schulze reports that the cows were sold for 40 Marks and from that sum, two other cows can be bought. He profusely explains that he did not receive a cent and that he himself has bought two cows, but they died. He tenaciously pursues the claim, from which we can conclude how important the cows are to his ability to get by. On June 30, 1633, Administrator Johann König is authorized to henceforth procure the cows for the pastor.

Whether all this is enough to provide sufficient income is hard to judge. The only sure thing is that the pastor has to earn his money twice – once as a theologian in the pulpit and pastor of the congregation and one more time farming the land and making use of what is produced. He has to earn it himself, earn it twice, because he receives no pay for his preaching. So we see Sebastian not only as pastor, but also, in the spring, striding across the land, hands outstretched, sowing seeds. In the fall, he is in the barn threshing. Toward winter, he is dividing up feed for pigs and splitting wood for fires in the kitchen and living space. Early in the morning and in the evenings he has to milk the "iron cows." On Easter, the pastor's wife stands astonished before the "blessing of eggs." Incidentally, a bemused Finder reports that some of the farmers who have to provide the pastor with half a pig's head, keep the meat for themselves and deliver the bones to the pastor.

Donated 400 Years Ago - The Finkenwerder Altar Candle Holders

On the altar of the church in Finkenwerder stand two bronze candle holders that were donated in 1604. Each stands 33.5 cm high and weighs 2 kg. Their craftsmanship is admirable.[534]

They are the oldest altar objects in Finkenwerder. They have withstood wars and the turbulence of time. They have now served the congregation for 400 years. At the time they were donated, the old church still is standing. It is the one Lorich shows on his 1568 Map of the Elbe. They adorn the altars of the churches built in 1617 under Sebastian König, 1756 under Pastor Evers, and finally 1881 under Pastor Bodemann. The candle holders are always there. In spite of their importance, the congregation members are not particularly conscious of them. Evers does not mention them at all. Bodemann only alludes to them in a footnote, without naming either the altar or the donor.[535]

The candle holders are noted for the first time by Ewald Goltz in his 1981 work: *St. Nikolai-Kirche in Hamburg-Finkenwerder – Geschichte und Geschichten* [History and Stories]. Goltz makes a systematic, permanent, itemized list and mentions the candle holders with their donation information:

HONORABLE BASTIANUS.REGIUS.CLAUS.SUFRIAN. DE.HABEN.DISN.LUCHTER.VOR.ERT.DERKARKEN. ANNO. 1.6.0.4.

Honorable Sebastian Regius, Claus Sufrian first acknowledge these candle holders in 1604 and

PETER.FINK.UND.JACOB.VAN.RIGE.DE.HABEN.VOR. ERT.DISEN.LUCHTER.DER.KARKEN.ANNO.1.6.0.4.

Peter Fink and Jacob Van Rigen first acknowledge these candle holders in 1604.

Peter Fink at that time is a member of the church council. He is in this position for at least 27 years. Between 1590 and 1617 he is mentioned more often in the church accounts and correspondence than any other person. Jacob van Rigen is named as Lüneburg administrator from 1597 to 1616. Both are Sebastian's companions for many years.

ILLUSTRATION 86: The Finkenwerder candle holder from 1604. Produced by Bastianus Regius, master bell caster Claus Sufrian, church administrator Peter Fink, and Lüneburg Administrator Jacob van Rigen. It is only here that Sebastian König uses his former name of "Regius."

Claus Sufrian is the bell caster who completed his master's examination in Hamburg in 1595.[536] He executes several works for St.

Jacobi in Hamburg, including two candle holders in 1596 – 97.[537] If a pastor and master bell caster work together, they must know each other well. It is important for a bell caster to stay in contact with the pastors and hope new bells are needed in the future. It is not known whether Claus Sufrian is still active in 1617 and casts the bells for the new church.

It is noteworthy that in 1604, when Sebastian has been in Finkenwerder for 16 years, he has his old family name of Regius engraved on the candle holders. We do not know his motivation. The following is speculation. After so many years in which he does not see his home, is he fulfilling a wish to identify once again with his origins and his family? Does he this time at least want to leave a record of the old name in Finkenwerder? For research into the family geneology, his decision is a stroke of luck, because it shows that Bastianus Regius and Sebastian König are one and the same person.

Page 154

What can be the reason for the bequest? Is there a special occasion in 1604, an abundant harvest, the lucky survival of a storm surge, a plague that is overcome? No horrendous event is known, and the donors have left no record behind. A possible answer may lie in other happenings at the time. In the previous year, on October 20, 1603, Duke Otto II dies after reigning for 54 years. Sebastian König must have been present and representing the Finkenwerder Church at his burial celebration on November 24. He takes part in the funeral procession along with his pastoral colleagues from the other Harburg congregations, according to the protocol: "...the clergy walk in pairs. They are each to give the honorable superintendent and the head court pastor a "Milreis"[538] [1,000 Reals] or one and one-half Thaler. They also have to give the school boys, organists, and others a Thaler."[539] The money that Sebastian gives is probably collected from the Finkenwerder congregation members because the amount does not appear in the church accounts. If one considers that daily amounts are reckoned in pennies, then the expected amount cited here is a large sum!

The funeral order of procession is proscribed in minute detail in the court's protocol. The invited participants have to inform the parade officers beforehand how many horses they intend to bring so that the animals can be taken care of and sheltered. At 10 am, a bell is rung and the procession forms. It is led by a jousting steed with a noble boy in full Kürass [cuirass: a piece of armor consisting of breastplate and backplate fastened together] next to the band, followed by more horses decorated with the Braunschweig, Lüneburg, and other coats of arms.

The pastors, as spiritual leaders, are placed near the head of the procession, before the casket. Also ahead of the casket are noble boys and standard bearers on horseback, "...the princely casket follows. It is draped with a long black velvet coverlet upon which is sewn a cross of white silken satin, on the front of which is the entire coat of arms embroidered in gold..." The coffin is carried by 12 nobles. As in a pageant, they are announced by name and followed by 12 noble torch bearers and the duke's family. Naturally, the dukes von Braunschweig and Lüneburg from Celle and Wolfenbüttel are present as well as the bishops of Verden and Minden, mayor and city council of Hamburg, dukes, counts, nobles, and representatives of many Evangelisch countries and cities.

ILLUSTRATION 87: Duke Otto II dies on October 20, 1603 at Schloss Harburg. Pastor Sebastian König participates in the internment celebration as the clerical representative of Finkenwerder. Above the engraving of the duke it reads, "OTTO IVN. D. BR. ET. LVN" (Otto II, Duke of Braunschweig and Lüneburg).[540]

What an impression all this must make on Sebastian: the duke's huge household, the ingeniously planned ceremony, the solemn quiet, the respectful words! Added to all this are the meetings with the rulers of neighboring countries, whom Sebastian has only known through hearsay. It is probably the deepest experience of his professional life.

When Duke Wilhelm and his brother Christoph take over, they probably govern jointly.[541]

Page 155

Duke Wilhelm capably takes on the reclamation project surrounding all of Finkenwerder. An atmosphere of gratitude and fundamental change emanates from the experience of Duke Otto II's funeral, the homage to the new rulers, and construction of the huge dikes. It is comforting to consider that the idea of casting the altar candle holders originates from this mood.

In the meantime, the candle holders themselves have their own moving history. In November 1839, they are stolen from the church. Apparently, while fleeing from a flash flood, the thieves hastily throw them into one of the canals that separate tracts of land. Decades later, excavation in the canal brings the candle holders to the surface.[542] Pastor Bodemann writes in his 1860 book, *Memories of the Elbe Island of Finkenwerder*, that the candle holders are back.[543] It can therefore be deduced that at the very latest, the candle holders were recovered around 1860.

The Year 1617 – A New Church and a Larger Congregation

Toward the end of his tenure as pastor, when Sebastian is about 60 years old, he is confronted with two huge tasks that will demand all his energy. The church, date of construction unknown, has been in disrepair for a long time. It was possibly erected in 1400 or shortly thereafter. There is a clue in the August 21, 1400 will of Hamburg resident Timm von Urden. He claims to have paid "10 Marks Pfennige" to help build a church in Finkenwerder.[544]

Repairs no longer suffice. Building a new church must be envisioned. A similar situation confronts the congregation in Nienstedten, whose residents belong to the Hamburg side of Finkenwerder. The Nienstedten chronicle states: "In those times, the Elbe must have had to flow through a much smaller channel, so narrow, that at the time, the Finkenwerder parishioners could request a bridge be built to Nienstedten. But the Elbe expanded due to the Hamburg dike construction and political considerations fueled by regulations of river traffic on Hamburg's main waterway to the Northern Elbe. The result is that Finkenwerder's marshes are gradually sacrificed to the floods. Nienstedten residents were forced to pull back to the north. The aforementioned can also be concluded from the church's history. In 1589/90, the cemetery around the church has to be elevated. In 1596, the tower collapses and is rebuilt in 1602. In 1636, the 'new church' on its present site is mentioned."[545] Thus, the people in Nienstedten must also be concerned about rebuilding.

In the three decades of his pastorate on Finkenwerder, Sebastian experiences how laborious, even dangerous, it is at times for residents of the Hamburg side to fulfill their religious rights and obligations on the other bank. In all kinds of wind and weather, they have to cross the water to attend Sunday services, christening celebrations, and emergency baptisms. They attend wedding celebrations – with their many merry-making river crossings. Also, the deceased have to be taken across the river in rowboats or sailboats. Lastly, it is often impossible to cross the Elbe in winter when it is full of ice.

The Nienstedten residents, who live on the Hamburg side of Finkenwerder, wish to share the costs of building a new church, however, the discussion soon shifts to whether it is wise to join with the southern half of the island to build a new church there.

The logic of the issue is often different from people's emotions and customs. In the church, which the people of Hamburg-Finkenwerder now attend, hang portraits of the dukes zu Braunschweig and Lüneburg, as well as the brothers Wilhelm, Otto III, and Johannes.[546]

Page 156

Braunschweig and Lüneburg are far removed from the Hamburg-Finkenwerder residents since they have been subjects of the Counts zu Holstein for centuries. Their memories are of "their" church, where they were baptized, confirmed, and married, and where they buried their mother and father.

The diplomatic issues are quite delicate. If their residents want to be included in a different church organization, the Hamburg mayor and city council members must agree to it. The Hamburg city council wants to avoid a disagreement with the Danish court. The city council values this relationship so highly, it will not allow the contract to be signed without "connivendo." [547] Bodemann calls it "...to close one eye and look through the fingers with the other..."

Also, the congregation from Nienstedten does not want to agree to the contract without obtaining some sign of approval from the Hamburg or Danish authorities. The Danish authorities are not willing to give up all their longstanding claims against Finken-werder-Nienstedten. For many years, the Danish authorities demand money from Finkenwerder-Nienstedten. Finally, in 1881 Hamburg pays 1,800 Reichsmarks to Finkenwerder-Nienstedten and settles all longstanding claims.[548]

In this situation, Sebastian and the Harburg office are faced with the task of finding workable solutions acceptable to three governmental parties and preparing a contract which two of the parties will not sign, but rather simply tolerate.

We can well imagine how Sebastian is rowed in a boat across the Elbe to Nienstedten, then talks again with representatives of the Hamburg side of Finkenwwerder, and finally, rides on horseback to Harburg with the results in order to obtain an agreement. He receives a great deal of help from his older son, Johann, who has been married to Ilsche Fock since 1607. She is the daughter of Simon Fock, the former Lüneburg administrator. In the meantime, Johann has a position representing the church at court.

Everything is finally settled on March 17, 1617. Duke Wilhelm signs the contract for the Harburg office. For the Lüneburg side, Administrator Simon Fock, Heine Wenten, Hinrich von Riegen, Johann von Riegen, and Johann König are present. Representing

Hamburg are Heinrich Rust, Hermann Wulff, Heine von Riegen, and Jacob Finke. The "Hamburg subjects" are accepted into "Your Princely Grace's church in Finkenwerder" for all time. The Hamburg subjects' rights and responsibilities are to be the same as those of the Lüneburg residents on the other side.

The clergy of the now united island are also taken care of in the contract – "...annually or on Christmas they receive 12 lübisch Schillings and a piece of ox meat that has been dried and smoked on a wooden rack[549] and is good enough to make broth out of. They also receive all things that are necessary in advice and service, be they horses, wagons, or plows...plus they provide all things desired by the church and their personnel..."[550] These orders are issued to the new members of the congregation on the Hamburg side. For Sebastian, who has often had reason to complain about his small income over the years, it means his situation is improved by the growth of his congregation and by the new items of practical assistance. In 1617, the size of the Lüneburg congregation is estimated to be 400 members, in addition to 200 – 250 members from Hamburg.[551] From these numbers, Sebastian's income from the congregation has increased by about 50%.

Page 157

There is nothing in the archives about the rebuilding of the church in 1617. The chroniclers Evers, Bodemann, and Finder do mention the church, but they do not know the dates, size, cost, or appearance. In our search for an illustration, we ran across a small drawing from the 1650 *Nobilis Fluvius Albis* [*The Noble Elbe River*][552] by Merian.

ILLUSTRATION 88: There is no definitive visual
representation of the church that was built in 1617. Merian's
small drawing of 1650: NOBILIS FLUVIUS ALBIS
shows a simple church in the middle of Finkenwerder
Island, probably with its bell tower. In comparison,
the church in Altenwerder is definitely larger.

Other than that, the only remaining memory of the church appears
to be what Bodemann deduced from later church financial records.
In addition to the previously cited portrait of the duke, he names
three more paintings that are in the church in 1617, "...which were
cherished by friends in Hamburg: *die Verkündigung Mariä* [*Mary's
Announcement*]; the *Ecce Agnus Dei*; and the *Hirten zu Bethlehem* [*Shep-
herds' Arrival in Bethlehem*]." The paintings had been placed in the
pastor's widow's house following demolition of the old church. In
the flood of October 7, 1756, the house was inundated, and all the
paintings drifted away."[553]

Bodemann reports: "There was a tower near the church in 1568.
Without a doubt, there was also one by the church in 1617, because
in 1659, there is a statement about the tower, and in 1676 the tower
is described as being very dilapidated." Also, according to the new
church's bills, the wood from the old tower is sold. That means the
old church must have been dismantled at the same time the new one
is built.[554]

Does this limited information allow us to conclude that the church
built in 1617 is similar to the one that Lorich drew in his *Map of the
Elbe* in 1568? The Harburg Church's financial resources are extremely
limited, so that a simple building with a separate tower to the side,

perhaps with only a belfry, suffices. It is evident that construction costs are cut because just a few decades later extensive repairs have to be made. In a contract between the Lüneburg and Hamburg sides dated September 9, 1672, an "extremely run-down" church is discussed.[555]

However limited our picture of this church may be and however modest the church building is, we are able to conclude from it that Sebastian is satisfied with "his" church and that uniting the people of the island into one congregation is the realization of his personal dream. That both happened exactly 100 years after the beginning of the Reformation may be a special joy to him.

Duke Wilhelm in Harburg may also look favorably upon the unification of the two congregations because it helps him increase his influence.

ILLUSTRATION 89: The church built in Finkenwerder in 1756 probably looks similar to its predecessor of 1647.

Page 158

Susanna Outlives Her Husband by Ten years, But Who Is She? (403 on the family tree)

PASTOR SEBASTIAN KÖNIG DIES AFTER 33 YEARS OF SERVICE

The joy of building the new church and the increasing size of the congregation have hardly passed when the first clouds of a mighty catastrophe, later called the Dreissigjährigen Krieg [Thirty Years' War], appear on the horizon. With the Fenstersturz zu Prag [Defenestration of Prague] on May 23, 1618, a process is set in motion that will devastate the country and bring unending suffering to the nations, a religious war that will alter the religious and political map of Europe.

Sebastian is about ten years old in 1569 when his grandmother, Anna Weissbrücker, dies in Celle. She could have told Sebastian about the beginning of the Reformation – her husband's struggle to negotiate his way between Zwingli and Luther, as well as the Imperial Diet in Augsburg where the Augsburg Confession was presented to the emperor and to which his grandfather, Urbanus, contributed. In three generations, the Reformation has become part of the family history. Now, at the end of his life, Sebastian sees that everything is in danger of collapse.

In the 1620 church accounting records, we find his last handwritten notes. After 33 years of serving his first and only congregation, he dies on Finkenwerder Island in the Elbe. His family establishes roots there. His oldest son, Johann, is the Lüneburg administrator and begins a four generation family tradition of serving the Guelph princes. In 1622, his daughter, Ilsche, marries Sebastian's successor. Nothing more is known about the circumstances of Sebastian's death. He is at least 62 years old in 1621, possibly even three or four years older.

His successor, Pastor Johann Schulze, assumes the position on November 4, 1621. Schulze notes the beginning of the first Finkenwerder church records. Where is Sebastian buried? He rests in peace either in the Finkenwerder Cemetery or in the church built in 1617. There is solid evidence for the latter possibility.

Evers reports about Johann Schulze, Sebastian's successor. "In 1646 Schulze's gravestone indicates his remains are in the former church."[556] If the gravestone stands in the church, that also means he is buried there.

Michael Pflug, Pastor Schulze's successor, "...constructs his own gravesite for himself and his family under the pulpit of the old church, where he is then buried on May 17, 1714."

If succeeding pastors are laid to rest in the church, it is very possible that Sebastian König is also buried there, since the church was constructed during his tenure as pastor.

It is a shame and may even be an injustice that the pastors' wives in the first decades of church records are listed only by their first names. For example, they are often mentioned simply as "Hans Harmen's wife" or "Jacob von Rigen's widow." For those tracing family geneaology, the above mentioned procedure makes matching the wives to their proper families more difficult. Such is the case with Susanna, Sebastian's wife.

Little is known about Susanna. Her death is listed in the Finkenwerder church records as February 11, 1631. Her name is mentioned in the bell registry in 1631. She survives her husband by about 10 years.

Page 159

A reference to Susanna is found in Bodemann, who cites a 1629 note by Pastor Schulze in which the land cultivated by Susanna's husband is said to be "subdivided."

> "Simon Külper's pasture land is now in the hands of many people. Present occupants are: 1) Hinrich Focke, 2) Carsten Bannit, 3) Peter Meyenschin, 4) Berend Külper,

5) Susanna Königes.

Sub-tenant farmer Harm Külper's pasture land is then "sub-divided" among 1) Harm Külper 8 heaps of sheaves plus 2 sheaves of oats, 2) Carsten Bannit 8 heaps of sheaves, 3) Susanna Königes 5 1/2 heaps of sheaves, 4) Peter Tinsdahl."[557]

Susanna therefore owns land that formerly belongs to Simon and Harm Külper. This fact could indicate that Susanna belongs to the Külper family. Both Külper properties are in financial difficulty in 1594. Sebastian König buys a parcel of land from Simon Külper in 1605. Can we surmise that Sebastian buys the land in order to lighten the Külper brothers' financial burden because his wife is a Külper?

Further possibilities about Susanna's heritage are connected to the von Rigen, Köpke, Finke, and especially the Steers families. Susanna's younger son is named Gerd. This name is not common on Finkenwerder Island, but it does occur in the families named above. A Gerd von Rigen appears in 1600 in Alten Land. From 1653 – 1691 there are Gerth von Rigens, father and son, on Finkenwerder. From 1657 – 1686 Gerd Köpke, father and son, live on the island. In 1630, a Gerd Finke dies, and in 1642, a Gerd Finke is born. That Susanna may originate from these families is a possibility, but not conclusive.

Susanna's clearest ties are to the Steers family. On August 7, 1628 Peter Steers' wife, Susanna, dies. This is the first time the uncommon name Susanna appears in the Finkenwerder records. On September 15, 1639 Johan Steers is baptized. Johann König is his godfather and gives him his name. At their marriage in 1646, Carsten Mewes and Cillie Steers, have three pairs of godparents. Ilsche König becomes godmother to Armgard in 1647 and to Illsche Mewes in 1650. Both godmother and godchild again share the same name.

As already stated in this text, the church registry indicates that Hinrich Steers is a designated heir of Sebastian and Susanna. This fact further documents the close family connection.[558] Peter Steers' wife, Susanna, could be a cousin of Sebastian's wife, Susanna, and both could have been named for a common grandmother. Many genealogical puzzles can be solved by tracing who is named after whom. Perhaps conclusive agreement is reached whenever help comes fortuitously or from an expert reader.[559]

In the chapter, "It Started with a Call for Help from Harburg," we establish that Susanna cannot be a native of Finkenwerder, since her oldest son, Johann, is born in 1587 and Sebastian is still in Strassburg in the fall of 1586. It therefore follows that Susanna must be Sebastian's second wife. There are two almost conclusive clues that support this supposition:

· Gerd König (503) inherits previously mentioned land from his mother, Susanna.

· Gerd marries on November 18, 1621 and names his daughter Sanna (Susanna). Sanna is born on July 28, 1622. At that time, the custom for naming children is:

   · The oldest son is named after the paternal grandfather.

   · The oldest daughter is named after the paternal grandmother.

   · The second son is named after the maternal grandfather.

   · The second daughter is named after the maternal grandmother.

Gerd König obviously names his children according to this rule because his daughter is named Sanna and his son is Bastian. When his daughter, Sanna, dies on January 27, 1624, and a second daughter is born on April 7, 1629, she is also named Sanna. We can see that it is very important to Gerd that his mother's name be carried on.

How does Gerd's naming compare to that of his older brother, Johann? Johann also follows tradition and names his son after his father, Sebastian, however, there is no Susanna among Johann's daughters because he has a different mother than his brother, Gerd. She is his father, Sebastian's, first wife. Sebastian's second marriage in Finken-werder also clarifies his interrelationships with the local families, his land holdings, and his lifelong residence on the island in the Elbe.

Children of Pastor Sebastian König
(401 on the family tree)

The children's birth order is recorded, except for the first born, Johann.

1.	Johann König (501).	Born January 10, 1587. Dies June 28, 1649.
		Circa "Jacobi" [July 25TH – the Holy Day of the Apostle Jakobus], 1607 marries Ilsche Fock (502). She is born approximately 1586. Dies December 19, 1667 "at about 81 years old." Daughter of Administrator Simon Fock.
		More about Johann in the following chapter.

2. Gerd König (503)

Birthdate unknown. Dies April 27, 1645.

Marries November 18, 1621 Gretsche Focken (504). She is born approximately 1599. Dies April 27, 1645. Daughter of Administrator Simon Fock.

The brothers Johann and Gerd König marry the sisters Ilsche and Gretsche Fock.

More about Gerd König and his descendants in Appendix 45.

3. Ilse König (Ilsche) (505)

Born approximately 1603. Dies February, 24, 1657.

1622 marries Pastor Johann Schulze (506). He is born approximately 1585, probably in Salzwedel. Dies October 2, 1646 in Finkenwerder at age 61.

Pastor Schulze is a descendant of Sebastian König. His first entry in the church record book is the wedding of his brother-in-law, Gerd König.

It has already been noted that Pastor Sebastian König may have had other children by both his first and second wives. These children may have died before 1621 or have eventually married and moved to other congregations. In both instances, the children would not be included in the Finkenwerder church registry. It is also possible that there are other daughters who are listed only by their first names in the church registry.

Johann König (1587 – 1649)
(501 on the family tree)

FARMER, INN OWNER, CHURCH COUNCIL
MEMBER, LÜNEBURG ADMINISTRATOR

Education, Family, and Early Responsibilities

Johann König is born on January 10, 1587. His birthplace is probably what is today Hann.-Münden, at that time called Münden. A
year later, he comes to Finkenwerder and grows up with his younger
siblings in the parsonage there. The Elbe island becomes his home,
and he dies there on June 28, 1649 after a lifetime of working hard
for his large family and his fellow citizens.

There is no school on Finkenwerder during his childhood. We
assume that he learns to read and write at home. Later, as administrator, he is recognized for his elegant penmanship and refined speech
suitable for an office position. He probably acquired this speech
through a lengthy apprenticeship at the Harburg office, where his
father has close contacts and whose members are very interested in
training young men with Johann's background as future office staff.

Page 161

At age 20, Johann marries Ilsche Fock(en) (502). She is the daughter of administrator Simon Fock. The wedding takes place on July 25,
1607. We know this from the entry of Johann's death in the church
registry. The marriage is blessed with 15 children. Ilsche survives

Johann by 18 years. She dies on December 19, 1667 at age 81, which is an advanced age for that time.

Johann and Ilsche have many children, but the family is also an example of the high infant mortality rate. How do these families, especially the mothers, who lose so many children fare? Are these people used to death knocking so frequently and so early at their doors? At that time, death is seen as a part of life and as one's fate as decreed by God. But is this easier said than done?

In spite of all the unfortunate happenings, the family also experiences joy. On July 27, 1634, Johann and Ilsabe (Ilsche is the North German version of the name) become grandparents. Their daughter, Margreta (601) gives them a granddaughter named "Cirke," a very unusual name for Finkenwerder. According to Homer in the *Tenth Canto* of the *Odyssey*, Circe is the beautiful enchantress of Greek mythology who lives on an island and "casts such a spell over" the hero, Ulysses, that he stays for a whole year.

Margreta König and her husband, Hinrich Fock, must have a good reason for giving their daughter such a name. Margreta's great-grandfather, Urbanus Rhegius, is a scholar of the Greek language. Is the Cirke adventure one of the favorite tales that is handed down by Urbanus' descendants?

Among other charms, the beautiful enchantress Circe is able to turn men into swine. Does "our" Circe threaten to do this to her playmates when they tease her about her name? In any case, her parents are quite brave to give her this "peculiar" name.

The residents of this island in the Elbe could be the first North German people to hear about this chapter by the ancient poet Homer because this is prior to 1781 when Johann Heinrich Voss from Otterndorf near Cuxhaven translates the *Odyssey* into German.

Cirke Fock marries Hinrich von Rigen on October 20, 1650 at only 16 years of age. He is the owner of the second largest farm in Finkenwerder.[560] Their marriage lasts a brief nine years. Cirke dies on April 9, 1659 when she is only 25 years old.

A daughter from the marriage of Hinrich von Rigen and Cirke Fock, Trina von Rigen (born December 25, 1651, dies April 11, 1719), marries Ludolph (Lülff) Geerkins on October 29, 1682. Their daughter, Wübbke (Wiebke) Geerkens marries Hinrich Popp on November 6, 1712 in Finkenwerder. Hinrich is from Neumühlen on the northern bank of the Elbe.

The Popps' descendants are seafaring fishermen, ship captains, and ship owners. Experienced captains command their own ships and are known in harbors on all continents. Hinrich Popp dies in his prime at age 37 while transporting freight in his schooner-brig, "Popp."[561] The Finkenwerder church record book states, "It apparently capsized in the beginning of December 1847 in a storm off the eastern coast of Scotland, from which it set sail in November carrying various cargo."[562]

Page 162

The Popp family generally has their ships built in Finkenwerder at the J.C. Wriede Dock Yards or the von Cölln Dock Yards. Wilhelm Friedrich Wulff (1808 – 1882), in an 1834 watercolor over pencil drawing, shows their commercial fishing galley, "VENUS," built in 1832.[563]

ILLUSTRATION 90: The commercial fishing galley, "VENUS," built in 1832 by J.C. Wriede in Finkenwerder for Hans Jacob Popp. Wriede is descended from the Popp and Rhegius families. Watercolor over

pencil by Wilhelm Friedrich Wulff. (Museum für
Hamburgische Geschichte am Holstenwall).

A current descendant from this line – also a descendant of
Rhegius – is a ship's pilot who will gladly provide us with a look
into Finkenwerder's past whenever he guides modern ships from all
over the world past Finkenwerder Island.

For further details about Johann König's children, see Appendix 46.

Lüneburg Administrator in Hard Times

Sebastian König's predecessor, Simon Fock, is mentioned in the 1617
church records as administrator, but when Duke Wilhelm writes
in March 1619 to Sebastian König about the poor dike conditions,
Simon Fock, who was supervising the dike reconstruction project,
is no longer mentioned. The administrator's position is apparently
vacant at this time. Johann König is probably appointed to this position later.[564]

Finder calls the administrator "the most important official in
the country" and says that "this person is selected from the most
long-standing landowners and land owning farmers in the country."
Also, the administrator should have "flexibility to handle all kinds of
disputes."[565] What real estate does Johann König own that proves
he qualifies for the position? According to Pastor Schulz's note
from 1629, he owns two parcels of land that previously belonged
to Carsten Horstmann.[566] In 1602, Simon Fock assumes the property,
which is 2,300 Marks in arrears.[567] Most likely Johann and his wife
receive this parcel of land at their wedding in 1607. Thus, Johann

qualifies for the office of administrator via his education, his position as son-in-law of the previous administrator, and his land ownership.

The old oath of office is still available in the Low German language. The original text with its translation into modern German is found in Appendix 47.[568]

On an island threatened by storm surges, the condition of the dikes is of utmost importance. The administrator is responsible for every aspect of the dikes' condition. He also has a judge assigned to dike matters who has himself sworn an oath, as well as two witnesses coordinating these matters.

Page 163

Further obligations are added: the rights and orders, collection of fees for the landowners, pledges, taking inventory in cases of death, notorizing other necessary legal documents, twice yearly inspection of the fire prevention equipment, and carrying out instructions from the Harburg office.

During his tenure as administrator Johann König has to deal with a series of storm surges. Particularly devastating are two floods on January 21 and February 26, 1625 – the so-called Flood on the Evening of Lent. Thick chunks of ice shift and spill over the dike. The water level rises. This is called an ice flood, in which the dikes are smashed by chunks of ice.

In 1627 the dike on the Lüneburg side is still in poor condition. On July 9 Johann König is ordered by the Harburg office to submit a report at the office.[569] In a petition dated February 27, 1620, the people on the Finkenwerder side of the island implore Duke Wilhelm to request the Hamburg city council to bring Hamburg's part of the Finkenwerder dike up to standard. Hamburg had promised this in the collaborative dike project "...because of Hamburg's weak, crumbling, and neglected dike, Osterfeld is often flooded[570] and both the summer and winter plantings ruined."[571] Johann König personally presents this complaint to the Dukes of Harburg on February 18, 1628. The duke issues an edict, and on March 3 asks the Hamburg city council to restore the dike.[572]

Looking at the previously cited transcript from another perspective is revealing: "...we can agree to report and not leave out that for a number of years there was an agreement between your fore-fathers and the faithful congregation. According to their memories, this was already agreed to in the duke's dike unification plan.[573] The petition is addressed to Duke Wilhelm: "Your Gracious Lord's father" is Duke Otto II. This re-surfaced evidence shows that the plan to unify the dikes was already undertaken by Duke Otto and could not be attributed only to Duke Wilhelm because the dike's unification agreement between the Harburg office and the city of Hamburg already existed during Duke Otto II's reign. In addition, Pastor Sebastian König reports in his letter of May 30, 1600 about a dike association comprising both sides of the island. The actual construction work takes place in 1603 – 1612 during Duke Wilhelm's reign. The document, dated February 27, 1628 may be found in Appendix 48.

Shortly thereafter, in 1630, a Sommerfult [summer flood] solves a puzzle for the people on the Elbe. On a calm, beautiful summer day, the water continuously climbs, the dike breaks, and the land floods. There is no known cause. The water recedes as calmly as it comes. Today, distant undersea earthquakes would be the explanation.[574] What is a mystery to the people in the Harburg marshes of 1630 we know today is a huge tsunami, such as the one on the second day of

Christmas 2004 that ravages the coast of the Indian Ocean, killing over 200,000 people.

The flood of 1630 is not the last one that Johann König has to deal with as administrator. The Elbe is unrelenting to the region's inhabitants. On October 11, 1634; February 4 – 5, 1642; January 21, 1643; and New Years Day and Shrove Tuesday, 1648 other storm surges are briefly recorded.[575] Johann has to contend with these weather conditions until his death and has to try to alleviate the islanders' distress as best he can.

Page 164

Disputes Over Fishing Rights on the Elbe

In olden times, fish are abundant in the Elbe River. Generations of our ancestors live from its bounty. The Hamburg side of Finkenwerder gets more from the Elbe than does the Lüneburg side with its distinctive agriculture. In earlier centuries there are sharp differences in customs and lifestyles between "land and water," between farmers and fishermen. The farmers marry mainly among themselves and the fishermen do likewise. The Kinau brothers are throughtful observers of their fellow countrymen, and their writings provide us with a firsthand glimpse into the lives and activities on the island.

Fishing in the Elbe is already in the news in 1343. Count Adolph VII von Holstein sells his fishing rights in the waters around Finkenwerder to Arnold von Brügge, a citizen of Hamburg, who in turn leases them out.[576]

The Harburg inheritance registry of 1667 mentions fishing in the Elbe: "The Elbe is full of many varieties of fish, but especially large burbot and lamprey in November, December, and January; in February lamprey, but no burbot; in March and April salmon and smelt; in May, June, and July salmon and sturgeon; in August Nesen and Bressem; in September Nesen and snipe; and October Schnepel and lamprey. Otherwise, throughout the year are pike, perch, and all kinds of small fish..."[577]

Disputes about fishing rights go back decades. Johann König, as Lüneburg administrator, is often involved in them. In 1641 – 1664, there are reports of stolen nets and commercial fishing boats. In these years there are also quarrels between Altenwerder and Dradenau, about which the fishermen from Krusenbusch are also questioned about the thefts.[578] Finally, from 1639 – 1728, the disputes about thefts are between Finkenwerder and Blankenese.[579]

In the last cited dispute, the Blankenese fishermen claim that fishing rights on the Elbe extend only as far as authority on land. Thus, fishermen from Finkenwerder are allowed to fish only around Finkenwerder, whereas fishermen from Blankenese, because they live in the duchy of Holstein, may fish on the entire right bank of the Elbe, up to the North Sea. The authority of the government of Harburg, especially the duchy of Braunschweig-Lüneburg ends for all practical purposes with Finkenwerder. At that point, the left bank of the Elbe up to the North Sea is governed by the archbish-opric of Bremen. It appears that the Blankenese fishermen want to keep their Finkenwerder competitors at a distance by redefining the Elbe fishing rights.

The people of Finkenwerder defend themselves against these claims. In his capacity as Lüneburg administrator, Johann König writes Frantz Stapeldorf on July 31, 1647. The salutation begins, "Honorable Grace, Duly Installed Counselor and Senior Official of

Pinneberge for the archbishop of Bremen." The letter goes on to state that not only the plaintiff, the residents of Blankenese, but also the defendants, the residents of Finkenwerder, and many others "have recognized beacons and buoys as landmarks of the Elbe waters since time immemorial along with the right to fish wherever one wishes up to the North Sea, wherever one is most comfortable, in order to find food for one's family."[580]

The senior official of Pinneberg sees things differently. He answers on August 27, 1647 that should the Finkenwerder fishing boats come too close to the Blankenese boundaries, they will be charged a tariff. Johann König should "seriously urge the Finkenwerder fishermen to restrict their fishing to their side of the Elbe." The tone is diplomatic, but the content is irreconcilable. Johann König takes his time answering. He discusses the situation with the fishermen and stays firm in his opinion.

Page 165

He writes to his counterpart in Pinneberg that Finkenwerder stands by its conviction that all are allowed to fish in the Elbe waters up to the North Sea. Their ancestors were never prohibited from doing so until the people of Blankenese recently stopped it by force.[581]

ILLUSTRATION 91: Johann König, administrator, on September 20, 1647, writes to Frantz Stopeldorff, senior official of Pinneberg and advisor to the Archbishop of Bremen, about fishing rights that since

> "time immemorial" have allowed all to fish without
> any restrictions on the Elbe up to the North Sea.

The transcribed letter is in Appendix 49. He rejects the opinion from Pinneberg and in clear language reminds him that all inhabitants of the Elbe waters from as far back as people can remember had the right to fish without restraint. This fact is the cornerstone of the law and customs. He flatters his counterpart by telling him that he is too wise to allow these plaintiffs to enforce their claim. He warns that continuing the pursuit of such minor complaints often brings harm to those involved.

ILLUSTRATION 92: Das Ampt D. Fischer.
Only fishermen in possession of this mark have
fishing rights for the engraved year.[382]

Finkenwerder in the Thirty Years' War

Johann König's time in office falls almost completely within the dates of the Thirty Years' War (1618 – 1648), yet he and his fellow Finkenwerder citizens are fortunate during this time of national misfortune. The horror of the merciless war does not reach Finkenwerder, at least not directly.

On September 27, 1622, Duke Wilhelm clearly decrees his concern about the future course of the war. He asks the superintendents and pastors of the Harburg region to hold special days of prayer. He directs them to refrain from the prevailing spirit of the time "which involves punishing others in God's name. This punishing attitude will only endlessly spill more blood through war and revenge in other kingdoms, principalities, countries, and states throughout Germany." The first Wednesday of every month at 7 am there is to be a special day of prayer for the peasants and clergy, men and women, young and old, young boys and young girls.[583]

From the text of the decree, we realize how important the prayer days and their content are to Duke Wilhelm. The sermons are not to last more than half an hour, so that the craftsmen and farmers can participate. The people are to be instructed in the main points of the Christian religion, which are derived from the best source – *Luther's Small Catechism.*

Page 166

Everything should be explained clearly and briefly so that the people do not get bored by lengthy sermons and fall asleep, rather, they are to be uplifted and renewed. (See Appendix 50.)

An "Assecuratio,"[584] an official notice about the financial burden to the people of Finkenwerder incurred by the war, dated March 5, 1629, to be paid to Duke Wilhelm by the Finkenwerder administrator and the people amounts to over 150 Reichstaler. (See Appendix 51.) Apparently this document is about a pledge made by the Finkenwerder residents for war expenses which they are not in a position to pay due to the expenses associated with the prior storm surges. The duke reduces the original high amount and agrees to 150 Reichstaler, which is to be paid by Michaelmas [Feast of St. Michael on September 29]. The promissory note is agreed to by "Administrator Johann König, Johann von Riege, Peter Fincke, and Heinrich von Riege as a general mortgage for all residents of Finkenwerder."[585]

Imagine the position the administrator is in! He is responsible for collecting the payment due. The farmers are still suffering from the damage caused by the storm surges. The duke is also in financial distress. The war necessitates preparation. How frequently does Johann negotiate with the farmers? How often does he ride to Harburg, to report and to negotiate until the 150 Reichstaler pledge cited above can be secured by the necessary financial backing? Is a general agreement sufficient for implementation, or is a more detailed agreement required? What complications are going to arise when the duke has to put the agreement into effect?

These are difficult times. Up until the end of the long war, additional contributions will be required.

In the closing years of the war, people from various parts of the country are seeking refuge in Finkenwerder. We find many examples of these conditions in the church accounting records:

> "On March 28, 1639 a sick man from the Stift [monastery] Minden is given 12 Schillings by order of Johan Konig and Hinrich von Rigen.
>
> On May 19, 1645, two men from Stehnal (Stendal) by Johan Konig's authorization received 6 Schillings. I gave them 2 Schillings of my funds, but the money was withdrawn from a different account[586] because the men came with a document stating they had met the administrator in the inn and he recommended that I, as pastor, pay the men.
>
> On June 14, 1645, a displaced man, Johan Bahrlib, born in Osterburg and previously a school master at Winsen, received 6 Schillings per order of Joh. Konig.
>
> On September 23, 1645, a man from Halberstadt named

Hans Bawemeister is given 6 Schillings per Joh. Konig's authorization.

March 18, 1647 a wretched exile received 12 Schillings."

The strangers must first report to the administrator and he decides whether or not the newcomers may be given funds from the poor box account.

In 1639, Johann König Commissions the Holy Communion Chalice That is Still Used Today

The 367 year old chalice has served countless parishioners at Holy Communion, confirmands beginning their new life after Confirmation, hopeful young married couples, sorrowful mothers, and elderly people seeking consolation. Nevertheless, hardly anyone knows how old the chalice is or where it comes from because the name of the person doing the casting and the date are not engraved on it.

We do find more enlightening information in the church registry:

Page 167

"The year 1639, on the 28TH... Johan Köning gave me 11 Reichstaler. The chief coin artisan got 10 additional Reichstaler. Johann König wanted to commission the goldsmith to inscribe some letters on three plates for four Marks."[587]

The chalice is 19 cm. high. The diameter above is 10 cm. The base has six rounded exterior corners called "fillets," decorated with three round plates on which Christ's cross, the Lamb with the flag of victory, and a cross are engraved.

In the year in which the chalice was commissioned, Johann König has been the Lüneberg administrator for 20 years. Possibly, this is the occasion for the making of the chalice.

Pastor Bodemann commissions a similar chalice in 1871, which at 23.5 high is larger than Johann König's. The Bodemann chalice bears the inscription: "Geschenk von Pastor Bodemann 1871" [Gift of Pastor Bodemann 1871]. At the base is the motif of the so-called clover leaf cross, which symbolizes the union of the cross of Christ and the Trinity.[588]

The commission year of the the Bodemann chalice is the end of the war in 1870 – 1871 and the year of the founding of the German Empire. The donor is probably expressing thanks for the war's end. Up until this time, the chalice is not mentioned in any publications nor is the "alms box," which is purchased in 1637 during the tenure of Pastor Schulz, the successor and son-in-law of Pastor Sebastian König. We read about this in the Finkenwerder church record book in 1637:

"From this time on the church deacons have put an alms box in the church. Money is placed into the alms box for safekeeping, to be used at the deacons' discretion, but for which they will give an accounting."[589]

There is no disbursement for the chalice in the church accounting records so it must be a donation. The foregoing text can be a clue that members of the church council are the donors. From 1623 – 1637, this is Hinrich von Riegen, from 1624 – 1632 Harm Wulf, and from 1636 – 1637 Hinrich Wulf.

ILLUSTRATION 93

ABOVE: The Holy Communion chalice commissioned in
1639 by Lüneberg Administrator Johann König.

BELOW: At the end of the Deutsch-Französischer
Krieg [known as the Franco-Prussian War in the US],
Pastor Bodemann commissions this Holy Communion
chalice for his church. (Photos by Klaus Elle).

The offerings for the "Blocks" are intended for charitable purposes, hence, it is also called the "alms box."

ILLUSTRATION 94: The impressively handcrafted
"alms box" is assumed to be commissioned by
church council members in 1637 through pledges
to the church. (Photo: Klaus Elle).

Page 168

The First School Established on Finkenwerder's Lüneburg Side During Johann König's Tenure as Administrator

The Hamburg School in Finkenwerder is established "...in order
that our children and their descendants will be capable and faithful
industrious teachers and instructors of the correct Christian education and upbringing from the time of their youth to their true knowledge of God Almighty. In addition, to foster the Christian virtues
and customs. And also, to be able to read, write, and calculate." That

is what it says in the founding document of the Hamburg School in Finkenwerder, dated March 12, 1660.[590]

Finder proudly reports that this is the only old school in Hamburg for which we have original documentation.[591] He not only documents the information, but also provides the complete handwritten evidence for the founding of the school, signed by Administrator Hein Von Riegen and by 20 farmers with their court seals. All of them pledge to provide funds to maintain the school.[592]

The founding of the school on the Lüneburg side is less definite. Since the time of Pastor Evers, all chronologists report that all the children on the Hamburg side attend an existing school on the Lüneburg side established before 1660. Evers mentions that in the beginning, the people living on the coast do not also serve as teachers. Rather, the Lüneburg side has a "special person" to whom they entrust their children's education.[593] Instruction probably takes place at various farmsteads. But, in which year is this the case?

Otto Schmidt, the teacher at the Lüneburg School, maintains in an unfortunately undated newspaper article, that in 1932 "his" school could be 300 years old. In that case, the school was founded in 1632. But, he adds that there are no records from the 17TH century to consult on the subject. Wilhelm Kölling states the same thing in his article, *Schulen auf Finkenwerder von 1660 bis 1919* [*Schools on Finkenwerder from 1660 to 1919*].[594]

Our interest in Johann König's time as Lüneburg administrator is augmented by another point of view regarding the founding of the school on the Lüneburg side. On May 6, 1621 Duke Wilhelm issues a "Gracious Reminder about the Worship Service." Point 3 reads: "The pastors should establish schools in the villages." The pastors are thereby directly instructed to be concerned about education in their congregations. In a different handwriting in the decree's text there are numerous annotations on the left side of the page, presumably from an office official, among others, regarding point 3. It says, "A sexton should be installed in Finkenwerder."[595]

ILLUSTRATION 95: Duke Wilhelm of Braunschweig and Lüneburg in a 1622 portrait. The Harburg branch of the lineage ends with his death in 1642.

Page 169

Here is a direct connection between "school" and "sexton." According to the document, the residents must be provided with education. Evers gives an example of the first sextons and teachers: "The first sexton mentioned is Heinrich Focke being godfather on January 27, 1622 ... "[596] This was eight months after Duke Wilhelm's decree. So, Heinrich Focke can be the "special person" mentioned by Evers. In our opinion, this seems to be a new building block in the educational foundatioin of the people of Lüneburg-Finkenwerder, which starts before that on the Hamburg side, as we previously assumed.

Whether the duke's proclamation in May 1621 goes back to the time of Pastor Sebastian König's death in the same year is unknown. In any case, Sebastian König's successor and son-in-law, Johann Schulze, carries through on the duke's wishes without hesitation.

The End of an Era - Duke Wilhelm Dies after a 39 Year Reign

With Duke Wilhelm's death on March 30, 1642, the Harburg lineage of the dukes von Braunschweig and Lüneburg dies out after 115 years. Wilhelm never married and dies without a successor. Harburg is now under Celle's domain. According to his final wishes, his remains are burried in the ducal tomb of the city church.[597]

Is Johann König, now the Lüneburg administrator, appointed by "his" duke, whom he served for over 20 years, present at the celebration of the duke's life in Celle, as his father, Sebastian König was present for Duke Otto II's funeral in 1603? The answer to this question is "no." Only two people from Harburg are invited to the celebration of the duke's life in Celle on May 16, 1643. The city magistrate lists only Mayor Peter Rosenbruch and city council member Christoffer Reinhardt.[598] No one from the Harburg congregations is present! At the end of the epoch, many people at that time may have wished for a sweeping, broad-minded handling of the reorganization by the duke in Celle.

Upon Duke Wilhelm's death, a silver coin worth one Taler is issued. On the front is an image of the duke in armor, with the inscription:

WILHELMUS.D.G.DUX.BRUNSUIC.ET LU
(Wilhem by God's Grace Duke of Braunschweig and Lüneburg)

The reverse side bears the following inscription:

NATVS.XIV.MART.
AO.MDLXIV.
OBIIT.
HARBURGI
XXX.MARTH.
HORA.IV.MATVTINA.
ANNO.MDCXLII
AETAT.LXXIIX.DI ERVM.XVI
H.S.

(Born on March 14, 1564. Died in Harburg on March 30 at 4 am in the year 1642 at age 78 years and 16 days. H.S.)[599]

There is an interesting version of the Taler commemorating the duke's death. The engraver inserted an extra "X," so that the duke's age, instead of being engraved LXXIIX (78 years) is mistakenly issued as LXXXIIX, making the duke 88 years old.

Page 170

ILLUSTRATION 96, Left: Taler coin commemorating the death of Duke Wilhelm. To err is human: the engraver cuts one "X" too many into the coin's stamp. Thus, Wilhelm's age is mistakenly 88, instead of the actual 78. The coin, illustrated below, is the only known version of this engraving error. Right: The 1619 commemorative Taler showing the image of Duke Wilhelm in armor with a Spanish ruffled collar. In his hand he has a scepter, the sign of his sovereignty. Six of these commemorative Talers are known to exist today.

After Duke Wilhelm's death, Finkenwerder is governed by Celle, just as it was prior to the establishment of the Harburg lineage in 1527. Duke Friedrich, a grandson of Duke Ernst the Confessor, is the reigning duke .[600] Harburg becomes only an Ambt [branch office], governed by Celle's Hofmarschall [senior marshall], Hans von Petersdorf, who bears the title Oberhauptmann [senior leader].[601] He is now Johann König's direct superior and his fellow administrator of the Harburg district.

Times remain tense. The Thirty Years' War in its third decade demands financial support. In Harburg, these levies allow Duke Friedrich to redesign the castle according to the most modern plans by Dutch architects. The castle must have five equal sized corners, with bastions projecting from each of the moats.[602] The duke believes that it is absolutely necessary to redesign the castles as fortresses because the war will not end in the foreseeable future.

And in Finkenwerder, Administrator Johann König has to explain the new levies to the residents. In order to finance the construction of the Harburg fortress, the tax on owning livestock is to be doubled, along with the announcement that additional increases could follow.[603]

ILLUSTRATION 97: In 1644 – 46 Duke Friedrich wants the Harburg Fortress built according to the latest architectural design. The residents of Finkenwerder, including Rhegius' descendants, must "burgfesten," that is, contribute their physical labor to "build the mighty fortress by hand." Merian's 1654 sketch shows "Die jetzige Newe Vestung Harburg" [The current new fortress in Harburg].

A Latin Text Honors Johann König

The Finkenwerder church registry contains a Latin entry pertaining to Johann König's death. He dies on June 28, 1649 at age 62:

> "H. Johan Konig Senior. Natus 1587. Die 10 Januan Conjug(ationem) duxit 1607. Circa Jacobi, Genuit Liber(os) Orator ultra 30 annos. Denatus anno 1649, die 28. Junii."

Page 171

The text in the church registry is almost unreadable because of an ink blot. With the help of the Staatarchiv in Hamburg, which we again thank, it is possible to reconstruct the text. The German text, [translated into English] states:

> "Mr. Johan Konig senior: Born 1587 on January 10TH. He marries in 1607, circa Jacobi [July 25, the holy day of the Apostle James].[604] He fathers 15 children. For over thirty years, he was a speaker/spokesman. Dies on June 28, 1649." [605]

While the usual entries in the church registry are tersely written, this entry is pleasantly rich in details. Who knows such details, and who is the person who honors Johann with this unusual entry? Since 1647, Eibert Janzen holds the pastor position, and it is he who composes the above entry. Where does such intimate knowledge of the deceased come from? The answer is simple. On January 20, 1647, Eibert Janzen marries Margreta Schulz, the daughter of his predecessor, Pastor Schulz, and granddaughter of Pastor Sebastian König. Once again history repeats itself because previously in 1621 Johann Schulze marries a daughter of his predecessor, Sebastian König.

In writing about the deceased administrator, Johann König, the new pastor honors his wife's uncle.

Sebastian König, Jr. (1621 – 1667) (615 on the family tree)

FARMER, INN OWNER, LÜNEBURG ADMINISTRATOR

"We do not know anyone more qualified and talented than Bastian, the son of the deceased administrator..."

On July 21, 1649, three weeks after Johann König's death, the senior leader of the Harburg office, Hans von Petersdorff, writes to Pastor Eibert Jantzen that in accordance with the laws and regulations, the administrator position must be filled. Thus, he has asked the land owning farmers whether they would like to submit the names of qualified men.

He further writes: "We do not know anyone more qualified to be the new administrator than Sebastian König, the son of the deceased administrator. If you are all agreed, then we will try to have him accepted and installed in office. Older people reside in the land, and these people cannot write. Would it not be unsettling if the administrator has to have all pieces of paper and commands addressed to him read aloud by someone else? Bastian König has learned to write and already knows what an administrator has to deal with, since he learned this from his father. On his behalf, we implore you to install him as your administrator."[606]

For his part, Sebastian König is not particularly happy about the suggestion, and he points out that he "...would like to be spared having to accept it because he would be performing the same service as his blessed father, who on account of his many good deeds, had little joy and encountered much personal damage. He imploringly continues by saying that because he is married and also does not know whether his mother wants to transfer her widow's home to him, he questions whether it would not be better for him to look for a different position and to spare himself accepting the job requirements until he can support a household on his own.

At least, he wants to accurately and faithfully report the daily conditions under which an administrator industriously works and how a faithful administrator would decide."[607]

The senior leader agrees, and with a handshake confirms Sebastian König's tentative duties. The senior leader requests suggestions from Pastor Jantzen per the duke's instructions regarding who among the Finkenwerder farmers would be able to take over the assistant administrator's office. But three decades after the first modest attempts to establish schools, there is no other single candidate who can read and write and who has united support.

Page 172

At age 28, Sebastian König has garnered so much support that everyone "wanted him to become" the administrator. He is therefore requested to appear in the prince's office in Harburg at 10 am on July 25 to accept his appointment.

Since Sebastian still does not know whether his mother will transfer her widow's residence to him, the rules of protocol now revolve around the existing Gasthof [Inn] Schwartau on the south Elbe, which the König family currently occupies.

According to the date on the front entrance of Gasthof Schwartau, the building was established in 1667. It is described as the oldest building on this Elbe island.[608] From the above document, it is clear that the building is even older. It can be traced back to Johann König (1587 – 1649) who was connected to the inn. (See chapter: "Finkenwerder in the Thirty Years' War.")

The question of inheritance is soon clarified in Sebastian's favor. Thus, he takes the oath as administrator. He is officially installed on January 30, 1650 at Schloss Harburg. The protocol of his official appointment is available in his original handwriting. A translation is provided in Appendix 52.

Senior Leader Hans von Peterstorff, Pastor Jantzen, the church elders, and several other important people from Finkenwerder are present at the swearing in. The oath is presented to Sebastian König who "with his arms raised swears to God to faithfully perform the duties of the office." He is then named administrator and appropriately introduced.[609] The protocol is drawn up by Secretary Frantz Richters and Administrator Gerdt Bredehols.

ILLUSTRATION 98: On January 30, 1650
at Schloss Harburg, Sebastian König, Jr. is
sworn in as Lüneburg administrator.

In the search for the new administrator, we have to mention as we have done previously that Pastor Jantzen is a cousin by marriage of Sebastian König, Jr. As in past generations, there is a close relationship between the pastor and the administrator.

Page 173

Sebastian König, Jr. (615 on the family tree), Marries the Hamburg Administrator's Daughter

ANNKE HARMENS AND HER FAMILY

What a very important year 1650 is for Sebastian König, Jr.! Just 29 years old, he takes over his father's position, is sworn in as Harburg administrator, and on Sunday, July 17, 1650, marries Annke Harm(en)s. She is also called Anna and Antje in the church registry. Annke is born on January 21, 1629 and is 21 years old at the time of her marriage.

What a celebration this must be in Finkenwerder! The crippling years of the long wars are over, and the people can again breathe freely. Sebastian is administrator and at the same time owner of the well known Gasthof Schwartau in Finkenwerder. Now he marries Annke Harm(en)s, the daughter of Hamburg administrator, Hans Harm(en)s. In 1650, Hübbe does refer to Hans Harms as one of the largest landowners on the Hamburg side, but he is not certain whether he is administrator.[610] We can clear up these uncertainties through the discovery of a document, the 1648 "duly appointed list of Finkenwerder administrators."[611] It reads:

"I, in the presence of others, hereby acknowledge for the first time that I am standing here today as the successor to the honored and respected Hanss Harmen and others, duly appointed administrators, in my church in Finckenwerder. From Mr. Hanss Harmens and Albrecht Focken, I purchase property for 80 lübisch Marks including the properties from his heirs, for me to use and reside in. According to his will and benefit, I have signed and sealed this document or letter of purchase. Done in Finckenwerder a week before Easter day, in 1648.

HZS" (official seal of the duke)

The Finkenwerder church registry of 1657 contains a seating chart for the church pews. According to it, Sebastian König, Jr. sits up front on the Lüneburg side near the church council members. There are allocations in the pews for men and woman that can be purchased or rented. The seating placement is strictly divided into Lüneburg and Hamburg sides. Even today this seating order is kept by the older Finkenwerder residents, even though it has not been officially valid for quite some time.

Hans Harms has been the official administrator of the Hamburg side for some years. It is most likely that Sebastian and Annke met when their fathers were discussing business. The familial relationships after Sebastian's marriage to Annke Harms are shown below:

Sebastian König, Jr., the Lüneburg administrator,

and Hans Harms, the Hamburg administrator are son-in-law and father-in-law.

In 1657, Jacob Harms succeeds his father.

Pastor Eibert Jantzen is Sebastian König, Jr.'s relative by marriage.

When we follow Finder's line of thinking, then the administrator is "the most important official in the country." Therefore, the decades from 1620 to 1667 present an interesting photo of our family history on Finkenwerder from a genealogical perspective. At the same time, the minister's tenure from 1588 to Sebastian König to Johann Schulz and Eilbert Jantzen depicts the closest family ties.

Based on the collective evidence, it can be assumed that many difficult and pressing questions are likely resolved by the administrators before being brought before the Harburg or Hamburg offices. But the familial ties are not always advantageous. In 1654, Sebastian has to resolve a case which cannot be pleasant for him.

Page 174

For ten years, Simon Focke has not taken Holy Communion and has not attended church services. Simon claims this is due to a heated land dispute with Martin Ockelmann in which the two men "lived as enemies." Simon has been jailed for 10 days and paid 60 Reichstaler in compensation. The administrator and the church council members are duty bound to resolve this matter.[612]

Who is Simon Focke? Very probably he is Sebastian's uncle or, stated more clearly, a brother of the wives of Johann and Gerd König and son of Simon Fock, the previous administrator by the same name. The document cited above may be a key to the question of why Simon Fock, Jr. does not inherit the acreage, but on the contrary, the acreage is divided between the sisters Ilsche and Gretsche Fock. Simon Focke, Jr. dies unmarried in 1658.

Annke Harms has nine siblings, six of whom die young. Also, Annke's twin sister, Ilsche, is barely two years old when she dies.

Only Annke and her brother Jacob, later administrator and heir to the acreage, and her brother Hinrich live long enough to marry.

The only gravestone, called either a Grabplatte [grave slab] or Leichstein [corpse stone], still in Finkenwerder is dedicated to Annke's brother Jacob. It is located at the entrance to the church. Up until the 40TH year of the last century it lay in the Benidt-Hof [Farm]. It was brought to the church before the land was plowed to construct the Fleugzeugwerke [Airplane Factory] Blohm & Voss. The gravestone had lain on the outer perimeter of their land.

This type of period gravestone often depicted Christ on a cross in the middle of the stone. To the right of the cross the father is named with the sons. At left are the mother and daughters. There are the five sons and five daughters, which the church registry names as the children of Jacob Harms and his wife Ancke Steers:

	BORN	DIED	MARRIAGE
HANS	(Baptized) April 13, 1656	December 3, 1688	February 10, 1684 to Grete v. Rigen
TRINA	December 13, 1657	April 11, 1664	
ALHEIT	October 24, 1658	October 26, 1658	
ALHEIT	October 30, 1659	December 19, 1659	
ALHEIT	December 9, 1660	March 7, 1669	
PAUL[613]	January 2, 1663	July 24, 1712	Hamburg administrator Marriage I: November 24, 1687 to Catharina von Rigen Marriage II: July 14, 1691 to Rebecca Foken[614]

CATHAR.	July 16, 1665	April 19, 1689	June 1, 1686 to Johann von Rigen
HINRICH	April 21, 1667	November 18, 1727	December 16, 1696 to Gesche Lüdders
JACOB	December 21, 1668	January 3, 1703	October 27, 1691 to Cilje Wullfs
JOHANN	June 9, 1672	Unknown	October 24, 1699 to widow Anna Quast, Moorende, Königreich/Estebrügge

Because they are so heavy, these impractical grave stones are not used in the 18TH century. Farmers relocate some of them to higher ground where they remain to this day. The Harms family owned the Benidt-Hof at that time. A biblical verse can be deciphered from a 1639 preserved stone in the Altenwerder belltower. Both the belltower stone and the previously mentioned Jacob Harms stone are engraved with verses from Job 19: 25 – 27 that were slightly altered by Luther:

Page 175

"As for me, I know that my Redeemer lives, And at the last He will take His stand on the earth.

Even after my skin is destroyed, Yet from my flesh I shall see God;

Whom I myself shall behold, And whom my eyes will see and not another. My heart faints within me!

If you say, 'How shall we persecute him?' and 'What pretext for a case against him can we find?'

Then be afraid of the sword for yourselves, For wrath brings the punishment of the sword, So that you may know there is judgment."

Luther replaced the old pre-Reformation grave inscriptions about salvation, purgatory, and damnation with more optimistic sayings. The grave stones cited above use the recommended inscriptions.

In about 1700, grave stones such as the one shown in the illustration below cost about 100 Marks. That is equivalent to about 22 hundredweights of rye or two fat, yoked oxen.[615] In Finkenwerder, only the wealthy farmers can afford them.

ILLUSTRATION 99: The only remaining grave stone in Finkenwerder is on the grave of Jacob Harms, Hamburg administrator (1627 – 1676), brother-in-law of Lüneburg administrator Sebastian König, Jr. (1621 – 1667).

Dike Issues Continually Recur

There is really no Finkenwerder administrator who does not have to address concerns about the dikes because maintenance of the dikes is fundamental to everyone's livelihood, whether landowners, fishermen, artisans, male servants, or female servants.

In the year of his installation as administrator, Sebastian König receives a "*DOMINORUM CONSILARIORUM*."[616] It is an "order to the Finkenwerder administrator that subjects of this principality should render aid to Hermann Wulff in repairing the damage to the dike because the city has pledged such help." It is dated August 5,

1651.[617] It is impossible for Hermann Wulff to raise funds to repair the dike by himself. Sebastian König is instructed to strongly urge the subjects of Finkenwerder-Lüneburg to lend a hand to the inhabitants of the Hamburg side in order to prevent the whole island from being endangered.

In the legally ordered, cooperative work involving both sides of the island, the new family ties of the two administrators are shown to be effective for the first time. In the next years to come, the work on the dike will remain a recurring theme.[618]

"He Has a Free Parcel of Land as Long as He is Administrator"
THE HARBURG INHERITANCE REGISTER OF 1667

A meeting of note takes place from March 20 – 22, 1666 at Schloss Harburg. For two years the Braunschweig-Lüneburg government in Celle has been trying to get an exact accounting of the existing tax payments in the land. An inheritance registry needs to be established because the efforts thus far have had little success. An examination of the existing situation takes place in March 1666 at Schloss Harburg. In attendance are a representative of the ducal treasury in Celle, the Lüneburg advisors and chancellors in Harburg, Heinrich Bessel, other Harburg Officials, the Harburg administrators, and the administrator of the Harburg administrator's association.

Page 176

The only ones absent are representatives from Kirchwerder and Jehrden, so that we can safely state that the administrators from

Finkenwerder and Altenwerder, namely Sebastian König and Carsten Lüdders, are present.[619]

We are grateful for the excellent information about the property ownership and living conditions of this time stemming from the founding of the inheritance registry. Here we learn, for example, that the "Finckenwärder Tithes" must not be paid off in-kind because a tenth of the amount due is lacking and there are difficulties transporting these in-kind goods via water. For that reason, the duke's subjects do not have to pay a tenth of their harvest, but rather, for every Morgen of interior land, they pay two Marks ($2/3$ Taler) and for every Morgen of reclaimed land, they pay $1/2$ Taler.[620]

The owners of inns, restaurants, taverns, and other such establishments appear to play a special role at that time because their properties are still counted among the farmers' real estate:

"In the village, the land parcels have five parts for taxation purposes:

1. Sebastian König, the present administrator, because of his official duties, has a tax-free parcel

2. Hans Külper annually gives 4 Rtl. acres for tax purposes

3. Hein Wüpper also gives 4 Rtl.

4. Henrich Schulte also gives 4 Rtl.

5. Hein Loep also gives 4 Rtl. for taxes."

We find Sebastian König in fourth place among the farm owners: "Sebastian König, the current administrator, lives near the dike[621] on the property he inherited from Simon Vocken. Sebastian co-owns inherited land with Henning Linnemann. For his share, Simon has 7 $1/2$ Morgen inland property and 3 Morgen reclaimed land. Of these combined 10 ½ Morgen, 7 Morgen are right in front of his door. The ½ Morgen of Sebastian's land between Henning Linnemann's land on the west and Henrich von Riegen's on the east means that Sebastian has to maintain 50 rods of the dike. The annual amount of Sebastian's annual tithing is 6 ½ Taler and 2 smoked chickens. He also keeps the money earned from the property cited above because the money is a fringe benefit for serving as administrator. Sebastian is also obligated to pay 1 Taler, 32 Schillings tax on the cattle on the parcel of land. He has a free parcel of land as long as he is the Finken-werder-Lüneburg administrator.[622]

The administrator must submit a document specifying the tenure status of the government's land in his district. Thus, the above text was composed by Sebastian König himself and is therefore authentic. We learn from Sebastian that he inherited his parcel of land from "Simon Vocken" and that he shares the parcel with Henning Linnemann. Simon Fock, the former administrator, is Sebastian's grandfather. Simon divided his estate between his two daughters, Ilsche and Gretsche. Ilsche and Gretsche Fock marry brothers Johann and Gerd König. Now half of the estate comes to Sebastian König through Ilsche Fock/Johann König. The other half goes to Henning Linnemann, Sebastian's brother-in-law through Gretsche Fock/Gerd König. Sebastian König and Henning (Hennke) Linnemann are also cousins.

Henning Linnemann pays a tithing tax of 6 Taler and 40 Schillings so that he "gives the administrator with whom he shares the estate that money instead of the money from Sebastian's salary." In other words, Sebastian not only has his parcel of land tax-free, but he also receives the additional amount of his cousin's tithing fee mentioned above.

Page 177

The Children of Sebastian König, Jr. and Annke Harms

Before the protocol for the inheritance registry is written in July 1667, Sebastian König dies on March 30, 1667. The entry of his death in the Finkenwerder church registry states that he is 46 years old. He was therefore born in 1621, before November 4, which is the first entry in the church registry.

Sebastian and Annke are married barely 17 years. Of their eight children, three die. Their sons, Johann and Hans, are 17 and 15 years old at the time of their father's death. Their two daughters, Illsche and Greta, are 10 and eight years old. Their daughter, Trina, dies at age 13 in 1668, a year after her father's death.

Now Annke, who is 38 years old, has to manage the house, the farmland, and the inn, in addition to taking care of the children – a superhuman task. She evidently is soon helped by Claus Baje, a farmhand, who also managed the farm during Sebastian's lifetime, probably as a foreman. Annke is a great support to her elderly father, Hans Harmens, the former Hamburg administrator, whom she mentions in her will of 1670.

Annke König and Claus Baje marry on April 5, 1670. In the following year, on December 17, 1671, a daughter is born to Annke. The marriage is short-lived. Claus Baje dies on November 20, 1676. Annke dies two months later on January 28, 1677 at the age of only 48.

Two months before Annke Harms marries for the second time, she specifies in her will of February 18, 1670 that every child 14 years of age or older should receive 200 lübisch Marks. Furthermore, "... when the child is advised to marry..." it receives a horse or 50 Marks and a cow. Then it is detailed what every son should receive from the bed to the hat, while it is listed that the daughters receive blankets, shirts, kettles, pots, and stockings to handkerchiefs. Everything has been thought through.[623]

The final condition, "Whoever lives the longest should keep the family possessions and give the others what belongs to them..." which means the inheritance of the estate is also regulated by the will. "Whoever lives the longest" means the oldest living child at that time. We later see that Hans König (720), rather than the first born Johann (719), inherits the estate. Johann is named in the 1670 will when he is 19 years old. There must be a special reason why Johann does not inherit the estate.

The previously mentioned will is the oldest handwritten document of this type known to us and is shown in Appendix 53. Appendix 54 also gives information about the children of Sebastian König, Jr. and Annke Harms.

A 1688 list of contributors indicates Hans König is executive owner of the farm land.[624] Here is the inheritance list:

> "Hanss König   current primary farmer
>
> Claus Baje   2ND farmer
>
> Bastian König   3RD farmer
>
> Johann König   4TH farmer"

The above clarifies that after Sebastian König, Jr.'s death, Claus Baje serves as interim farmer before the estate and the inn are inherited by Hans König, which probably means when Bastian reaches the age of legal maturity.

The 137 years of service that the R(h)egius/König family has rendered the Guelph princes ends with Sebastian König, Jr.'s death in 1667. For five generations the family has served the dukes von Braunschweig and Lüneburg in various responsible positions, beginning with the 1530 Imperial Diet of Augsburg when Duke Ernst the Confessor secures a promise from Urbanus Rhegius to move to Celle. The early death of Sebastian, Jr. prevents the tradition from continuing because Sebastian's children have not reached legal age.

Page 178

Hinrich von Riegen, whose first wife is Cirke Fock, succeeds Sebastian König as Lüneburg administrator. We have already described her family in the chapter entitled: "Johann König – Education, Family, and Early Responsibilities." Von Riegen dies two years later on August 8, 1669.

Interestingly, the office of administrator remains in Hinrich von Riegen's family after his death. When Hinrich's widow, Alheit von Riegen, born Nibben, marries Cord Schwartau on October 8, 1670, Cord, who was born in Altenwerder, is appointed administrator.

Cord Schwartau, who is born August 23, 1649 in Altenwerder and dies February 14, 1688 on Finkenwerder Island, comes from an estate on the neighboring island of Altenwerder. His father, just like Cord, is a landowner and church council member in the part of the island that belongs to Bremen. Coincidentally, five generations later, one of his descendants, Jacob Schwartau, marries Anna Feldmann, whose mother, Rebecka König, brings the acreage and inn into the marriage. The present day Gasthof Schwartau at Finkenwerder's southern dike comes about from this connection to the König's original acreage.

How did Pastor Evers say it? "The people of the island are closely intertwined through both social and family relationships."

More Rhegius Descendants on Finkenwerder

ONE INN, TWO PASTORS' FAMILIES, THREE POETS, AND FOUR ACREAGES AS EXAMPLES

The Gasthof [Inn] Schwartau on the *Süderdeich* [Southern Dike]

THE ORIGINAL ACREAGE AND THE CENTER OF THE KÖNIG FAMILY

The idyllic farming and fishing island of the Kinau brothers disappeared a long time ago. Only a few homesteads and their land have been able to withstand the change of time. And what do we know today about fishing on the high seas? Gorch Fock in his main work, *Seefahrt ist not! [Seafaring is Necessary!]*,[625] describes the scenery of the fishermen in Finkenwerder in the year 1887. "...the fishing on the high sea with full sails blooms in summertime. Fishing on the high sea has reached its peak, and the Finkenwerder fishermen are masters of the sea." The Elbe is home to three hundred well smacks [traditional fishing boats with a well that is filled with circulated external water to keep fish alive] and cutters, 187 of which have their home port in Finkenwerder and display H.F. on their brown sails..."[625] Today, fewer than a handful of fishermen still venture forth.

We find the earliest piece of information about old Finkenwerder in the former Lüneburg section. Here we can still enjoy blooming fruit trees in the spring. Tall poplars and old walnut trees remind us of days gone by. Since the great flood of 1962, there is no longer a direct way to the open sea on the Elbe's southern bank, but there are still tranquil nooks that invite us to explore them. This portion of the dike has a long history. It is a part of the old dike from former Gorieswerder, about the year 1200.

In 1988, Jakob Schwartau, the owner of Gasthaus Schwartau, proudly welcomes us guests with a framed handwritten document, a 1667 excerpt from the Harburg inheritance registry. " ... he has free income from the inn, as long as he is the administrator." With a sly smile Jakob adds, "If I were now administrator, I would not have to pay any taxes..." We are here in the inn and surrounding land of Sebastian König, Jr. (1621 – 1667). The year in which the Harburg inheritance registry was created, 1667, is inscribed over the door of the main entrance, which also verifies the age of the inn.

We take a huge leap backward to the time before 1667, as far as that is possible, to tell about the origins of the land. Bodemann reports in 1629: Johann König and Simon Fock are Carsten Horstmann's heirs. When Simon Fock inherits land, Johann König already has two parcels of it. Johann pays Simon 17 bundles of oat sheaves.[626]

From this information, we can deduce that Carsten Horstmann is the previous owner of Simon Fock's estate. That acreage is served a public notice of indebtedness on March 29, 1602.[627] The estate owes 3,128.3 Marks.

On March 19, 1602, there is a meeting, and the debt is reduced to 2,323.0.0 Marks. This notice follows: "if a buyer is found and within a week (8 days) official notice is provided to our office, the amount due is 2,300.0.0 Marks."

Apparently, Carsten Horstmann cannot satisfy the church members' conditions and the estate is to be sold for 2,300 Marks. The condition is that Simon Fock take it over, probably for 2,300 or fewer Marks. Is Simon Fock an unknown buyer? Bodemann says that "Carsten Horstmann's heirs, therefore Simon Focke..." inherits the estate. Presumably he is the son-in-law who certainly will take over the acreage, but not with its huge debt. Thus, before the transfer of the land, the terms of purchase described below are made. The terms of purchase document is found in Appendix 55.[628]

Presumably, the inn already exists before 1600. The farmers and fishermen of the island need a place where they can discuss their common concerns. There are notices from the Harburg office to look over. Messages are brought from the duke to the administrator and the minister. It is known that Duke Otto II sends his "messages by horseback."[629] Horses have to be sheltered and guests have to be given lodging and food. What better place to conduct these activities than an inn. Or rather, did the inn develop from these needs in the first place? Also, the historic traveling arrangement between the duchy and those living in South Finkenwerder can include taking care of additional guests.

The archives contain sparse information about the time before 1600. Did Carsten Horstmann inherit the acreage? Who is the previous owner? An unsigned written document in Pastor Sebastian

König's handwriting, dated June 1597, leads to the conclusion that Lawrentz (Laurentz) Herman preceded Carsten Horstmann.

"June... 1559 Lawrentz Herman's son-in-law[630] is ordered to pay... Albert Schildes, who has filed a court claim, the following pension and expenses of 160 Marks. From this sum Carsten Horstmann will immediately pay Lawrentz Herman 30 Marks and an additional 30 Marks at Michelmas. Repeatedly Carsten Horstmann has acknowledged that he owes the sister-in-law 50 lübsch Marks, which Carsten Horstmann should receive during his lifetime."[631]

From all of the circumstances above, we can conclude that Laurentz Hermann marries the widow of Albert Schildes and functions as interim operator for several years. This supposition is supported by looking through Carsten Horstmann's 1602 notification of debts. He owes 800 Marks solely to "Albert Schildes' blessed surviving daughter" and 600 Marks to "Lawrentz Herman, the guardian of the old maid Catharine Schildes," probably Albert Schildes' sister, who works on his estate during her unmarried years. Laurentz Hermann acts as her guardian so that she does not get her share of the estate.

Who is Albert Schildes? He is probably the same person as "Albert Schilt" whose name appears among the farmers who are questioned regarding the 1571 missal incident (see chapter: "The Official Records of the Harburg Synod: Treasure Trove...").[632]

There is no uniformity of spelling at this time in history. People write the same way they speak.

Page 180

Keeping this in mind, the reader might not become so irritated when the same person is called Hostmann and Horstmann; Linnemann and Lindemann; Fock, Focke, Focken, Vock, and Vocke;

Harms and Harmens. The Finkenwerder church registry alone contains nine different variations of the König family name: Koning, Koniges, Koninges, Konig, Köning, Konings (1630), König (1667), Königs. From 1679 on it is usually spelled "König," but once in 1714 the name appears as Köhnig.

There is also no uniform spelling of first names. Someone can be named Anna-Anntje-Annke, but she is always the same woman. The same applies to Catharina, Catrina, Trina. Also, Sebastian becomes Bastian; Susanna becomes Sanna; Margarethe becomes Grete, Gretje, or Gretsche.

The following is a list of the previous owners of Gasthof Schwartau for the last 400 years:

1. Albert Schildes, listed in the years 1571, 1597, 1602.

2. Lawrentz Hermans is interim owner[633] in 1597. He apparently marries the widow of the previous owner and runs the estate until Carsten Horstmann, the son of Schildes' widow, can take over the property.

3. Carsten Horstmann, the son-in-law of Albert Schildes and son of Administrator Hans Horstmann is listed in 1597 and 1602. Because of numerous notices of outstanding debts, he has to offer the estate up for sale in 1602. After successful negotiations with the church members, his son-in-law, Simon Focke, takes possession of the property.

4. Lüneburg Administrator Simon Focke is listed in 1617 in the church registry and in 1667 in the inheritance registry, page 122. His son, also Simon Fock, dies unmarried in 1658. The estate is equally divided between his daughters, Ilsche and Gretsche Fock.

5. LÜNEBURG ADMINISTRATOR JOHANN KÖNIG.[634] Born 1587, dies 1649 (501). In 1607, he marries Ilsche Fock, daughter of his predecessor. Whether he becomes the official owner of the estate cannot be ascertained. In 1645, he is mentioned for the first time as owner of the inn.

6. LÜNEBURG ADMINISTRATOR SEBASTIAN KÖNIG, JR. Born 1621, dies 1667 (615), estate owner 1650 – 1667.

    According to the 1667 Harburg inheritance registry, he inherits the estate from Simon Fock/Vocke, jointly with his cousin Henning Linnemann. Sebastian König, Jr. receives 10 ½ Morgen [0.6 – 0.9 of an acre], his cousin 11 Morgen. With 21 Morgen, the estate (before the splitting of the land) is the largest in Lüneburg-Finkenwerder. Even after the division, both portions of the estate are still larger than most of the others. The increased size of the original estate may be due to the astute work of Sebastian's three predecessor administrators: Simon Fock, Johann König, and Sebastian König, Jr.

7. Annke König, nee Harms, innkeeper. Born 1629, dies 1677 (616). She is the estate owner after the death of her husband, Sebastian, in 1667. She manages the estate for her dependent children. In 1670, she writes the details of her children's inheritance.

8. Claus Baje, interim innkeeper from 1670 – 1676 (617). Annke König, nee Harms, marries Claus Baje on April 5, 1670. He serves as interim innkeeper until his death on November 20, 1676. Annke dies two months later on January 28, 1677.

9. HANS KÖNIG, INNKEEPER AND OFFICIAL ON THE DIKE COMMITTEE. Born 1652, dies 1710 (720). Estate owner from 1680 – 1710.

Hans König is the second oldest son of Sebastian and Annke König.

In 1680 he marries Gesche (last name not known) and at this time apparently becomes heir to the estate and inn. He is 25 when his mother dies. It is safe to assume that he has been managing the estate since 1677. As a member of the dike committee, on January 6, 1704 Hans König signs "specifications concerning what the outstanding damage caused by the December 8, 1703 sea storm and strong winds was to the Finkenwerder dike and what repairing it would cost."[635] The total damage amounts to 3,274 lübisch Marks.

Page 181

10. BASTIAN KÖNIG, INNKEEPER, CHURCH COUNCIL MEMBER. Born 1685, dies 1766 (819).

As the eldest son, he becomes the heir, either upon his father's death in 1710 or at his marriage to Margareta Harmens on November 3, 1711.[636] Bastian König is responsible for many church bills for the years 1742 and 1744.[637] Fifty-two pages comprise the "monetary account for income and expenditures of the Finkenwerder Church, supervised by Harburg office, from January 1742 up to January 1, 1743, done by Bastian König, leader" which he himself signs "Bastian König, Rechnungsführender Jurat [member of local church council in charge of accounts]."[638]

As far as we know, Bastian König, at age 81, lives longer than any of his known ancestors. His wife dies on April 29, 1762 at age 70. (She is born on August 20, 1692.)

11. GERD KÖNIG, INNKEEPER, MEMBER OF THE LOCAL CHURCH COUNCIL. Born 1726, dies 1796 (914).

Gerd König is the youngest of the five sons and becomes the heir. The reason may be that his four brothers may already be married and "be provided for" when Gerd marries. Gerd and Ilsabe have three daughters, two who marry and one who dies at age three.

Gerd's second marriage is on November 18, 1770 to Rebecca Rusten. They have eight children. None of their three sons survive. Of the five daughters, only two marry. After five generations, the last "König" inhabits the estate and the inn. Gerd dies from a pulmonary disease at age 70 on December 9, 1796. He leaves no male heirs.

For the years 1743 and 1745, Gerd König is "member of the local church council in charge of accounts,"[639] although he is only 17 and 19 year old, respectively. In these years he twice replaces his father, who occupies this position in 1742 and 1744.

In the year of his first marriage there is a dowry chest bench with the inscription: GEHRDT KÖNIG ANNO 1758. The bench measures 193 cm. long and 45 cm. deep. The seat height is 50 cm. and the back rest is 95 cm. high.

12. Paul Feldmann, innkeeper, head of church record books. Born September 10, 1783, dies October 25, 1833 (1039).

On June 5, 1806, Paul Feldmann marries REBECKA KÖNIG, Gerd König's daughter from his second marriage. On November 24, 1807 the pair has a daughter, Rebecca, who marries Carsten Benidt on July 13, 1826.

ILLUSTRATION 100: "Lüneburg-Finckenwärder." The excerpt from the Topographischen Landesaufnahme des Kurfürstentums Hannover 1777 [Topographical Land Divisions of the Prince Elector of Hannover in 1777] shows the course of the dike and the streets, with organization of the farmers and their fields divided by irrigation ditches.

[Paul Feldmann, con't]

They occupy the former Harms estate, where Rebecca's ancestors, the Administrators Hans and Jacob Harms, had lived. Rebecca Feldmann marries into the estate of her forefathers, which may be the basis for her not inheriting the Schwartau estate, even through she comes from Gerd's first marriage.[640]

Paul Feldmann and Rebecka König are married only seven years. She dies on August 12, 1813 "just eight days before her 28TH birthday...of dropsy [an old term for swelling or edema of the soft tissue due to the accumulation of excess water] and is buried with a celebration of her life on the 15TH."[641] This would be the end of the König lineage on this estate if Paul Feldmann's second wife were not a descendant of Rhegius.

Remarriage is a question of economics during this era because otherwise, who will care for the children and the household? That is the reason for Paul's second marriage to MAGDALENA MEYER on August 25, 1814. She is "the daughter of Hinrich Meyer, a Hausmann [homeowner] on the Lüneburg side of the island." His daughter "is a young maiden wearing a wreath[642] on her head. A wedding sermon is given." Magdalena Meyer is born on December 6, 1792.

Paul does not go far to look for a wife. The mother of the bride is none other than Margareta König, born on June 29, 1761. She is a half sister of his first wife and the daughter of Gerd König from his first marriage. For this reason, descendants of Paul Feldmann's second marriage are also König and Rhegius descendants. This remains the case today for the owner of the Schwartau estate.

Gerd König dies in 1796, 10 years before his daughter Rebecka marries Paul Feldmann. It is not known who manages the estate during these ten years. It is probably the eldest daughter from Paul's first marriage. Margareta König and her daughter, who is Paul's second wife, are also members of the extended family.

In 1825, 1827, and 1829, Paul Feldmann serves as supervisor of the church record book.

ILLUSTRATION 101: The dowry chest bench from 1758, the year of Gerd König's marriage, was on display in Gasthof Schwartau until a few years ago. The backboard and the side arms are original. The chest was replaced. (Photo: Rudolf Meier).

ILLUSTRATION 102: The Finkenwerder Room in the Bomann-Museum in Celle has two chairs inscribed "J. Metta König 1809" (1114), as well as a bench inscribed "Jungfer Metta König 1809." Additionally, there is a bench inscribed "Jacob König, 1745," (903). (Postcard from the Bomann-Museum).

Page 183

13. Jakob Schwartau, innkeeper. Born November 15, 1811, dies April 12, 1888.

On June 26, 1834 Jacob Schwartau marries ANNA FELDMANN, born on July 3, 1815. She is a daughter from the second marriage of Paul Feldmann to Magdalena Meyer. A year after his father-in-law's death, Jacob takes over the inn. Jacob Schwartau is a descendant of the Schwartau estate on the southwest part of Finken-werder. Cord Schwartau, who came from Altenwerder, was married there in 1670.

14. PAUL SCHWARTAU, INNKEEPER. Born August 14, 1837, dies December 4, 1914.

    Paul Schwartau marries Anna Feldmann on May 20, 1869. She is born on August 10, 1842 and dies on January 4, 1905. His father, Jacob, lives to be 77 years old. It is not known when Paul takes over the inn.

15. JAKOB SCHWARTAU, INNKEEPER. Born February 25, 1875, dies April 14, 1961.

    On May 23, 1902 he marries Elise Margarethe Wriede, daughter of Finkenwerder shipyard owner Johann Wriede and his wife Katharina Maria Schwartau from Altenwerder.

16. PAUL SCHWARTAU, INNKEEPER. Born November 6, 1902, dies November 23, 1969.

    He marries Elisabeth Fock on July 27, 1929.

17. JAKOB SCHWARTAU, INNKEEPER. Born July 23, 1930.

    He marries Elke Kamp on May 22, 1954. She is born March 21, 1933. Jacob Schwartau inherits the inn in 1969. His family still owns it.

ILLUSTRATION 103: Jacob Schwartau, born in 1930, owner of the Gasthof Schwartau, with the goblet donated in 1857 at the inaugural inspection of the dike. The goblet holds .7 liters. Red wine is usually drunk from it. At the time of the dike's inspection, it has to be emptied in one draught.[643] One person is said to have done it in 19 seconds! (Photo: Walter König).

The inscription on the goblet described in Illustration 103 reads:

Good health
To His Royal Highness
To the well being of the country
To the Halls of Justice
And to the members of the Dike Inspection Committee

To the Finkenwerder Dike's Inspection
Donated by E.C. Compe
Senior Leader of Harburg
1857

Older Finkenwerder residents fondly remember the wedding celebrations at Gasthof Schwartau and many a joyous time dancing during their youth. How it was during the "Kaiser's time" is reported by Finkenwerder Regional Poet, Dietrich Stehr:

"The greatest enjoyment and the main celebration at Gasthof Schwartau was on the Kaiser's birthday. Merriment and joy prevailed. At 7 pm the musicians began to play. Seven musicians and two drummers made "Bleckmusik" [played with brass instruments]. Around 11 pm the banquet was served, consisting of fresh soup, oxen and pork on bread, potatoes, gravy, baked apples with cooked plums, and red beets. On this occasion, some veterans from 1870 – 71 were called forward to tell of their war experiences. This became extremely interesting.

When the speeches ended, the music started with: 'Ich hab' mich ergeben' ['I Devoted Myself to It'] or 'Heil Dir im Siegerkranz' ['Hail to You Wearing the Victor's Crown'] or 'Es braust ein ruf wie Donnerhall' ['A Cry Erupts Like the Sound of Thunder'] and other patriotic songs. And when everyone has had enough singing, the hall is cleared, chairs are put away, and the really serious dancing and feasting starts. At the Gasthof Schwartu, eating and drinking are first rate. Seven half-liters of beer are sold for a Reichsmark. A delightful grog costs one Dohler. The women drink 'Love Flowers,' a mixture of eggs, cognac, and raspberry vinegar."[644]

Page 184

ILLUSTRATION 104: Gasthof Schwartau, around 1904. To the right of the façade is the salon. A coachman from the Elbschlossbrauerei [Castle of the Elbe Brewery] delivers drinks to those seated at the table in front of the entrance. Jacob Schwartau, born in 1875, is pictured with his wife, Frau Elise Margarethe Wriede, holding their son, Paul, in her arms. All of the Schwartaus mentioned above are Rhegius descendants.

With the marriage of Johann König and Ilsche Fock in 1607 the long history of the König family on this property begins. After six generations, the family name dies out with Rebecka König in 1813. Nevertheless, up to the present day, Rhegius' descendants live on this beautiful piece of land in Finkenwerder on the Southern Elbe.

Rhegius Descendants in the Finkenwerder Parsonage

In his handwritten document, Pastor Evers reports two instances in which the Finkenwerder ministers marry their predecessors' daughters.[646] Specifically, Eibert Jantzen marries the daughter of his predecessor, Schulze, and Johann Friedrich Overbeck takes the daughter of his predecessor, Michael Pflug, as his wife in 1722.

Such unions happen frequently in these times. A new pastor almost always comes from outside the area. He knows no one in his new surroundings. He is first introduced to the "old" pastor's family and often lives with them. Is it surprising that he is attracted to the lovely daughters of the household? Certainly, it is well within the realm of possibility that marrying a daughter of someone in the desired position is an unwritten prerequisite of the job.

Pastor Evers does not know that there is a third case in 1622, which we today consider the first instance. In that year, Sebastian König descendant, Johann Schulz, marries a "daughter of the König family." Accordingly, starting with Sebastian König, there is an unbroken chain of three generations of Rhegius descendants in the Finkenwerder parsonage.

· Pastor Sebastian König (401), serves in the position from 1588 – 1621. His daughter, Ilsche König, marries her father's successor, Johann Schulze, in 1622.

ILLUSTRATION 105: Vigorous trade on the Southern
Elbe River around 1888 – the Schiffswerft [shipyard]
Behren with the houses at the dike on the Southern Elbe
in the background. Gasthof Schwartau is the second from
the right. (Hinrich Paul Lüdders, 1828 – 1897, mentor to
the maritime painter, Joh's Holst, Altenwerdeer[645])

Page 185

Pastor Johann Schulze (506), holds the position from
1621 – 1646. Evers[646] states about him: "...according to this
gravestone in the former church building, he dies in 1646.
The words are: Born Johannes Schulze, pastor, Died in
Finckenwerder 1646 at age 61, 25 years as pastor, married
24 years ... Some of his descendants still live in Harburg."[647]

Johann Schulze and Ilsche König marry in 1622.[648] (Pastor
Schulze calls his wife Ilse, the High German form of her name.)
The couple has four children:

DATE OF BIRTH	NAME	
May 14, 1625	Günther	Godfather: Only Johann König! Günther is pastor in Kuhstedt from 1658 – 1689. While there, he "commissions" a communion chalice. In 1660, he is transferred to Kirchwisstedt and also serves in Kuhstedt until 1663.[649] He dies in 1689 in Kirchwisstedt.

December 6, 1626	Anna	Godparents: "Hans Schwartau's wife, Johann König's wife, Hans Harmen's wife, Johann von Rigen and Johan Wulffes" (Anna marries Hans Wiseke on December 2, 1645).
January 8, 1629	Margreta	Godparents: "Annerl di Schenk, wife of pastor and superintendent of Harburg; wife of senior civil servant, Henrici Schrader; Johann König's daughter Margret; Herr Ernst Christian Wermaring, pastor of Hollensted; and Hans Harmenss."
June 6, 1633	Johann	Godparents: "Hans Schulze, citizen of the new city of Salzwedel; Gerhardus Meyer, choirmaster and organist of the Harburg School; and the wife of my brother, Jochim Schulzen."[650]
		(Johan dies on January 4, 1635).

That Pastor Schulze marries a daughter of Sebastian König is confirmed in his report to Administrator Johann König, regarding the "iron cows." Here he speaks of Johann König as his brother-in-law.[651]

- Eibert Jantzen succeeds Pastor Johann Schulze in 1647. Evers reports that Jantzen marries Margreta Schulz, his predecessor's daughter. The wedding takes place on January 20, 1647 in Finkenwerder. The couple has six children, of whom at least three die in childhood. In 1664, after 18 years of marriage, Eibert Jantzen records his wife's death in the church registry: "...Margreta Jantzen is buried on May 12. My wife, who piously went to meet the Lord, died on May 8 between 2 – 3 in the afternoon, at age 37, and in the 18TH year of our marriage."

On November 20, 1666, Pastor Jantzen marries Elisabeth Anna Ludeman from Harburg. Three children result from this second marriage.

Eibert Jantzen serves as pastor on Finkenwerder for 31 years and is buried here on January 23, 1678. His age is unknown. His second wife survives him by 28 years. She dies on April 5, 1706 at the age of 76. (Details about the children from both marriages are in Appendix 56.)

Following an old tradition, the eldest son (here Johann David Jantzen) becomes a clergyman. In the next generation, Johann David Jantzen's eldest son, Johann Otto Jantzen, also becomes a clergyman.

Page 186

In this generation, there is another connection to Finkenwerder because Johann Otto Jantzen is a grandson of Pastor Eibert Jantzen. Johann Otto Jantzen marries Dorothea Eleonora Evers on October 30, 1729. She is a sister of Daniel Conrad Heinrich Evers, the Finkenwerder pastor who has frequently been cited as the Finkenwerder Island's chronologist.[652]

When Pastor Eibert Jantzen's wife, Margareta Schulze, dies in 1664, her children are not yet of legal age so they stay a few years in the parsonage. Beginning in 1588, when Sebastian König arrives in Finkenwerder, we have a span of almost 90 years in which Rhegius descendants live in the Finkenwerder parsonage.

How must we imagine this parsonage? Albershardt says in his unpublished 1945 description of the house that the location is "at the end of the old 'Nurddieks' [North Dike], the rest of which has almost disappeared. The 'ool Pastoren hus' [old parsonage] is in the middle of the island. Formerly, the old parsonage stood next to the 'Karken-wurt' [Kark=Low German for Kirche (church), Wurt=Large manmade mound of earth upon which structures are constructed in low-lying areas to protect them from flooding.]

The church registry mentions that a barn was built for 139 Marks in 1600. The "iron cows" and the other domestic animals have to be sheltered and the field crops must be preserved. There is also peat and brush to be burned.

In 1604, a member of the local church council, Peter Finck in Harburg, buys two glazed tile stoves, one for the parsonage and a second one for the sextonry.[653] He pays 16 Marks for both stoves. Installation and necessary building materials are an added 15.13.0 Marks. The tile stove is located in the Dönz [old-fashioned living room], while in the kitchen, on the other side of the wall, is an open fire, over which the pots are hung. Smoke and heat pull upward through the chimney. In the shifting smoke, hams, bacon, and sausages are hung and stored. In addition, the smoke makes it easier to keep the grain that is stored on the floor dry. Now we can really envision what is today shown in open-air museums.

"The tile stove was the first and most significant piece of equipment to make people's houses comfortable. This could not be accomplished with the iron 'Füerschapp' with its coal embers. There is evidence that the stoves first appear in Hamburg in the second half of the 15TH century. In the upper marshes on the Elbe, this innovation occurs at about the same time as in Finkenwerder."[654] From this perspective, we can see that the Finkenwerder parsonage keeps up with its era and that our ancestors treasure this "modern convenience" on cold winter days.

A further improvement in housing conditions occurs almost simultaneously. In 1607, Pastor Sebastian König enters a sum into the church accounts for "patches to the windows in the church and the parsonage." The glazier, Otto Hessen in Harburg, and his assistant receive 15.8.0 Marks for this work and 2.4.0 Marks for food and beer. The amount is almost as high as the cost of the tile stoves. This is an indication of the era's high glass prices. There are probably small green or blue irridescent "Bohemian glass" panes, composed of lead. They soon become opaque from the constant smoke. At the end of the Middle Ages, the citizens of Hamburg still do not have glass windows, rather, the houses have hatches that can be closed in bad weather and on cold days.[655] How much longer can it take until these conveniences are in the homes of farmers, fishermen, and daily wage earners?

In 1615, 14 Marks are spent for "installing a new tile stove and building a wall in the Schwibbogen [flying buttress]." An open hearth is probably being rebuilt into an enclosed place for cooking, covered by a "flying buttress," which will better draft the smoke upward and lessen flying sparks.[656]

Page 187

In 1615, extensive repairs are made to the parsonage. Larchwood planks are purchased and repairs to the "living quarters" are paid for. First, we think it is a bedroom, but, as it turns out, it is the privy that has to be redone.

During Pastor Schulz's tenure, expenses for an oven are listed in the church accounts.[657]

"July 6, Hinrich Focken, Carsten Bannit's stepson, for sod, the same as he put in the parsonage[658] so that an oven could later be placed over it – paid...Mark 0.4.4;

Claus Köpken, citizen of Hamburg, for 700 stones for the oven...Mark 7.8.0; Taking these stones to the sailing barge[659] to transport back here...Mark 1.1.0;

Item for payment for fetching 2 barges from the Holstein Authority...Mark 1.8.0."

The oven is also paid for out of church funds. It will not only be used by the pastor's family, but also by congregation members if they do not have their own oven. Living is organized for self-sufficiency.

Since olden times, the quality of the water appears to be a public health problem of special concern. In 1762, Pastor Evers complains that he... "has to use water from the irrigation ditches and does not have the slightest chance to have healthy water brought in."[660] Where does the pastor get water for baptizing? Even at the beginning of the last century, one of the Lüneburg school children, who has to sing at a church function, is sent to the ditches to fetch baptism water. Since it was summer, the boy in the story fetched water containing crushed grain duck food. This event is repeated from generation to generation

What does the parsonage look like where Rhegius descendants live for three generations? We are grateful for the fortunate circumstance that a 1759 drawing of the parsonage has been preserved. Otherwise, we could not answer the question. It compares the observable new construction to the old parsonage, which is the one in which the families of Pastors König, Schulze, and Jantzen reside.

Illustration 106 shows the plan of the ground floor (A) and the profile (B) of the old parsonage. Originally, the size of the house is

50 feet wide (14.32 m) and 77 feet long (22.05 m), including the stables. Without the stables, it is about 47 feet (13.46 m). That is almost 200 square meters of living space, plus the two rooms in the attic.[661] The rooms are described in the drawing as follows:

"Special drawing of the parsonage located on the Elbe Island of Finkenwerder in Harburg district, No. 1:

A) The ground floor plan contains:

a. the vestibule of the house; b. the living room; c. kitchen; d. bedroom above the cellar; e. entrance to the cellar in the kitchen; f. spiral staircase to two bedrooms diagonally across from one another; g. 3 small rooms and bedroom for children and domestic servants; h. an empty, unused small room and bedroom (wüst = empty bahr = probably not in use); i. entrance to the side of the root cellar; k. exit to the garden; l. horse and cattle stalls; m. additions for storing peat and wood; n. cattle entrance

Page 188

B) Profile of the old building toward the porch of the transcept. That part is enclosed by yellow lines. It includes the multi-purpose room for the cattle and the small rooms for the fruit. The part of the harvest agreed upon by the community for its use would be stored here along with salvaged wood for rebuildling and other construction purposes such as the cattle pen and the small rooms for storage and preservation of fruits and feeds."[662]

In the drawing, we can clearly see the house's "Wurt," the small manmade mound upon which it is built to protect it from storms and floods, as well as the steps leading to the Wurt. The illustration shows a structure from Lower Saxony that has two purposes: 1) living quarters and 2) stables. The "I" denoting both horse and cattle stables and the "n" indicating the cattle entrance confirm how numerous and important the cattle are.

Pastor Evers provides documentation for the reasons the new construction on the parsonage in 1756 exceeds cost estimates. The total cost of Reichstaler 2292.19.3½ cents is about 112 Reichstaler over projected costs. Evers is not sparing in his criticism of the architect, who fails to inspect the building site. Since the old parsonage sat on ground that was much too low, it was ruined by the flood of 1756. Through the pastor's intercession, it was raised 10 feet so that it could also serve as a refuge during floods.

ILLUSTRATION 106: Floor plan and view of the gable of the old Finkenwerder parsonage.[663]

In addition, if the total cost had been based on accurate measurements, from the lengthening of the staircase to the raised foundation to "finishing the pig stalls with two new troughs and providing a two-seated lavatory for the servants,"[664] there would not have been the excess costs.

Three generations of Rhegius descendants are not the only ones to grow up in the parsonage. Over the centuries, numerous Rhegius descendants come to the parsonage to commemorate births, marriages, and deaths. Not to be forgotten are the many confirmands who receive Biblical instruction in the meeting room of the "ool Pastorenhus" [old parsonage].

Page 189

The Kinau Family of Poets as Rhegius Descendants

"With the homeland in the heart, embrace the world." These words appear in the *Hamburger Abendblatt* [*Hamburg Evening Paper*] as a slogan on the masthead. These words are similar to those above the Gorch Fock Halle [Hall] in Finkenwerder: "The homeland is the key to the people's soul, but then there are also people who are the key to their homeland."[665]

Gorch Fock, whose real name is Johann Kinau, is one such key to his North German homeland. He is the key to seafaring, to the life of the farmers and the fishermen on his home Island of Finkenwerder, and to its tradition of fighting for survival on land and sea. His pseudonym has elements of both the farmers and fishermen, as he himself writes:

> "Georg is the farmer,
> And Fock the fisherman,
> But Gorch [Low German for Georg] Fock is still waiting,
> And looks at both of them."

347

The farms and farm people certainly play an important role in Gorch Fock's short stories, but his real passion is for the sea, which he views as a living force of nature, as an adventure, as fate. The sea nurtures, but also demands risks from the seafarer and fisherman. The first sentence of Fock's major work, *Seefahrt ist not!* [*Seafaring is Necessary!*], already shows us his life's theme when he starts by letting the character, Pastor Bodeman, preach, "Especially, we beseech you for those who seek their nourishment upon the water. Bless, bless the fishermen on the sea and on the rivers, protect the men and the ships in all perils! ... And he may have the inner strength to sail through the tempest...And the sea seizes the word 'sea' – the Nordsee [North Sea] becomes the Mordsee [Murderous Sea] - their clouds hunting things down, annihilating them, tearing them to pieces. With her whistling, thundering storms, the gigantic foaming, roaring sea, with fire and lightening, with ground swelling and tempest, with shredded sails and broken masts...and there was no one there who would dispute this description."[666]

ILLUSTRATION 107: On July 19, 1912, Gorch Fock writes to Goldschmidt, the owner of Glogau Publishing, that he will be finished with his book, Seefahrt ist not, on August 1. (We gratefully acknowledge permission from Hans-Joachim Gabriel)

The work, published in 1913, makes Fock's name well known far beyond the borders of his homeland. He unleashes a groundswell at that time. The emperor seeks more funds for a German navy. The protagonists of the novel have the perfect character traits for the emperor's goal: obedience, risk taking, testing the sea, dependability, close ties to their homeland, patriotic reminiscences in their diaries, and letters from the front, all of which lead the Third Reich to fervently embrace them to suit its own purposes. On May 8, 1933 the new sailing ship for training the Reich's navy is christened the *Gorch Fock* in memory of his "hero's death" as a volunteer in the Skagerrakschlacht [Battle of Jutland/Skagerrak] in 1916.[667] The Oberbefehlshaber [commander-in-chief] of the navy, Generaladmiral Raeder, gave the christening speech from the launch. Its national pathos sounds strange to us today.[668] It is a type of redemption for Germany that following the war, the country names its naval training ship *Gorch Fock*, after an author whose work it had adopted for its own purposes. It is a message of goodwill to all on the world's seven seas and is recognized as such throughout the world.

Page 190

Writing is in the Kinau family's blood. Rudolf, who is seven years younger than Johann (Gorch Fock), begins writing when he is displeased with his brother's obituary. He composes his own obituary, called *Achtern 'n Dick* [*Behind the Dike*]. It is a dialogue with his fallen brother, a little story written in simple, touching words as can only be exchanged between those who trust one another.[669] These words begin a long series of over 30 books, radio plays, and theater dramas. For the radio series, *Fief Minuten gooden Wind* [Five Minutes of Good Wind], *Sünnschien op'n Weg* [Sunshine on the Path], and *Hör mol'n beten to* [*Listen for a Moment*], he writes over 1,000 broadcasts. They are packed with regional North German humor and folk wisdom applied to daily life.[670] Often he reads from his own works and repeatedly tells about the world of his carefree childhood days and about the exciting celebrations on the island, about the world of the farmer on the land and the capable fisherman on the sea, of the world of the common people with their daily cares, and of their thoughts about how the years go by.

Rudolf Kinau entertains many generations. His *Thees Bott dat Woterküken* [*Thees Bott – The Water Maiden*] is read aloud to us by our parents on winter evenings before we could read for ourselves. How often it makes us laugh! In all his humor, he writes about things that are very deep and thought provoking. Over 1.5 million copies of *Kamerad und Kameradin* [*Boy and Girl Companions*] are printed. In his autobiography, *Mit eegen Oogen – Biller ut mien Leben* [*With My Own Eyes – Pictures of My Life*], which he publishes when he is 70 years old, he presents us with pictures of his life.

Often Rudolf visits the grave of his brother, Gorch Fock, on the small rocky Swedish island of Stensholmen, where the waves from the Skagerrak strait wash upon its shores and Swedish farmers build Gorch Fock a simple but impressive grave of rocks from the cliffs. Rudolf's poem for his brother, who died at a young age, suggests Rudolf had many talks with Gorch about the condition of the world.

ILLUSTRATION 108: The four Kinau siblings. From above left to lower right: Johann (Gorch Fock), Jakob, Rudolf, and Katharine (Katharine in Finkenwerder costume, 1936, during the 700TH anniversary celebration).

"As you are like a silvery beam,
  So still and rocky is the coast,
  So modest and simple is your grave,
  Far, far from the city and marshes
  You lie and sleep. The joyful seas
  Play with the mussels and stones.
  The seagull sounds out, the sea wind is silent.
  A steep and shining spray arises.
  Without a cross or crown a grave stone.
  Here lies Gorch Fock!"

Jacob Kinau, the last of the three brothers, also starts writing. He publishes his first work, *Die See ruft* [*The Sea is Calling*] in 1924 when he is 40 years old. The story takes place around 1760 during the tenure of Pastor Evers. The plot centers around the people from "Buschhof," which is easily recognizable as the Nesshof on Finkenwerder Island. Just like the Königs, the Kinaus have ancestors there. Jakob frequently mentions the name "Keunig," which shows he is well acquainted with family ties, even if not directly tied back to Pastor Sebastian König.

Jakob Kinau seems to be the brother most interested in family lineage. In 1935, he publishes his book, *Gorch Fock. Ein Leben im Banne der See* [*Gorch Fock: A Life Under the Spell of the Sea*]. It is the history of the Kinau family, which originates in the village of Kinau in the foothills of the Riesen Mountains. The family's destiny takes the Kinaus via Halberstadt to Northern Germany. His great-grandfather, Johann Friedrich Kinau (apothecary, surgeon, and doctor), arrives in Moorburg around 1820 and shortly thereafter comes to Finkenwerder. The restless man dies an early death on June 1, 1834.[671]

A Life Under the Spell of the Sea becomes a highly productive resource for our family history. We learn about Gorch Fock's early interest in his ancestors. "He considers it his highest duty to keep the family traditions and blood line proudly alive. At age 17 he maintains a correspondence club with all related people in his "cosmos" [extended family] in Amsterdam, in order to research his ancestors."[672] He probably has no time to write up this material. But Jacob Kinau's efforts to learn about his grandfather, Johann Nikolaus Kinau, put us on track to connect the Kinau-König families. (See Appendix 57).

"Johann Nikolaus did not only have eyes for the sea. He had also cast his eyes upon Katharina Fock, the daughter of Bastian Fock, who farms a Grönland [Greenland] acreage and is Finkenwärder administrator. Johann Nikolaus marries Katharina Fock on February 18, 1844." (See Page 28 of *Gorch Fock. Ein Leben im Banne der See.*) Bastian Fock's mother is Rebecka König (1017), born February 20, 1756. She is the great-great-grandmother of the Kinau brother poets.

Among other things, we are grateful to Jakob Kinau for his three novels about Finkenwerder: *Die See ruft [The Sea is Calling]*, *Freie Wasser [Open Waters]*, and *Leegerwall [Leeward]*.[673] All three describe the fate of the people living on the Nesshof. In *Leeward*, he describes the expansion of the Hamburg metropolis and how it threatens to annihilate old Finkenwerder. His brothers also frequently re-work this theme. They see their childhood paradise and the land of their ancestors being sacrificed to the new times.[674]

In his publication of his older brother's collective works, Jacob Kinau demonstrates the utmost dedication to the preservation of old Finkenwerder.[675] A decade after his seafaring brother's death, he finishes the task of "assembling the treasures," as he describes it in the preface. Let us speak about the Kinaus as Jakob Kinau best depicts his family's heritage: "Our father, Heinrich Kinau, devoted his life to fishing in the North Sea after having stood on all masts and rigging of the tall sailing ships of this world.[676] In 1876 our first Ewer was built on the southern dike. [A Ewer is a type of fishing boat found only in Northern Germany, designed especially for shallow waters. It is an earlier version of the Kuter (Cutter in English) and is sometimes refered to as a Ewer-Cutter.]

Page 192

During these years, father was a 'Hartdrieber' [tough fisherman] who fished in the open sea when the other fishing boats were laying behind the islands. Too soon, he had to learn that sea fishing is more a matter of luck than willpower and that luck cannot be taken by force ...

Abject poverty reigned in our parents' humble abode. The only furnishings were four chairs, a bench, a table, and an armoire for storing the commode. Straw was the material in the two small bedrooms. But the whole day, the sun peeked through the two little windows and Mother's joyful laughter carried over the dike.

ILLUSTRATION 109: Heinrich Wilhelm Kinau's fishing boat H.F. 125 at the mouth of the Elbe. For him, it is a hard way to earn the family's daily bread. For his sons, it is a child's paradise. The ship is "large and mighty, the biggest and most beautiful ship in the whole wide world!"[677]

The eldest, Johann Kinau [Gorch Fock], was born on August 22, 1880. Within three years, there were already three children in the hut. Greta and Heiner were carried in their mother's arms and little Johann tugged on her apron! And Meta Holst's eyes were brighter and happier as they glanced over the dike upon the fishing smack, whose sails became more tattered and torn. I arrived two years later, and Rudolf came two years after that. Now the huts were full. Four boys and a girl. Father had to make a little wooden cubby hole in the wall into which I was placed each evening to sleep. Five little 'animals' to feed, which were always hungry. Five little 'Schieten-pedder,' for whom pants and boots easily wore out unlike things made of stronger materials. All these expenses on small wages — with all kinds of hard knocks and pressing debts bearing down on the farmers. Mother, how great you were that in spite of all these woes, you planted your sunny laughter into our hearts."[678]

To their great credit, all three brothers maintain the Finken-werder Plattdeutsch [Low German] language as it was spoken around 1900. Rudolf Kinau preserves the Low German language, a heartfelt cause he often emphasized. Jakob Kinau writes only in Hoch Deutsch [High German], interspersed with many dialogues in Low German. Also, the "Finkwarder Speeldeel" founded by Gorch Fock, is committed to the preservation of the Finkenwerder culture and language.

The youngest of the Kinau siblings, Metta Katharina, born December 15, 1893, dies August 25, 1988. She remains unmarried and lives at 6 Nessdeich until her death in Finkenwerder. She is a bank employee in Hamburg and lovingly takes care of her parents. In 1983, at age 90, she hosts the Finkenwerder reunion in her parents' home, now a museum. "If there is a Claus-Groth-House and a Matthias-Claudius House, then there should also be a Gorch-Fock-House." In that way, the Kinau-House comes to honor all Kinaus.[679]

Even though the literary works of the three brothers are very different, they make a harmonious whole. For each one of them, the home Island of Finkenwerder and seafaring, especially sea fishing under sail, are the foundation and backdrop of their passions and writings, shaped by their own experience in the family.

Page 193

ILLUSTRATION 110: Gorch Fock's
parents shortly before 1914.[680]

They have a flair for observing the daily lives and personality traits of their fellow citizens. They wrap these observations in the poetic art of storytelling, so that their works become much read "literature of the homeland."

ILLUSTRATION 111: Gorch Fock gives his father a present
of this door plate. It reads, "Heinrich Kinau, Sea Fisherman."

"...And Because this House Is Exposed at Land's End..."
THE NESSHOF ON FINKENWERDER

The sea is not quite here, but she is not far away. In stormy fall and winter weeks she presents her commanding calling card. Wind and waves whip the island. Built on reclaimed land, crowned and protected by mighty treetops, the Nesshof is buffered by the dike, which wards off the ravages of nature to which the island is exposed.

"The Ness" is the outermost western point of Finkenwerder, toward the broad part of the Lower Elbe, toward the "nose" of the former Gorieswerder. The largest farm on the island is located here, standing alone in the floods, outside the encircling dike. The landowner of the "Ness" is "an important man among the farmers of the Elbe archipelago, known far and wide, just as is the innkeeper of the Brocken, the highest point in the Harz Mountains. Rich and very independent, he lives on his island pinnacle according to Louis XVI's principle, 'I am the state.'"[681]

The reconstructed history of the farm goes back to the year 1568, when Tewes Quast buys the Ness from the Hamburg treasury. Two years later he builds the first farmhouse here. He becomes the first farmer of the Ness known to us.[682]

He owes his wealth to the lush meadows and productive fields to which the annual floods bring fertile mud when the water overflows the low lying summer dike. The mud provides sufficient soil to build and repair the dike, which happened in 1793 to an especially endangered section of the "Auedeich," later the "Steendiek."

Around this time the Ness farmer Carsten Benidt looks for a wife. On October 13, 1803, he marries twenty year old Anna König (1110). From the Finkenwerder church record book we learn that the wedding takes place at home:

Page 194

> "On October 13, 1803, young Casten [sic] Benit, marriageable son of Peter Benit Sr., who is a homeowner on the Ness, marries Anna König, daughter of the the late Hinrich König from the Hamburg side, at home, with the wedding sermon."

In 1746, Anna König's grandfather, Hinrich König, (909) (1718 – 1781) marries Anna Harmens, (910) (1705 – 1763). She is 13 years older than he. Anna Harmens is the widow of Hinrich von Riegen, homeowner and member of the local church council. She is the daughter of Administrator Paul Harmens (the latter is a descendant of Administrators Hans and Jakob Harms, Landscheideweg 110, according to Hübbe, acreage number 30).

The young woman comes from the farming tradition and knows life on the farm. Jakob Kinau describes first hand the status of a Ness farmer's wife. Getting married is not the couple's only obligation. Carsten Benidt and Anna König have their hands full with everything that has to be done. The antiquated house is dilapidated and in need of urgent repair. They get to work and by 1806 construct one of the most magnificent farm houses on the island.

For over a century, the house conveys the wealth and social status of its builders. In 1920, it is destroyed by arson. The main beam bears the inscription:

MAY GOD ALMIGHTY'S HIGHEST
BENEVOLENCE PRESERVE

THOSE WHO NOW GOVERN THIS HOUSE.

TO PROTECT MAN WIFE AND CHILD.

AND BECAUSE THIS HOUSE IS
EXPOSED AT LAND'S END,

WE BESEECH GOD TO WARD OFF

ALL HARMFUL MATTERS.

Gloria in Exelsis Deo. A.D. 10 July 1806[683]

In 1936, in celebration of Finkenwerder's 700ᵀᴴ year, Johann Jakob Fock, who was 76 years old at that time and is the son-in-law of Nesshof farmer, Carsten Schwartau, writes about the layout of the house and its furnishings:

ILLUSTRATION 112: The Nesshof, the magnificent Niedersachsenhaus [Lower Saxon] style farm house on the westernmost point of Finkenwerder Island. For over 100 years, it is the hearth and home for several generations of Rhegius descendants.

"As we step into the house, to the right is the Döns [small, heated old-fashioned living room] with the well-known 'Finsterschapp' [aperture], through which one can see the vestibule. In the small room there are two curtained beds built into the wall. One of them is close to the oven, the other is in the outer wall. An old player piano, a sofa, a table, and various chairs all turned on a lathe, and an armchair were the furniture in the living room. There was no 'best room' [parlor] at that time. The 'Flett' or the vestibule was covered with flooring and separated from the outer room, which was for the livestock.

Left of the vestibule is another small room, the so-called 'hooge Döns' [high Döns, meaning the floor was laid higher, so that the living room could be heated better]. This room was not always occupied. Behind the living room on both sides – the left side was the parent's apartment - lay the kitchens. To the right was a very large kitchen because the household was large. At the table every day, besides the farmer and his wife, there were nine children, two male servants, and three hired hands, as well as several female maids.

We step away from the entrance into the large room. There we see the steps that lead to the granary and the room for smoking meats and fish, which is also on the same floor.

Page 195

This was all there was to see. Let us now look at the 'Grootdeel' [the common room and rooms for the live-stock]. First are the servants' rooms, then the stalls for the horses, the cattle, and many calves. Just behind the farm house is the barn. On one hillock were located another pig sty and a building referred to as the 'bake house.' I do not know whether they actually baked in the bake house, but it is probable."

The author, a Rhegius descendant, allows us a glimpse into life on the farm. By herself, Anna König has to supervise the food preparation. Food for every meal for the family and the hired help, a total of about 20 people, has to be taken care of. And every day, the many children require the mother's full attention and energy.

Anna König's marriage at the Ness farm is not the Rhegius family's only connection to the farm up to this point, as we can surmise from the following chronology of Ness owners.

1. Tewes Quast from the Altes Land acquires the Ness in 1568 from the Hamburg treasury, erects a large manmade mound of earth, and builds the first Nesshof.

359

2. Hinrich Rust, apparently the administrator mentioned by Hübbe in 1612, 1617, and 1624, dies on March 15, 1625. He is most likely a son-in-law of the previous owner. His wife, name unknown, dies on August 20, 1625.

3. Hans Harms, Hamburg administrator, is mentioned in 1645 by Bodemann, page 33. As owner of the Nesshof, he is the father-in-law of Sebastian König, Jr. (615), who marries Hans Harms' daughter, Annke Harms, in 1650. Whether Harms is the son-in-law of the previous owner is unknown.

4. Hinrich Harms, son of the aforementioned Hans Harms. Born September 22, 1622, dies on March 21, 1667. On July 12, 1646 he marries Margreta Köpken, who dies in May 1698. Hübbe mentions Hinrich as owner of the Nesshof in the years 1650, 1660, and 1661.

5. Hans Stehr, born 1643 (calculated), dies March 5, 1717. He is mentioned by Hübbe as owner of the Nesshof in 1680 and 1713. His first marriage is to Margreta Harms on July 4, 1669. Her maiden name is Köpke, and she is the widow of the previous owner, Hinrich Harms. Margreta Stehr dies in May 1698. On October 10, 1699 Hans Stehr marries a second time to Catharina Focken.

6. Jacob Harms, Born October 21, 1688, dies May 7, 1729. Hübbe lists him as the Nesshof owner in 1726. (Hübbe writes 1726, but likely means 1762). Jacob Harms is the son of Administrator Paul Harms and Catrina von Rigens. Jacob's second marriage is to Rebecca Fock, donor of the church chandelier. See, "The Finkenwerder Church's Chandelier ." On November 2, 1717, he marries Catharina Focken, the widow of Hans Stehr.

7. Carsten Benit, born January 4, 1706 "on the Ness," dies October 17, 1757. Hübbe mentions in 1740 that he is the son of the Landvogt [provincial administrator], Carsten

Benit. His first marriage on July 4, 1730 is to Catharina Harmens, born Fock. She is the widow of the prior owners, Jacob Harmens and Hans Stehr. Therefore, she is the wife of three Ness farmers: first Hans Stehr, second Jacob Harms, and third Carsten Benit. She dies on January 7, 1740. Her marriage to Carsten Benit is childless.

His second marriage is on October 4, 1740 to Margarethe Rütern. She is born July 20, 1720 and dies February 22, 1785.

8. Peter Benit, baptized December 8, 1749, dies March 2, 1812. He is not mentioned by Hübbe.

On July 22, 1777 he marries Anna Fock. She is born August 28, 1760 and dies on March 22, 1832.

(Peter Benit's younger brother, Johann (1030), (1755 – 1822) marries Gesche König (1029) on October 30, 1781. She is born June 30, 1759 and is the oldest daughter of the innkeeper, Gerd König. They own the farm house built on the Osterfelddeich 136 in 1786.[684] Listed in the Kössenbitter [a periodical in Low German] in August 1791, page 11 and in Finder's book, page 201).

When Peter Benit's father, Carsten, dies in 1757, Peter is just eight years old. His mother, Margarethe Rütern, does not remarry. She lives until 1785. Whether she operates the farm by herself or eventually with a farm manager from 1757 up until the marriage of her son, Peter Benit, is unknown. It is possible that there is an interim manager.

Page 196

9. Carsten Benit, born October 12, 1778 on the Hamburg side of the Ness, dies October 1, 1860 (1111). Hübbe mentions him as Nesshof owner in 1809. He marries ANNA KÖNIG on October 13, 1803 (1110). She is born on October 2, 1783

and dies on November 21, 1856. In this generation, all of the Nesshof's farmers and some of their wives are Rhegius descendants.

10. Hinrich Schwartau, born April 5, 1803, dies May 24, 1891. Hübbe mentions him as Nesshof owner in 1832. He marries ANNA BENIT on November 10, 1825. She is born on February 4, 1805 and dies on September 18, 1874. She is the only daughter of the previous Nesshof owner, Carsten Benit.

11. CARSTEN SCHWARTAU, provincial administrator and recognized horse breeder. Born January 14, 1827, dies March 1, 1890. Hübbe mentions him as Nesshof owner in 1863. He marries Margaretha Feldmann on October 10, 1856. She is born March 30, 1829 and dies on March 29, 1913. She comes from Gasthof Schwartau and is a daughter of Paul Feldmann (1783 – 1833) and his wife, Magdalena Meyer. Thus, she is a granddaughter of Margaretha König (1761 – 1828) and great-granddaughter of Gerd König (1726 – 1796), the last of the Königs from Gasthof Schwartau to bear the König family name. The family connection is explained in the chapter "Gasthof Schwartau." Both Carsten and his wife, Margaretha, are Rhegius descendants.

Carsten Schwartau and Margaretha Feldmann have nine children:

1.	MAGDALENA ANNA 1857 – 1880	Marries Martin Barghusen, the son of Dike Administrator Hinrich Barghusen.
2.	MARGARETHA 1858 – 1919	Marries Johann Jacob Fock from Uhlenhof. (See Uhlenhof description.)

3.	CARSTEN HINRICH 1859 – 1905	In 1879 emigrates to America/Minnesota to live with relatives of his grandmother, Anna Benitt. There, he marries Meta Catharina Bade from Neuenfelde.
4.	WILHELM 1860 – 1882	Becomes a fisherman and drowns in the Elbe.
5.	PAUL 1861 – 1883	Inherits the farm. On a hot summer day, he is found dead of a sun stroke in the garden. (See J.J. Fock's work. Fock lived on the Uhlenhof and in 1903 wrote a piece about Finkenwerder, which refers to the death of Paul Schwartau.)
6.	RUDOLF 1865 – 1881	Becomes a fisherman and drowns in the North Sea at age 16.
7.	ADOLPH 1867 – 1942	In 1883, travels at age 16 to his older brother in the USA, but returns to Germany after a few months at his father's request to become owner of the Nesshof.
8.	ALWINE 1870 – 1872	Dies at age two.
9.	EMMA 1873 – 1963	Marries homeowner Amandus Popp from the Lüneburg side.

ILLUSTRATION 113: To the left, Carsten Schwartau, provincial administrator and horse trainer. Marries Margaretha Feldmann in 1856. Their son, Carsten Hinrich (1859 – 1905) emigrates to America in 1879, where today over 100 Rhegius descendants live. In 1892, Margaretha Feldmann travels to the New World to visit her son. The photo to the right shows her and her daughter, Emma, in Red Wing, Minnesota. (Photo from the descendants in the USA).

Page 197

ILLUSTRATION 114: Carsten Hinrich Schwartau (1859 – 1905) becomes a successful farmer in America. In 1882, he marries Meta Catharina Bade from Neuenfelde. The photo shows the couple in 1903 with their 10 children. Two years later, Carsten Hinrich dies at age 46. (Photo from the family in the USA).

In 1883, the family's situation on the Nesshof is affected by fate. Carsten Schwartau and his wife had already lost their eldest daughter, 22 year old Magdalena Anna, in 1880. She dies giving birth to her second child. Their sons, Wilhelm, Paul, and Rudolf, lose their lives in their youth. Because Adolph follows his older brother, Carsten, to America, the Nesshof now has no heir running the farm.

In this situation, Carsten sends an emissary across the Atlantic to his sons. The two of them are to decide which one will return. According to the American *Chronicle of an American Family in 1976*, they discuss the situation for 2 ½ days. Then, it is decided that 16 year old Adolph will return to Finkenwerder.

The fact that the older brother, Carsten Hinrich Schwartau, is already married at this time plays a role in their discussion. Carsten marries Meta Catharina Bade (1866 – 1940) on October 31, 1882 in Goodhue county, near the town of Red Wing on the Mississippi. She is from Neuenfelde. The couple has 10 children:

	BIRTH/DEATH	SPOUSE	MARRIAGE DATE
MARGARETHA	1883 – 1957	Unmarried	
JOHN CARSTEN	1885 – 1929	Ida Bleckman	1916
HENRY PAUL	1887 – 1965	Elin Frenn	1925
RUDOLPH DIETRICH	1889 – 1982	Alma Ehlen	1916
ANNA EMMA	1891 – 1965	Adolph S. Bender	1929
ADOLPH WILLIAM	1893 – 1968	Edith Erickson	1921
CLARA MARIE	1896 – 1987	Erwin R. Hinrichs	1925
GEORGE FREDERICK	1898 – 1982	Eva Husby	1924
LAURA REGINA	1900 – 1982.	Walter H. Nelson	1924
HELEN FRIEDA	1902 – 1994	Clark Crandall	1937

In 1892, 63 year old Margaretha Feldmann travels with her youngest daughter, 19 year old Emma, to visit her son, Carsten Hinrich, in America. She stays for several months. All the children, except Margaret, Anna, and Helen, continue the family's farming tradition.

Page 198

The oldest daughter, Margaretha, visits Finkenwerder in 1908/09 for an entire year. In her diary, in English, she records her observations and experiences in Finkenwerder.

12. ADOLPH SCHWARTAU Born July 26, 1867, dies November 16, 1942. Marries Emma Aline Fock (1869 – 1952) on June 18, 1890. His father, Carsten Schwartau, dies in 1890, so that Adolph becomes heir to the Nesshof at age 23. It is no easy task, as we shall soon see.

Around 1900 Finkenwerder "is chosen as a future harbor area because of its favorable location...In the following years, the state of Hamburg acquires a large number of farms on the island."[685] Adolph Schwartau sells the Nesshof in 1906, but continues to manage it as a lessee. After 338 years, the land goes to Hamburg. Throughout the industriousness of twelve generations, it was a productive, cultural area that fed the city.[686]

ILLUSTRATION 115: In 1915, Adolph Schwartau and Emma Fock celebrate their silver anniversary at this house built by great-grandparents Carsten Benit and Anna König. The four unmarried daughters in the photo wear full length dresses. The three sons are not there because they are serving in World War I. (Foto: Privately owned).

Even if it is not light hearted, the last big family celebration at the Nesshof takes place on June 18, 1915. Adolph Schwartau and Emma Fock celebrate their silver anniversary.

Those present at the anniversary pose in celebratory clothes in front of the proud gables of the house, adorned with an outsized black, white, and red flag. Of the four sons, three are serving on the war front. Carsten comes back from France uninjured. The youngest, Paul and Wilhelm, are both killed and never see their family and the Nesshof again.

After the war, the large farm declines. In 1920, invaluable treasures and the centuries old "essence" of the Nesshof are lost in a fire. The house is rebuilt, however, it has a flat, corrugated sheet metal roof. The farm is only a shadow of its former self, which was rich in tradition.

Economic inflation soon follows, as well as the devaluation of the Ness farmers' funds gained in the sale of the estate in 1906. These factors, along with many difficulties due to fate, bring the once prosperous and independent Nesshof to the brink. The death of two sons in the war adds immeasurably to the decline.

The isolation of the Nesshof creates a desire for photographs and paintings. The Finkenwerder artist, Eduard Bargheer (1901 – 1979) from time to time lives in the Ness cottage where the day laborers previously lived.[687] As a young man, Bargheer has little money. Instead of rent, he offers Ness farmer, Adolph Schwartau, a portrait, which he paints in the expressionist style. When Bargheer delivers the finished portrait, the Ness farmer looks at it critically for a while and then says, "I cannot recognize myself in this painting. Take it back and do it over!" He does accept the second portrait, which is painted conservatively. Unfortunately, the painting was burned in Adolph Schwartau's daughter's home in Hamburg during WWII.[688]

Page 199

The Schwartau family farms the Nesshof for nearly 30 years, however, gone are the days in which the Ness farmers control the land. In 1937, engineering crews move in, fell trees and demolish buildings. A year later, the Nesshof is swallowed up by heaps of sand used to construct the Fleugzeugwerft [Aircraft Works] Blohm & Voss. [The Company originally built ships and was called into service building planes in WWI.]

Today, at the beginning of the 21ST century, the DASA Daimler-Chrysler Aerospace Airbus GmbH [Ltd.] is located there. This is a sign of globalization and competition for world-wide market share in the aircraft industry. More than a thousand people, including Rhegius descendants, work there.[689]

ILLUSTRATION 116: This excerpt from an early landscape photograph shows the Ness cottage in 1865. The four children in front of the entrance are from left to right: Unidentified child; Margaretha Schwartau (born 1858); Carsten Hinrich Schwartau, who goes to America (born 1859); and Magdalena Anna Schwartau (born 1857). In the background is the North Elbe. (Archiv Kulturkreis Finkenwerder).

A Seafarer Marries a Daughter of the Grönland [Greenland]

THE RHEGIUS DESCENDANTS ON THE GRÖNLAND FARM

On the Hamburg side, stretched between the Ness dike on the north and the Landscheideweg on the south, lies a farm rich in tradition. It is one of the few remaining functioning farms. Hans Förster is enchanted by this "ancient picturesque Grönland farm," as he meanders around the island with pen in hand to recapture the past, attentively looking about for natural beauty.

> "For those who are interested, there are two possibile ways the farm got its name. One way simply involves the green pasture [the literal translation of Grönland]…The other interpretation - I believe, Gorch Fock also mentions this – maintains that previously, probably before there was arable land on the north side of the dike…, before the sound of the seafarers laying anchor off Grönland – it might have been – that the perceptive eye sees the elevated mounds of land. As their elaborately rigged ships lie at anchor awaiting favorable winds, this land is also viewed by the North Sea sailors as artistically paintable. In the 17th to the 18TH century, the hunt for Grönland whales by many dominions, including Hamburg, leads many whales to bleed to death and to become extinct in many areas. This area, located in the navigable waters and with favorable wind conditions, protected by the north dike, between the Steendike and the Ness, might have appeared to arctic whalers as a pleasant place to lay anchor and wait for better weather conditions…" [690]

We also find this interpretation of the Grönland farm's name in Jakob Kinau's work.[691] Gorch Fock in *Seefahrt ist not!* definitely espouses this version ... Klaus Mewes often glances at the farm in the distance on large man-made mounds of earth as high as the dikes. The old residents still call it the Grönland farm because in days of yore, the Hamburg whalers had anchored near it.

Page 200

The entire far-flung Mewes clan originated there. The former administrator, who was of Dutch descent, had "ruled like a king" at Grönlandhof. His name, Bartel Mewes, was derived from the orginal name, "Bartholomäus." His sons and grandsons later learned that it was better to cultivate the green sea than the brown land. Hence, they were pulled away from the dike and became sailors and fishermen.[692]

We have seen in the chapter about the Kinau family how Rebecka König (1017), the great-great-grandmother of the Kinau brothers, becomes the connecting link to the Grönlandhof. From the perspective of the family history, it is good to see that her poet-descendants establish a literary memorial here.

ILLUSTRATION 117: The Grönlandhof. Gorch
Fock writes in *Seefahrt ist not!* that whalers
from Hamburg lay anchor in the area.

That Finkenwerder farm houses are threatened by other events besides flooding is impressively and tragically illustrated at the

Gröndlandhof. In 1821, it burns down to the foundation walls. The residents lose all their possessions and livestock. The house is rebuilt, and a year later, fate strikes again. Lightening ignites the straw roof. All is again lost! Bastian Fock (1787 – 1848), Rhegius descendant and owner of the farm at the time of the fire writes down this dramatic account of the event, which the family preserved. The following is the unaltered text:

> "I feel deeply that it is my solemn duty and debt to write down the unforgettable events which shock every one of our known compatriots, as well as us, to our very core.
>
> It was on January 10, 1821 at approximately 3 o'clock in the afternoon that we were overwhelmed by a highly unexpected fateful event. In the blink of an eye, our house and barn were engulfed in flames. It was amazing to us that next the fire ignited the straw in the cow stalls in the house, where we never went about with any kind of fire in hand. The little bit that I could save through sheer determination and bravery were the horses, a table, and benches and beds from the little room. In a few minutes, everything else was lost. There were two cows in a stall. One burned to death, the other escaped alive from the fire. But, she was so badly wounded that within the hour, she had to be slaughtered. Four thin pigs, all the ham and meat, in sum, everything, fell prey to the flames.
>
> We stood there dismayed and frightened by the engulfing flames ascending skyward. We cried with our children about our cruel fate.
>
> After much consideration, we again turned to the widow of the baker, Dethel, for shelter, where we

stayed for a few days. But after further advice, we negotiated with Gerd Meyer, where we lived in a small room.
Several weeks after the fire I contracted[693] with a carpenter from the southern uplands of Northern Germany
by the name of Johann Ratge who lived in Ehestorf. For
1,800 Marks he agreed to build a new house with flooring, doors for the house and small rooms, and all window
frames in the gable.

Page 201

I gladly agreed to this, but I also prepared for more
danger. How would we gather our courage if he did not
keep his word? Also, there was a farmer who was renting
a room in the house. Who would make sure he kept his
word? For that reason alone, I lived in constant fear that
he would renege on his promise, which was also often
true. As May Day approached and the house should have
been finished, construction proceeded slowly. Nevertheless, when the house was completed, I was overjoyed and
still had 300 Marks left. In the course of several weeks,
I erased my debt to the contractor.

After we were able to settle reasonably comfortably in
our house, we were soon happy there. But our home did
not remain calm and peaceful for long – hardly a whole
year. Because, as my wife and I were sitting in our small
room on Sunday, July 21, 1822 around 3 o'clock in the
afternoon, and our children were playing there, a strong
clap of thunder accompanied by a blazing flash of lightening arose. This flash hit the front of the rooftop with
such force that the wood and window split apart as they
collapsed.

Our dismay was so great that it is easy to imagine that our ability to think was lost. On the contrary, we hurried out of the room toward the door. Now we saw smoke and fire. We wanted to put the fire out, but our efforts were in vain. Now we threw bedding and housewares out the door. My hands are trembling whilst remembering this. We were barely outside when the fiery roof collapsed, burning everything we had taken out of the house.

In order to escape, we now had to hurry through the window of the room. All that remained was some clothing that we had tossed out of the house. But, full of faith, we looked up to God who gave us His blessing as he did in the first fire. He was not going to abandon us this time, but rather give us some of his blessings.

Now the harvest was at hand, for the rye had already been mowed. Then we brought the grain to the pastor's home and to Gerd Meyer's home, where we also were staying once again."[694]

As far as this emotionally moving, straightforward, eyewitness account from 200 years ago is concerned, there is no complaining about the loss of goods and land, no call upon the authorities to provide compensation for the damage, no question about the debts. On the contrary, there is much more resignation to the fate suffered and a glimpse into God's blessings sustained by full faith and trust in Him! The report is not dated. It was probably written in 1823 or 1824, while the influence of these life experiences is fresh and clear in the writer's mind. If the account were written after 1825, it surely would have mentioned the flood that accompanied the storm of February 1825, which inundates the entire island. Even the houses built on the high man-made mounds of land are partly standing in water over a meter high: in the church up on a high point, there are more the 50 centimeters of water.[695] On the Gröndlandshof, the water is reported to stand "a foot high in the small heated rooms.[696]

In the above material on Gröndland, we have jumped ahead. Now, in order to bring the sequence of owners and history of the farm up to date, we are backtracking to pick up what we skipped over:

1. Symon Fock is cited by Hübbe "around 1568" as owner Farmstead 25 with 25 Morgen [the amount of land a farmer could plow in one day].[697] He buys the farm from the Hamburg treasury for 830.15.4. Marks. (This Symon Fock is not to be confused with Simon Fock, the fourth owner of Gasthof Schwartau on the Lüneburg side.)

2. Hans Rychardes probably takes over the farm from Symon Fock shortly after 1568. Hübbe indicates, "1568 Symon Fock, then Hans Rychardes."

3. Hein von Riegen is cited by Hübbe as owner in 1612, 1617, and 1624. In the 1617 church record book he is mentioned as a member of the church council. He plays a role in the unification of the churches on the Hamburg side with those on the Lüneburg side. He dies July 20, 1627.

Page 202

4. Hein Ripke is cited by Hübbe as farm owner in 1650, 1660, 1661.

    His first marriage is on November 19, 1629 to Anna von Rigen, daughter or widow of the previous owner. She dies on January 28, 1649 at age 68.

    His second marriage is on July 24, 1649 to Anna Struhs (Steers?), who dies on January 5, 1653.

His third marriage is on May 15, 1653 to Wöpke Wüpper (born February 10, 1633, dies March 17, 1679). Her father is Johann.

Hein Ripke and Wöpke Wüpper have seven children.

He dies on June 21, 1666 at age 66.

5. Otto Fink(en) from Altenwerder is cited by Hübbe as farm owner in 1680 and 1681.

Born before 1640, his father's name is probably Peter Fink.

His first marriage is on June 2, 1667 to Wöpke Ripke, widow of the previous owner. She is born on February 10, 1633 and dies on March 17, 1679 at age 36. She brings the farm into the marriage.

His second marriage is on May 5, 1681 to Gretje Diereks (Dirichs)

They have five children, among them are Peter, the heir, born June 4, 1683; Otto Fink V, born September 26, 1693; and Gretje (dies May 30, 1740 at about age 80).

6. Peter Fink is cited by Hübbe as owner in 1713 and 1724. He is a son of the previous owner's second marriage.

He is born on June 4, 1683 and dies October 22, 1725.

His first marriage is on December 12, 1705 to Anna Fink(ens), "Jacob's daughter."

His second marriage on June 20, 1719 is to Anna Plaas.

7. Albert Fink is not cited by Hübbe.

He is born July 24, 1707 and dies in 1749. He is a son of the previous owners.

On June 19, 1742, he marries Anna Schulten (born March 30, 1722, dies May 29, 1782).

8.   Johann von Riegen is cited by Hübbe as owner in 1762.

He is born February 16, 1727 and dies November 19, 1795.

He marries Anna Fink on December 1, 1750. She is "Albert's Vidua" [widow], nee Schulten.

He is probably the interim manager of the farm since he marries the widow of the former owner.

9.   Paul von Riegen is cited by Hübbe as owner in 1802 and 1809.

He is born July 9, 1753 and dies December 8, 1833.

He marries Adelheit Fink on October 10, 1782. Her parents are Albert Fink and Anna Schulten. Albert Fink was the owner prior to Johann von Riegen.

Born March 30, 1747, dies April 13, 1811

(Paul von Riegen is from the Lüneburg side, and his wife is from the Hamburg side. He is not the son of Johann von Riegen.)

10.   BASTIAN FOCK. He is provincial administrator and is mentioned by Hübbe as owner in 1832.

He is born March 2, 1787 and dies January 9, 1848.

Bastian Fock is the first Rhegius descendant on the Grönlandhof. His father, Jakob Fock (1018), marries Rebecka König on July 31, 1783. See the chapter about the Kinau family.

On January 18, 1811 he marries Catharina von Riegen, daughter of the previous owner. She is born on August 5, 1786 and dies on October 8, 1864.

The house burns down twice, in the years 1821 and 1822. See above. In 1844, their daughter, Catharina Fock (1817 – 1866), marries Johann Nikolaus Kinau, seafarer and great-grandfather of the Kinau brothers.

ILLUSTRATION 118: Hope chest, inscribed, "BASTIAN
FOCK CATRINA FOCK ANNO 1823." Provincial
Administrator Bastian Fock is the the first Rhegius descendant
on the Grönlandhof and great-grandfather of the poet
brothers Kinau. (Photo: Privately owned by Rudolf Meier).

Page 203

11.   JACOB FOCK is cited by Hübbe as farm owner in 1848. He is the son of the prior owners.

   He is born December 7, 1820 and dies July 9, 1861.

   On January 26, 1849, he marries Catharina Fock. She is born on December 9, 1821 and dies March 15, 1885.

12.   Hans Benit is cited by Hübbe as interim owner in 1863. He is born April 3, 1830 and dies November 6, 1896. (Father Hinrich Benit, mother Cecilie Butendeich)

   On March 20, 1863 he marries Catharina Fock, widow of the previous owner.

13.   Peter Stehr is cited by Hübbe as farm owner in 1897. He is born November 7, 1844 and dies May 3, 1935 at almost ninety-one years of age. On March 22, 1877 he marries CATRINA FOCK (only daughter of Jacob and Catharina Fock)

   She is born October 20, 1851 and dies December 22, 1923.

14.   JOHANNES STEHR, son of the prior owners

   He is born February 10, 1878 and dies September 22, 1968.

   On December 17, 1903, he marries Margarethe Müller, born March 17, 1880, dies March 28, 1946.

This history of the farm once again shows that even though residents of the farm have different surnames, they are actually members of the same branch of the family tree.

Beginning with the third owner, Hein von Riegen, there is an unbroken genealogical line up to the present. It is also possible that Hein von Riegen can be a son-in-law of the former owner, Hans Richardes. If that is the case, Hans Richardes would be a son-in-law of Symon Fock, the first listed owner. But, the proof is lacking.

The Meier Cottage on the Osterfelddeich Nr. 6 (Today Nr. 30)

The cottage is not associated with the prominent names on the island. It is a welcoming, well-maintained cottage in what was formerly the Lüneburg side of Finkenwerder. In 1945, A. Albershardt describes the straw roofed, half-timbered cottage of the farm worker, Hinrich Meier, as an interesting example of intermediate social status, that is, between a farm worker's cottage and a farmer's house. It is 14 meters long and 11 meters wide.

The house, with its cozy mansard roof, still looks neat and trim. The half-timber panels remain only in the front gable. Albershardt puts the time of construction at the second half of the 18TH century. Since then, it has seen many alterations and renovations. Until about 1810, the front part contains the open hearth. The rear part is open on the sides. It is where the cattle stand between the stanchions. This layout has long gone out of use. Even more recently, the house's owners have made changes suitable to modern times.

In the first generation known to us, Dirck Meier marries Gesche Meinschien in 1702. The Harburg inheritance registry of 1667 indicates that Hans Meyenschien has a 2 ½ Morgen plot of interior land, which is later divided by inheritance. The additional term "wüste" [fallow land], means that the cottage land is no longer plowed in 1667 or thereafter. [698]

The connection between Hans Meyenschien, the owner in 1667, and Gesche Meinschien cannot be exactly established. She probably inherits the aforementioned cottage and farm.

From 1702 to the present, the farm is owned by the Meier family, as shown in the following list:

1. Dirck Meier is born in 1677 (estimated) and dies September 27, 1752. He marries Gesche Meinschien on May 7, 1702, on the Hamburg side.[699] She is born on June 5, 1670 and dies on August 5, 1736.

2. Dietrich Meier is born May 24, 1714 on the Lüneburg side and dies December 23, 1799 on the Lüneburg side. His first marriage to Beke Rust is on June 2, 1738 on the Lüneburg side. She is born on October 2, 1709 and dies on May 15, 1739 on the Lüneburg side.

    His second marriage is on December 1, 1739 to Gesche Schulten. She is born November 29, 1719 and dies on February 25, 1740.

    His third marriage is on November 8, 1740 to Magdalena Roloff/Rolf from Altenwerder.[700] She is born in January (approximately) 1717 and dies on January 22, 1799.

3. Hinrich Meier is a son from Dietrich Meier's third mar-
    riage.[701]

    He is born October 26, 1747 on the Lüneburg side and
    dies June 16, 1820 on the Lüneburg side.

    His first marriage is to Anna Steer on May 26, 1778.
    She is born November 26, 1752 and dies August 28, 1780.

    His second marriage on October 4, 1781 is to MARGA-
    RETHA KÖNIG (1031), who is 15 years younger than he.
    She is born June 29, 1761 and dies on February 28, 1828.

From this generation on, all of the following owners are Rhegius
descendants.

We already know Margaretha König from the chapter, "Gasthof
Schwartau." The 12TH owner of the inn, Paul Feldmann (1783 –
1833), marries Magdelana Meyer on August 25, 1814. She is born
on December 6, 1792. She is the daughter of the above mentioned
Hinrich Meier and Margaretha König. (Through this marriage of
Paul Feldmann and Magdalena Meier the König lineage is preserved
at Gasthof Schwartau.)

4. PETER MEIER is son of the previous owner from his
    second marriage to Margaretha König. He is born January
    14, 1798 and dies August 21, 1859. On October 27, 1825
    he marries Katarina Fock on the Lüneburg side. She is born
    March 6, 1807 and dies January 27, 1868.

5. HINRICH MEIER is the oldest son of the previous owner.
    He is a sailor and quarter time farmer. He is born on Sep-
    tember 20, 1826 and dies January 25, 1866. On March 24,

1852 he marries Gesche Köpke. She is born January 28, 1826 on the Hamburg side and dies August 16, 1859.

6.   NIKOLAUS MEIER is son of the previous owner. He is a sailor on a freighter. He is born November 20, 1858 and dies December 26, 1929. He marries Meta Cath. Jürgina Schuldt on January 3, 1883. She is born October 23, 1859 and dies on July 29, 1893.

7.   HINRICH HERMANN NIKOLAUS MEIER is son of the previous owner. He is a sailor and farmer. He is born September 30, 1887 and dies September 7, 1957. On April 16, 1910 he marries Helene Margr. Struhs. She is born June 3, 1887 and dies September 24, 1956.

The cottage remains in the family's possession in the eighth and ninth generations (HINRICH JACOB NICHOLAUS and HINRICH PETER JULIUS MEIER). In no other instance of family history has possession remained in an unbroken chain with the same surname over so many generations.

ILLUSTRATION 119: The Meier family's cottage at Osterfelddeich Nr. 6 (today Nr. 30) has seen many alterations over time. (Photo privately owned).

A Blooming Paradise and Ornamented Gable
THE UHLENHOF AND ITS RHEGIUS DESCENDANTS

July 9, 1787 is an important date in the history of the Uhlenhof family. On this date, three Finkenwerder farmers make their way to Hamburg. Between 11 and 12 o'clock they are sitting in the home of Hermann Christian Uhlenhoff in the hops market. The men sign a contract with him, which brings an old Finkenwerder farm back into the possession of local farmers. It had belonged to Hamburg merchants for several decades: first Carl Albrecht Roose, then Hermann Christian Uhlenhoff.

In 1568, the farm is probably taken over from the Hamburg treasury by Dyrick Bonnytt because the farmer owners can no longer afford the dike's upkeep. When Carl Albert Roose and his wife assume ownership in 1747, they build one of the most beautiful farm houses on Finkenwerder and call it the "Roosenhof" [Rose Farm]. The inscription over the gable's uppermost ledge reads:

CARL ALBRECHT ROOSE. ANNA CATRINA
ROOSEN. ANNO 1747.DEN 1. JUNIUS.

The lintel above the door to the house bears the inscription:

FOR THE LORD GOD IS A SUN AND SHIELD.
THE LORD GIVES US

GRACE AND GLORY.

NO GOOD THING WILL HE WITHHOLD FROM

THOSE WHO WORKETH RIGHTEOUSLY.

O LORD OF HOSTS, BLESSED IS THE MAN THAT

TRUSTETH IN THEE.

PSALM 84, VERSES 12,13[702]

ILLUSTRATION 120: In the photo above all is right
with the world. It shows the splendid Uhlenhof farm
with its blossoming fruit trees and women in their white
Sunday aprons. To the right is Hinrich Fock (1826 – 1910)
in a straw hat. On the left is his wife, Catharina Mewes
(1827 – 1909), shorn sheep, wool hung out to dry, and
the farm's dog. It is a picture of a safe haven, affluence,
and tranquility. (Photo from a postcard around 1895).

The postcard is printed with the inscription, "Finkenwerder at
Blossom Time." It is a carefully composed idyllic scene of the farmer's world on the island. Old Finkenwerder residents still recall the
tranquil path, which leads from the boundary of the land to the farm
house. A visitor on the path passes blooming fruit trees, goes along
a wooden fence, comes to the man-made high ground, and stands in
front of the magnificent high gable of the house.[703]

Whether the Roose family lives on and manages the farm is uncertain. Possibly, it is rented out until Herman Christian Uhlenhof takes
it over in about 1762.[704]

Page 206

Uhlenhoff remains unmarried and sells the farm in 1787. He left the Finkenwerder Church a bequest and is buried in the old church.

The three farmers who signed the contract in Hamburg in 1787 are Jacob Fock, Johan Koepke, and Hans Meyer. They acquire the farm, designated in the contract as "Roosengehöft," along with its 13 ½ Morgens of land for "roughly 3,000 Dänish Courant." The astonishing thing is this: Jacob Fock, who is barely 20 years old, assumes 75% of the sale price. He is the principal buyer.[705] Who is this young man? The reseachers submit that he is a Rhegius descendant, which is verified from the following dates:

	DATE OF MARRIAGE(S)	SPOUSE(S)
SEBASTIAN KÖNIG (615) Born 1621 (estimated) Dies March 30, 1667	Marries on July 17, 1650	ANNKE HARMS (616) Baptized January 21, 1629 Dies January 28, 1677
GRETA KÖNIG (725) Born October 9, 1659 Dies February 3, 1733	First Marriage: January 30, 1683	JACOB WITTORF (726) Not from Finkenwerder Dies March 31, 1709
	Second Marriage: September 8, 1711	JOHANN LÜNSSMANN (727)
	Third Marriage: November 21, 1713	HARMEN WULFF (728)
HINRICH WITTORF Born January 3, 1701 Dies December 30, 1757	Marries April 20, 1732	MAGDALENA NIBBEN Born July 5, 1699 Dies December 21, 1767

ADELHEIT WITTORF	First Marriage:	H(E)INRICH FOCKEN, FARMHAND
Born October 8, 1745 on the Lüneburg side Dies July 27, 1800	December 20, 1763	Born April 2, 1706 Dies November 26, 1767 (Drowns)[706]
	Second Marriage November 22, 1768	HINRICH ROLF Born December 12, 1748 on the Lüneburg side Dies February 26, 1817 on the Lüneburg side
JACOB FOCK	Marries December	ANNA BENITT
Born February 10, 1767 Dies November 7, 1823	1, 1785	Born February 27, 1764 on the Hamburg side Dies February 8, 1841

At age nine months, Jacob Fock, the principal buyer of the farm, loses his father. On September 9, 1903, J.J. Fock reports that the father drowns "near Sodenholen on the Southern Elbe" four years after his marriage to Jacob's mother, who becomes a widow at age 22. A year later, she marries Hinrich Rolf. Both children from the second marriage, Jacob and his two year older brother, Hinrich, apparently have their claim settled so that the ancestral home goes to the children from the second marriage.

ILLUSTRATION 121: The elaborately decorated sled for the marriage of the couple, Jacob and Anna Fock. Albershardt describes it thusly in 1945: "Frilled sled from 1796 with adjustable, removable seats, back rest with symbolic pictures of life, leaf and flower motif. The wood carving is flat and painted in many colors. On the rear internal panel is a large tulip and an angel of good fortune along with the inscription, 'Jacob-Anna Focken Year 1796' as well as the Bible verse, 'Obey the Lord on your path in life and trust in Him. He will be righteous unto you.'" This precious historical piece went up in flames in 1945 when the farm was bombed. (Photo from Albershardt).

Anna Benitt, Jacob Fock's wife, has a very similar biography. She is just 8 months old when her father, Carsten Benitt, dies at age 28. Her mother, Gesche Horstmann, becomes a widow at age 24. She marries for a second time to Carsten Fock from Aue [marsh] on November 25, 1766. In Finkenwerder, the farm is known as "Au-Cassen-Fock Hoff." It is located on the boundary line, where the ESSO gas station is today.[707]

Neither Anna nor Jacob has elder parents to care for, so they probably have Mr. Uhlenhoff stay on with them in his later years until the end of his life.

From that, we can deduce that Uhlenhoff is well acquainted with Jacob and Anna's parents and grandparents. Finally, Hein Benitt, Anna's grandfather, is still administrator when Uhlenhoff is in Finkenwerder. Uhlenhoff, like all farmers, had dealings with him.

The following information about the Anna Benitt's ancestors shows that she comes from a good and apparently wealthy family:

Her great-grandparents:

CARSTEN BENITT, PROVINCIAL ADMINISTRATOR
Born February 12, 1697
Dies January 31, 1729
Marries October 21, 1703
on the Hamburg side

CATH. HARMENS (HÜBBE NR. 11)
Born February 7, 1675
Dies September 24, 1762

Her grandparents:

HEIN BENIT, PROVINCIAL ADMINISTRATOR[708]	MARRIES CATHARINA SCHWARTAU 1735
From Farm Nr.26 (Hübbe)	1712 – 1764
1708 – 1783	

Her parents:

CARSTEN BENITT	MARRIES ON JUNE 29, 1762 GESCHE HORSTMANN
Born September 17, 1736	Born May 27, 1740
Dies October 12, 1764	Dies July 12, 1820
	Second marriage on November 25, 1766 to Carsten Fock (1744 – 1817) from Auefock-Hof

Jacob Fock and Anna Benitt are the first married couple with the surname "Fock" on the Uhlenhof farm, which remains a Fock family farm for 200 years. Even though the Fock family lives there, the farm is still called the "Uhlenhoff-Hof," [Uhlenfarm Farm] because its former owner's surname was Uhlenhoff and the farm was originally named for him.

At the end of their youngest son, Carsten's, 18TH year in 1822, Jacob and Anna think about bequeathing the farm to the next generation. Jacob is 55 years old and his wife, Anna, is 58. By this age, most farmers have already given over their house. The couple does not wait to transfer their home. They do so before their son's marriage on February 13, 1823 to 22 year old Anna Wriede, daughter of master baker H. Wriede. Anna Wriede is designated as their son, Carsten's, future bride and is present at the signing of the transfer contract.

The contract mentioned above is an enlightening document from that time period. It contains information about the typical regulations for transferring farms, particularly for safeguarding the "part of the farm reserved by the parents for their own use." Often such a contract is completed when the young couple marries. The parents are considering the uncertainties of life. Another factor is what will happen after the elder couple is unable to continue the hard physical labor needed to maintain the farm and its cultivation.

In 1787, Jacob Fock takes over 75% ownership of the farm. Twenty-five years later, nothing more about the 75% is mentioned in the transfer contract. The farm belongs solely to Jacob. He must therefore have bought out his partner. He buys the farm for 3,000 Mark Courant at the current rate and it is now appraised for 5,000 Mark Courant at the current rate. Since the administrator of the Butendeich is present, the appraised value of the property is correct.

The young couple is to provide the parents with a horse and saddle for riding to church. This is not only a sign of social status, but also an indication of the lack of established roads at that time. Every week a pound of coffee beans is due, which indicates a certain standard of living that the parents want to maintain as they age.

Page 208

If invited to a wedding or a child's baptism, guests traditionally bring chickens, milk, and butter. The young couple is responsible for supplying the elder couple with these gifts for them to take to the ceremony.

After everything is stipulated in the contract, finally this concluding important – and touching – sentence appears: "The parents bequeath the items to their son and daughter-in-law, the entire farm for them to serenely enjoy,[709] live upon, and manage, as their own property.[710] We wish our descendants all the best as it is now incumbent upon them to preserve the farm." The contract is in Appendix 58.

The elder couple must have felt that it was time to put their affairs in order. The contract has just been signed for 13 months when Jacob Fock drowns on November 2, 1823 at age 56. Only the entry in the church registry reveals the drama that must have accompanied the drowning, considering the recent transfer of the farm.[711]

His wife, Anna, outlives her husband by 18 years. She lives to age 77 and resides on the farm until 1841. Only three of their ten children survive their parents.

The next generation is:

1. CARSTEN FOCK Born November 28, 1805 on the Hamburg side Dies October 5, 1874	Marries on February 13, 1823	ANNA WRIEDE Born September 26, 1801 Dies November 29, 1856 of cholera
2. HINRICH FOCK Born January 16, 1826 on the Hamburg side Dies January 5, 1910	Marries January 10, 1850	CATHARINA MEWES[712] Born March 25, 1827 Dies 1909

Both Hinrich and Catharina are Rhegius descendants. They celebrate their golden wedding anniversary on January 10, 1900. The anniversary photo shows 74 year old Hinrich Fock sitting on a Finkenwerder Chair [this is a special type of chair on Finkenwerder], while Catharina stands beside him, as was customary in that era. Their son, Jan, writes about his parents as follows: "They were pious people, faithful to the church and God's word and we children also adhered to the church and God's word. Not to hear an angry word at home and then not to hear a good word spoken in the barracks took some getting used to."

ILLUSTRATION 122: The golden anniversary on the Uhlenhof in 1900. Hinrich Fock, who inherits the farm from his parents, marries Catharina Mewes on May 10, 1850. She is the daughter of deep sea fisherman Hans Mewes. Both Hinrich and Catharina are Rhegius descendants.

Page 209

3. CARSTEN FOCK	Marries June	ANNA STEHR
Born October 21, 1851	5, 1879	Born November 18,
on the Hamburg side		1859 in Alte Land
Dies March 9, 1938		Dies August 24,
in Buxtehude		1936 in the village
		of Francop

Among Carsten Focks's six siblings is Johann Jacob Fock (1859 – 1949) who in 1883 marries Margaretha Schwartau from the Nesshof. In this instance, both of them are also Rhegius descendants, each from a different branch. For those who are interested, here is is the information:

Johann Jacob Fock is first a Rhegius descendant through the Fock/Wittorf/König line described previously. The second line is through his mother:

· Catharina Mewes, whose father is Hans Mewes, a deep sea fisherman.

· His father is Johann Mewes, whose mother is Anna Schulten.

· Her father is Hermann Schulten, whose father marries Metta König (807).

Johann Jacob Fock's wife, Margaretha Schwartau from the Nesshof, is first a Rhegius descendant through her mother, Anna Benitt, whose mother is Anna König (1110). (See chapter: "Gasthof (Inn) Schwartau.") The second line comes through her mother, Margaretha Feldmann, whose mother is Margaretha Meier, whose mother is Margaretha König (1031) (See chapter: "The Meier Cottage on the Osterfelddeich Nr. 6"), daughter of Gerd König (914) of Gasthof Schwartau. There are also related cross references among the Uhlenhof, Nesshof, Gasthof Schwartau, and Hofstelle Meier and to Aue-Fock-Hof.

Johann Jacob Fock is among Professor Ernst Finder's interviewees when the professor makes his frequent trips to Finkenwerder over the thirty years during which he gathers material for his book.

ILLUSTRATION 123: The orchard owner Johann Jakob Fock (1859 – 1949), principal owner of the farm, brother of Carsten Fock (1851 – 1939). In 1883, he marries Margaretha Schwartau from the Nesshof. Both are Rhegius descendants. They are shown here on their silver anniversary in 1908.

In the summers of 1935 and 1936, Johann Jakob Fock and Professor Finder sit under the large pear tree at the orchard's boundary, deep in conversation, the professor with a writing pad on his knee.

In Finkenwerder, the professor's appearance is conspicuous. His white hair is longer than is customary and his multi-colored smock is never buttoned, even when the weather is bad. The two understand each other well. Much that Johann Jacob reports from his vast knowledge of Finkenwerder traditions is included in Finder's book, *Die Elbinsel Finkenwärder* [*The Elbe Island of Finkenwerder*]. For quite some time, the book has been in demand as one of the most definitive books about the island.

Page 210

In Appendix 59 there is an excerpt from the J.J. Fock memoir that Finder encouraged him to write.

At the beginning of the 20TH century, the Uhlenhof, which is still known by this name, suffers the same fate as the Grönlandhof. The city of Hamburg needs flat land for the expansion plans and in 1907 buys the Uhlenhof, which becomes state property. Former owners become tenant farmers.[713]

With the proceeds of the sale, Carsten Fock acquires a farm in Neuenfelde and moves there with his two youngest sons. His eldest son, Hinrich, stays behind as a tenant on the farm.

4. CORD HINRICH JOH. FOCK	Marries	ANNI GESINE CECILIE SCHACHT
Born June 24, 1880	April 22, 1906	Born November 8, 1880
Dies September 18, 1958		Dies January 5, 1944

Hinrich Fock and his family had to witness the bombing of the farm shortly before the end of the war on Good Friday, March 30, 1945. It burns to the foundation walls. The older son, CARSTEN FOCK, born July 3, 1910, returns home from an American prisoner of war camp in 1947 and sees the world of his childhood laying in ruins. Together with his father, he cultivates the farm for several years until he falls from a tree during the 1967 fruit harvest and dies at a young age.

The Finkenwerder Church's Chandelier

A DONATION FROM THE YEAR 1727

Upon entering the St. Nikolai Church in Finkenwerder one's eye beholds an unusually beautiful chandelier. Ten arms in the Baroque style come together around a brass sphere. Engraved on the sphere is the donor's name. The imaginative elements are placed so that the smaller ones proceed upward where they are crowned by an angelic figure with outstretched wings. This is the third church the chandelier has adorned.

ILLUSTRATION 124: In 1727 Rebecca Fock donates the chandelier displayed in this photo. (Photo: Klaus Elle).

After it is first donated, the chandelier hangs for 30 years in the church built by Pastor Sebastian König in 1617. The dedication reads:

"This crown was given to adorn the Finkenwerder Church in 1727 by the esteemed Mrs. Rebecca Focken, the widow of the honorable and respected Paul Harmens, administrator of Hamburg-Finkenwerder. Their surviving children are honorable and respected Jacob Harmens, Hans Harmens, and Anna Harmens, wife of Heinrich von Riegen, and the young maiden Catharina Harmens.

Lord Jesus, from this time forward, may the crown of righteousness, which this chandelier signifies, be bestowed upon those who love thee with heart and soul. So beseeches Joh. Fried. Overbeck, Past. Finkenwerder."

What do we know about the donor? Who is she and how is she related to the König family? The donor, Rebecca Fock(en), born March 31, 1673, dies December 15, 1737 is the widow of Paul Harms, born January 2, 1663, deceased administrator, who dies on July 24, 1712 at age 49.

Page 211

When Paul was baptized on January 9, 1663 in the Nienstedt Church, among his godfathers is Lüneburg administrator, Sebastian König, Jr. (615). He is baby Paul's uncle, married to Annke Harms, a sister of his father.

For over three generations, the Harms family that made the donation has had a member who is administrator of the Hamburg side (Farmstead Number 30, according to Hübbe, Landscheide 110, later the Benitt-Hof.) Family members are:

Hans Harms, Hamburg administrator around 1648. He is Sebastation König, Jr.'s (615) father-in -law. Probably

394

born in 1595. According to the Finkenwerder church registry, he dies on March 13, 1673 or, according to the Nienstedt church registry, he dies on December 30, 1676. See chapter: "Sebastian König, Jr. Marries the Daughter of the Hamburg administrator."

Hans Harms' son, Jakob Harms, (born November 18, 1627, dies October 15, 1676). On July 8, 1655, he marries Anke Steerss. He is Hamburg administrator after 1660, according to Hübbe and is mentioned by Bodemann as administrator in 1672. His sister, Annke Harms, is the wife of Sebastian König, Jr. (615).

Jakob Harms' son, the previously mentioned Paul Harms, is cited by Hübbe as administrator in 1709. He is born on January 2, 1663 and dies on July 24, 1712.

Paul Harms has nine children, two from his first marriage to Catrina von Rigen, seven from his second marriage to Rebecca Fock, the donor of the chandelier. From the children of the second marriage, three are alive at the time of the donation, but from the first marriage, only Jakob is alive. They are listed by name in the donation's text:

1. Jacob Harms, born October 21, 1688, is the son from the first marriage to Catrina von Rigen. He is heir to the farm. On November 2, 1717, he marries the widow from the Nesshof, Catharina Steers. Jacob dies in 1729.[714] His widow marries Carsten Bannit. See chapter: "The Nesshof on Finkenwerder," Generation 6.

ILLUSTRATION 125: Chest with rounded lid, with the inscription: "JACOB HARMS ANNO 1717 DEN 1 OCTO." In 1717, he marries the widow from the Nesshof, Catharina Steers, and brings this ornately worked chest into the marriage. The upper part is richly decorated above with elaborate leaf-work and the lower part with arches and pilasters in the Renaissance style.

The chest stays in the small heated room at the Nesshof until 1860. In that year, Anna, the youngest daughter of the Nesshof farmer, Hinrich Schwartau (1803 – 1891) marries Paul Heinrich from the Lüneburg side, who is part owner of a farm. After Paul's death, Anna moves in with her nephew, J. J. Fock on the Norderschulweg [North School Road], which is later on the boundary line. The chest stays in the attic there until 1942 – 43. Because of the fire danger from the bombing raids on Hamburg, the attic has to be cleared of all combustible items. From here the whereabouts of the the the more than 225 year old chest is unknown. (Photo: Landesmedienzentrum Hamburg Medienarchiv Bild).

2. Anna Harms, born March 4, 1705. First marriage on November 18, 1721 to Heinrich von Rigen from the Hamburg side. He is homeowner and church representative in legal matters. He dies on September 25, 1744.

 Anna Harms (910) marries for the second time on January 25, 1746 to HINRICH KÖNIG, son of BASTIAN KÖNIG (819) and Margaretha Harms (820), who is also a descendant of the König family.

 Through this marriage, Hinrich König acquires the house on Landscheide 100 (acccording to Hübbe, Farmstead Number 27). He is mentioned by Hübbe as the owner of the farm in 1762 and 1781. His children do not inherit the farm because they are from his second marriage.

3.   Hans Harms, born September 29, 1707, dies August 9,
     1729, probably unmarried. When he dies, that is the end
     of Paul Harms' male lineage.

4.   Catharina Harms, born April 20, 1710, dies October 10,
     1766. On January 17, 1730, she marries Hamburg adminis-
     trator, Tewes Bannit (born February 4, 1704, dies January
     31, 1751). It is interesting that the daughter of administra-
     tor Paul Harms also marries an administrator.

We do not know what moves Rebecca Fock to make this generous
donation of the chandelier to her church. Bodemann places its cost
at 100 Marks.[715] The significant dates in her life can give a clue. She
marries Paul Harms in 1691. He dies at age 49 in 1712 after 21 years
of marriage. She is ten years younger than he and is therefore still
a young woman. The first four of the children from her marriage to
Paul Harms, who are born in the years 1693, 1696, 1698, and 1701,
all die as children. Three of them die in July 1706 from smallpox.

When one considers these dates, one can assume that her stepson,
Jacob, the legal heir to the farm, works on the farm after the death of
his father in 1712 up until his own marriage in 1717 and takes over his
father's role as much as possible. When Jacob marries in 1717 at the
Nesshof, the largest farm on the island, it is possible that Rebecca
Fock considers her own son, Hans, heir to the farm. The extravagent
wedding chest for Jacob, including its lavish contents, may serve as a
diplomatic gift. Rebecca can certainly not foresee that her son, Hans,
dies in 1729 at age 22.

So Rebecca is alone. Hübbe mentions her in 1713 and 1727 as farm owner (farmstead number 30). She takes full responsibility for managing the farm for a long time. The marriage to Paul Harms is her first and only. She becomes a widow at age 39 and outlives her husband by 25 years. It appears that in spite of many twists of fate, she takes life by the hand and at age 54, full of gratitude, trust in God, and also pride in her lifetime accomplishments makes a generous gift of the chandelier to her church.

At the end of our wanderings from the Bodensee [Lake Constance] in Southern Germany to the River Elbe in the North we can hold onto the fact that Sebastian König, a grandchild of the reformer Urbanus Rhegius, left behind many footprints in Finkenwerder. His well-known positive relationship with the Guelph dukes in Harburg greatly facilitates the resolution of many problems. Let us think only about the years of the major construction of the dikes on Finkenwerder, the union of both sides of the island into one community, and the building of a new church in 1617.

The surname König is present on Finkenwerder until 1877. Eight generations after Sebastian König (401), Johann Hinrich König (1203), a ship's carpenter, goes to the Stülcken Ship Yards in Steinwärder where he finally assumes the position of dock supervisor.[716] A century later, several family members return to Finkenwerder. In the meantime, they live on the neighboring island of Altenwerder where they finally have to leave in favor of today's modern Container Terminal Altenwerder.

In the last part of our family geneology, we will look at how posterity has paid tribute to Urbanus Rhegius' memory. Immediately after his death, epitaphs are dedicated to him in Celle and Hannover. In 1858, the König of Hannover re-publishes Urbanus' *Welfischen Kat-*

echismus. Heimbürger and Uhlhorn write their Rhegius biographies. Emperor Friedrich III erects a statue to Rhegius in the Wittenburg Schlosskirche. In 1980, Liebmann writes a comprehensive Rhegius biography. In 2003, Scott Hendrix publishes Rhegius' work, *Wie man Fürsichtiglich predigen soll* for American theology students.

Section IV:
Posthumous Honors to Urbanus Rhegius

in the Cities of Celle and Hannover

Even recently, Celle honors Urbanus Rhegius' memory. In 1909/10, "Rhegiusstrasse" [Rhegius Street] is laid out in the new Hehlentor district.[717] In the spring of 1982, the Celle church district builds a new community center and names it the "Urbanus-Rhegius-Haus." Prof. Dr. Maximilian Liebmann presents a guest lecture in Celle in 1980 entitled, "Urbanus Rhegius – Vom Reformer zu Reformator" ["Social Reformer to Religious Reformer"].[718] On the occasion of Rhegius' 500TH birthday in 1989, Prof. Dr. Rainer Postel from Hamburg delivers the celebratory address.[719]

After his death, an epitaph honoring Urbanus is placed in Celle's City Church. Unfortunately, it becomes a victim of a later church renovation. Guden has a Latin version in his dissertation about Duke Ernst:[720] [Below are the Latin text and English translation. A German translation is in Appendix 60.]

"RHEGIUS heu! subita iam morte exstinctus obiuit,
Germani VRBANVS gloria magna soli.
Marmoreo inque adyto Cellae tumulatus in aede,
Qua populum docuit iussa verenda Dei.

Ingenio excellens, Musarum munere clarus,
Quarum sacra colens laurea serta tulit.
Grandior ast illum postquam cum ceperat aetas,
Ad sacrum stadium contulit ille suum.
Romanae et Graecae linguae Solymaeque peritus
Asseruit Christi dogmata sancta Dei.
Cuius erat vigilans prae cunctis pastor ovilis,
ERNESTO procul hinc rite vocante virum.

Hinc populis veram Cristo monstrante salutem
Consituisse scholas, maximus ardor erat.
Tum calamis, tum voce potens insurgere in hostes,
Sanctorum ense Dei monstra necare potens.

Integer et sancto morum candor probatus,
Quos potuit, iuvit pro pietate pios.
Hoc tandem Christi studiis immortuus orbe
Exiit, haud potuit mortuus esse tamen.

Namque viri egregium nomen florebit in orbe:
Sancta Abrahae requiem mens capit ipsa sinu."

"Oh! RHEGIUS has already ascended,
His flame extinguished by sudden death.
All Germans speak of his renown.
He lies enshrined in marble in the most holy place
In the Lord's house in Celle,
Where he taught the people God's commandments.

His holy spirit was radiant,
Made famous by the Muses' gift of talent.
Urbanus, who wore the Laureate's crown,
Was even greater
After receiving the crown,
Since he embellished it
By devoting his entire essence to the sacred scripture.

He knew well the Roman, Greek, and Hebrew languages,
Which he used to spread the holy teachings of Christ.
He was a man of God and was His watchful shepherd.
Duke Ernst called Urbanus from afar
To shepherd the flock in his duchy.
Urbanus' passion to found schools to bring people to Christ
Was exceedingly strong.
He was capable of standing up to enemies,
Sometimes with a shepherd's flute and sometimes with his voice.
He destroyed monsters with God's holy sword.

Without blemish and respecting the purest morality,
Urbanus helped reward the pious for their devotion to God's word,
Which he wanted to flourish.

Finally, Urbanus left this world,
After serving Christ's work until
His own death.
And thus, Urbanus is not dead,
Because his magnificent name
Will continue to bloom in this world.
His holy spirit lies peacefully
In the lap of St. Abraham."

Guden adds the following comment to the text: "As he looked over Urbanus' grave in Celle in the presence of Chancellor Balthasar Klammer[722] and Advisor Joachim Möller, scholarly, distinguished, and genuinely devout JOACHIM von BEVST[721] spontaneously composed and delivered the following tribute to Urbanus:

"What kind of man lies here?
Do not ask, pilgrim!
He was Regius, as his name signifies."

Page 214

The Hannover congregation also thanks Rhegius with an epitaph in the Marktkirche [Church at the Market Place] St. Georgi et St. Jacobi. It also has not survived. It was near the altar. The original Latin text and English translation are below. A German translation of the original Latin is in Appendix 61.

"Urbano Regio Theol(ogo) Alpigenas inter genitore colono
Editus estremo nomen in orbe tenet.
Accitus numero vatum cum laude docebat
Quod fovet in multis Teutona terra scholis.

At postquam nostris verbi lux fulsit in oris,
Post habuit Cristo dogmata vana suo.
Pontificum contemsit opes Babylone relicta,
Foecundi amplexus foedera casta thori.

Insignis Christi miles discrimina adivit,
Praebens Vandalico pabula laeta gregi.
Saxoniae tandem respexit ovilia nostrae,
Testantur tanti quod monumenta viri.

Ossa cubant Zellae virtus celebratur ubique
Illius et semper vita superstes erit."[723]
obit Cellis Anno Christi 1541 die 23.Maji

"To the theologian Urbanus Rhegius,
Who was born the son of a farmer,
And called by the name of Rhegius in the Alps.
Rhegius is world-renowned, as he was chosen
For the esteemed society of Laureates,
And he taught by distinguished example.

But since then, the radiance of his work has
Shone upon our lands.
As he abandoned false teaching for Christ,
He did not bow down to the pope's authority.
After Rhegius left Babylon,
He joined the alliance of pure Evangelisch believers.

As an exceptional fighter for Christ, he undertook
Very difficult assignments,
As he gave the common people the
Joyful nourishment of Evangelisch beliefs.

Lastly, he cared for the sheep of the fold,
Which the commorative artists
Attested to by the monument here
To this highly renowned man.

His mortal remains lie in repose in Celle,
But his virtue will be prized everywhere,
And he shall live forever."

He died in Celle on May 23, 1541.

A Memorial - The Schlosskirche In Luther's City Of Wittenberg

The Schlosskirche [Castle Church] in the Luther-City of Wittenberg, which was built by Elector Frederich dem Weisen [Frederick the Wise] in the years 1490 to 1499, becomes the birthplace of the Reformation on October 31, 1517 when Luther posts his theses on the door. Over the centuries, the church has been revered, but has also suffered repeatedly from wars and decay. During the Seven Years War, the castle and its church are in flames. The melted bells lie in the nave. The door on which the theses are posted is scorched. When Napoleon's troops occupy Wittenberg in 1813, the castle's tower is again burned to the ground.

As so often happens in history, something new arises from the ruins. In the 1815 Laxenburger Frieden [Peace of Laxenburg], Sachsen must cede Wittenberg to Prussia. But in the same year, Schinkel, the king's senior advisor, receives the order to do whatever is necessary to "repair and restore this treasured memorial."[724]

In the following decades, the Prussian kings do much to restore the exterior and interior of the Schlosskirche. In 1844, King Frederick Wilhelm IV has the large church door cast in bronze, and Luther's theses are written in gold.

From 1880 on, Kronprinz [Crown Prince] Friedrich Wilhelm (who becomes Emperor Friedrich III in 1888), takes personal charge of the the restoration of the Schlosskirche and repeatedly visits Wittenberg. He gives the building commission – not always to their joy – direct instructions. Even upon a trip to the south a few months after his deathly illness broke out, the emperor is heavily engaged in the plans, down to the minutest details. From Portofino, Italy, near St. Margheria (Genua) he writes to Minister of Culture Gossler on October 11, 1886:

"It is my sincere desire that the Wittenberg Schlosskirche and the beginning of the Reformation in Germany during the time period between Luther's nailing of the 95 theses in 1517 and his entering Worms in 1521 should be glorified. To this purpose, magnificent memorials should be placed above the graves of Luther and Melanchthon. Next, the memory of those men who established the tremendous work of the Reformation are to be immortalized by placing their statues on the church's columns or putting their pictures or epitaphs on the church's walls.

Page 215

I have put my personal effort into assembling a list of those respected reformers. As soon as possible, I am sending the list to the experts and architects so that they can render their professional opinions on it and so that they are cognizant of the antiquarian value of this material. Gez. [Signed] Friedrich Wilhelm"[725] The original writing is included as Appendix 62.

In one of the cited appendices, the crown prince mentions Urbanus Rhegius among those respected reformers. The building commission accepts the crown prince's suggestion and notes in the meeting minutes that "only these men may be placed here who are recognized as holy standard bearers of the Reformation's blessed work." Finally, the following are selected: Martin Luther, Philipp Melanchthon, Johannes Bugenhagen, Georg Spalatin, Justus Jonas, Johann Brenz, Urbanus Rhegius, Nicolaus von Amsdorf, and Caspar Cruciger. The statues, which are larger than life and made of French sandstone, are attached to pillars along the main aisle.

Appendix 63 gives a brief overview of the celebrated persons honored in the castle church. Their order of placement is also provided.[726]

The crown prince does not live to see the completion of the work to which he so passionately dedicated himself. In 1888, "the year of three emperors," he becomes heir to his father's throne, even though he himself is deathly ill. As Emperor Friedrich III he rules for only 99 days. It falls to his son, Emperor Wilhelm II, to complete the work in progress.

The dedication of the renovated Schlosskirche is celebrated on October 31, 1892, the 375TH anniversary of the theses' posting. All the Evangelisch princes from Germany and Europe are invited, as well as the senates of the three free cities and the Hanseatic League. All Prussian offcials, the chancellor, high military officers, mayors, rectors, deacons, superintendents, and Luther researchers participate. Two of Luther's descendants are personally greeted by the emperor.

These words, delivered at the time, bear witness to the ebullient fervor of this day: "With the commemorative speech, the dedication ceremony ends. Then the prayer of benediction, the most deeply moving moment of this magnificent hour, ensues. The emperor, empress, young princes, and the entire illustrious assembly of princes and powerful people of this earth fall down on their knees and pray that by performing this consecration they are releasing a stream of blessings that will flow forth from this sacred church. And while the prayer sounds through a half-opened church window, the sound of bells comes from all the towers of Wittenberg. This call to honor is accepted and spread by all the German church towers at the very same hour..."[727]

On December 7, 1996, the Reformation's sites in Wittenberg and Eisleben are designated as UNESCO World Heritage Sites. Among these are Wittenberg Schloss and Schlosskirche and the Wittenberg Luther and Melanchthon Houses. In Eisleben, the house where Luther was born and died is a site.

These commemorative sites are recognized as the heritage of humanity since they "represent a meaningful section of human history and, as authentic places of significance for the Reformation, have an extraordinary universal significance."[728]

Would Urbanus ever have imagined that 350 years after his death, he would be honored among the greatest public figures of the Evangelisch movement and that in another century he would be part of a World Heritage Site? It is a great tribute to his life's work!

Page 216

ILLUSTRATION 126: The statue of Urbanus Rhegius in the Wittenberg Schlosskirche (Photo: Studio Kirsch, Lutherstadt Wittenberg).

Page 217

ILLUSTRATION 127: Interior view of the Wittenberg Schlosskirche. Luther's crypt lies under the pulpit. On the right, behind the third column is Rhegius' statue.

Modern Design With an Old Portrait - The Rhegius Stained Glass Window in Langenargen

On Sunday morning, September 23, 2001, over 600 guests assemble in the Langenargen Festhalle [Celebration Hall] because the church is too small for an ecumenical service. The Urbanus Rhegius stained glass window is to be dedicated with a celebratory service. Invited guests include Protestant and Catholic congregations, Mayor Rolf Müller and Prof. Eduard Hindelang, who is the founder and long-standing director of the Museum Langenargen. We are grateful for his tireless initiative to honor Rhegius in the city of his birth.

On the evening before the ceremony, the Rhegius descendants, many of whom have traveled a great distance, gather in the Hotel Schiff. Some come from Northern Germany. Four come from the USA, in spite of the attack on the World Trade Center in New York City just 12 days previously. There are 16 direct descendants and nine spouses present. Most are descended through the lineage of Urbanus Regius, Jr. (303) and his son, Sebastian Regius/König (401). Present from the Königsberg lineage are Magdalene Weinberger and Charlotte Kickton.

ILLUSTRATION 128 below: Invitation to the dedication of the Urbanus Rhegius memorial stained glass window in the Evangelical Friedenskirche Langenargen on September 23, 2001:

We cordially invite you to the
Dedication of the memorial window
In the Evangelisch Friendenskirche [Church of Peace] in Langenargen
For the reformer, Urbanus Rhegius

Sunday, September 23, 2001 at 10 o'clock
In the Celebration Hall (next to the Friendenskirche) on Church Street

Ecumenical Worship Service

With Bishop of State Gerhard Maier and
Deacon Franz Scheffold.
The church choirs from the Friedenskirche
And from St. Martin will sing, directed by Rudolf Mader.

Accompanied by a wind ensemble
From the Youth Music Academy directed by
Music Director Gerd Lanz

In conclusion, the dedication address by
Dean and Univ. Professor Dr. Maximillian Liebman,
Board of Directors of the Institute for Kirchengeschichte [Church History] and
Kirchliche Zeitgeschichte [Contemporary Church History] of the Universität Graz.

Yours sincerely

Pastor Ulrich Fentzloff	Deacon Franz Scheffold
Evangelisch Church	Catholic Church Congregation of
Congregation	St. Martin
Rolf Müller	Eduard Hindelang
Mayor	Museum Langenargen

To the joy of all assembled, Professor Eduard Hindelang and Professor Maximilian Liebmann join the guests already present. It is a long awaited, festive, and informative evening. Professor Liebmann explains what an extraordinary situation it had been for him, a Catholic Church historian, to obtain his habilitation [a qualification required in order to conduct self-contained university teaching and to obtain a professorship in many European countries]. Liebmann says, "Finally the 'highest levels' in Rome gave their consent, and I received their permission to present my research on Rhegius' life's work to become a professor." [729]

Liebmann continues, "For quite some time Rhegius did not receive the attention in Church history that he deserves. We should not forget that he belongs to the fewer than one hundred persons who contributed to the success of the Reformation. And, the Augsburg Confession of Faith of 1530 is still the most important written document of the Evangelisch Church. This very document was largely influenced by Rhegius in cooperation with Melanchthon." For a moment, there was a special feeling in the air, a feeling that it was important for Professor Liebmann to give this summary not only for us, the Rhegius descendants, but also for Church history.

ILLUSTRATION 129: The Urbanus Rhegius stained glass window in the Evangelisch Church in Langengargen. Designed by Diether F. Domes, Langenargen, constructed by the A. Diering Glass Workshop, Überlingen.

ILLUSTRATION 131: A lively discussion. From left to right: Professor Eduard Hindelang, Professor Maximilian Liebmann, Diether F. Dome. (Photo: Kurt Feiner, Langenargen).

Page 219

ILLUSTRATION 130: Sixteen Rhegius descendants and nine spouses attend the dedication of the Rhegius stained glass window in Langenargen. They are pictured here along with the hosts in the Langenargen Friedenskirche. Photo: Kurt Feiner, Langenargen

Rhegius descendants are in uppercase.

Top row, from left to right: Prof. Liebmann, Pastor Fentzloff, RUDOLF MEIER, Diether F. Domes, Deacon Scheffold, Mayor Müller, Heinrich Bersuch, Michael Lohmann, HANS MEIER, MARGERETHE EHLBERG, Heinz Ehlberg.

Middle Row: Prof Eduard Hindelang, William Glew (USA), Anne Schmucker, BERTHA BROCKMANN, WALTER KÖNIG, ILSE AHMLING, Claus Ahmling, ANNETTE MARKS, RIA HENNING, GERTRUD BERSUCH, Elke Meyer, BURGHARD KÖNIG.

Front Row: KATHRYN SCHWARTAU MATTHEES (USA), MARIAN NELSON GLEW (USA), JUDITH SCHWARTAU (USA), Johannes Marks.

Behind the Front Row: Birgit Meier, MAGDALENA KÖNIG, MARTIN KÖNIG, Charlotte Kickton, Magdalene Weinberger.

The service of celebration is a wonderful experience: church choirs and wind instruments, the sermons by the Bishop of State Gerhard Maier and Deacon Franz Scheffold, the opening remarks by Pastor Ulrich Fentzloff, the dedication address by Prof. Maximilian Lieb-mann, the joyful congregation, and finally, the viewing of the church window. Everything culminates in a day to remember. Diether F. Domes, Langenargen artist in residence, explains the window's design to the interested guests. His explanation of the symbiosis between the ancient portrait and the typical direction of the lines in the stained glass is intellectually challenging and enlightening. Fol-lowing the presention of this information by the artist, a lively dis-cussion opens up among the guests and they perceive the window's harmony of design and color.[730]

Funds for the realization of the window are largely provided through generous donations by individual companies and organi-zations, the Evangelisch Church congregations in Langenargen and Finkenwerder, the Museum Langenargen, well-known people from the Bodensee area, and, to a considerable extent, through over 30 contributions from Rhegius descendants.

Untranslated Anlagen 1 – 66 [Appendices]

A Thank You to All Those Who Helped with this Book

This book would not be possible in its present form without the willing assistance of many helpers in museums, archives, libraries, city administrations and parish offices. Many families also assisted.

In hopes of forgetting no one, our thanks go to:

Dr. Harm Alpers, Superintendent i.R., Celle

Dr. Angelika Barth, Tettnang

Pfarrer Martin Bürkle, Langenargen

Prof. Dr. Karl Heinz Burmeister, Bregenz

Prof. Dr. Ralf Busch, Hamburg

Diether F. Domes, Langenargen

Pfarrer Heinz-Gerd Funke, Wartenburg

Hans-Joachim Gabriel, Hamburg

Horst E. Gerke, Burscheid

Martin Hässler, Tuttlingen

Jutta Haag, Finkenwerder

Gisela Haltrich, Leer

Wilhelm Kranz, Hamburg

Rolf Kummerfeld, Finkenwerder

Prof. Dr. Maximilian Liebmann, Graz

Dr. Christian Lippelt, Wolfenbüttel

Prof. Dr. Peter Lüdders, Berlin (deceased)

Prof. Dr. Inge Mager, Hamburg

Pfarrer Herbert Marder, Stieffenhofen

Dr. Hans Otte, Hannover

Jochen Permien, Hamburg

Prof. Dr. Rainer Postel, Hamburg

Jacob Schwartau, Finkenwerder

Willi and Henry Simon, Finkenwerder

[Continued]

Peter Heidtmann, Tettnang

Ria Henning, Hamburg

Prof. Eduard Hindelang, Langenargen

Charlotte Kickton, Köln

Carl-Albrecht Költzsch, Buchholz

Dr. Joachim Stüben, Hamburg

Kurt Wagner, Finkenwerder

Magdalene Weinberger, Eckernförde

Herbert Winkler, Finkenwerder (deceased)

Prof. Dr. Rainer Wohlfeil, Hamburg

Jost Wünsche, Tettnang

Our special thanks go to Ms. Anne Schmucker and her tireless effort uncovering many valuable finds in the Augsburg Archives. Also, thanks to Oberstudienkdirektor Georg Baldewein, Tuttlingen, for his expert translation of the Latin texts and final editing. The cordial advice and assistance of Prof. Scott Hendrix, Princeton, USA is very much appreciated.

The overall layout, including the cover design, was in the hands of Denise Mein. Her creative design ideas brought the book to life in the eyes of the readers.

The author thanks his sons Burghard, Winfried and Dierk König for overcoming computer hurdles and thanks Burghard for his many design suggestions for the text. The biggest thanks go to spouses Adalgisa König and Birgit Meier for their generous support and unending patience during the long years of this book's development.

ENDNOTES 1 – 730

The original German text has footnotes containing both source citations and explanatory information. In this English version, the footnotes have been converted to endnotes, with the source citations in
the original German and the explanatory information translated into
English and bracketed. The 66 appendices have not been translated,
so endnotes 1 – 730 are for the body of the text.

The following are some German terms that appear most frequently
in these endnotes:

GERMAN	ENGLISH
Band (Bände)	Volume(s)
Druck	Printed document
Fol.	Page, [Latin Folio]
Fussnote	Footnote
Handschrift	Handwritten document
Nr. (Nummer)	Number
S = Seite(n)	Page(s)
Siehe auch	See also
Signatur	Catalog number
Tafel	Table
Teil(e)	Part(s)

1.   [The three-digit numbers in parentheses after certain person's names indicate their position on the Rieger-R(h)egius-König family tree that is enclosed in the German version of this book.]

2.   Ernestus Regius: Opera Vrbani Regii Latine Edita, Cum eius Vita, ac Praefatione Ernesti Regii, Nürnberg 1562. "Geboren ist Urbanus am Bregenzer See (Bodensee), in jenem Landesteil, der als Herrschaft der edlen Grafen von Montfort gilt: in der Stadt Langenargen..." ["Urbanus was born in the city of Langenargen on Lake Constance in the part of the territory that was ruled by the Counts of Montfort."]

3.   Roland Weiss: Die Grafen von Montfort im 16. Jahrhundert, Geschichte am See 49, Kreisarchiv Bodenseekries, Markdorf/Tettnang 1992, S. 8

4.   Karl Heinz Burmeister: Graf Heinrich VII. von Montfort-Rothenfels 1456 – 1512, in: Lebensbilder aus dem Bayrischen Schwaben, Weissenborn 1993. S. 9

5.   Johann Kichler/Hermann Eggart: Die Geschichte von Langenargen und des Hauses Montfort, Friedrichshafen a.B. 1926, S. 183

6.   [Illustration 1: "Arge Castle in Lake Constance." Rebuilt after the fire of 1473. In the background are the Swiss Alps.] Matthäus Merian: Topographia Sueviae, 1643, aus: "1200 Jahre Langenargen Bodensee"

7.   [Since the references to the Counts of Montfort vary in different works, we are uniformly citing Johann B. Kichler's, "The History of Langenargen and the House of Montfort."]

8.   Ral Kichler/Eggart, S. 59/60

9.   Ralf Reiter: Das Heilig-Geist-Hospital zu Langenargen von der Urkunde Graf Hugos bis zum Ende des 19. Jahrhunderts, in: Langenargener Geschichte(n), Band 6, Langenargen 1991, S. 11

10. Mannfred Krebs: Die Investiturprotokolle der Diözese Konstanz aus dem 15. Jahrhundert, in: Freiburger Diözesanarchiv 66 – 74 Jahrgang, 1939 – 1954, S. 484

11. Alois Niederstätter: Grafen von Montfort als Studenten an den Universitäten Europas

12. Kichler/Eggart: S. 48

13. Roland Weiss: S. 17

14. Kichler/Eggart: S. 48

15. Elmar L. Kuhn: "Die buren Argen gwunnen", in: Langenargener Geschichte(n), Band 4, 1989

16. Langenargener Geschichte(n), Band 4, 1989

17. Maximilian Liebmann: Urbanus Rhegius und die Anfänge der Reformation, Münster 1980, S. 68

18. Gerhard Uhlhorn: Urbanus Rhegius – Leben und ausgewählte Schriften, Elberfeld, 1861, S. 2

19. Stefan Zweig: Triumpf und Tragik des Erasmus von Rotterdam, Frankfurt/M., 1981, S. 30

20. Karlheinz Deschner: Das Kreuz mit der Kirche – eine Sexualgeschichte des Christentums, Düsseldorf/Wien 1987, S. 158 – 175. Eine milde Strafe scheint es zu sein, wenn der Geistliche für ein uneheliches Kind einen Jährlichen Betrag an das Bistum zahlt, "In einem Jahr sollen wohl 1500 Pfaffenkinder in dem Constanzer Bistum geboren werden,...von jedem 5 Gulden, macht 7500 Gulden", sagt Deschner auf S. 175. [This appears to be a mild punishment if the cleric has an illegitimate child and pays an annual sum to the bishopric. "In one year 1,500 children of clergy were said to have been born in the Bishopric of Constance...a payment of 5 Gulden for each child would amount to 7,500 Gulden total," states Deschner, p. 175.]

21. [In a letter of February 1516 to Johann Fabri, Urbanus mentions that his brother is a letter carrier and a "puer rudis," an immature, as yet uneducated boy.]

22. Ferd. Eckert: Geschichte der Lateinschule Lindau, Festschrift von 1928, S. 8 und 9

23. Hans Winterberg: Die Schüler von Ulrich Zasius, Stuttgart 1961, S. 4

24. Boissardus, Bibliotheca chalcographica, 1669

25. Uhlhorn, S. 4

26. Statutenbuch des Coll. Sapientiae, um 1500, Universitätsarchiv Freiburg

27. Heinrich Schreiber: Geschichte der Albert-Ludwigs-Universität in Freiburg, I. Teil, 1857. S. 209

28. Winterberg, S. 59 und 85. [Winterberg refers to Count Johann II. as Johann III.]

29. [See the original German edition of this book, chapter entitled, "She Bears the Entire Burden, but No One Mentions Her," p. 100.]

30. Walter König: Urbanus Rhegius (1489 – 1541), Humanist, Dichter, Theologe, Reformator, in: Schwaben-spiegel – Literatur vom Neckar bis zum Bodensee, Ulm/Donau 2003, Band II, S. 692

31. Karl Heinz Burmeister: Geschichte der Stadt Tettnang, Konstanz 1997, S. 81 und Liebmann, S. 369

32. Liebmann, S. 83

33. Liebmann, S. 96

34. Liebmann, S. 80

35. Liebmann, S. 98

36. [Duke Ernst of Bavaria (1500 – 1560), from the House of Wittelsbach, is just 16 years old when he gives Urbanus the assignment to recruit Erasmus. Because of his noble lineage, Duke Ernst is already rector of the University of Ingolstadt.]

37. Uhlhorn, S. 10

38. Liebmann, S. 28 und 117

39. Karl Schottenloher: Kaiserliche Dichterkrönungen im Heiligen Römischen Reiche Deutscher Nation, in: Papsttum und Kaisertum – Forschungen zur politischen Geschichte und Geisteskultur des Mittelalters, Herausgeber Albert Brackmann, München 1926, S. 648

40. Will Winker: Kaiser Maximilian I., München 1950, S. 250

41. [See Illustration 8: Painting from the Rheinisches Bildarchiv, Stadt Köln]

42. [In the text, the words "Kai. Mai." are the abbreviation for Kaisierliche Majestät, meaning Imperial Majesty.]

43. Heinrich Fechter: Ulrich von Hutten – Ein Leben für die Freiheit, 1954, S. 223 – 224 [Description of poet Ulrich von Hutten's coronation, see Appendix Ia.]

44. [For more information refer to "Genealogia." See p. 216 of this translation, chapter entitled, "Court Singer, Secretary, Historian, Financial Administrator, Notary, Poet. The Multi-talented Rhegius Grandson, Franz Algermann"]

45. Uhlhorn, S. 10

46. Albert Brackmann: Papsttum und Kaisertum – Forschungen zur politischen Geschichte und Geisteskultur des Mittelalters, München 1926, S. 655

47. Winterberg, S. 69

48. Liebmann, S. 101, Fussnote 229

49. Winker, S. 256

50. Uhlhorn, S. 8, Liebmann S. 13

51. Liebmann, S. 112

52. Helmut Maurer: Das Stift St. Stephan in Konstanz, in: Das Bistum Konstanz, Berlin N.Y. 1981, S 150

53. Christina Egli: St. Stephan in Konstanz – Chorherrenstift und Pfarrkirche, Konstanz 1998

54. Liebmann, S. 118

55. H.Ch. Heimbürger: Urbanus Rhegius, Hamburg und Gotha 1851, S. 49

56. Liebmann, S. 115

57. Liebmann, S. 104

58. Joachim Fugmann: Humanisten und Humanismus am Bodensee in der ersten Hälfte des 16. Jahrhunderts, in: Schriften des Vereins für Geschichte des Bodensees und seiner Umgebung, 107. Heft, Friedrichshafen 1989, S. 140

59. Liebmann, S. 117

60. Liebmann, S. 12

61. Liebmann, S. 106

62. H.G. Wackernagel: Matrikel der Universität Basel, Basel 1950, Band I, S. 343/4

63. Winker: Kaiser Maximilian I., München 1950, S. 283

64. Klaus-Peter Schmid: Die Lutherstiege in Augsburg St. Anna, Augsburg 1984, S. 25

65. Liebmann, S. 135/36

66. Liebmann, S. 13

67. [Pen=derived from the Latin "poena," meaning "punishment."]

68. Wilhelm Rem: Chronica newer geschichten, zitiert bei Liebmann, S. 140

69. Urbanus Rhegius unter dem Pseudonym Henricus Phoeniceum von Roschach: Anzaygung dasz die Romisch Bull mercklichen schaden in gewissin manicher menschen gebracht hab vnd nit Doctor Luthers leer", Augsburg 1521, siehe auch Liebmann, S. 367

70. Karl Heinz Burmeister: Geschichte der Stadt Tettnang, Konstanz 1997, S 71

71. Liebmann, S. 139/40

72. Liebmann, S. 141

73. Chronik der Deutschen, Gütersloh/München 1983/1995, S. 308

74. Horst Jesse: Die Geschichte der Evangelischen Kirche in Augsburg, Pfaffenhofen 1983, S. 73: ["As a result of the 1521 meeting with Luther in Worms, Rhegius preaches against indulgences and the deplorable state of affairs in the Church." The documents for this are missing. Our research in Augsburg is unconfirmed.]

75. Fritz Reuter: Der Reichstag zu Worms von 1521, Reichspolitik und Luthersache, Worms 1971, S 210. Siehe auch Liebmann, S. 366, Druck 25 "Dialogus Simonis Hessi et Martino Lutheri"

76. Adolf Wrede: Zwei Beiträge zur Geschichte des Fürstentums Lüneburg im Reformationszeitalter, in: Zeitschrift des Historischen Vereins für Niedersachsen, 1894, S. 22

77. H.Ch. Heimbürger: Ernst der Bekenner, Herzog von Braunschweig und Lüneberg, Celle 1839, S. 29, sowie Dieter Matthes: Die welfische Nebenlinie in Harburg, Hamburg-Harburg 1962, S. 11

78. Urbanus Rhegius: Ain Serman von dem hochwirdigen sacrament des Altars, gepredigt durch Doctor Vrbanum Regium, Thumprediger zu Aug-spurg am tag Corporis Christi 1521. Siehe auch Liebmann, S. 366

79. Heimbürger: Urbanus Rhegius, S. 73/74. (Quelle: Joseph Friedrich Rein: Das gesamte Augspurgische Evangelische Ministerium in Bildern und Schriften, von den ersten Jahren der Reformation Lutheri, bis auff Anno 1748), Stadtarchiv Augsburg 1749

80. Uhlhorn, S. 45

81. [See Illustration 12.] Augustin Scheller: Chronica Ecclesiastica Augustana, Manuskript von 1749

82. Liebmann, S. 145/46 [The Chronicler Sender speaks of 5,000 deaths from the plague in Augsburg, footnote 174.]

83. Originalbrief in der Universitätsbibliothek Breslau, erwähnt bei Liebmann, S. 344, als Handschrift Nr. 19

84. Burmeister, S. 81.

85. Urbanus Rhegius: Ain vberschöne vnd nützliche erklärung über das Vater vnser des hailigen Cecilij Cypriani, durch Vrbanum Regium der hayligen geschrift Doctor verteutscht, datiert Augsburg, den 31.10.1521, siehe Liebmann, S. 368, Druck Nr. 30. [There are approximately 250 existing explanations of the Lord's Prayer going back to the early fathers of the Church and Cyprus, Bishop of Carthage.]

86. Urbanus Rhegius: Des hochgelerten hern Erasmi von Roterdam schöne vn clare ausslegung über die Epistel Pauli zu Tito. Durch Vrbanum Regiu der hayligen schrifft Doctor geteutscht, Augsburg Anfang 1522, siehe Liebmann S. 369, Druck 32

87. Liebmann, S. 155 und 344, Handschrift 20, Original in der Universitätsbibliothek Hamburg. [Citation by Liebmann: "There is nothing further to say about this prideful and arrogant letter. The high esteem in which I hold Rhegius forbids me to do so. Without a doubt, his expulsion by the Augsburg Church officials angers him, which excuses him somewhat..."]

88. Burmeister, S. 79

89. Andreas Jung: Geschichte der Reformation der Kirche in Strassburg und der Ausbreitung derselben in den Gemeinden des Elsasses. I. Band, Strassburg und Leipzig 1830, S. 38/39

90. Liebmann, S. 158

91. Helga Noflatscher-Posch: Die Jahrmärkte von Hall in Tirol, Hall i.T. 1992, S. 124

92. Noflatscher-Posch, S. 50 – 54

93. Liebmann, S. 160/61

94. Urbanus Rhegius: Ain Sermon. Von der kyrchweyche/Doctor Vrbani Regij. Prediger zu Hall jm Intal/ M.D.XXII. Jar. Siehe auch Liebmann, S. 369, Druck 34. [It is noteworthy that all the works Rhegius composed in Hall were printed in Augsburg. Perhaps it is an indication that it was through his book publishing connections that he came to Augsburg?]

95. Gemachl = Gemahlin = [consort]. On March 26, 1521, Ferdinand marries 18 year old Anna, Princess of Bohemia and Hungary. Thereby, Ferdinand becomes founder of the Habsburg lineage in Austria-Hungary.]

96. David Schönherr: Franz Schweyger's Chronik der Stadt Hall, 1303 – 1572, Innsbruck 1867, S. 83

97. Richard Reifenscheid: Die Habsburger Graz, Wien, Köln 1982, S. 125, und Paula Sutter Fichtner: Ferdinand I. – Wider Türkennot und Glaubensspaltung, Graz, Wien, Köln 1986, S. 28

98. Uhlhorn, S. 52

99. Liebmann, S. 191

100. Maximilian Liebmann: Kirche in Gesellschaft und Politik, Festgabe, Graz 1999, S. 54 und 55

101. Urbanus Rhegius: Himmlicher Applasbrief, Augsburg 1523, Liebmann Bibliographie Druck 39, S. 371

102. Der Ablassbrief ist erwähnt bei Liebmann, S. 167 und 371, Druck 39, sowie bei Uhlhorn, S. 52

103. Haller Heiltumbuch 1508/09 in: Tilman Falk: Hans Burgkmair, München 1969

104. Uhlhorn, S. 52, Liebmann, S. 169

105. Liebmann, S. 170

106. Liebmann, S. 17

107. Liebmann, S. 188

108. Brief Urbanus Rhegius' vom 21 Oktober 1524 an Johannes Oekolampad, erwähnt bei Liebmann, S. 346 als Handschrift 28, Original im Staatsarchiv Zürich

109. Uhlhorn, S. 60 – 62

110. Die Chronik von Clemens Sender von den ältesten Zeiten der Stadt bis zum Jahre 1536, in der Bearbeitung von Friedrich Roth, in: Die Chroniken der deutschen Städte, 23. Band, Leipzig 1894, S. 1 – 404

111. [Corpus Christi fell on June 15, 1525 so that the following Friday is June 16TH. Sender errs here. June 16TH, the date given by Liebmann, is correct.]

112. [The text means that according to the Lutheran rite, communion is given both in the form of bread and in the form of wine.]

113. Urbanus Rhegius: Ain Sermon vom eelichen stand wie nutz not gut vnd frey er jederman sey, Augsburg 1525. Siehe Liebmann, S. 378, Druck 53

114. Ausschnitt aus dem Stadtplan von Georg Seld (geziechnet 1510 – 21)

115. August Franzen: Zölibat und Priesterehe in der Auseinandersetzung des Reformationszeit und der katholischen Reform des 16. Jahrhunderts, Münster 1971, S. 30

116. Anne Schmucker: Frauen in der Reformationszeit - Die ersten Priesterehen in Augsburg, in: Geschichte quer, Heft 6, Augsburg 1998, S. 6 und 7

117. Wilhelm Schiller: Die St. Annakirche in Augsburg, Augsburg 1938, S. 35

118. Inge Mager: Theologenfrauen als "Gehilfinnen" der Reformation, in: Katharina von Bora, Die Lutherin, Wittenberg 1999, S. 127, Fussnote 109 [Mager likewise comes to the conclusion that Anna could be born around the year 1505.]

119. Friedrich Roth: Augsburgs Reformationgeschichte, 1517 – 1555, Band I, München 1901 – 11, S. 150

120. [Latin accusative: "Ad Doctorem Urbanum Rhegium," approximately translated as: "Dedicated to U.R."]

121. D. Wilhelm Schiller: Die St. Annakirche in Augsburg, ein Beitrag zur Augsburger Kirchengeschichte, Augsburg 1938, S. 57

122. Freiherr Johann Michael v. Welser: Die Welser - Nachrichten über die Familie, Nürnberg 1917, S. 62 und 74 – 77. [The author surmises that Lukas is a silent partner, since there is no other mention of him.]

123. [Duke Otto I. spends the year 1516 at the margrave's court and receives a 1,500 Gulden living allowance from his father. This amount is appropriate to his rank and class. Later, Duke Otto II facilitates sending lansquenets to the margrave's son, Albrecht Alcibiades.] Dieter Matthes: Die welfische Nebenlinie in Harburg, S. 11

124. Urbanus Rhegius: Von Reu, Beicht, Büsz., kurtzer beschluss auss gegrüter schrift nit auss menschen leer. Durch Doc. Vrbanum Regjum zu Hall jm Intal gepredigt. Im Iar MDXXiiij, Augsburg 1523, siehe Liebmann S. 370, Druck 37

125. [The chronologist Sender appears to be making fun of Lucas Welser: "a pious man, but not a very bright one, has joined the council." His son Sigmund, took part in the iconoclasm in Augsburg.]

126. Schiller, S. 57

127. Paul Arnold: Medaillenbildnisse der Reformationszeit, Berlin 1967, S. 56. [Translation of the circumscription on the coin: "Ambrosius Jung, Doctor of Arts and Medicine, at age 57."]

128. Arnold, S. 80

129. Josef Fleischmann: Die Ärztefamilie Jung, in: Lebensbilder aus dem bayrischen Schwaben, Bd. 4

130. Urbanus Rhegius: Von leibaygenschaft oder knechthait, wie sich Herren vnnd aygenleut Christlich halten sollend. Bericht auss götlichen Rechten. Durch D. Vrbanum Regium zu Augspurg gepredigt MDXXV, Augsburg 1525. Siehe auch Liebmann, S. 377, Druck 52

131. Adolf Laube/Hans Werner Seiffert: Flugschriften der Bauernkriegszeit, Berlin 1975, S. 148. Die Auffassung, dass Rhegius' Reformvorschläge faktisch auf eine schrittweise Aufhebung der Leibeigenschaft hinausliefen, scheint eine sehr wohlwollende Auslegung zu sein. [This is an early manifestation of Urbanus' conviction that serfdom is questionable, and moreover, it is wrong. Urbanus says this with some reservation because Luther is of a different opinion.]

132. Scott Hendrix: Die Bedeutung des Urbanus Rhegius für die Ausbreitung der Wittenberger Reformation, in: Humanismus und Wittenberger Reformation, Leipzig 1996, S. 54. [Special edition for the 500ᵀᴴ anniversary of Melanchthon's birth on February 16, 1997.]

133. Claus-Peter Clasen: Die Augsburger Steuerbücher um 1600, Augsburg 1976, S. 7 – 10. [Since the year 1509, excluding income and property tax, everyone pays a 30 cent tax for poor people, plus a 6 cent security tax. The actual tax is the property tax (no income tax!). A half percent is charged on cash and .25 percent on real estate. Household goods, silverware, and jewelry are exempt. Likewise, since the year 1581, 500 Gulden in harbor dues are charged, which is a very high rate. Since the tax to be paid, which only will be specified, the property tax will be included. Inheritance tax by the Weisbrücker/Fendt family amounts to 6 – 10% of the sum of the inheritance.]

134. Weinberger: S. 553. [Weinberger calls Caspar Weissbrücker "a relative" of Anna. In Weinberger's estate documents, however, this handwritten note is found: "Caspar is sometimes referred to as the father and sometimes the cousin. Judging from his age, he must be the father." Weinberger suspects the correct answer. Zschoch uses the term "relative" for Caspar Weissbrücker (p. 129, footnote 219).]

135. [Mayors are Marx Ustett and Georg Östreicher. R=Rheinsche Gulden.]

136. [The first amount is the tax that supports poor people, the second for property tax.]

137. ["Vom Diepold" comprises the present day streets of Mauerberg, Hinter Schwalbeneck, Hoher Weg and Spenglergässchen. "Vom Zimerleuthhaus" comprises the present day streets of Karolinen and Karlstrasse, Kesselsmarkt and Steingasse. "Vom Ror" is part of Karolinenstrasse along with Perlachturm and Peterskirche.]

138. Anthony Livesey: Die grosse Schatzkammer der Antiquitäten, Bayreuth 1984, S. 55

139. Protokollbuch Kaufleute Stuben, Bayrisches Wirtschaftsarchiv München, Fol. 38

140. Augsburger Stadtlexikon von 1998, S. 552.

141. [In the recorded citizens' names from 1288 – 1497 the name Weissbrücker does not appear (from 1498 until 1557 the names are virtually all missing.)]

142. Stadtarchiv Augsburg, Schätze 1441/2

143. [In the above mentioned, because of similar names, Mätthäus Fendt a goldsmith born in 1545, could be connected to a son of another Matthäus Fendt, who acted as the executor of Ursula Fendt's will, according to the tax records of 1547. (Helmut Seling: The Art of the Augsburg Goldsmith 1529 – 1868, vol. III: Fend, Matthäus, goldworker, born in Augsburg around 1545, master goldsmith 1570, marries 2.1566, 3.1604, died 1618)]

144. Liebmann, S. 196

145. [See Illustration 27.] Handschrift von Augustin Scheller aus dem Jahr 1749 in der Staats-und Stadtbibliotek Augsburg

146. [The east choir no longer exists.]

147. Paul von Stetten, Augsburger Geschlechter, nicht datiert

148. [Monseigneur = in France is a prince or high ranking clergy; Monsieur = Mister; Monsignore = higher ranked clergy or dignitary, Pictor = artist painter]

149. Uhlhorn, S. 139/40

150. Urbani Rhegii Lebens Geschichte, Celler Handschrift (auch als Anonyme Handschrift bezeichnet) Bibliothek des Predigerseminars Celle (bei Liebmann unter Landeskirchenamt, Archiv Hannover erwähnt), 2004 als Transkription von Horst E. Gerke, Burscheid, im Selbsverlagherausgegeben, dort S. 157

151. Liebmann, S. 347, Handschrift 36 (Original im Staatsarchiv Zürich)

152. Uhlhorn, S. 140

153. Liebmann, S. 198

154. Heimbürger: Urbanus Rhegius, S. 115

155. Heimbürger: Urbanus Rhegius, S. 118

156. Liebmann, S. 244. Siehe auch Hedios, in: Marburger Religionsgespräch, S. 14 sowie Köhler: Zwingli und Luther, Bd. 2, S. 75

157. Heimbürger, S. 126. Eine Aufzählung aller Teilnehmer des Reichstages in: Heinrich Wilhelm Rotermund: Geschichte des auf dem Reichstage zu Augsburg im Jahre 1530 übergebenen Glaubensbekenntnisses der Protestanten, nebst den vornehmsten Lebensnachrichten aller auf dem Reichstage zu Augsburg gewesenen päpstlich und evangelisch Gesinnten, Hannover 1829

158. Liebmann, S. 227

159. Liebmann, S. 229, zitiert Conrad Eubel: Hierarchia Catholica medii et recentioris aevi, III. Bd., 2. Auflage, Münster 19131 – 23, S. 117

160. Liebmann, S. 242 – 244 und 349, Manuskript 46. Original des Rhegiusbriefes in der Staats-und Universitätsbibliothek Hamburg

161. Scott Hendrix: Die Bedeutung des Urbanus Rhegius für die Ausbreitung der Wittenberger Reformation, in: Humanismus und Wittenberger Reformation, Leipzig 1996, S. 61: ["His main contribution to the final result of the Confession of Faith is his achievement of winning over Landgraf Philipp, with whom he has had a good relationship for some time. This relationship is crucial to the Confession and its delivery."]

162. Uhlhorn, S. 153

163. Uhlhorn, S. 154 – 55

164. [At this celebration, the observation of the eye witness Sender, who describes this event with a wink of his eye, does not quite fit. The kaiser's officiating advisors were so tired that their servants one after another removed their masters' shoes...]

165. Uhlhorn, S. 155

166. Urbanus Rhegius: Der Vier vnd Zwentzigst Psalm Sampt dem Ostergesang Cum Rex glorie Christus etc. Von dem herrlichen Sieg vnd Triumpf Christi, Wittenberg 1533. Siehe Liebmann, S. 390/91, Druck 98. Die Schrift is datiert "November 1530"

167. Rhegius an den Kurfürsten von Sachsen Johann Friedrich vom 22. Juni 1540 (Liebmann, S. 310 und 403, Druck 132)

168. Liebmann, S. 246 – 48

169. Liebmann, S. 240/41

170. Liebmann, S. 260

171. Liebmann, S. 303

172. Rhegius an Markgraf Georg von Brandenburg-Ansbach vom 11. Oktober 1528, siehe Liebmann, S. 304/05 und S. 348, Manuskript 39

173. [Margrave Georg, speaking before the Imperial Diet, tells the Kaiser that he would rather have his head chopped off than give up the teachings he believes in and God's word. To that the Kaiser replied in his broken Low German dialect, "Not off with your head, dear prince, not off with your head!" Georg, also called Georg the Pious, has an unshakeable religious belief, which even his opponents respect.]

174. Staatsarchiv Nürnberg, Signatur: Fürstentum Brandenburg-Ansbach, Religionsakten, Tomus II

175. [W.C. Ludewig erroneously reports in his "History of the City of Harburg and Harburg Castle," vol. I, pg. 49, that the third brother, Duke Otto I., "himself at the Imperial Diet of Augsburg" also signed the Confession of Faith. In actuality, Otto I. is not among the signers.]

176. Uhlhorn, S. 153

177. Liebmann, S. 256

178. Liebmann, S. 311

179. Urbanus Rhegius an: Freund in Augsburg, datiert 1534, siehe Liebmann, S. 390, Drucke 99

180. Zitiert nach Uhlhorn, S. 160

181. Ludwig Bechstein: Der Fürstentag, Historisch-Romantisches Zeitbild aus dem sechzehnten Jahrhundert, Frankfurt am Main 1834, Erster Teil, S. 196/97

182. [Because of Duke Heinrich's participation in the Hildesheim Prince-Bishopric Feud, Kaiser Karl V. charged the Duke under imperial decree. Following Heinrich's flight to France, the two older sons, Otto and Ernst, come to power. In 1527, Otto I. is compensated with Harburg, and Franz is compensated in 1539 with Gifhorn. Ernst thereby becomes regent of the country.]

183. Urbanus Rhegius: Eine vngehewre wunderbarliche Absolution der Closterfrawen jm Fürstenthumb Lüneburg mit jhrer auslegung durch Vrbanum Regium. Supperattendenten daselbst, Wittenberg 1532. Siehe Liebmann, S. 387, Druck 88

184. Uhlhorn, S. 163

185. Uhlhorn, S. 171

186. Uhlhorn, S. 172

187. Uhlhorn, S. 185. [Based on her appearance, Anna is about 5 months pregnant on the trip to Celle.]

188. Urbanus Rhegius: Christlyke Ordenynnghe van der Scholenn vnd kerckenn sackenn der Stadt Luneborch, datiert 9 Juni 1531, Manuskript im Evangelisch-lutherirschem Kirchenbuchamt Lüneberg (siehe auch Liebmann, S. 350, Manuskript 50)

189. Dieter Fabricius: Die theologischen Kontroversen in Lüneburg im Zusammenhang mit der Einführung der Reformation, Lüneburg 1988, S. 125. [In the agreement between the council and citizenry it is established that "ordained and worthy and scholarly doctoris Urbani regii asks for and desires…"]

190. Richard Gerecke: Urbanus Rhegius als Superintendent in Lüneburg (1532 – 1533), in: Reformation vor 450 Jahren, Lüneburg 1980, S. 72. In: Die Chroniken der deutschen Städte vom 14. bis ins 16. Jahrhundert, Lüneburg – Stuttgart 1931, S. 484, ist diese Begebenheit in plattdeutscher Sprache wiedergegeben: "Furgedachte doctor Urbanus Regius, so alhei im furstenthum die reformacion angestelt, ist auf anholdent der burger durch Helmige Lampen und Hans Poelden van Zelle anher vormucht und alhei vor seines superintendens tocius religionis bostahlt und angenommen. Diese haben den doctor mit sich gebracht den sontag Palmarum (Märtz 24), alhei auf die folgende Ostern (März 31) seine Lher und pridige anzufangen"

191. Uhlhorn, S. 189

192. Fabricius, S. 117/118

193. Hans-Otto Westermann: Das Verhältnis von lutherischer Kirche und Schule in Celle, in: Kirche in Celle, S. 212 ["It can be firmly documented that the Reformation in Germany advanced powerful methods of instruction. Luther and Melanchthon, along with Johann Bugenhagen and Urbanus Rhegius, were the most important figures in the North German school district who put their stamp on the cirruculum in North German school districts for centuries. The main instructional focus was the loyal, pious, and obedient Christ. The agreement about knowledge was naturally to be bound to the above desired goal. This basic foundation was nowhere as definitely clear as in the Protestant church organizational doctrine of the 16TH century which was simultaneously the school doctrine."]

194. Uhlhorn, S. 194

195. Fabricius, S. 119

196. Uwe Plath: Der Durchbruch der Reformation in Lüneburg, in: Reformation vor 450 Jahren. Eine Lüneburger Gedenkschrift, Lüneburg 1980, S. 214. [Among the 20 councilors, Witzendorff is the only disciple of the Reformation. Rhegius dedicates his work, "Gewisse lere bewerter vnd vnüberwindlicher trost wider verzweiflung der sünden halber" to Witzendorff. The work appears in 1532 in Wittenberg (Liebmann S. 388, Druck 93). Rhegius is also a godfather to one of Witzendorff's children.]

197. [Fabricius calls the Text "the foremost theological text in the history of the Reformation to emerge from Lüneburg" (p. 131) and cites it fully on page 135. "The disputed theses are a successful compromise of Evangelical doctrine that should be pertinent today. People should obey the authority of the govnenment with the stipulation that such obedience must take Christian ethics into account. Luther's support of the civil authorities casued a rift between him and the supporters of the Peasant Revolution.]

198. Elmar Peter: Geschichte einer tausendjährigen Stadt, Museumsverein Lüneburg 1999, S. 255. [The prince's drawing room is located on the second floor of the Lüneburg City Hall. Portraits of Guelph dukes and their consorts decorate the large walls, painted by Daniel Freese at the parliament of the Hanseatic League.]

199. Fabricius, S. 175

200. Staats-und Universitätsbibliothek Hamburg (siehe auch Liebmann, S. 363, Manuskript 64)

201. Rainer Postel: Die Reformation in Hamburg 1517 – 1528, Gütersloh 1986, S. 351

202. Heimbürger, S. 149 und 150

203. Hamburger Abendblatt vom 1. Juni 2004 in "Der Luther von Hamburg", aus Anlass des 475. Jahresstages der Schul-und Kirchenordnung

204. J. Geffcken: Doctor Urban Regius, seine Wahl zum ersten Hamburgerischen Superintendenten, und ein Paar Briefe in dieser Angelegenheit, in: Zeitschrift des Vereines für hamburgische Geschichte, zweiter Bd., Hamburg 1847, S. 341 ff

205. [Taken from the quotation in Low German. For the original, see Appendix 8.]

206. [Heinrich der Mittlere (the one in the middle) dies in 1532 in the Wienhausen Cloister]

207. Urbanus Rhegius: Psalmvs Octvagesimvs Septimus, de Gloriosa Christi Ecclesia (Liebmann, S. 394, Druck III), erscheint 1536 in Hamburg bei Franz Rhode, bis 1594 nachgedruckt, auch in englischer Sprache

208. Urbanus Rhegius: Dialogus oder Gesprech zwischen dem Teuffel vnd inem biessenden Sunder...(Liebmann S. 398, Druck 116), erscheint 1537 in Hamburg bei Franz Rhode, 1545 in Latein mit einer Widmungsrede von Hieronymus Weitzendorf, Lüneburg, auch 1588 in Genf.

209. Jürgen Ricklefs: Das Haus des Urbanus Rhegius, erster Superintendent der Superintendentur Celle und des Fürstentums Lüneburg, an der Bergstrasse 1A und 1B in Celle, in: Celler Chronik 2, Celle 1985, S. 103

210. [In the January 8, 1937 article in the Celle Newspaper, "The House on the Bergstrasse that was Cut in Two," author Anna Fuess posits that the division of the house had to have been handled by the duke and Rhegius, judging from the two portraits of the men. There is no proof of this assumption. Photo by: Han-Günther Bigalke: Framework of the Building, Decoration from the North German Building Frames, and their development in Celle, Hannover 2000, p. 38/9]

211. Urbanus Rhegius: Ain Bedenken vnd wolmeinung, vber etlich artikel des Babst vn keyserlicher Mayest, das kunftig Conciliu betreffend, (Liebmann S. 352, Handschrift 62)

212. E.F.G.= Euer Fürstliche Gnaden= [Your Princely Grace]

213. Uhlhorn, S. 211

214. Liebmann, S. 169

215. Liebmann, S. 193

216. Richard Reifenscheid: Die Habsburger. Sonderausgabe 1994 Wien, S. 114. [Karl V's empire, "upon which the sun never set" is partitioned. His son Philipp receives Spain, his brother Ferdinand becomes founder of the Austrian Empire.]

217. Uhlhorn, S. 213

218. Werner Siebarth: Herzog Franz von Braunschweig-Lüneburg und seine Zeit, Hannover 1953, S. 52

219. [In 1537 Johann von Amsterdam signs the Schmalkalden Articles for Bremen. In 1571 Johann von Amsterdam appears as pastor in Finkenwerder. See Appendix 40, the most complete list of Finkenwerder pastors.]

220. Uhlhorn, S. 219. Siehe auch Scott Hendrix: Validating the Reformation: The use of the Church Fathers by Urbanus Rhegius, in: Ecclesia Militans, Studien zur Konzilien-und Reformationsgeschichte, Zweiter Band, Paderborn 1988, S. 281 – 305

221. Heimbürger, S. 167

222. Martin Tamcke: Die reformatorischen Impulse zu Bildung und Glaube bei Herzog Ernst und im Uelzen seiner Zeit, Vortrag vom 26. März 1997 im Gildehaus Uelzen. Herausgeber: Verein Historisches Uelzen e.V

223. Stupperich, de Kroon, Rudolph: Martin Bucers Deutsche Schriften, Band 6,1, Wittenberger Konkordie, Gütersloh 1988, S. 131 (freundl. Hinweis von Prof. Scott Hendrix, Princeton, USA)

224. Urbanus Rhegius: Dialogus von der schönen predigt, die Christus Luc. 24. von Jerusalem bis gen Emaus den zweien jüngern am Ostertag aus Mose vnd allen Profpheten gethan hat. Wittenberg 1537. Sehr häufig nachgedruckt: Wittenberg 1537, 1539, 1545, 1551, 1553, 1558, 1565, 1566, 1573, 1584, 1590, 1591, 1606. 1647 Hamburg, 1651 Lübeck, 1689 Lüneburg (mit stark verändertem Titel), 1538 Plattdeutsch, 1557 und 1631 Holländisch, 1648 Dänisch, 1578, 1642 London, englisch, 1545 Protejov Tschechisch, 1571, 1573 und 1583 Prag Tschechisch, 1539 durch Rhegius ergänzte Ausgabe in Wittenberg 1539. Diese 1542 in Frankfurt Latein (von Johannes Freder) und einem Vorwort von Martin Luther (Nachruf auf Rhegius). Siehe Liebmann, S. 396 und 397, Druck 115 und 115,I Ein Exemplar im Stadtarchiv Lindau

225. Uhlhorn, S. 332

226. Inge Mager: Drei Frauen halten ihren Männern den Rücken frei: Walpurgia Bugenhagen, Anna Rhegius und (Anna) Margarethe Corvin, in: Jahrbuch der Gesellschaft für niedersächsische Kirchengeschichte, 97, Band 1999, S. 244

227. Uhlhorn, S. 332

228. Peter Handy, Karl-Heinz Schmöger: Fürsten, Stände, Reformatoren, Gotha, 1996, S. 9

229. Handy, S. 45

230. Handy, S. 45

231. Beschreibung des Reisezuges: Georg Schuster: Aus der Geschichte des Hauses Hohenzollern, Berlin-Lichterfelde, 1815, "Die Reise des Kurprinzen Joachim II. nach Nürnberg im Jahre 1522 und seine Rückreise nach Berlin im Jahre 1523"

232. Bechstein, Erster Theil, ab S. 147

233. Heimbürger, S. 205. Heimbürger führt noch folgende Teilnehmer auf: "In Gefolge des Kurfürsten Luther, Melanchthon, Bugenhagen, Spalatin, Jonas, Agricola, Amsdorf, Minius und Mykonius, mit dem Landgrafen Dionysius, Melander, sein Hofprediger, die Superintendenten von Kassel, Alsfeld und Marburg, Fontius, Tilemann, Schnabel, Adam Kraft, Anton Corvinus aus Witzenhausen, und die Marburgischen Professoren Draconites, Noviomagus und Dobanus Hessus"

234. Bechstein, Erster Theil, ab. S. 141

235. Bechstein, Erster Theil, S. 145

236. Handy, S. 46

237. Handy, 1996

238. Handy, S. 41

239. Martin Luther: Schmalkaldische Artikel, Heinrich-Jung-Verlagsgesellschaft mbH. Zella-Mehlis, 1995, S. 6

240. Heimbürger, S. 205

241. Bechstein, Erster Theil, S. 235

242. [The Sunday before Ash Wednesday is day of celebration for which the date varies. In 1537 it falls on February 11.]

243. Uhlhorn, S. 321

244. Urbanus Rhegius: Dialogus. Ain lustparlich nützlich gesprech vom künftigen Concilio zu Mantua: Zwischen einem Weltfrommen, ainem Epicuren und ainem Christen. Durch D. Urbanum Rhegium. Zu Zella in Saxen 1536, Gedruckt zu Hamburg durch Franciscum Rhodum 1537. Siehe auch Liebmann, S. 395

245. Köstlin, Julius: Luthers Leben, Leipzig, 1883, S. 515

246. Bechstein, Erster Theil, S. 259

247. Bechstein, Erster Theil, S. 97ff

248. Thüringisches Hauptstaatsarchiv Weimar. Ernestinisches Gesamtarchiv, Reg. H 124, B.37r-38v

249. Uhlhorn, S. 327, sowie Bechstein, Zweiter Theil, S. 147

250. Thüringisches Hauptstaatsarchiv Weimar, Signatur: ThHStA Weimar, Ernestinisches Gesamtarchiv, Reg. H 124, Bl.37v

251. [It is probable that Urbanus' deeds in Hannover around 1536 are connected to Duchess Elisabeth, who four years later wanted him to secure the whole country for the Reformation.]

252. Bechstein, Zweiter Theil, S. 149 ff., sowie Uhlhorn, S. 327

253. Werner: Dr. Martin Luthers Werke, Gesamtausgabe, Briefwechsel, Bd. 4, 1933, sowie Liebmann, S. 355

254. Liebmann, S. 397

255. Heimbürger, S. 209

256. Urbanus Rhegius: Wie man die falschen Propheten erkennen ia greiffen mag. Ein predig zu Mynden jnn Westphalen gethan, Braunschweig 1539, Liebmann Nr. 129, S. 402

257. Robert Stupperich: Urbanus Rhegius und die vier Brennpunkte der Reformation in Westfalen, in: Westfalen, Hefte für Geschichte Kunst und Volkskunde, 45. Band 1967, S. 22 bis 34

258. Uhlhorn, S. 329

259. Uhlhorn, S. 329, auch Liebmann, S. 403, Nr. 13

260. Ernestus Regius: Opera Urbani Regii Latine Edita. Dum eius Vita, ac Praefatione, Nürnberg 1562

261. Uhlhorn, S. 330

262. Uhlhorn, S. 337, sowie Wilhelm Havemann: Geschichte der Lande Braunschweig und Lüneburg, 2. Bd., Göttingen 1855, S. 145: [Verbatim: "The following is dated and in the prince's handwriting. It attests to the prince's concerns for the widow and children of his deceased friend: 'After Almighty God has taken the scholarly Urbanus Rhegius, Doctor of Theology, from this world, we want to thank him for his loyal and industrious service, which he rendered us and the church community and to provide his widow, Anna, 40 Gulden a year for life, plus 6 wichhimpten rye so that she may better care for her children. Because she has been blessed with many children, we want to support her four children, two sons and two daughters. If we find in the future that one of his sons wants to study further, we will provide him education for the clergy and an ecclesiasrical fief.'"]

263. F. Bonnels: Celle. Führer durch die Stadt Celle, Celle 1901, S. 37 und 38

264. [Duke Wilhelm the Younger dies in 1592.]

265. Jürgen Ricklefs: Zur Geschichte der Stadtkirche, in: 660 Jahre Stadtkirche Celle, Celle 1968, S. 23/24

266. [What is meant is Lower Saxony.]

267. Zitiert nach Uhlhorn, S. 334

268. Inge Mager: Drei Frauen halten ihren Männern die Rücken frei: Walpurga Bugenhagen, Anna Rhegius und Margarethe Corvin, in: Jahrbuch der Gesellschaft für Niedersächsische Kirchengeschichte, 97, Band 1999, S. 244

269. Hellmuth Zschoch: Reformatorische Existenz und konfessionelle Identität, Tübigen 1995, S. 129

270. Scott H. Hendrix: Toleration of the Jews in the German Reformation: Urbanus Rhegius and Braunschweig (1535 – 1540). Sonderdruck: Archiv für Reformationsgeschichte, Jahrgang 81, Gütersloh 1990, S. 189 – 2

271. Scott H. Hendrix: wie vor. Brief siehe Liebmann Bibliographie S. 391, Druck 104

272. [Margaritha publishes his work in 1530 in Augsburg: The Entirety of Jewish Beliefs Together with a Basic and True Account of All Standing Rules, Ceremonies, and Public and Private Customs, Which the Jews Keep Throughout the Year, Along With the Beautiful and Well-Founded Arguments of Antonium Margaritham, Hebrew Teacher in the Honorable City of Augsburg written and issued in April 1530. He teaches from 1523 to 1530 in Augsburg. In his concluding remarks, he says that the Jews will curse him for his statements on the Jewish faith and may try to kill him. The concluding sentence reads: Distributed in the ninth year of my rebirth in Wasserburg. He was expelled from Augsburg in 1530 or shortly thereafter following a dispute with Josel von Gosheim.]

273. Jöcher/Rotermund: Allgemeines Gelehrten-Lexikon, 1787 – 1819

274. [Chaldea is the original name of a region in southern Mesopotamia. The Chaldeans were a Semitic-Aramaic tribe.]

275. Karl Schottenloher: Die Widmungsvorrede im Buch des 16. Jahrhunderts, Münster 1953, S. 63. [Schottenloher's information is based on a statement by the Saxon preacher Aurifaber who published an edition of Luther's letters in 1556 and reported that he made a trip through Saxony and Upper Germany a half year ago. He maintained that many of Luther's letters from that time were destroyed, for example, because both Rhegius' library and Lübeck's Superintendent Curtius' library burned down.]

276. Heinrich Johann Bytemeister: Commentarius Historicus de Vita, 1726

277. Clemens Cassel: Geschichte der Stadt Celle, Celle 1930, I. Bd. S. 480

278. Ev.-luth. Landeskirche Hannovers Landeskirchliches Archiv: Celler Stadtkirche K.R. 13

279. Uhlhorn, S. 337, sowie Weinberger: Nachkommen des Reformators von Niedersachsen Urbanus Rhegius, in: Norddeutsche Familienkunde, Band 14, Heft 2, April – Juni 1989, 64. Jahrgang

280. Vierzehn Kinder nennen: Clemens Cassel in: Geschichte der Stadt Celle, S. 428 und die Celler Handschrift, S. 204

281. Siehe vorletzte Fussnote

282. Albert Brauch: Die Verwaltung des Territoriums Calenberg-Göttingen während der Regentschaft der Herzogin Elisabeth (1540 – 1546) in: Quellen und Darstellungen zur Geschichte Niedersachsens, Band 38, Hildesheim und Leipzig 1930, S. 40. sowie Helmut Samse: Die Zentralverwaltung in den südwelfischen Landen, Hildesheim 1940, S. 281

283. Adolf Wrede: Ernst der Bekenner, Halle 1888, S. 110 und 111

284. Erhard Gorys: Lexikon der Heiligen, S. 45. [Further explanation of names is also from this source.]

285. Urbanus Rhegius: (LBI) Catechesis, Illustriss. Principi Francisco Otthoni, Brunsuicensium Luneburgensiumpue Duci, puero generosissimo, et toti Scholae Ducali dicata. Magdeburg 1541, sowie zahlreiche Nachdrucke, 1858 in Hannover von August Wellhausen in deutsch herausgegeben, 1908 in Warschau in polnisch, siehe Liebmann S. 404, Druck 138

286. Karl Kayser: Die reformatorischen Kirchenvisitationen in den welfischen Landen von 1542 – 1544, Göttingen 1897, erwähnt auf S. 479 Hermann Quedlenburg als Urbanus Rhegius' Schwiegersohn, siehe auch Uhlhorn, S. 337

287. Freundlicher Hinweis von Christian Lippelt, Wolfenbüttel

288. Ernestus Regius: Opera Vrbani Regii Latine Edita. Cum eius vita, ac Praefatione, Nürnberg 1562. Siehe Liebmann Bibliographie S. 406, Druck 142, Ernestus Regius: Vrbani Regii Weylandt Superintendenten im Fürstenthumb Lüneburg Deutsche Bücher vnnd Schrifften. In welchen die fürnemsten haubtstück Christlicher lehre sampt etlichen büchern der heylichen Schrifft trewlich vnd reyn erkläret vnd viler schedlicher Secten irrthum widerleget. Nürnburg 1562. Siehe Liebmann Bibliographie S. 409, Druck 143

289. Ant. Theod. Effner: Dr. Martin Luther und seine Zeitgenossen dargestellt in einer Reihe karakteristrender Züge und Anektoten, Augsburg 1817, S. 134

290. Marcel Fournier et Charles Engel: Gymnase, Academie et Universite de Strasbourg, Premiere Partie 1525 – 1621, Paris/Strasbourg 1894, S. 104 – 168 Charles Engel: ["The Latin School and Former Academie of Strasbourg (1538 – 1621), Strasbourg 1900, p. 127, mentions Ernest Regius as Professor in Strassbourg beginning in 1565."]

291. Heinrich Joh. Bytemeister: Commentarius historicus de vita, scriptis et meritis supremorum praesulum in ducata Lunaeburgensi, Celle 1726, pg. II. [Remark: Veldenz: District of Bernkastel-Wittlich, originally a fief of the Bishopric of Verdun. The Palatine Veldenz is founded in 1543 by Count Pataline Ruprecht and exists as an independent principality: Administrative offices are Veldenz, Lauterecken and Cloister Remigiusberg, later also the Earldom of Lützelstein and half of the territory of Guttenberg] (Th. Gümbel: Geschichte des Fürstentums Pfalz-Veldenz, 1900.)

292. C. Krause: Melanchthoniana, 1885, S. 152 – 154 Nr. 64.

293. D. Daniel Heinrich Arnold: Kurzgefasste Nachrichten von den seit der Reformation an den lutherischen Kirchen in Ostpreussen gestandenen Predigern. Königsberg 1777, S. 35 sowie D. Daniel Heinrich Arnold: Historie der Königsbergischen Universität, Zusätze, Königsberg 1756, S. 178

294. Erich Wetzel: Die Geschichte des Königlichen Joachimsthaler Gymnasiums 1607 – 1907, Halle 1907

295. Handbuch historischer Stätten Deutschlands, Berlin/Brandenburg 1989, S. 228/229

296. Lubecus, Franciscus: Göttinger Annalen, Göttingen, S. 392

297. Oberlehrer Walther: Dr. Joachim Mörlin – Ein Leben aus der Reformationszeit, II Theil, in: Gymnasium zu Arnstadt, von Carl Theodor Pabst, Arnstadt 1863, S. 3

298. Heimburger, S. 218. "Christus mundum transigit" [approximately: Christ's Acceptance Throughout the World]

299. Uhlhorn, S. 336/37

300. Friedrich Keyser: Reformations Almanach für Luthers Verehrer auf das evangelishe Jubeljahr 1817, Erfurt, S. 81

301. Stadt-und Verwaltungsarchiv Erfurt: Matrikel der Uiversität Erfurt

302. J.C. Hermann Weissenborn: Acten der Erfurter Universitaet, II. Teil, Halle 1884, S. 318

303. F. W. Kampfgschulte: Die Universität Erfurt in ihrem Verhältnisse zu dem Humanismus und der Reformation, Erster Teil, Trier 1858, S. 80 und 258 Eckhard Bernstein: Der Erfurter Humanistenkreis am Schnittpunkt von Humanismus und Reformation. Das Rektoratsblatt des Crotus Rubianus, in: Der polnische Humanismus und die europäischen Solidäten, Wiesbaden 1997, S. 139, 153 und 164. [We thank Mr. Walter Blaha from the Erfurt City and Administrative Archives for his valuable support.]

304. Wilhelm Havemann: Geschichte der Lande Braunschweig und Lüneburg, Erster Band, Lüneburg, 1837, S. 339

305. Heimbürger: Ernst der Bekenner, Herzog von Braunschweig u. Lüneburg, Celle 1839, S. 85

306. Uhlhorn, S. 337

307. Urbani Rhegii Lebens Geschichte, Anonyme Handschrift in der Bibliothek des Predigerseminars Celle, S. 130, transkribiert und kommentiert von Horst Gerke, Burscheid 2004

308. [Werner von König (Born December 8, 1561 in Münden, died May 10, 1621 in Bückeburg). His gravestone is in the Lutheran Church in Bückeburg: "Werner von König – Chancellor for Duke Ernst in Holstein-Schaumburg. Previously Chancellor for Duke Heinrich Julius of Braunschweig und Lüneburg. Inherited Lochtum and Vienenburg. Born 1561, died in 1621": Student years 1581 Helmstedt, 1583 Wittenberg, 1587/88 Basel. Doctor of Jurisprudence 1589 in Münden. Previously lawyer in the imperial court, 1594 senior civil servant in Wolfenbüttel, 1603 chancellor, 1607 beknighted, from 1616 in Bückeburg.]

309. [Zell in Saxony= Celle in Lower Saxony]

310. Relics = [Culturally revered remains. (Meaning here is not clear)]

311. [Regum = of the kings, Latin genitive plural of Rex = König= king]

312. [Ex rege, Latin ablative = from the king]

313. [We thank Horst Gerke from Burscheid for the Latin text.]

314. Karl Heinz Burmeister: Geschichte der Stadt Tettnang, Konstanz 1997, S. 78/79

315. Original im Pfarrarchiv Grünenbach, Allgäu, Nr. 78

316. Pfarrer Herbert Mader: Grünenbacher Chronik, S. 65. [We thank Pastor Mader for his willingness to provide information.]

317. Thilo Ludewig: Oberstaufen. Heimatbuch des Marktes Oberstaufen und der ehemaligen Reichsherrschaft Staufen. Weiler im Allgäu 1983, S. 287

318. Mannfred Krebs: Die Investiturprotokolle der Diözese Konstanz aus dem 15.Jahrhundert, in: Freiburger Diözesanarchiv 66.–74 Jahrgang 1939–1954, S. 484: "alt S. Fridilini. –1492 III 31 data est confirmacio ad alt. S. Fridolini in cap. Langenargen, dot. p. Hugonem comit. In Montfort et Rotenfels seniorem. I fl." [The investiture protocol of 1473 still has the following entry (translated into German): "On February 22, 1473 Conr. Riegger is installed as sinecure clergyman of the church in Winnenden Castle. The position is vacant due to the death of Johann De Naw. Riegger was recommended by Georg von Welmershausen from the house of the German Order of Winnenden." Whether this is "our" Conrad Rieger cannot be determined. It is in the realm of possibility. He would then have to have been born before 1450 and have been more than 40 years old at the birth of his son Urbanus. His earlier cited death in 1494 would be plausible. Other possibilities to investigate further could be the following: Conrad Roger, July 7, 1467 in Fellbach in Cannstadt, Conradus Reger, October 9, 1471 in Hofen (Cannstadt). On this date Johann Gnann exchanges with Conradus Reger, chaplain of the Altar of St. Katherin in Winnden (!), Conr. Raigger dies in 1481 in Hofen (Cannstadt) and on April 12, 1481 is replaced by Joh. Sailer. Conr. Rigel is installed in Mauracherhof/Emmendingen on September 2, 1469, Conr. Rigel, 1464 is named chaplain of the Altar St. Jacobi in Sebrun (Seebronn/Rottenburg). Count Hugo XV. is married to Countess Anna of Zweibrücken. Ernst Regius is in the service of the Counts of Zweibrücken-Bitsch starting in 1568. Whether this is coincidence or a connection cannot be confirmed.]

319. Kichler/Eggart, S. 143

320. Ralf Reiter: Das Heilig-Geist Hospital zu Langenargen von der Urkunde Graf Hugos bis zum Ende des 19. Jahrhundert, in: Langenargener Geschichte(n), Band 6, Langenargen 1991

321. Kichler/Eggart, S. 144.

322. Original von Prof. Edinger im Museum Langenargen

323. Karl Heinz Burmeister: Graf Heinrich VII. Von Montfort-Rothenfels 1456–1512. Domherr zu Augsburg und Konstanz, in: Lebensbilde aus dem Bayrischen Schwaben, Weissenborn, Schwaben 1993, S. 9–32

324. Stadtarchiv Augsburg, Ratsämterbuch 1520–1533

325. [The fact that in the Königsberg line the baker's profession once again dominates, though a few generations later, is perhaps a coincidence, but nevertheless noteworthy.]

326. Augsburger Steuerbuch 1533, 13b: "Jerg Konigs hab ist verteilt"

327. Stadtarchiv Augsburg, Urgichten 1525 April–1528 August. [Sixt Pfefferlin is chief official of the fishermen and one of the most important people in the trade.]

328. Stadtarchiv Augsburg, Strafbuch Nr. 94, S. 183

329. dt. = dat., Latin = [gives]

330. Michael Streez: Das Fürstentum Calenberg-Göttingen in Niedersächsisches Jahrbuch für Landesgeschichte, Band 70, Hannover 1998, S. 194

331. Edgar Kalthoff und Alheidis von Rohr: Calenberg-Von der Burg zum Fürstentum, Historisches Museum am Hohen Ufer, Hannover 1979, S. 6

332. Streetz, S. 196

333. [The Order of the Golden Fleece was founded in 1430 by Philipp the Good, Duke of Burgundy. Burgundy comes to the Habsburgs through the marriage of Maximilian I to Duchess Maria of Burgundy, the granddaughter of Philipp the Good. The Order is, on the one hand, inspired by the Greek mythology (the coat of the Golden Aries), on the other hand by the Burgundian dukes "for the protection and promotion of the Christian faith" and later conferred by the Habsburg rulers as a high distinction.]

334. [Heimbürger confirms Elisabeth's request to Duke Ernst, to allow Rhegius to come to her (p. 213)]

335. Niedersächsisches Hauptstaatsarchiv Hannover, Signatur: Cal. Br. 22 Nr. 59

336. Paul Tschackert: Antonius Corvinus, Leben und Schriften Quellen und Darstellungen zur Geschichte Niedersachsens, Band III, Hannover und Leipzig 1900, S. 119

337. Wilhelm Havemann: Geschichte der Lande Braunschweig und Lüneburg, Göttingen 1855, S. 304 – 305, sowie Tschackert, S. 151

338. Tschackert, S. 150

339. Veröffentlicht von Friedrich Karl von Strombeck: Deutscher Fürstenspiegel aus dem sechzehnten Jahrhundert, oder Regeln der Fürstenweisheit von dem Herzoge Julius und der Herzoginn = Regentinn Elisabeth zu Braunschweig und Lüneburg, Braunschweig 1824

340. Havemann, S. 305/306. [The landgrave was annoyed. Erich's father had already agreed to young Erich's betrothal to the landgrave's daughter, Agnes. In 1539, the landgrave substituted his younger daughter, Anna, for Anges.]

341. Streetz, S. 202

342. Edgar Kalthoff u. Alheidis von Rohr: Calenberg – Von der Burg zum Fürstentum, S. 21

343. Dietrich Kausche: Harburg und der süderelbische Raum, Köln 1969, S. 400

344. [In contrast to their father, Urbanus Rhegius, all his children spell their name "Regius."]

345. Signatur: Acta Ecclesiastica, Biographien III, Faszikel 5, Folio 140 – 313

346. Rudolf Steinmetz: Die Generalsuperintendenten von Lüneburg-Celle, in: Zeitschrift der Gesellshaft für niedersächsische Kirchengeschichte 1916, 21. Jahrgang (Freundl. Hinweis von Dr. Harm Alpers, Celle). [Horst F. Gerke, Burscheid Dünweg 62, made a transcription of it in 2004 entitled "Communications from Over the Centuries, No. 12.]

347. Albert Brauch: Die Verwaltung des Territoriums Calenberg-Göttingen während der Regentschaft der Herzogin Elisabeth, Hildesheim und Leipzig 1930, S. 31

348. emploiret=angestellt=employed. In the beginning he was probably employed by Duchess Elisabeth.

349. Brauch: S. 52. [According to information obtained from the Main State Archives of Lower Saxony in Hannover on August 15, 2000, Das Register des Rentmeisters Rode was destroyed by fire during WWII.]

350. Brauch, S. 24

351. Tschackert, 153

352. Niedersächsisches Hauptstaatsarchiv Hannover. Signatur: Ca. Br. Nr. 105 – 115, Nr. 110, 1548 – 1552

353. [St. Walpurga Day on May 1ST]

354. Niedersächsisches Hauptstaatsarchiv Hannover. Signatur Ca. Br. 23 Nr. 105 – 115, Nr. 110, 1548 – 1552

355. Albrecht Saathoff: Aus Göttingens Kirchengeschichte, Göttingen 1929, S. 156

356. Wilhelm Havemann: Elisabeth, Herzogin von Braunschweig-Lüneburg, geborene Markgräfin von Brandenburg, Göttingen 1839, S. 93

357. Havemann: Elisabeth, S. 93

358. Havemann: Elisabeth, S. 94

359. Havemann: Elisabeth, S. 97

360. Havemann: Elisabeth, S. 104

361. Havemann: Elisabeth, S. 107

362. Wolfgang Kunze: Leben und Bauten Herzog Erich II., Hannover 1993, S. 69

363. Niedersächsisches Hauptstaatsarchiv Hannover, Signatur: Hann 72 Celle Nr. 273, Stadtbuch, A01405 ad anno 1561, Bl 168/9,7. April 1553

364. Niedersächsisches Hauptstaatsarchiv Hannover. Signatur: Cal. Br. 23 Nr. 187

365. Saathoff, S. 152

366. Heuerpfaff = Mietpfarrer = [clergyman collecting all rents, taxes, etc.]

367. Franciscus Lubecus: Göttinger Annalen – Von den Anfängen bis zum Jahre 1588, Quellen zur Geschichte der Stadt Göttingen, Band I, Göttingen 1994, S. 359

368. Stadtarchiv Göttingen. Signatur: A A Kirchensachen, St. Albani Nr. 2

369. Saathoff, S. 159

370. Niedersächsisches Hauptstaatsarchiv Hannover. Signatur: Calenberger Briefschaften, Nr. 1587, Br. 23 Nr. 187. [Fall-back = at the death of the recipient of a feudal grant, the grant returns to the feudal lord.]

371. Brauch, S. 52, Fussnote 280. ["Feudal tenure awarded by Duke Erich to the 3 Sons of Senior Civil Servant Urbanus: Sebastian the Elder, Christoph and Erich on Sept. 17, 1576". The grant is also in the so-called "Jörns-Bestand" in the City Archives of Nordheim. Their origin is not available. According to communication from the Main State Archives of Lower Saxony in Hannover from August 15, 2000, a large part of the manuscripts department was destroyed by fire in WWII, including these documents.]

372. Klaus Kürschner: Ein Beitrag zur Geschichte des Reinhäuser Waldes, Anhang Seite 2, Amtmänner und Drosten des Amtes Reinhausen von 1542 – 1885 (dort allerdings sehr fraglich) und "Anonyme Handschrift, Celle 1750, "dieser (Urbanus ein Sohn gleichen Nahmens) succidierte Joh. Ruden Nbb. Hasstano = canon. Frieslariensi et Marchallo autae Ducis Erici jun: 1557 zu Reinhausen und ward Amtmann und Verwalter des Kloster, Leznerus in LXXVII." Cap (entnommen aus: Horst Gerke: Jühnder Mitteilungen, Heft 4, Urbanus Rhegius. Die Familie und Nachkommen des Reformators von Niedersachsen, Februar 2001)

373. Hospital Rechnung, Archiv Stadt Hann.- Münden

374. Helmut Samse: Die Zentralverwaltung in den südwelfischen Landen, Hildesheim 1940, S. 321

375. J.H.Z. Willigerod: Geschichte von Münden in vorzüglicher Hinsicht auf Handlung und Schiffahrt, Göttingen 1803, S. 303 – 305

376. Urkundenbuch Reinhausen, Seite 350, Nr. 468

377. Herzog August Bibliothek, Wolfenbüttel: Cod. Guelf. 610 Helmst. Fol I-323, letzte Seite, handschriftlicher Stammbaum der Familie Rhegius. [...last page, handwritten family tree of the Rhegius family. Note: this finding was a breakthrough in the authors' research on the Rhegius family.]

378. Archiv Stadt Hann. – Münden, Hospital Rechnung Anno (15)59 bis auff Ao (15)60

379. Zwanzig Taler für zehn Fass Bier. Archiv Stadt Hann.-Münden

380. Leopold Ranke: Deutsche Geschichte im Zeitalter der Reformation. Bd. I, S. 255 ["The brave Erich of Braunschweig sent him into the crowded assembly to get a drink of Einbecker beer in a silver tankard"]

381. Michael Streetz: Das Fürstentum Calenberg-Göttingen (1495/1512 – 1584), in Niedersächsisches Jahrbuch für Landesgeschichte, Folge: Zeitschrift des Historischen Vereins für Niedersachsen, 1998, Band 70, S. 197

382. J.H.Z. Willigerod: Geschichte von Münden in vorzüglicher Hinsicht auf Handlung und Schiffahrt, Göttingen 1803, S. 303 – 305

383. Wolfgang Kunze: Leben und Bauten Herzog Erich II. von Braunschweig-Lüneburg, Hannover 1993, S.100

384. Wilhelm Lotze: Geschichte der Stadt Münden nebst Umgebung mit besonderer Hervorhebung der Begebenheiten des dreissigjährigen und siebenjährigen Krieges, Münden 1909, S. 49/50

385. Albert Brauch: Die Verwaltung des Territoriums Calenberg-Göttingen, Hildesheim 1930, S. 279 und 281

386. Niedersächsisches Hauptstaatsarchiv Hannover. Signatur: Cal. Br. 19 [For the original information we heartily thank Carl-Albrecht Költzsch]

387. Niedersächsisches Hauptstaatsarchiv Hannover. Signatur: Cal. Br. Arch. Des. 2, XXXV Münden, Nr. 1799

388. Michael Streetz: Das Fürstentum Calenberg-Göttingen, S. 206/207

389. Niedersächsisches Hauptstaatsarchiv Hannover. Signatur: Cal. Br. Arch. Des. 2, XXXV Münden, Nr. 1779

390. Samse, S. 321

391. Klaus Kürschner: Ein Beitrag zur Geschichte of the Reinhäuser Waldes, Amtmänner und Drosten des Amtes Reinhausen von 1542 – 1885, Anhang

392. Manfred Hamann: Urkundenbuch des Klosters Reinhausen, Hannover 1991, Pos. 468

393. Tobias Ulbrich: Zur Geschichte der Klosterkirche Reinhausen, Göttingen 1993, S. I und 63.

394. Uhlhorn, S. 337 und Fussnote 9

395. [The document contains information from Niedersächsischen Hauptstaatsarchivs Hannover from 5.10.1999, which could not be found. It is possible that it was destroyed by fire in WW II.]

396. Erich Weise: Geschichte von Schloss Nienover im Solling, Hildesheim 1989, S. 68 und 194/95

397. Weise 1989 [(friendly note from Christian Lippelt, Wolfenbüttel). The following presentation is based on this work.]

398. Niedersächsisches Hauptstaatsarchiv Hannover, Signatur: Cal. 2 XXXVIII Nr. la (In dem zitierten Werk von Erich Weise als Anhang I beigefügt)

399. Niedersächsisches Hauptstaatsarchiv Hannover, Signatur: Cal. Br. Arch. Des. 2, XXXV Münden Nr. 1799

400. Niedersächsisches Hauptstaatsarchiv Hannover, Signatur: Cal. Br. Arch. Des. 2, XXXV 1779

401. Signatur, wie vorige Fussnote

402. Niedersächsisches Hauptstaatsarchiv Hannover, Signatur: Cal. Br. 22 C 1587

403. Niedersächsisches Hauptstaatsarchiv Hannover, Signatur: Cal. Br. 22, Nr. 1587 (Fürstliche Hausschulden)

404. Niedersächsisches Hauptstaatsarchiv Hannover, Signatur: Cal. Br. 22 Nr. 1587

405. Niedersächsisches Hauptstaatsarchiv Hannover, Signatur: Cal. Br. 22 (Fürstliche Hausschulden) Nr. 158

406. Charles Engel: L'Ecole Latine et L'Ancienne Academie de Strasbourg, Strasbourg 1900

407. Karl Evers: Geschichte der Familie Evers, Celle 1913, S. 14

408. Evers, S. 19

409. Supplizieren = ein Bittgesuch einreichen = [to deliver a request]

410. Illustrissimus = Durchlaucht, der Erleuchtetste = [Your Excellency, the Enlightend One (here it refers to Duke Julius)]

411. Karl Kayser: Die General-Kirchenvisitation von 1588 im Lande Göttingen-Kalenberg, in Jahrbuch für Niedersächsische Kirchengeschichte Bd. 8, 1904, S. 173

412. Weinberger, S. 553

413. Herzog August Bibliothek Wolfenbüttel, Signatur: Cod. Guelf. 610 Helmst. Fol 1-323

414. Niedersächsisches Hauptstaatsarchiv Hannover, Signatur: Cal. Br. 22 Nr. 1587

415. Klaus Kürschner: Ein Beitrag zur Geschichte des Reinhauser Walder, Anhang

416. Heinz Kelterborn und Wilhelm Wegener: [The name "von Dransfeld" is mentioned as a Göttingen family of advisors and scholars] in: Familienkundliche Kommission für Niedersachsen und Bremen sowie angrenzende ostfälische Gebietee.V., Forschungsberichte Neue Folge Band 5, Hannover 1988

417. Christian Gottlieb Jöcher: Allgemeines Gelehrten-Lexikon, Hildesheim 1960, S. 170: ["Algermann Franc., a musician and poet...lived until the end of the 16TH century and resided in Hamburg ..."]

418. Niedersächsische Landesbibliothek Hannover: Signatur C 10 462, Nr. 1 (unvollständiges Exemplar bis Zeile "Ein Fürst zum Krieg von Gott erkorn", restliche Zeilen bis Ende: Niedersächsisches Staatsarchiv Wolfenbüttel, Signatur 11.121:8

419. [Algermann's approach is similar in 1593 in "Symbolism" for Duke Heinrich Julius and in 1606 in his funeral oration for Duke Heinrich Julius, Doctor of Jurisprudence (friendly note from Christian Lippelt, Wolfenbüttel)]

420. [The format, 273 X 122.5 cm, is partially a woodcut and partially a pen drawing colored on linen. The sketch is by Franz Algermann, woodcut by Georg Scharffenberger, printed by Konrad Horn in 1584. Another copy is available in the Kupferstichkabinet Berlin. (Ausstellungskatalog Nr. 27 der Herzog August Bibliothek Wolfenbüttel: Sammler, Fürst, Gelehrter: Herzog August zu Braunschweig und Lüneburg 1579 – 1666, Wolfenbüttel, 1979, S. 53)

421. [Anna's father is Ernst von Campe, born in 1488. Metta's father is his brother Ja(h)n von Campe, born in 1485 V before 1515, eldest son of Heinrich von Campe, born in 1462] (Auszugaus: Robert Lucht: Der Rechtfertigungsbrief Otto I. von Harburg in: Harburger Jahrbuch 1958, HH-Harburg 1959 und J.H. Steffens, Geschlechts-Geschichte des Hochadlichen Hauses von Campe auf Isenbüttel und Wettmarshagen ec. Zelle, 1783, Tab-II).

422. Guelphen = Welfen

423. Ausstellungskatalog Nr. 27: Sammler, Fürst, Gelehrter: Herzog August zu Braunschweig und Lüneburg 1579 – 1666, Wolfenbüttel 1979, S. 53

424. [According to Philipp Meyer: The pastors of the churches in the countries of Hannover and Schaumburg-Lippes since the Reformation, Hildesheim 1942. According to Samse in 1575, Joh. Algermann died in 1549. This is probably incorrect, since after 1549 Johann Cornerus is named as a sucessor in Beedenborstel.]

425. Karl Kayser: Die reformatorischen Kirchenvisitationen in den welfisichen Landen 1542–1544, Göttingen 1897, S. 473, "M. Johann Algermann" Prediger laut dortigen Pfarrnachrichten für die Zeit von 1534–1548"

426. Brauch, S. 24. [In this source Maria is called "Marie Madeleine."]

427. Urbanus Rhegius: Dialogus von der schönen predigt, die Christus Luc. 24. von Jerusalem bis gen Emaus den zweien jüngern am Ostertag aus Mose vnd allen Propheten gethan hat, siehe Liebmann, S. 396. Die Schrift wurde bis 1689 nachgedruckt, u.a. in Niederdeutsch, Holländisch, Dänisch, Englisch, Tschechisch

428. Brief der Herzog August Bibliothek Wolfenbüttel vom 21.04.2004 ["The family tree is on page 323, to the right, and is most likely as you have already correctly presumed. It is written by Franz Algermann." Also, Christian Lippelt considers this assumption to be obvious.]

429. Uhlhorn, S. 337

430. Inge Mager: Gott "ohne vnterlass frü vnd spat rühmen loben und preisen", Ein evangelisches Hymnar von Franz Algermann aus dem Jahre 1596, Festschrift zum 100. Geburtstag von Christhard Mahrenholz am 11. August 2000, Langenhagen 2000, herausgegeben von Hans-Christian Drömann. Dagegen gibt Samse an: "2 Jahre Cantor in Neustadt, in Helmstedt 4 Jahre Schreiber, 1.3.1580 notarius publicus ebd."

431. Bibliotheks-Registrator Albrecht: Nachrichten von Franz Algermann Leben und literarischem Wirken, in Feier des Gedächtnisses der vormahligen Hochschule Julia Carolina zu Helmstedt, Helmstedt 1822, S. 167

432. Mager, siehe vorletzte Fussnote

433. F.K. von Strombeck (Herausgeber): Leben, Wandel und tödtlichen Abgang weiland des Durschlauchtigen Hochgeborenen Fürsten und Herrn, Herrn Juliussen, Herzogen zu Braunschweig und Lüneburg, hochlöblichen, christmilden Gedächtnisses, durch Franciscum Algermann, Sr. Gnad. Landfiscalen und Diener, Anno 1598, in: Feier des Gedächtnisses der vormahligen Hochschule Julia Carolina zu Helmstedt, veranstaltet im Monate Mai des Jahres 1822, Helmstedt 1822

434. Duncker & Humblot: Allgemeine Deutsche Biographie, Band I, Leipzig 1875 und andere Quellen

435. Herzog-August-Bibliothek Wolfenbüttel

436. Niedersächsisches Hauptstaatsarchiv Wolfenbüttel. Signatur: I Alt 9 Acta publica aus der Regierungszeit des Herzogs Julius Nr. 280

437. Niedersächsisches Hauptstaatsarchiv Wolfenbüttel, 4 Alt I, Nr. 1037

438. Niedersächsisches Hauptstaatsarchiv Wolfenbüttel, 3 Alt I, Nr. 119, fol. 89–95

439. Christian Lippelt: Hoheitsträger und Wirtschaftsbetrieb: Die herzogliche Amtsverwaltung zur Zeit der Herzöge Heinrich der Jüngere, Julius und Heinrich Julius von Braunschweig-Wolfenbüttel (1547–1613), in Vorbereitung befindliche Dissertation an der Universität Oldenburg. Eine komplette Publikationslist Algermanns enthält: Christian Lippelt: Franz Algermann: Verwaltungsbeamter und Historiograph. Biographische Studien zu einem fürstlichen Diener am Wolfenbütteler Hofe, voraussichtliche Veröffentlichung im Braunschweigischen Jahrbuch für Landesgeschichte, Nr. 86, 2005. [We thank Christian Lippelt for his valuable contributions.]

440. Niedersächsisches Hauptstaatsarchiv Wolfenbüttel: 3 Alt, Nr. 104, fol. 21–22. [The literature and the accompanying family tree of Hermann Quedlenburg (number 317 on the family tree enclosed with the original German edition of this book) indicate that he marries Rhegius' daughter, Appolonia (number 316 on the family tree.)]

441. Dietrich Kausche: Harburg und der süderelbische Raum, Köln 1967, S. 366, Veröffentlichung des Helms-Museums Nr. 19

442. Kausche, S. 366.

443. Scheidt/Wriede: Die Elbinsel Finkenwärder, München 1927, S. II

444. Niedersächsisches Hauptstaatsarchiv Hannover, Vorwort zum Findbuch Hannover 74, Amt Harburg

445. Scheidt/Wriede, S. 14

446. Melchior Lorichs: Die Hamburger Elbkarte aus dem Jahre 1568, Original Staatsarchive Hamburg

447. Ernst Christian Schütt: Die Chronik Hamburgs, Dortmund 1991, S. 22

448. Kausche, S. 367

449. Friedrich Wilhelm Bodemann: Denkwürdigkeiten der Elbinsel Finkenwerder, Hamburg 1860, S. 49

450. Finder: Die Elbinsel Finkenwärder, S. 16, Bodemann, S. 51, H.W.C. Hübbe, Beiträge zur Geschichte der Stadt Hamburg, Hamburg 1897, S. 68, Scheidt/Wriede, S. 15

451. [For 1,200 Rheinische Gulden made of good gold with good weight.]

452. Ernst Christian Schütt: Die Chronik Hamburgs, S. 161

453. Kausche, S. 393 – 398, sowie ausführlich Dieter Matthes: Die welfische Nebenlinie in Harburg, Hamburg-Harburg, 1962, Veröffentlichung des Helms-Museums Nr. I

454. [The numbers refer to the "family tree Rieger, R(h)egius, König" that is included in the original German edition of this book.]

455. Niedersächsisches Hauptstaatsarchiv Hannover, Signatur wie vor

456. Philippo Julio Rehtmeier: Braunschweig-Lüneburgische Chronica, Braunschweig 1722, S. 1065, sowie Rudolf Meier: "Herzog Otto III. zu Braunschweig und Lüneburg" in "Harburger Jahrbuch" 19/1996, S. 50

457. [Also called Scheiblich]

458. Philipp Meyer: Die Pastoren der Landeskirchen Hannovers und Schaumburg-Lippes seit der Reformation, Göttingen, 1942, S. 392.

459. H.W.C. Hübbe: Beiträge zur Geschichte der Stadt Hamburg, S. 78/79

460. Ausschnitt aus dem mehrfach erwähnten Prachtstammbaum der Welfen von Franz Algermann

461. Niedersächsisches Hauptstaatsarchiv Hannover: Hann. 74, Harburg 5012

462. Niedersächsisches Hauptstaatsarchiv Hannover: Hann. 74, Nr. 5011

463. [Derived from Latin: Rex = König. Regius as an adjective "kingly", as substantive attribute "of the kings." (Letter from the German Association for Language from April 20, 2000)]

464. Niedersächsisches Hauptstaatsarchiv Hannover: Hann. 74, Nr. 5011

465. Signatur: Harburg 74, Nr. 5011

466. Niedersächsisches Hauptstaatsarchiv Hannover, Karte der Elbniederungen bei Harburg um 1620

467. [In Harburg, the official church regulations are those developed by Antonius Corvinus for the church in Calenberg. "According to those regulations, by order of Duke Otto, the spiritual leaders of Harburg were sworn in."] (Paul Tschackert: Antonius Corvinus, Leben und Schriften, S. 120) [With the death of Duke Wilhelm in 1642, the so-called Harburg lineage fell back to the Duchy of Lüneberg and therefore the Church Regulations of Lüneberg dated 1564 became valid also for Harburg.] Siehe Torsten Schweda: Harburger Jahrbuch 20/1997, S. 54/55

468. Urbanus Rhegius: Wie man fursichtiglich vnd on ergernis reden sol von den furnemsten Artikeln Christlicher lere, latein 1535 (Formulae quaedam...) deutsch 1536, 1537, 1538, 1544, 1554 (polnisch) 1575, 1576, 1590, 1602, 1605 (schwedisch) 1646, 1672 und 1714. 1908 ediert und kommentiert von Alfred Uckeley, Leipzig, 2003 lateinisch-englische Edition durch Scott Hendrix, Princeton/USA: Preaching the Reformation: The Homiletical Handbook of Urbanus Rhegius, Marquette University Press 2003, siehe auch Liebmann, S. 390 –391

469. [Books that present the official teachings]

470. ["Corpus Docrinae." This is the zenith, format, and complete picture of the purist Christian teaching, pulled together from God's holy scripture of the prophets and aspostles, Helmstedt, 1603. Preface has unnumbered pages. The "Useful Booklet" refers to Rhegius' booklet.]

471. [To swear to God]

472. Alss = Also, demgemäss = [therefore, appropriate thereto]

473. g. F. und H. = gnädiger Fürst und Herr = [Gracious Prince and Liege]

474. newes = neue = [new]

475. Später Wüper oder Wüpper genannt = [Later called Wüper or Wüpper]

476. Caspelleute = Kirchspielleute, Gemeindemitglieder = [church consistory, members of the congregation]

477. Bodemann, S. 149

478. Bodemann, S. 139

479. I.F.G = Ihre Fürstlichen Gnaden = [Your Princely Grace]

480. [The people clearly do not want to be a godfather, or they cannot afford the Pfennig fee for the baptism, which is a gift to the child. Gefattern = Paten = godfather]

481. Gegen den Befehl des Fürsten = [Against the prince's order]

482. [Hamburger = Resident of the "Hamburg Side" of Finkenwerder. Their church originally belonged to Nienstedten on the other side of the River Elbe. In 1617 they were merged with the church in Finkenwerder, and from then on, they had to pay the respective costs involved.]

483. Einsammeln = [Gather up, collect]

484. Bodemann, S. 142, Finder, S. 87

485. Archiv des Kirchenkreises Alt-Hamburg, Neue Burg, Hamburg, Signatur: Finkenwerder II, Nr. 78/1

486. Allein Gott die Ehre = [Only honor God]

487. [Chair of St. Peter = February 22 This feast commemorates Christ's choosing Peter to sit in his place as the servant-authority of the whole Church.]

488. [At this time, Gulden are Rheinische Gulden. 100 Gulden are equivalent to 150 Lübische Gulden, which will be mentioned in the text that follows]

489. p = Latin pagina = seite = [page]

490. [This is the first mention of Johann König, Sebastian's son. Since he and church council member, Heine Wentgen, take on debt for the church congregation, it is concluded that Johann König is also a church council member. Some years later he becomes Lüneburg administrator.]

491. [Portrait of Duke "Otto IV N" (Jr.) from a medallion dated 1585 and described by Ludewig in 1845. The illustration appears to have been forgotten, but it was rediscovered in 1989. Unfortunately, the medallion has not been found.]

492. Matthes, S. 100/101.

493. Niedersächsisches Hauptstaatsarchiv Hannover: Hann. 74, Harburg 4302. Brief datiert "Eilig im Vinkenwerder, den 7. Januar", ohne Jahresangabe, aber vermutlich 1611

494. [Bodemann is in error here. According to the church accounts, there is no entry of 150 lübische Mark.]

495. Bodemann, S. 128–9

496. D.C.H. Evers, Pastor auf Finkenwerder von 1756–1765, Handschriftliche Aufzeichnungen: "Nachricht von der Elb-Insul Finckenwärder" vom 15.9.1762, Staatsarchiv Hamburg: Handschriftensammlung 1063. Diverse maschinenschriftliche Übertragungen bei Finkenwerder Heimatsforschern

497. Lübsch, lübisch = lübische Mark (abgeleitet von Lübeck) = [(derived from Lübeck)]

498. [Verheuren = verpachten, vermieten = lease, rent]

499. Finder, S. 105 Hundeloch = Gefängnis = [jail]

500. Niedersächsisches Hauptstaatsarchiv Hannover: Hann. 74, Harburg Nr. 2542, Brief datiert 31. März, ohne Jahresangabe, vermutlich 1604

501. Finder, S. 26

502. Finkenwerder Kirchenrechnungen 1590–1663, S. 23. Kirchenkreis Alt-Hamburg, Archiv Neue Burg, Hamburg: Finkenwerder II, Nr. 78/I

503. [We find no proof of such transactions, but from that, one can assume that the process happens in Harburg and must have been agreed to there.]

504. Niedersächsisches Hauptstaatsarchiv Hannover: Hann. 74, Harburg

505. Finkenwerder Kirchenrechnungen, S. 40/41 [Besides Johann König two additional heirs are mentioned: Hinrich Steers and Johann Wulff. They probably represent the missing heirs of Gerd König (503 on the family tree enclosed with the original German editions of this book) and Ilse König (505 on the family tree). Wedumb = parsonage]

506. [Johann König probably does not appear so that in his capacity as administrator he does not oppose his brother, Gerd König, who must make the payment.]

507. Finkenwerder Kirchenrechnungen, S. 49

508. Urbanus Rhegius: "Ain Sermon von der kyrchweyche", Augsburg 1522

509. Evers, S. II, Staatsarchiv Hamburg: Handschriftensammlung Nr. 1063. [The sermon could have been given in celebration of the 25TH anniversary of Sebastian's time as pastor in Finkenwerder.]

510. Meyer, S. 377

511. [Should any reader have knowledge of these writings, we would be very grateful.]

512. Niedersächsisches Hauptstaatsarchiv Hannover, Synodalprotokolle: Hann. 74, Nr. 5011

513. [Instituieren = install, initiate. The installation of a sexton is to occur in accordance with the duke's instruction that "the pastors have to establish schools in the villages." There is more about this in the chapter entitled, "The First School Established on Finkenwerder's Lüneburg Side During Johann König's Tenure as Administrator."]

514. Communicanten = Teilnehmer am Abendmahl = [participant in holy communion]

515. [Mark 2401.2.6 = 2401 Mark, 2 Schilling, 6 Pfennig. Until 1621/22 a Mark had 16 Schilling, a Schilling had 12 Pfennig, a Taler equaled 2 Mark. By that reckoning, a Taler had 32 Schilling, a Schilling had 12 Pfennig. In about 1621/22 a Taler was three Mark, a Mark 10 2/3 Schilling or 96 Pfennig], siehe Max Bahrfeld: "Neue Münzordnung vom 14. September 1621 des Herzogs Christian von Braunschweig und Lüneburg in Celle" in: Niedersächsisches Münzarchiv IV. Band (1602–1625), Halle 1930, S. 499

516. [Peter Finck, Hans Harmens, Jacob von Rigen, Heine Wolf and Heine Wenthen, the administrator]

517. Bodemann, S. 149. [On pg. 148, Simon Külper is called the main builder.]

518. Rhatten = raten, Ratenzahlungen leisten = [to pay the legal fees]

519. Bodemann, S. 149

520. Die Gläubigerprotokolle Simon Külper vom 23.5.1594 und Hermann Külper vom 14.8.1594 sind ein zusammenhängendes Schriftstück im Niedersächsischen Hauptstaatsarchiv Hannover: Hann. 74, Harburg 4302

521. Harald Schloz: Finkenwerder – Von "Fischeridyll" zum "Industrie-standort"? Hamburg 1996, S. 17ff

522. Wilhelm Marquard: "950 Jahre Sturmfluten" in Harburger Kreiskalender 1963, S. 23 ff

523. Hübbe, S. 97, sowie Finder, S. 26 und andere

524. Niedersächsisches Hauptstaatsarchiv Hannover: Hann. 74, Harburg

525. Niedersächsisches Hauptstaatsarchiv Hannover: Hann. 74, Harburg 5314

526. Finder, S. 27

527. Niedersächsisches Hauptstaatsarchiv Hannover: Hann. 74, Harburg 2542. [Finder erroneously dates this letter from 1629 instead of 1619], Siehe dort S. 28

528. Freundliche Mitteilung von Archivdirektor Dr. Hans Otte, Ev.-luth Landeskirche Hannover, Landeskirchliches Archiv, vom 7 Februar 2002

529. [Reconstruction based on the topographical drawing of the Elector of Hannover's realm, 1777.]

530. Dietrich Kausche: "Harburger Erbregister von 1667", Hamburg 1987, S. 121

531. Finder, S. 103

532. Bodemann, S. 146ff

533. Niedersächsisches Hauptstaatsarchiv Hannover: Hann. 74, Harburg 4984 [Finkenwerder and Altenwerder school affairs, erroneously assigned to this file.]

534. B. Brockmann, W. König, M. König, R. Meier: Der Segen der guten Tat, in: De Kössenbitter, April 2000

535. Bodemann, S. 133

536. Renate Klee Gobert: Die Bau-und Kunstdenkmale der Freien und Hansestadt Hamburg, Band III, 1968, S. 269

537. Konrad Hüseler: Das Amt der Hamburger Rotgiesser, Braunschweig/Hamburg 1922, S. 59

538. [Milreis = 1,000 Reis (plural of Real), Portuguese gold coin from 1580 –83. According to the above, a gold "Milreis" coin is worth 1.5 Taler] (Friedr. Frh. v. Schrötter: Wörterbuch der Münzkunde, Berlin/Leipzig 1930, S. 391)

539. Niedersächsisches Hauptstaatsarchiv Hannover: Organisationsplan Für die Begräbnisfeierlichkeiten Herzog Otto II. am 24. November 1603 zu Harburg. Celler Briefe 71, XI, Nr. 7

540. A.C. Förster: Ursprung und Name des Dorfes Ovelgönne, Kreis Harburg 1566 –1966, Buxtehude 1966

541. aus: W.C. Ludewig: Geschichte der Stadt und des Schlosses Harburg, Harburg 1845, S. 78

542. [Kleigraben = As the years passed, the earth erupted through the clay ditches. The clay, a very fermenting slime, was spewn forth on both sides of the fields or cultivated lands.]

543. Bodemann, S. 133 und Ewald Goltz: St. Nikolai-Kirche in Hamburg-Finkenwerder, S. 23

544. Hans-Dieter Loose: Hamburger Testamente 1351 bis 1400, Hamburg 1970, S. 132: ["Henceforth I will give 10 Mark Penninge to help build a church in Finkenwerder."]

545. Rosemarie Halbrock: Nienstedten – Geschichte eines Dorfes an der Elbe, S. 8, ferner Rudolf Meier: Finkenwerder ging zur Kirche in Neuenstedten, in: De Kössenbitter, April 2002, S. 35

546. Evers, Handschrift Seite 18 (In der maschinenschriftlichen Übertragung S. 10)

547. [Connivendo = Stillschweigende Duldung, bewusstes Übersehen = Tacit permission, consciously overlook, disregard]

548. Finder, S. 97

549. [Wiemen, nordd = Lattengerüst zum Trocknen und Räuchern auch Sitzstange für Hühner = In Northern Germany it is scaffolding used in drying and smoking, as well roosts for chickens.]

550. [In the Finkenwerder literature these are called "Rezess," which are comparable to settlements with creditors.] Die Original befindet sich im Niedersächsischen Hauptstaatsarchiv Hannover: Hann. 74, Harburg 5314, ebenfalls bei Evers als Anlage, bei Bodemann auf den S. 64–66

551. [Bodemann gives these figures for the year 1658] mit 491 bzw. 305 an, S. 99

552. [If one of our readers can supply a better illustration, we would be very grateful.]

553. Bodemann, S. 124

554. Bodemann, S. 138

555. Bodemann, S. 77. [Among others, the contract is signed by Henning Linnemann as one of the Lüneburg church council members. He is married to Gretsche König, a granddaughter of Sebastian König.]

556. Evers, Handschrift S. 19 (in der maschinenschriftlichen Übertragung S. II)

557. Bodemann, S. 149

558. [See chapter in this translation: "Church Land – Leasing, Sale, Complex Entanglements"]

559. [According to Finder, the name Steer/Stehr first appears in Finkenwerder in 1498.]

560. Dietrich Kausche: Harburger Erbregister von 1667, Hamburg 1987, S. 122 [(Farm number I on the southwest part of the island with 18 Morgen land)]

561. Bleiben, geblieben = ein besonders auf Finkenwerder geläufiger Ausdruck für den Seemannstod = [To remain, remained = a common expression, peculiar to Finkenwerder, for a sailor's death]

562. [Finder, S. 251/2: that "to preserve his well-earned memory" a so-called "personal" was read in the church and is preserved in the church archives]

563. Bracker/Prange: Alster, Elbe und die See, Hamburgs Schiffahrt und Hafen in Gemälden, Zeichnungen und Aquarellen des Museums für Hamburgische Geschichte, Hamburg 1981, S. 295, auch bei Adi Albershardt: Als Finkenwerder noch Insel war, Hamburg 1981, S. 36, ferner auf einer Briefmarke Paraguays von 1978

564. [The "Gresche Focken, Simon's blessed widow" who died on November 3, 1638 is probably the wife of administrator, Simon Fock.]

565. Finder, S. 72 (Irrungen = Streitigkeiten) [errors = disputes]

566. Bodemann, S. 149

567. Niedersächsisches Hauptstaatsarchiv Hannover: Hann. 74 Nr. 4302 "Carsten Horstmanns Im Finckenwerder Schuldt Verzeichnuss" vom 29. März 1602. [The debtor should seek a buyer within 8 days] Dies ist laut Bodemann, S. 149, Simon Fock.

568. Finder, S. 73/74. [This text applies to the administrators on the Hamburg side. The oath of the Lüneburg administrators will be similar.]

569. Niedersächsisches Hauptstaatsarchiv Hannover: Hann. 74 Harburg 2542

570. Übergangen = hier: überflutet. [Went over = here it means: flooded]

571. Niedersächsisches Hauptstaatsarchiv Hannover: Hann. 74 Harburg 2542 "Supplication der Fincken-werder ann Herrn Wilhelm Herzogenn zu Br: undt Lüneburgk"

572. Finder, S. 28, [cited verbatim from the document named above, but erroneously lists the date as October 18, 1628]

573. [Teichbandt = Deichverband = Dike Unification Plan. Deich (dike) is usually written "Teich."]

574. Wilhelm Marquardt: 950 Jahre Sturmfluten, in: Harburger Kreiskalender 1963, S. 23–38

575. Hübbe, S. 108

576. Scheidt/Wriede, S. 32

577. Dietrich Kausche: Harburger Erbregister, S. 48.

578. Krusenbuch = unbedeichte Landspitze der Kattwyk, von Neuhof durch die Rethe getrennt = [point of land without a dike separating Kattwyk from Neuhof (New farm) by the reef]

579. Niedersächsisches Hauptstaatsarchiv Hannover: Han 74, 3709 und 3710

580. Siehe letzte Fussnote.

581. Dietrich Kausche: Harburger Erbregister, S. 53: ["Finally, all the fishermen of the administrative units of the Elbe, including those in the Brunssbüttel administrative units, may sail the Elbe to the North Sea and fish without paying anyone anything." Authorized by Johann König.]

582. Langermann: Hamburgisches Münz- und Madaillen Vergnügen, Hamburg 1753

583. Niedersächsisches Hauptstaatsarchiv Hannover: Hann. 74, Nr. 5011 (Synodalprotokolle)

584. Versicherung, Zusicherung, Bestätigung = [Insurance, assurance, confirmation]

585. Niedersächsisches Hauptstaatsarchiv Hannover: Hann. 74 Harburg

586. [This is supporting evidence that Johann König already had the inn which his son, Sebastian, later ran. This place is now the Schwartau Inn located at Finkenwerder's southern dike.]

587. Finkenwerder Kirchenbuch, S. 114 rechts

588. Gerd Heinz Mohr: Lexikon der Symbole

589. Kirchenbuch Finkenwerder, S. 108 links

590. Niedersächsisches Hauptstaatsarchiv Hannover: Ham. 74 Harburg 4984 "Fink- und Altenwerder Schulsachen", auch bei Evers, S. 50/51, [with the full text provided]

591. Finder, S. 107/108

592. De Kössenbitter, März 1991, S. 14

593. Evers, in der Übertragung S. 25

594. Wilhelm Kölling: "Schulen auf Finkenwerder von 1660 bis 1919" in: De Kössenbitter, August 2002

595. Niedersächsisches Hauptstaatsarchiv Hannover: Harburg 74, Nr. 5011 (Synodalprotokolle). Instituie-ren = einsetzen = [establish]

596. Evers, S. 67

597. Ludewig, Band I, S. 113, sowie Rudolf Meier: Finkenwerder und die Herzöge zu Braunschweig und Lüneburg auf Schloss Harburg, in: De Kössenbitter, Dezember 1992, S. 16

598. Ludewig, Band I, S. 114–116.

599. Max Bahrfeldt: Beiträge zur Münzgeschichte der Lüneburgischen Lande im Ersten Drittel des XXVII, Jahrhunderts, Wien 1893, S. 68. [Ludewig erroneously names Hans Stucke instead of Henning Schlüter as the designer of the coin, p. 143. Dieter Matthes give the duke's birth date as March 15, 1564], siehe: Die welfische Nebenlinie in Harburg, Veröffentlichung des Helms-Museums Nr. 14, S. 84 Tafel 1b

600. Matthes, Tafel 1c

601. Ludewig, Band I, S. 149

602. Dietrich Kausche: Die Hansestädte und der Bau der Festung Harburg (1644 –46) in: Niedersächsisches Jahrbuch Band 54, 1982, S. 189 –216

603. Viehschatz = Abgabe auf den Viehbesitz = [tax on livestock]

604. Jacobus = 25. Juli, Heiligentag nach dem Apostel Jakobus = [July 25th, holy day of the Apostle James]

605. [The word "orator" in German also means negotiator, speaker/orator. Here it probably refers to his activities as member of the local church council and as administrator]

606. Niedersächsisches Hauptstaatsarchiv Hannover: Hann. 74, Harburg 2057

607. Niedersächsisches Hauptstaatsarchiv Hannover: Hann. 74, Harburg 2057

608. K. Wagner, R. Meier, H. Stroh: Finkenwerder auf den Spuren der Vergangenheit, Hamburg 1986, S. 69

609. Niedersächsisches Hauptstaatsarchiv Hannover. Signatur: Hann. 74, Harburg 2057

610. Hübbe, S. 133 ["Farmstead number 30 now (1897) 22 hectares." According to Hübbe, only the Nesshof with its mud flats is larger. Farm number 30 is known in Finkenwerder as the "Benitt-Farm," Landscheideweg 110.]

611. Akten des Kulturkreises Finkenwerder e.V. [A further confirmation is on pg. 49 of the Finkenwerder Kirchenrechnungen, where Hans Harmens is mentioned on January 30, 1650 as the Hamburg administrator.]

612. Niedersächs. Hauptstaatsarchiv Hannover: Hann. 74, Harburg 4667, datiert Anno 1654, den 25. Octobris

613. [Baptized in Nienstedten January 9, 1663. Godfather, among others, is Sebastian König, 615, administrator of the Lüneburg Side of Finkenwerder.]

614. Donor of the chandelier, see chapter of this translation entitled, "The Chandelier of the Finkerwerder Church."

615. Jost Grolle: Die Predigt der Steine. Totengedenken in Kirchwerder, Hamburg 1997. [The explanations of the gravestones are taken from this work.]

616. Ratsherren = [Councilors]

617. Niedersächsisches Hauptstaatsarchiv Hannover: Hann. 74, Harburg 2542

618. Niedersächsisches Hauptstaatsarchiv Hannover: Hann. 74, Harburg 2542 "Alten- und Finckenwerder Teichsachen" datiert 9. Januar 1661

619. Dietrich Kausche: Harburger Erbregister von 1667, S. 11/12. [Jehrden is a place on the Seeve River between Fleestedt und Horst.]

620. Kausche: Harburger Erbregister, S. 55. [In 1667, one-half Taler equaled 1.50 Mark. The tax on the reclaimed coastal land was therefore about 25% less than on interior land. Kausche mentions on pg. 22 that Emil Waschinsky's investigation of money's purchasing power in Schleswig-Holstein at the time of the inheritance register shows that the 1667 Mark would be multiplied by about 16 to be comparable to 1970.]

621. Teich = Deich = [Dike]

622. Kausche: Harburger Erbregister, S. 121/122

623. Staatsarchiv Hamburg

624. Niedersächsisches Hauptstaatsarchiv Hannover: Hann. 74 Harburg 4669, datiert vom 27. Februar 1688

625. Gorch Fock: Seefahrt ist not! Hamburg 1913, Vierter Stremel, S. 53

626. Bodemann, S. 149

627. Niedersächsisches Hauptstaatsarchiv Hannover: Hann. 74 Harburg 4302

628. [Pastor Evers mentions an administrator named Hans Horstmann in an entry of the church regulations (Protokollabschrift) from June 27, 1581. This is the father of Carsten Horstmann.]

629. Ludewig, Band I, S. 61.

630. Swiger = Schwiegervater [father-in-law] bzw. [respectively] Schwiegermutter [mother-in-law]

631. Niedersächsisches Hauptstaatsarchiv Hannover: Hann. 74 Harburg 4302 [Simon Külper's name is on the creditor's list of May 23, 1594, probably filed here in error.]

632. Hübbe, S. 134, [lists the Hamburg administrator around 1500 –1508 as a Swede named Schilt/Schylt, probably an ancestor of this old Finkenwerder family.]

633. Zwischenwirt, ohne Erbberechtigung = [Interim owner, without the right to pass the property on to his heirs]

634. [In this and the following presentations the Rhegius descendents are highlighted in bold faced type.]

635. Nieders. Hauptstaatsarchiv Hannover: Hann. 74 Harburg 2542

636. [Margareta Harmens is from the family of Annke Harms, wife of the administrator Sebastian König, Jr. Margareta is a great granddaughter of administrator Hans Harms and a granddaughter of administrator Jacob Harms.]

637. Nieders. Hauptstaatsarchiv Hannover: Hann. 74 Harburg 4972

638. Jurat = Kirchengeschworener, heute Kirchenvorstand = [old German "Kirchengeschworener" = modern German "Kirchenvorstand". Both mean member of local church council.]

639. Niedersächsisches Hauptstaatsarchiv Hannover: Hann. 74 Harburg

640. [According to Hübbe, farm number 30 (22 hectares) in Finkenwerder is known as the Benidt farm, Landscheideweg 110.]

641. Parentation = Totenfeier = [funeral celebration. Most of the deceased are quietly interred. It costs extra to ring the church bells and to have a graveside oration.]

642. "im Kranze" = als Jungfer (Jungfernkranz) = [Wearing a wreath at a funeral oration, as a young maiden would wear a wreath.]

643. Gustav Wülfken: Diechschauen auf Altenwerder in alter Zeit, in "So schön war Altenwerder," 1989, S. 10/11

644. Dietrich Stehr: Heimatglocken, Hamburg 1947, S. 86

645. Walter König: Marinemaler Joh's Holst, Hamburg 1998, S. 9, 10, 38 und 39

646. Evers, In der Übertragung S. 11

647. [In one document in Evers' handwriting Pastor Schulze is listed as 67 years old, however, the original indicates age 61.]

648. Im Finkenwerder Kirchenbuch ist ihre Hochzeit nicht verzeichnet = [The marriage is not recorded in the Finkenwerder church register.]

649. Chronik Kuhstedt = [Kuhstedt Chronicle]

650. Alle Paten laut Finkenwerder Kirchenbuch = [All godparents are from the Finkenwerder church register]

651. [See chapter: "Between Spiritual Welfare, Dike Construction, and 'Iron Cows.'"]

652. Geschichte der familie Evers, nebst Stammntafeln und Stammregister, zusammengestellt von Oberlandesgerichtsrat Karl Evers in Celle, Celle 1913

653. Archiv Neue Burg, Hamburg, Kirchenkreis Alt-Hamburg: Finkenwerder II, Nr. 78/1 Finkenwerder Kirchenrechnungen, S. 19

654. Finder, S. 191

655. Finder, S. 192

656. Finder, S. 191. [Also shows an illustration of such a hearth]

657. Finkenwerder Kirchenbuch, S. 113 links

658. Wedum, Wehme = Pfarrhaus = [parsonage]

659. Ewer = [fishing smack, coastal craft]

660. Evers: Nachricht von der Elb-Insul Finkenwärder

661. [Finkenwerder uses two measurement systems: Finkenwerder rods and Hamburg Marsch rods (Hübbe Appendix 6). 1 Hamburger Marsch rod = 14 Hamburg feet = 4.01 meters (1 foot = 28.64 cm)]. Helmut Jäger: Methodisches Handbuch für Heimatforschung in Niedersachsen, Hildesheim, 1965, S. 66.

662. Fourage = frz., Lebensmittel, Futter = [Fourage is French for provisions and food for cattle]

663. Niedersächsisches Hauptstaatsarchiv Hannover: Hann. 74 Harburg 4963

664. Niedersächsisches Hauptstaatsarchiv Hannover: Hann. 74 Harburg 4964 "Finkenwärdrische Pfarrhaus-Baurechnung vom Jahre 1759 bis 1766 mit 88 Beylagen"

665. ["The statement was selected by Axel Springer in 1948. (The *Evening News* gives the dates as October 14, 1948). Springer was conceptualizing a newspaper that had not previously existed: newspaper that was independent, non-partisan, dedicated to Hamburg, its readers, its neighbors in the immediate area, and those neighbors living on the Elbe and the Alster Rivers. The newspaper's purpose was to unite the aforementioned regions in difficult times ('With the homeland in their hearts...'). Above all, the ruins (of WWII) were to symbolize to those in distant lands that the formerly world class city of Hamburg was willing and able to find the means to resume its previous world class status ('...embracing the world'). To accomplish this purpose, the slogan by Johann Kinau fits perfectly with the newspaper's editorial goal...". Email message from the Hamburg *Evening News*, July 30, 2003.]

666. Gorch Fock: See fahrt ist not! Hamburg 1913, S. 5–6

667. Jacob Kinau: Der Kampf um die Seeherrschaft, München 1938, S. 164–235. [Jacob Kinau describes the Battle of Skagerrak in great detail.]

668. Walter Schnoor: Gorch Fock und seine Heimat, Berlin 1937. S. 267–269

669. Rudolf Kinau: Achtern'n Diek, in: Blinkfüer, Hamburg 1918, S. 9–16

670. Ulli und Hinnik Kinau: Dat grotte Rudl Kinau Book, Hamburg 1986, aus dem Vorwort

671. Jacob Kinau: Gorch Fock. Ein Leben im Banne der See. München 1935, S. 25–27. [According to the church register, he was a "surgeon." He died in the Hamburg City Hospital on June 4, 1834 and is buried there.]

672. Jacob Kinau: Gorch Fock. Ein Leben im Banne der See. München 1935, S. 157

673. [Leegerwall, Legerwall, Leeküste: The wind is coming from the sea towards the coast. In the event of an oncoming storm, it is dangerous for sailors if they are unable to free the ship from the coast. The expression is also used in a metaphorical sense to mean an aggravating situation.]

674. Eine Bibliographie der Kinaubrüder enthält: W. Wagner, R. Meier, H. Stroh: Finkenwerder – Auf den Spuren der Vergangenheit und Wilpert/Gühring: Erstausgaben deutscher Dichtung, Stuttgart 1967

675. Jacob Kinau (Herausgeber): Gorch Fock. Sämtliche Werke, fünf Bände, Hamburg 1925

676. [Heinrich Kinau is the first Rhegius descendent named Kinau.]

677. Walter König: Marinemaler Joh's Holst – Sein Leben, sein Werk, seine Welt, Hamburg 1998, S. 124

678. Jacob Kinau (Herausgeber) Gorch Fock: Sämtliche Werke, Erster Band, Hamburg 1925, S. 10/11

679. [Open the first Thursday of every month from 2 to 4 pm and by appointment.]

680. Abbildung aus: Gorch Fock – Ein Leben im Banne der See

681. Norddeutsche Skizzen [North German Sketches, further details unknown. Unabhängig = independent. L'etat c'est moi = I am the state, quotation of Louis XIV.]

682. Hübbe, S. [lists the size, including the mud flats as 51 hectares (plot number 33). The next largest plot, farmstead number 30 (Harms, later Benitt, Landscheideweg 110) has 22 hectares.]

683. Finder, S. 187

684. Finder, S. 187

685. Finder, S. 62. ff.

686. [Hübbe reports on p. 87 that in 1568 the senate of the city of Hamburg purchased land from Finkenwerder peasants who could no longer afford the dikes' upkeep.]

687. Schloz, S. 318

688. [Oral report from Hinrich Schwartau's grandson, born in 1927]

689. [For example, Peter Bersuch, son of Heinrich Bersuch and Gertrud König, 1510/1509]

690. Hans Förster: Schönes Finkenwerder in Wort und Bild, Hamburg 1959, S. 84–86

691. Jakob Kinau: Freie Wasser, Hamburg 1926, Seite 8–9 und 12

692. Gorch Fock: Sämtliche Werke, Dritter Band, Hamburg 1925, S. 54/55

693. Veraccordieren = vereinbaren = [to come to an agreement with]

694. [The original information is privately held. Both fires are mentioned by] Bodemann: Denkwürdigkeiten, S. 199

695. Bodemann, S. 191

696. Zeitungsbericht: Norddeutsche Nachrichten vom 27. Juli 1939, ["Protection for the Greenland Farm,"which states that the house has been designated a protected historic site.]

697. Hübbe, S. 131 [Hübbe is referring only to the farms on the Hamburg side]

698. Dietrich Kausche: Harburger Erbregister von 1667, Hamburg 1987, S. 125 wüst = [desolate/waste] brach = [fallow/unplowed] unbewohnt = [uninhabited/vacant]

699. HS = Hamburger Seite = [Hamburg Side], LS = Lüneburger Seite = [Lüneburg side]

700. [Bodemann reports on p. 116, that on October 31 and November 1, 1746 "the wife of Dietrich Meyer in Lüneburg Finkenwerder gave birth to live triplets, 2 sons and 1 daughter, but that all 3 died soon after being baptized."]

701. [His younger brother, Dietrich Meier, born January 22, 1753, marries Anna Maria Külper on January 6, 1780 in Altenwerder. She is the widow of farm laborer and wagoner, Hans Rüter. He founds the Meier lineage on Altenwerder's southern dike ("Muus-Meier"); four generations later the lineage continues, including Adolf Meier, dairyman on the Altenwerder Kirchenweg ("Pussel" – Meier). His son, Rudolf Meier, returns to Finkenwerder and in 1936 marries Paula Oehms, see also Appendix 64, "An example of the multiple branches of the Rhegius family tree on Finkenwerder."]

702. [Note by Johann Jacob Fock, see also Finder, p. 188, also Rudolf Meier: The "Uhlenhof" in:] De Kössenbitter, Mitteilungsblatt des Kulturkreises Finkenwerder e.V., Dezember 1996, S. 10

703. [Builder Carl Albrecht Roose is the son of the Lüneburg administrator Jürgen Ro(o)se. Because of a governmental change in 1688, Finkenwerder and Altenwerder, formerly separate administrative units, are combined. The administrators are no longer selected only from the farmers' ranks, but are "officially appointed by the government." Thus, beginning in 1738, they are government officials. The farmers thereby lose considerable influence. In 1695, Jürgen Rose from Celle, whose former job was to assist with challenges to tax assessments, becomes administrator for combined Finkenwerder and Altenwerder] (aus: Altenwerder, Bezirksamt Harburg 1980, S. 39/40)

704. [An undated newspaper article,"The Uhlen Farm, a Jewel of the Island" reports: "Roose never lived on the farm. He was a citizen of Hamburg and, because the estate was deeply in debt, he acquired the farm and had the house built.This information directly contradicts that from the church register, which states that "Carol Michael Albrecht Roosen" is baptized in Finkenwerder on July 19, 1696. Also, his 6 children are baptized in Finkenwerder, so one can assume the family lived here.]

705. [The entire contract becomes public record around 1935 when it is published in the newspaper in three installments. Unfortunately, the date and newspaper are unknown.]

706. [According to the Finkenwerder church register, H(e)inrich Fock's body was never found. He drowned along with: Margreta Detels, age 16 –17 and her brother Johann Fock, age 20 –30.]

707. Rudolf Meier: Der "Auefock-Hof" in: De Kössenbitter, Dezember 2000, Seiten 20/21. [The eldest son of Carsten Fock and Gesche Horstmann, also named Carsten (born October 4, 1767, died November 27, 1851), married Anna König, (1046), on May 30, 1797 so that the descendents from this farm are also Rhegius descendents.]

708. Hübbe, S. 131 [lists Hein Benit, provincial administrator, on farmstead #26 in 1734 and 1762]

709. Possession = Besitz = [own]

710. Eigenthümlichkeit = Eigentum = [property]

711. Entry in the Finkenwerder Church Register: "Jacob Fock. Dies 2 days short of 56 years, 9 months, homeowner on the Hamburg Side, was a victim of the demon drink and therefore not able to confess his sins, was buried without the ringing of the bells on November 11th."

712. [Catharina Mewes is the daughter of sea fisherman Hans Mewes and his wife Anna Meier, born 1787 on the Lüneburg Side. Anna Meier is the daughter of homeowner Hinrich Meier and his wife Margaretha König, (1031). This is a cross-connection to the Meier place on the Osterfelddeich #6, see the previous chapter.]

713. [In this part of the city of Hamburg there were plans to expand the port, however, they were not carried out because of World War I.]

714. [Children of Jacob Harms: Hans – born January 22, 1720 dies January 17, 1777. Catharina – born January 27, 1722 dies May 26, 1767. Her first marriage is to Hinrich Bannit, second marriage to Carsten Schult. Paul – born June 24, 1725 dies May 4, 1754 by falling off a horse.]

715. Bodemann, S. 141

716. Hildegard v. Marchtaler: Hundert Jahre Stülcken-Werft 1840 –1940, S. 167

717. Stadtarchiv Celle, Schreiben vom 13.12.2002

718. Maximilian Liebmann: Urbanus Rhegius – Vom Reformer zum Reformator, Jahrbuch der Gesellschaft für Niedersächsische Kirchengeschichte, 78. Band, 1980, S. 21 –44

719. Evangelisch – lutherischer Kirchenkreis Celle, Kirchenkreisamt, Celle, Schreiben vom 9. Januar 2003

720. Heinrich Philipp Guden: Dissertatio saeccularis de ERNESTO duce Brunsvigensi et Luneburgensi, principe sapiente, pio, forti, felici, Augustanae confessionis assertore et vincice. Göttingen 1730, S. 54/55. [In a manuscript from Celle, the text is cited in varying styles of penmanship on p. 339/340.]

721. [Joachim von Beust, born 1522 in Möckern near Magdeburg, dies 1597 at his knightly estate Planitz near Zwickau, founding father of the Barons of Beust, early acquaintance of Luther, promoted in 1548 in Bologna to Doctor of juris utriusque, under Elector Moritz of Saxony, 1570 advisor and professor at the University of Wittenberg. One of his descendents is the chief mayor of the Hanseatic League city of Hamburg, Ole von Beust (telephone conversation with Achim Baron von Beust on May 12, 2005, father of the mayor, as well as in Biographic-Bibliographic Church Lexicon on the internet)]

722. [Klammer, who is chancellor for Duke Ernst the Confessor, is a close confidant of Rhegius. Klammer is Duke Ernst's highest ranking secular advisor. Rhegius is the highest ranking cleric. Among other things, both are participants at the Schmalkalden Convention in 1537], siehe Albrecht Eckhardt: Der Lüneburger Kanzler Balthasar Klammer und sein Compendium Juris, Hildesheim 1964, Quellen und Darstellungen zur Geschichte Niedersachsens, Band 63, S. 16/17. [Joachim Möller succeeds him as chancellor.]

723. Text zitiert nach Sabine Wehking: Die Inschriften der Stadt Hannover, Wiesbaden 1993, S. 52. Die Celler Handschrift enthält den Text in leicht abweichender Schreibweise (S. 311)

724. Leopold Witte: Die Erneuerung der Schlosskirche zu Wittenberg, eine That evangelischen Bekenntnisses, Wittenberg 1894, S. 10/11. Die folgende Darstellung ist grösstenteils diesem Werk entnommen

725. Geheimes Staatsarchiv Preussicher Kulturbesitz, Berlin, Fundort: Zentrales Staatsarchiv Merseburg, Signatur BPH Rep. 52 F/IV/Nr. 3/1

726. Helmar Junghans: Wittenberg als Lutherstadt, Berlin 1979, S. 185

727. Leopold Witte: Die Erneuerung des Schlosskirche zu Wittenberg, eine That evangelischen Bekenntnisses, Wittenberg 1894, S. 79/80

728. Luther's commemorative sites in Eisleben and Wittenberg, Internet text of the GERMAN UNESCO COMMISSION.

729. Habilitationsschrift: Sein Häufig zitiertes Werk: Urbanus Rhegius und die Anfänge der Reformation

730. [Diether F. Domes has published two books: Werksübersicht and Spuren Legen Nach Vorne, published by Prof. Eduard Hindelang, Museum Langenargen.]